Inside Rebellion

Some rebel groups abuse noncombatant populations, while others exhibit restraint. Insurgent leaders in some countries transform local structures of government, while others simply extract resources for their own benefit. In some contexts, groups kill their victims selectively, while in other environments violence appears indiscriminate, even random. This book presents a theory that accounts for the different strategies pursued by rebel groups in civil war, explaining why patterns of insurgent violence vary so much across conflicts. It does so by examining the membership, structure, and behavior of four insurgent movements in Uganda, Mozambique, and Peru. Drawing on interviews with nearly two hundred combatants and civilians who experienced violence firsthand, it shows that rebels' strategies depend in important ways on how difficult it is to launch a rebellion. The book thus demonstrates how characteristics of the environment in which rebellions emerge constrain rebel organization and shape the patterns of violence that civilians experience.

Jeremy M. Weinstein is Assistant Professor of Political Science at Stanford University. His research focuses on civil war, ethnic politics, and the political economy of development in Africa. He has published several articles in academic and policy journals, and he has received grants and fellowships from the Russell Sage Foundation, the Harry Frank Guggenheim Foundation, the Center for Global Development, the Brookings Institution, the Woodrow Wilson International Center for Scholars, the World Bank, and the U.S. Department of Education.

Cambridge Studies in Comparative Politics

General Editor
Margaret Levi   *University of Washington, Seattle*

Assistant General Editor
Stephen Hanson   *University of Washington, Seattle*

Associate Editors
Robert H. Bates   *Harvard University*
Helen Milner   *Princeton University*
Frances Rosenbluth   *Yale University*
Susan Stokes   *Yale University*
Sidney Tarrow   *Cornell University*
Kathleen Thelen   *Northwestern University*
Erik Wibbels   *University of Washington, Seattle*

Other Books in the Series

Continued after the Index

Inside Rebellion

THE POLITICS OF
INSURGENT VIOLENCE

JEREMY M. WEINSTEIN
Stanford University

CAMBRIDGE
UNIVERSITY PRESS

CAMBRIDGE UNIVERSITY PRESS
Cambridge, New York, Melbourne, Madrid, Cape Town, Singapore,
São Paulo, Delhi, Dubai, Tokyo, Mexico City

Cambridge University Press
32 Avenue of the Americas, New York, NY 10013-2473, USA

www.cambridge.org
Information on this title: www.cambridge.org/9780521677974

First published 2007
Reprinted 2008 (twice), 2009

A catalog record for this publication is available from the British Library.

Library of Congress Cataloging in Publication Data

Weinstein, Jeremy M.
Inside rebellion : the politics of insurgent violence / Jeremy M.Weinstein.
    p. cm. – (Cambridge studies in comparative politics)
Includes bibliographical references and index.
ISBN 0-521-86077-6 (hardback) – ISBN 0-521-67797-1 (pbk.)
1. Insurgency. 2. Insurgency – Case studies. I. Title. II. Series.
JC328.5.W45   2006
322.4'2–dc22   2006005048

ISBN 978-0-521-86077-2 Hardback
ISBN 978-0-521-67797-4 Paperback

For Rachel

Contents

Contents

List of Figures, Tables, and Maps

Figures

List of Abbreviations

AFDL	Alliance des Forces Démocratiques pour la Liberátion du Congo-Zaire (Alliance of Democratic Forces for the Liberation of Congo–Zaire)
AIS	Armé Islamique du Salut (Islamic Salvation Army)
CIO	Central Intelligence Organization, Rhodesia
CPN(M)	Communist Party of Nepal (Maoist)
CRH	Comité Regional del Alto Huallaga (Regional Committee of Alto Huallaga), Shining Path, Peru
DINCOTE	Dirección Nacional Contra el Terrorismo (National Counterterrorism Directorate), Peru
FARC	Fuerzas Armadas Revolucionarias de Colombia (Revolutionary Armed Forces of Colombia)
FIS	Front Islamique du Salut (Islamic Salvation Front)
FLN	Front de Libération National
Frelimo	Frente de Libertação de Moçambique (Front for the Liberation of Mozambique)
FRONASA	Front for National Salvation, Uganda
GIA	Groupe Islamique Armé (Armed Islamic Group)
MPLA	Movimento Popular de Libertação de Angola (Popular Movement for the Liberation of Angola)
NPFL	National Patriotic Forces of Liberia
NRA	National Resistance Army, Uganda
NRC	National Resistance Council, Uganda
NRM	National Resistance Movement, Uganda
PRIO	International Peace Research Institute, Oslo
RC	Resistance Council

Renamo	Resistencia Nacional Moçambicana (Mozambican National Resistance)
RUF	Revolutionary United Front, Sierra Leone
UHV	Upper Huallaga Valley, Peru
UNITA	União Nacional para a Independência Total de Angola (National Union for the Total Independence of Angola)
UNLA	Uganda National Liberation Army
UNLF	Uganda National Liberation Front
UPC	Uganda People's Congress

Preface and Acknowledgments

My first exposure to the politics of rebellion came in South Africa in 1995, only months after Nelson Mandela's election. An idealistic college sophomore, I moved into the township of Guguletu outside of Cape Town, seeking a connection to the powerful political changes and social transformations under way in the country. Through countless conversations with friends and acquaintances, I grew to understand the history of South Africa's remarkable transition. I learned about the meaning of resistance from those who had participated in nonviolent protest, joined the African National Congress and its guerrilla army, Umkhonto we Sizwe, and sought to make the townships ungovernable, under the banner of the United Democratic Movement. Seeing Mandela take the reins of power was the culmination of decades of *their* struggle for human rights, economic opportunity, and political power.

Four years later, then a Ph.D. student at Harvard, I returned to southern Africa, this time on a summer fellowship. I headed to Mwange refugee camp in northern Zambia, which was flooded with tens of thousands of people fleeing the fighting in eastern Congo. My aim was to learn something about the brewing rebellion and to understand why people felt the need to flee the country. The former dictator of Zaire, Mobutu Sese Seko, had been overthrown only a year earlier by Laurent-Désiré Kabila, who, after his victory, acted more like his predecessor than the revolutionary his supporters had expected. Decades of misrule and neglect in eastern Congo had created the conditions for resistance, and I wondered whether the new movements taking shape would bring the Congolese people the freedoms and opportunities for which they hoped. Sitting under the hot sun, recording the personal experiences of countless refugees, I found out the answer: No. Not one of the refugees expected that these movements would bring about a political transition. Fleeing to Zambia, I was told, was not an easy decision. Many left their relatives and most of their possessions behind. But when confronted by the brutality of the insurgents and their external backers, few could imagine an alternative to leaving.

Returning to graduate school, the intellectual question became quite obvious to me. Can social science help us to understand the conditions under which rebellion mobilizes the disenfranchised for political change, and when it serves only the narrow interests of its leaders? Extending the arena of research beyond these two cases, I became fascinated by the horrific violence perpetrated by insurgent movements in Sierra Leone and Liberia and the disciplined strategies of social mobilization pursued by communist rebellions in Latin America. I decided to concentrate my inquiry on the abuse of noncombatant populations, asking why insurgent movements commit high levels of violence in some conflicts and not others. My timing was fortuitous as the research questions I found fascinating gained currency in political science. Civil war replaced interstate war as the dominant form of international conflict, motivating a flood of new research on why some countries experience civil war and others do not. Yet, while the study of civil war onset lent itself to analyses conducted from afar, my interest in the strategies and behaviors of perpetrators drove me to the field. Understanding rebellion from the perspective of those who experienced it became my central preoccupation.

In the pages that follow, I offer an explanation that helps to resolve the puzzle of insurgent violence. To advance it, I generalize from the personal stories shared with me by countless individuals in Uganda, Mozambique, and Peru. I use the collective wisdom embodied in their experiences to compare and contrast insurgent behavior in different contexts, over time, and across countries. While the resulting narrative offers readers a look inside four rebel groups, it references commanders and combatants, and reports the experiences of particular towns and villages, without including the names of the individuals who served as sources during my research. For reasons of confidentiality and for the protection of their security, I promised them anonymity. I respect that promise in the presentation of my argument and evidence.

I am indebted to the individuals who patiently told me their stories and answered my questions. They opened their homes, sharing what little food they had to offer. They introduced me to others in their villages and communities, making it possible for me to hear diverse perspectives and experiences. Each shared with me a piece of their autobiography. These gifts of time, trust, and life experience cannot be easily repaid. Although this book cannot possibly give voice to each of their individual experiences, I hope that it does make a contribution to the historical record and provide part of an explanation for the violence experienced in Uganda, Mozambique, and Peru. I also hope that the lessons learned from making comparisons across conflicts will provide important insights to policy makers who seek to prevent the violence now perpetrated against civilians in much of the developing world.

I am often asked how I managed to identify the insurgent leaders with whom I needed to speak for this project. Thankfully, I benefited from the goodwill, genuine interest, and assistance of key individuals in each country who proved willing to open doors for me at every stage. Lieutenant General Elly Tumwine (Uganda) encouraged members of the National Resistance Army to tell me their stories and brought me into the Luwero Triangle for the first time. William Pike (Uganda) shared recollections of his first visit with the insurgents "in the bush," made valuable introductions to many in the movement leadership, and took the arresting photograph that graces the cover of this book. Senior party leaders entertained my requests for assistance from Renamo's political hierarchy; their letters of support gave me access to Renamo cadres in central and northern Mozambique. Benedicto Jiménez, a former head of Peru's counterterrorism police and distinguished analyst of the Shining Path in his own right, recognized the enormous value in comparing Sendero's strategy to that of other movements. His support opened the door to research among incarcerated Sendero militants, enabled my access to the police department's private archive of captured Shining Path documents, and made possible my field work in the tense, drug-growing region of the Huallaga Valley.

My research in Uganda, Mozambique, and Peru also would have been impossible without the hard work of three tremendous research assistants. Each, a social scientist in training, joined me in the field as a partner and colleague, conducting interviews, writing field notes, and challenging my thinking at every stage. Without their probing questions, keen insights, and careful attention to telling me honestly what was and was not possible, this project could never have been completed. My special thanks go to Phoebe Kajubi (Uganda), Laudemiro Francisco (Mozambique), and Abdie Ramirez (Peru). I am also grateful to three institutions that provided me with an academic community in which to base my research in the field: the Makerere Institute of Social Research (Uganda), the Higher Institute of International Relations (Mozambique), and the Institute for Peruvian Studies (Peru). At each one, administrators and colleagues offered valuable advice, guidance, friendship, and the opportunity to employ many of their excellent students in various aspects of my research. My six months of field work in Uganda were enriched also by the friendship and intellectual cama- raderie of a truly extraordinary group of researchers. Together, Ron Atkin- son, Devra Coren, Gina Lambright, Craig McIntosh, and Karen Evenson made up a social and intellectual cabal I never found myself ready to leave behind.

This book began as a doctoral dissertation in the Program in Political Economy and Government at Harvard University. I owe a substantial intellectual debt to my four dissertation advisors, Robert Bates, Jorge Domínguez, Stephen Walt, and Monica Toft. They were wonderful men- tors, offering a constant stream of inspiration, encouragement, and support from the project's inception to its conclusion. Their shared commitment to analytical rigor, creative field work, and clarity of presentation – expressed consistently in their incisive comments and feedback – is, I hope, reflected in the final product. I am also indebted to a group of colleagues and friends at Harvard, who contributed in formal and informal ways to my intel- lectual development and the growth of this project: Karen Ferree, James Habyarimana, Macartan Humphreys, Kosuke Imai, Alan Jacobs, Andrew Karch, Robert Mickey, Daniel Posner, Peter Singer, Naunihal Singh, Smita Singh, and Dan Zuberi. Macartan Humphreys, in particular, has been a source of tremendous insight and perspective; our collaborative work has shaped my thinking in innumerable ways.

The Development Economics Research Group at the World Bank, the Woodrow Wilson International Center for Scholars, the Brookings Institu- tion, the Center for Global Development, and the Department of Political Science at Stanford University provided extremely supportive environ- ments in which to complete this project. I received useful feedback on var- ious pieces of the manuscript in seminars at Cornell University, Columbia University, Emory University, Georgetown University, Harvard Univer- sity, Stanford University, the University of British Columbia, the Univer- sity of Michigan, and the University of Pennsylvania. In addition to the useful critiques offered by participants in these seminars, I received valu- able comments and suggestions from Ron Atkinson, Christopher Avery, Ian Bannon, David Capie, Dara Cohen, Paul Collier, Suzanne Cooper, Alexan- der Downes, Jesse Driscoll, James Fearon, Raymond Hopkins, Herbert

Howe, Macartan Humphreys, Stathis Kalyvas, Nelson Kasfir, David Laitin, Cynthia McClintock, Pablo Policzer, Will Reno, James Ron, Michael Ross, Nicholas Sambanis, Ethan Scheiner, Peter Singer, Gayle Smith, James Snyder, Sidney Tarrow, Elisabeth Wood, Richard Zeckhauser, students in my graduate seminar on African Civil Wars in Comparative Perspective (Fall 2005), and anonymous reviewers of the manuscript.

I am particularly grateful for the considerable institutional support that has made this project possible. The Jacob Javits Fellowship of the U.S. Department of Education, the Center for International Development at Harvard University, the Sheldon Fellowship of Harvard University, the Development Economics Research Group at the World Bank, the Woodrow Wilson International Center for Scholars, the Brookings Institution, the Center for Global Development, the Center for International Security and Cooperation, and Stanford University all provided funding for field work or during the writing phase of this project. I also acknowledge Sage Publications, which provided clearances to reprint extracts of copyrighted material. Chapter 3 is a revised version of an article that first appeared as "Resources and the Information Problem in Rebel Recruitment" in the *Journal of Conflict Resolution*, August 2005.

Lew Bateman, the senior editor for political science and history at Cambridge University Press, recognized the importance of the manuscript and made every effort to assist me in preparing it for publication. Ruth Homrighaus brought the skills of an editor and the perspective of a general-interest reader to these pages. I believe the book is much stronger for her contribution.

Finally, the very existence of this book owes much to the support and encouragement of colleagues, friends, and family. For lively intellectual debates and unstinting friendship, I am indebted to friends and colleagues from California, Swarthmore, Harvard, and beyond. My twin brother, Joshua Weinstein, has been with me from literally the beginning and his interest in finding out "what my argument was" consistently challenged me to clarify and refine my thinking. My parents, Harvey and Rhona Weinstein, with their professorial caps and academic red pens, have challenged me (since childhood) to ask big questions and collect empirical evidence in support of my arguments. They have also emphasized the importance of investing the necessary time and energy to complete a final product of which I can be proud. That lesson took a while for me to learn, but I hope they will see here that I have taken it to heart. Most of all, without my partner and best friend, Rachel Gibson, this book might never have been completed. Her willingness to sacrifice some of my energy and attention in support of my research and writing were a constant reminder of the importance of this project. Her love and affection were constant reminders of the wonderful things I can enjoy more fully following its completion. This book is for her.

Inside Rebellion

Introduction

Lukumbi Village, Uganda, 1981

Word of the rebels came first in the form of rumors. "There are men who move at night," he was told. "They live deep in the forest." "They are strangers to this zone." But Samuel had never seen them with his own eyes.[1]

Government soldiers, however, were known to Samuel and his neighbors. They came in packs, demanding to know where the guerrillas were hiding. Out of fear, people would sometimes offer information. Samuel recalled one person who volunteered to take government soldiers to a rebel camp. They shot him from behind as he led them into the forest. The government troops claimed he was plotting to have them ambushed.

Soldiers maintained a regular presence in the village: knocking on doors, hurling threats, and exacting punishment on those who refused to cooperate. Most of the soldiers were of another ethnic group from another region of the country, and the enmity between locals and those in the military stretched back decades into Uganda's colonial and immediate postcolonial experience. Political sympathies in the village thus lay with the men hiding in the forest. But the soldiers had some local collaborators – representatives of the government's political party, chiefs who owed their authority and wealth to political elites in the capital, and groups of youths from minority ethnic groups in the area. They informed government soldiers about the presence of guerrilla units and identified community members who were offering support and comfort to the insurgents.

---

[1] Interview, Semuto, November 19(B), 2000. The letter following the interview date is used to distinguish among multiple interviews conducted on a single day. "Samuel" is used as a pseudonym to protect the anonymity of the respondent.

These collaborators often disappeared. At the time, Samuel knew nothing more than that the rebels had come to take them away. He later learned that informers underwent a process of political indoctrination in the forest. If they accepted responsibility for their actions and agreed to support the rebellion, the rebels welcomed them into the movement. If they refused, they were killed.

So, the first time Samuel saw the rebels, he was scared. It was 2:00 in the morning. He and his father were outside herding cattle that had escaped from their kraal. They were stunned to see a group of men moving in the dark, entering the forest with bags on their heads. His father shrieked, catching the attention of the men who rushed over quickly to quiet them down. Samuel recognized a local leader among the men in the group. He spoke to the father and encouraged him to offer his support to the rebels. But he also warned them: "in case you report us, we will come and kill you with your children."

Soon after this encounter, Samuel and his father began to supply food to the insurgents in the forest. Although they feared the rebels at first, the behavior of the government soldiers solidified their support for the insurgency. Government troops continued to wreak havoc in the village, killing people and raping women. Samuel recalled thinking that the rebels were different. While the government soldiers were intent on killing them, the insurgents played by different rules.

In the ensuing months, the rebels dispatched political cadres into the villages, tasked with organizing resistance councils in support of the movement. Formed following a public meeting in which cadres described the political goals of the insurgency, the councils were elected by community members to administer the areas with "justice and impartiality." They had primary responsibility for maintaining security in the zone; local militias were organized to track the movements of government troops and warn of impending attacks. The councils also ensured a steady supply of recruits to the insurgents, using their local knowledge to root out thieves and lazy types. Samuel moved quickly to join a resistance council for his village.

This brought him into closer contact with the rebels. He found that the rebels were "so disciplined because they hated the government soldiers for their misconduct among the civilians." There were acts of indiscipline because, as Samuel remembered, "it's human." But resistance councils were encouraged to report this misbehavior to insurgent commanders. And these violations of the "laws the soldiers had" were punished.

Introduction

Maríngue Village, Mozambique, 1979

Luis was only seventeen when the rebels arrived without warning in September 1979.[2] They first cornered a local leader and sliced off his ear, accusing him of supporting the government. The insurgents then gathered the population in the center of the village. They killed seven people in a public display of violence. Each victim was accused of having family members that supported the government. Young boys were also abducted that day, Luis recalled – taken away from the village and not seen again during the course of the war.

The rebels remained in the village for three months following the first attack. Life under the insurgents was difficult. Luis's father was a wealthy cultivator who was quickly identified by the group as it sought to secure sources of food. The rebels arrived at their home one day, on the outskirts of the village, and shot their guns in the air, demanding contributions of food. Luis' family complied by offering a contribution, but it was deemed insufficient. The soldiers then robbed them of all the food in their house. Neighbors also suffered at the hands of the rebels. Luis explained that husbands with beautiful wives were obligated to make trips to the rebels' base to deliver food; when they arrived, the wife would be asked to stay, while the husband was sent home. If they refused to leave their wives behind, they were beaten severely.

On occasion, the insurgents spoke of "political things." They organized one public meeting in which a rebel commander explained the purposes of the war: "they were fighting against the government and its system," Luis remembered. An antigovernment posture had resonance in central Mozambique because the government was viewed as biased in favor of the ethnic groups of the south. Moreover, its campaign of socialist transformation in the countryside, which was just getting underway, threatened to undermine local practices of governance, land rights, and cultivation that were highly valued by the population. But the message of the insurgents was clouded by their behavior. Theft, abduction, and rape were common practices even during this first visit of the rebels to Maríngue.

The rebels' stay in the village was short-lived. After three months, a government counterattack forced the insurgents to flee to the bush. To protect people and make the village easier to defend, dispersed patterns of land

---

[2] Interview, Maríngue, May 23(B), 2001. "Luis" is used as a pseudonym to protect the anonymity of the respondent.

holding were quickly replaced by communal villages at the government's behest. On a daily basis, villagers went to the fields to work the land, but returned to the confines of the communal village at night, where they were watched closely by soldiers and locally organized militias.

The insurgents returned in 1982, again without warning. They launched a daylight raid on four communal villages near Maríngue, including the one where Luis and his family now stayed. When villagers heard the shooting, they fled to the bush and hid wherever they could. The rebels looted household belongings and then burned each and every home to the ground. Government soldiers were unable to repel the attack, and members of the local militia, like everyone else, fled quickly to protect their lives. Luis and his family, along with many of his neighbors, remained on the outskirts of the village. They constructed ramshackle houses near the land they worked and never returned to the center of town.

They elected instead to live in a zone of rebel influence. The village itself was too much of a target, and government forces had proven unable to offer them protection. But insurgent areas were not much better. Luis described life under the rebels as "very bad." People were forced to make weekly contributions of food to the insurgents; those who refused were punished severely. Civilians had no choice but to comply with the requests made by the rebels. While Luis understood the purposes of their military campaign, he could not make sense of their coercive tactics or brutality.

An old African saying likens the experience of civilians in wartime to that of the grass underneath the feet of dueling elephants. The grass is trampled by two outside forces over which it has little control. But it would be a mistake to imagine that civilians lack agency in all civil wars or that the abuse of noncombatants is simply a by-product of the battle between opposing armies. Civilian populations – their interests, their resources, and their support – figure centrally in the political and military struggles that plague many developing countries. And we see in these stories that the civilian experience of war differs across contexts. Understanding why requires a sustained look "inside rebellion" in an effort to determine why some insurgents who choose to challenge the state turn out to be thugs, and others, revolutionaries.

The Puzzle

One conservative estimate of the direct death toll from civil wars since 1945 exceeds 16 million, more than five times as many people as have died in interstate wars.[3] In the 1990s, over 90 percent of deaths caused by war occurred in internal conflicts.[4] The lingering effects of violence, including disease, famine, and the destruction of economic and social infrastructure, substantially (even exponentially) increase the numbers of those who perish as a result of fighting in developing countries.[5]

Journalists and scholars who write about civil war assume that violence against civilians is one of its fundamental characteristics. War correspondents report on untold human suffering in the Democratic Republic of the Congo and Colombia but never stop to ask why the war in Congo has claimed nearly 100,000 lives directly in battle, while Colombia's civil war, which has lasted more than four times as long, is responsible for only one-fifth the killing. Analysts explore the tactics and strategies of insurgents fighting in the bush in Sierra Leone and Nepal but fail to grapple with the reality that while rebels in both countries sought to capture state power and remove undemocratic regimes, those in Sierra Leone hacked, raped, and pillaged their way through the countryside in a war that cost more than 10,000 lives, whereas insurgents in Nepal transformed local structures of governance, mobilized large numbers of civilians, and killed fewer than 1,000 people in nearly 10 years of fighting. Scholars discuss the hundreds of thousands of innocent civilians who have perished in Chechnya and Mozambique but never think to inquire why the Russian government bears responsibility for most of the killing in Chechnya, but insurgent forces were largely responsible for the violence in southern Africa. From conflict to conflict, we are made keenly aware that the primary victims of violence in civil war are noncombatants caught in the midst of fighting. Yet we know surprisingly little about why some civil wars are so much more violent than others or why some groups commit horrendous atrocities and others do not.

Scholars who write about the violence that characterizes civil war tend to begin by exploring state behavior as a critical first step in making sense

---

[3] James Fearon and David Laitin, "Ethnicity, Insurgency, and Civil War," *American Political Science Review* 97 (2003): 75–90.

[4] A new dataset on battle deaths in civil war offers a strong empirical basis for comparing human suffering in warfare across conflicts and over time. See Bethany Lacina and Nils Petter Gleditsch, "Monitoring Trends in Global Combat: A New Dataset of Battle Deaths," *European Journal of Population* 21 (2005): 145–66.

[5] The best recent study documenting the indirect consequences of war is Hazem Ghobarah, Paul Huth, and Bruce Russett, "Civil Wars Kill and Maim People – Long After the Shooting Stops," *American Political Science Review* 97 (2003): 189–202.

of the consequences of warfare.[6] One cannot fault that starting point: some of the most extreme cases of civilian brutalization have come at the hands of national governments and their militaries. State violence has included communist mass killings such as those in the Soviet Union, China, and Cambodia; ethnic genocides like those of Armenia, Nazi Germany, and Rwanda; and counterinsurgent massacres of the type perpetrated in Guatemala and Afghanistan. Yet rebel groups often share responsibility for the violence inflicted upon noncombatants, and the tactics, strategies, and patterns of violence exhibited by nonstate actors in civil war remain largely unexplored.

Some rebel groups abuse noncombatant populations, while others exhibit restraint, discipline, and control. Insurgent leaders in some countries transform local structures of governance, engaging civilians in the process of affecting political change; others build administrative machineries that do nothing more than extract resources. In some contexts, rebel groups kill their victims selectively, while in other environments violence appears indiscriminate, even random. Movements sometimes loot and destroy the property of civilian populations, while at other times they protect it from government attacks. In this book, I present a theory that accounts for the different strategies pursued by rebel groups in civil war, explaining why patterns of insurgent violence vary so much across conflicts. By "violence," I refer both to the *character* of insurgent attacks (the extent to which groups use force selectively to punish and prevent defection) and its aggregate *level* (the number of killings, abductions, rapes, and so on). Drawing on interviews with nearly two hundred combatants and civilians in three countries, I build my explanation by looking inside rebel organizations at their origins and structures. In focusing on origins, I highlight the factors that shape a rebel group's membership. In examining structures, I demonstrate how the profile of a group's membership constrains the organizational strategies its leaders can pursue, the structures of governance it can build in liberated

---

[6] There is no shortage of sophisticated research on the causes of mass killing as perpetrated by states. For recent academic perspectives, see James Ron, *Frontiers and Ghettos: State Violence in Serbia and Israel* (Berkeley: University of California Press, 2003), and Benjamin Valentino, *Final Solutions: Mass Killing and Genocide in the Twentieth Century* (Ithaca, NY: Cornell University Press, 2004). For a more popular history of genocide in the twentieth century, see Samantha Power, *A Problem from Hell: America and the Age of Genocide* (New York: Harper Perennial, 2003).

zones, and its capacity to use violence in a strategic, selective, and limited fashion.

The Argument

I argue that differences in how rebel groups employ violence are a consequence of variation in the initial conditions that leaders confront. Factors that raise or lower the barriers to organization by insurgent leaders – in particular whether material resources to finance warfare can be easily mobilized without civilian consent – shape the types of individuals who elect to participate, the sorts of organizations that emerge to fight civil wars, and the strategies of violence that develop in practice. My central finding is that rebel groups that emerge in environments rich in natural resources or with the external support of an outside patron tend to commit high levels of indiscriminate violence; movements that arise in resource-poor contexts perpetrate far fewer abuses and employ violence selectively and strategically.

The Mechanisms

Fighting an insurgency involves building an organization capable of challenging a government militarily. Many barriers to the organization of insurgency exist. Potential rebels must raise capital to finance the logistics of a military campaign, recruit foot soldiers willing to risk their lives in battle against a stronger government force, and generate support from civilians who can supply food, information about the location and strategies of government forces, and valuable labor in support of the movement. In confronting these challenges, rebel leaders may draw on two types of endowments: economic endowments, which come from diverse sources, including natural resource extraction, taxation, criminal activity, or external patronage; and social endowments, including shared beliefs, expectations, and norms that may exist in (or be mobilized from within) certain ethnic, religious, cultural, or ideological groups.

This book shows how the initial endowments to which rebel leaders have access shape the organizations that emerge and the ways in which different rebel groups ultimately use violence. First, resources shape the membership profile of a rebel group. That is, initial endowments constrain the set of recruitment tactics leaders can employ, altering the benefits and costs of joining in such a way as to affect the calculations individuals make about whether to participate in an insurgency. My argument begins, then, with the most fundamental – and perhaps most studied – aspect of rebellion: participation.[7]

Attracting recruits to participate in civil war is not an easy task. The work of rebellion is difficult and potentially dangerous. And when a rebel group sweeps to power and transforms the political regime in a country, it is difficult for it to exclude nonparticipants from the new freedoms that come with political change.[8] So while the potential costs of participation make joining unattractive, the promised benefits may not tip the balance. The onus is on leaders of rebel groups to develop appeals that motivate participation in high-risk collective action.

Recognizing that potential recruits trade off the costs and benefits of participation, rebel leaders often offer selective incentives to motivate participation.[9] As Samuel Popkin first argued, they find ways to distribute material benefits such that participants are rewarded for exerting effort and nonparticipants are excluded. At the same time, rebel leaders develop appeals around ethnic, religious, cultural, or ideological claims, reminding individuals of their membership in or affiliation with aggrieved groups, playing on their allegiance to a particular set of ideals, or activating norms of cooperation and reciprocity in order to motivate participation.

This book builds on the insight that recruitment strategies depend a great deal on the incentives that are likely to motivate individual participation, but it extends the discussion to reflect an additional consideration. I break with the common assumption that all potential recruits are of the same value to a rebel group, recognizing instead that rebel groups can attract both

---

[7] James Scott's research on the sources of peasant protest provides the intellectual foundation for many subsequent studies of political violence and civil war, including this one. In exploring the causes of anticolonial movements and protests against the expansion of markets, Scott highlighted the ways in which market forces disrupted traditional peasant ways of life, threatening local institutions and, ultimately, peasants' ability to survive. His focus on the logic underlying an individual's calculus to resist social change is reflected in the major studies that have followed. While many have varied their assumptions about how peasants behave, key contributions have continued in Scott's tradition of highlighting the choices peasants make. See *The Moral Economy of the Peasant: Rebellion and Subsistence in Southeast Asia* (New Haven: Yale University Press, 1976).

[8] Olson's classic statement on barriers to collective action has influenced subsequent work on organization in contexts ranging from insurgency and war to political organization and community action. See *The Logic of Collective Action: Public Goods and the Theory of Groups* (Cambridge, MA: Harvard University Press, 1965).

[9] Samuel Popkin, *The Rational Peasant: The Political Economy of Rural Society in Vietnam* (Berkeley: University of California Press, 1979).

high-commitment and low-commitment individuals. High-commitment individuals are *investors*, dedicated to the cause of the organization and willing to make costly investments today in return for the promise of rewards in the future. Low-commitment individuals are *consumers*, seeking short-term gains from participation. The problem is that even though potential recruits are aware of their level of commitment, rebel leaders do not have access to this information. The recruitment process therefore involves both motivating participation and attempting to attract the right kind of recruit to the organization.

A group's endowments shape the potential strategies that its leaders can employ.[10] Groups with access to economic resources are able to translate those endowments into selective incentives, or payoffs, in order to motivate individuals to join the rebellion. Resource-constrained groups must develop alternative strategies. They make promises about the material benefits that may accrue to individuals in the future and the collective benefits that the country will reap from a rebel victory, but these promises are only credible where leaders draw on social endowments that tie them to potential followers by means of ethnic, religious, or ideological ties. They can also mobilize within ethnic networks, religious organizations, formal and informal associations, and communities to activate norms and expectations that promote or reinforce cooperation.

Different initial endowments, then, create a situation in which there is variation in the opportunity that participation presents to potential rebels, and rebel groups attract different types of people depending on the costs and benefits of participation. Where participation is risky and short-term gains are unlikely, rebel groups tend to attract only the most committed investors. I call the movements in which they engage *activist* rebellions. Where

---

[10] My focus on variation in the initial conditions rebel leaders confront has its roots in the literature on social movements. Resource mobilization theories focus attention on how the resources and organizational capabilities of groups help to explain their mobilization potential. See J. Craig Jenkins, "Resource Mobilization Theory and the Study of Social Movements," *Annual Review of Sociology* 9 (1983): 527–53. A second strain of argument highlights the importance of political opportunities in paving the way for collective action. Exogenous changes in the environment, such as openings in access to power, electoral realignment, and cleavages within elite groups, make it possible for resource-poor movements to emerge. A key work in the literature on political opportunity structures is Sidney Tarrow, *Power in Movement* (Cambridge: Cambridge University Press, 1992). More recent research links variations in endowments and opportunities to the strategies movement leaders employ, demonstrating how broad structural factors constrain the repertoires of action available to different groups. See Doug McAdam, Sidney Tarrow, and Charles Tilly, *The Dynamics of Contention* (New York: Cambridge University Press, 2001).

participation involves fewer risks and individuals can expect to be rewarded immediately for their involvement, groups tend to attract consumers, who take part in what I call *opportunistic* rebellions.

The membership profile of a rebellion then affects its internal organization and the strategies it pursues in war. Rebel leaders confront a series of difficult choices as they design their organizations and engage civilians. Two merit particular attention here. They must decide how to ensure that orders are followed and they must extract the resources they need from civilians without destroying their base of support and sustenance. The nature of the strategic dilemma leaders face at each step in this process of organizational growth, and the options available to them as they respond, are themselves a function of the resource environment in which the group formed and its profile of recruits. Activist movements can maintain internal discipline by drawing on established norms and networks enabling them to decentralize power within their armies; opportunistic rebellions must permit indiscipline in order to maintain their membership, while holding on to the reins of military strategy. Activist insurgents can often obtain resources by striking cooperative bargains with noncombatant populations; opportunistic groups tend to employ coercive tactics because they cannot credibly commit to non-abusive behavior.

The outcome I ultimately seek to explain is how rebel groups use violence. Linking differences in the initial conditions leaders confront to variation in the membership and internal structure of groups helps to make sense of the character and level of violence committed by rebels against civilian populations. Structures of internal control and external governance shape the capacity of rebel groups to discipline the behavior of their members and influence the expectations of civilians about the types of behavior they will see when the rebels come to town. Where social and political ties can be employed to develop effective organizations, rebel leaders have a greater capacity to use violence strategically. Because they have clear guidelines about how combatants should behave and strong mechanisms for enforcing discipline, activist insurgencies are better able to selectively identify targets, implement attacks, and discipline the use of force. The short-term orientation of opportunistic insurgencies, on the other hand, tends to be detrimental to civilian populations. Without local ties, opportunistic groups have more difficulty identifying potential defectors and are prone to make mistakes. A constant demand for short-term rewards also drives combatants to loot, destroy property, and attack indiscriminately. A group's early missteps then initiate a cycle of civilian resistance and retribution by group members that spirals quickly out of control. The indiscriminate character of insurgent behavior results in higher aggregate levels of violence as civilian resistance makes it increasingly difficult for opportunistic insurgencies to operate.

These patterns of insurgent behavior, established early on in the conflict, tend to persist over time. This is true in particular for opportunistic movements that, as they attempt to maintain their membership in response to battlefield losses and changing government strategies, have little flexibility to adapt their internal organizational structures and a limited capacity to alter the expectations of civilians about how the rebels will behave. Activist rebellions also exhibit tremendous resilience, although the norms and expectations that tie members together and link groups to the communities in which they operate are vulnerable to fraying in the face of disruptive shocks that alter the membership of the group or undermine its internal structures that facilitate cooperation. When such changes do occur, activist movements tend toward opportunism, a change in strategy which is difficult to reverse. Figure 0.1 summarizes the relationship between resource endowments and rebel violence described in this study.

This book thus treats the question of why rebel groups abuse civilian populations in some contexts and not in others as the result of a process of organizational formation.[11] In particular, it shows how the initial endowments accessible to rebel leaders shape and constrain their strategies as they respond to five distinct challenges of rebel organization. Other scholars interested in civil war violence have overlooked the different origins and internal characteristics of groups, focusing instead on dynamics of contestation and territorial control. Theories of contestation locate the sources of insurgent violence in the desire of losing rebel groups to signal their resolve; theories of control predict high levels of violence in places where insurgent groups are present but unable to control territory

---

[11] This argument implies substantial path dependence in rebel behavior. Theories of path dependence were initially applied to explain the divergence in economic performance across countries. Douglass North showed how North and South America embarked on distinct trajectories of economic development even though after independence they shared constitutional forms, abundant resources, and similar international opportunities. The key difference is that North America benefited from its English colonial legacy of decentralized patrimony, whereas South America was stuck with the centralized authoritarianism and clientelism of its former Spanish rulers. See *Institutions, Institutional Change, and Economic Performance* (Cambridge: Cambridge University Press, 1990). More recently, such arguments have been applied to explain divergence across forms of political organization. See Robert Putnam, *Making Democracy Work: Civic Traditions in Modern Italy* (Princeton: Princeton University Press, 1993).

Five challenges of rebel organization

Two organizational strategies

	Initial endowments	Economic endowments → Opportunistic strategy	Social endowments → Activist strategy
Challenge 1	Recruitment: Motivating participation, obtaining high-quality recruits	Appealing to short-term, material interests → attracts a membership pool of "consumers"	Making promises, activating norms, appealing to nonmaterial interests → attracts "investors"
Challenge 2	Control: Ensuring that combatants follow orders	Permit indiscipline to maintain membership but control military strategy from the top	Maintain discipline by establishing norms and sharing power within the army
Challenge 3	Governance: Managing civilians in areas of territorial control	Extract resources through coercion	Obtain resources by striking a bargain with civilians
Challenge 4	Violence: Punishing individuals or groups for acts of defection	Employ violence indiscriminately and to a significant degree	Use force selectively and in a limited fashion
Challenge 5	Resilience: Maintaining rebel membership over time	Coercive tactics persist as groups find it difficult to change their membership and alter civilians' expectations	Disciplined behavior often persists, but activist insurgencies are more vulnerable to disruptive shocks that change membership and alter expectations

Figure 0.1. The Relationship between Resource Endowments and Rebel Violence.

unilaterally.[12] Both approaches link insurgent violence to the relative weakness of an insurgent group. In contrast, this book finds that insurgent violence follows from an organization's material strength. Perhaps surprisingly, it argues that resource wealth, which one might imagine would be a prerequisite for a group's possessing long time horizons and forward-looking behavior, is associated more often with high levels of indiscriminate violence, as leaders prove unable to use their wealth in support of their groups' social purposes.[13]

To demonstrate how a group's initial endowments condition its strategies, I draw on empirical materials related to four rebel groups that were engaged in three different conflicts: the National Resistance Army (NRA) in Uganda (1981–86), the Mozambican National Resistance (Resistencia Nacional Moçambicana, or Renamo) in Mozambique (1976–92), and two factions of Peru's Shining Path, or Sendero Luminoso (1980–92). The NRA, which successfully challenged and overthrew the regime of Milton Obote, was responsible for comparatively little of the violence Uganda experienced; it was government-sponsored massacres that resulted in the deaths of hundreds of thousands. The NRA was recognized instead for its discipline and restraint and for the cooperative relationships it built with an ever-growing network of civilian supporters. Renamo received international attention unprecedented at the time for the abuses it committed against Mozambique's civilians during a nearly twenty-year struggle against the government. Abduction, rape, and the hacking off of limbs and other body parts were all-too-common parts of the civilian experience of the war in Mozambique. In Peru, the national organization of the Shining Path adopted violence as a strategy for cleansing the countryside yet built an organization that implemented that violence strategically and

---

[12] Lisa Hultman makes the argument about signaling resolve in a paper on civil war violence. See "Killing Civilians to Signal Resolve: Rebel Strategies in Intrastate Conflicts" (paper presented at the annual meeting of the American Political Science Association, Washington, DC, September 3, 2005). On territorial control, see Stathis Kalyvas, *The Logic of Violence in Civil War* (New York: Cambridge University Press, 2006).

[13] Resource wealth has been linked to short-term-oriented behavior in other contexts as well. The impact of sudden, unexpected wealth on small firms is covered in Olivier Blanchard, Florencio López-de-Silanes, and Andrei Shleifer, "What Do Firms Do with Cash Windfalls?" *Journal of Financial Economics* 36 (1994): 337–60. As with the behavior of states in the context of resource booms, the authors find that managers invest cash windfalls inside the firm, even when the investment opportunities are not attractive, as a way of ensuring the success of the firm with *them at the helm*. They call this the "agency model of managerial behavior."

systematically, with errors and missteps punished severely. Its regional committee in the Upper Huallaga Valley (UHV), on the other hand, made a name for itself for its indiscipline and mistreatment of civilians who lived in its zones of control.

The specific question that I address is why rebels in the National Resistance Army and the Shining Path showed such restraint in the use of force against civilians, while insurgents fighting under the banner of Renamo and the regional committee in the UHV committed serious abuses. My answer is that the strategies rebel groups pursue follow from their organizational structures. I show that groups organized largely on the basis of economic endowments, such as Renamo (supported by an external patron) and the regional committee of the Upper Huallaga Valley (supported by the drug trade), are populated by opportunists, lack mechanisms for disciplining behavior, and tend to commit widespread abuses against civilians. Rebellions organized around social endowments, such as the National Resistance Army (organized around ethnicity) and the Shining Path (organized around ideology), attract committed recruits, establish structures that facilitate cooperation and discipline, and employ violence selectively, controlling combatant behavior to a significant degree. Table 0.1 compares rebel violence across these four groups.

The interpretation I advance in this book is not intended to draw out all the pathways through which variation in the initial conditions rebel leaders confront shapes the strategies their groups ultimately pursue. The particular initial conditions I emphasize (economic and social endowments) are only one part of the larger landscape from which groups emerge. Other factors matter for the viability of insurgency, shaping both who decides to rebel and the nature of the organizations that evolve to wage civil war. The most important factor outside of those discussed here is the strength of the state's bureaucratic and military machinery. Where national governments are strong – able to implement their policies and police the countryside without challenge – the barriers to organization are often too high for insurgent groups to develop. Where no state exists or the government is so weak it does not rule outside of the capital, the barriers to organization may be so low that almost anyone can launch a rebellion. In this book, I consider civil wars in which the relative power of the state was similar and state power therefore cannot be the major explanation for variation in the structure and strategy of the insurgent groups. In all three countries, the state was weak enough that an insurgent organization could develop a rural base for insurgency; at the same time, it was strong enough that,

Introduction

Table 0.1. *Variation in Rebel Violence*

	Estimate of Battle Deaths	Government-Sponsored Mass Killing?	Share of Killings Attributed to Rebels	Character of Rebel Violence
Uganda (1981–1986)	104,800	Yes		Selective
Mozambique (1976–1992)	145,436	No	Vast majority	Indiscriminate, brutal
Peru (1980–1992)	69,280	No	Difference between rebel and state killings not statistically significant	Selective
Peru–Huallaga Valley (1980–Present)	ca. 14,000	No	Difference between rebel and state killings statistically significant, with rebels killing more	Selective at first, later indiscriminate, increasing brutality

Sources: For data on combat-related deaths in Uganda, Mozambique, and Peru, see Bethany Lacina and Nils Petter Gleditsch, "Monitoring Trends in Global Combat: A New Dataset of Battle Deaths," *European Journal of Population* 21 (2005): 145–66. Coding of government-sponsored mass killing is from Benjamin Valentino, Paul Huth, and Dylan Balch-Lindsay, "Draining the Sea: Mass Killing and Guerilla Warfare," *International Organization* 58 (2004): 375–407. The share of rebel killings in Mozambique is taken from Africa Watch, *Conspicuous Destruction* (New York: Human Rights Watch, 1992). For the share of rebel killings in Peru and Peru–Huallaga Valley, see Patrick Ball, Jana Asher, David Sulmont, and Daniel Manrique, "How Many Peruvians Have Died?" (AAAS report, American Association for the Advancement of Science, Washington, DC, August 2003). Assessments of the character of rebel violence in Uganda are made in Ondoga Ori Amaza, *Museveni: From Guerrilla to Statesmen* (Kampala: Fountain, 1998). For the character of rebel violence in Mozambique, see Alex Vines, *Renamo: Terrorism in Mozambique* (London: James Currey, 1991). The characterization of rebel violence in Peru and Peru–Huallaga Valley is from the Final Report of the Comisión de la Verdad y Reconciliación, available at http://www.cverdad.org.pe, vol. 1, Chapter 3, and vol. 4, Chapter 1.4.

from the perspective of the rebels, the conflict was asymmetric, with the government's military representing a real and credible threat.

My purpose here is to develop a simple, general model that links the resources groups have at their disposal in organizing violence to the strategies rebels pursue in their relations with noncombatant populations.

The recognition that internal conflict represents a significant threat to human well-being in developing countries and that understanding the origins and nature of civil war is a pressing intellectual challenge is already reshaping the academic and policy agenda as it relates to conflict. Recent research linking natural resources to the onset and duration of conflicts raises as many questions as it answers about the motivations of insurgent groups and the factors that affect their viability. The emergence of powerful rebel groups whose behavior is as abhorrent and destructive as that of states that maim and massacre in fits of genocidal destruction has drawn critical attention to the task of opening the black box of insurgent organizations. The principal purpose of this book is to bring these strands of thinking together, first, by shifting the focus of a burgeoning body of research from the causes of civil war to the equally pressing question of the determinants of violence within civil war; second, by highlighting the essential role that nonstate actors play in the process of organizing violence; and, third, by developing theory and empirics that link factors we already know are critical to understanding the viability of insurgency to the question of why and under what conditions insurgent groups abuse innocent civilians.

Civil War, Violence, and Organization

To investigate issues of rebel strategy and behavior and to link patterns of violence to the characteristics of insurgent organizations is to adopt a focus on civil war, violence, and organization that not only builds on a growing tradition of research but also departs from conventional approaches in a number of important ways. It is common practice to treat civil wars as a form of political violence with three major characteristics: (1) they involve fighting between agents of a state and organized nonstate groups that seek to capture control of the government or over a region or to influence government policy by means of violence; (2) the fighting kills at least 1,000 people over its course and 100 on average in every year; and (3) at least 100 people die on both sides of the conflict.[14] While a transparent and defensible definition has allowed for significant progress in understanding

[14] Fearon and Laitin, "Ethnicity, Insurgency, and Civil War." A similar definition of civil war is employed in most quantitative studies of violence. See J. David Singer and Melvin Small, "Correlates of War Project: International and Civil War Data, 1816–1992," ICPSR study no. 9905 (Ann Arbor: Inter-University Consortium for Political and Social Research, 1994); and Michael Doyle and Nicholas Sambanis, "International Peacebuilding: A Theoretical and Quantitative Analysis," *American Political Science Review* 94 (2000): 778–801.

the causes of civil war, recent research challenges the idea that the mechanisms leading to conflict can be usefully compared across a large set of countries and types of warfare.[15]

In shifting our analysis of civil war from the macro level to the micro level, it is important to distinguish among different types of conflicts, as the distinct characteristics of warfare shape the strategies of organization that groups ultimately pursue. Rather than draw difficult-to-defend distinctions between wars based on the expressed motivations of belligerents, I adopt a more transparent typology that distinguishes among wars in which groups seek to capture the center, conflicts fought over secession, and wars in which belligerents use violence but have no interest in achieving territorial control of any sort (notably terrorist groups). Trying to understand the organization of violence in a broad range of civil wars is a worthy goal; however, a more narrow focus on theory building in the context of the classical case of insurgency offers enormous leverage in identifying the distinct organizational challenges groups confront and the various factors that shape the choices of rebel leaders. In particular, the imperative of capturing a national territory creates a unique set of opportunities and constraints that may or may not hold in other types of warfare. The prospect of territorial control disciplines rebel behavior across geographic regions because it embeds insurgents in an interaction with civilians that, if they are successful, will be repeated over time. Rebel groups seeking control of the state constitute 56 percent of belligerent groups in civil wars fought since 1945, making the set of cases under consideration here part of a considerable population of armed groups.[16] Of course, one implication of this approach is that, to the extent that the organization and strategies of violence differ in secessionist wars and conflicts not fought over territory, the account presented here is limited in its explanatory power. I return to the question of how my model applies to secessionist movements in the conclusion.

In addition to the way in which it defines civil war, this account differs from many treatments of conflict in the outcome it seeks to explain. Whereas most studies of civil war analyze where and when conflict takes place or the conditions under which wars can be brought to an end, this

---

[15] Nicholas Sambanis, "Using Case Studies to Expand Economic Models of Civil War," *Perspectives on Politics* 2 (2004): 259–79.

[16] Monica Toft has gathered as yet unpublished data on the objectives of belligerent groups since 1945.

study considers why some civil wars are more violent, brutal, and destructive for civilian populations than others. This approach recognizes that patterns of violence and abuse vary in important and measurable ways across conflicts, over time and across space within conflicts, and across belligerent groups.

Following the lead of scholars of genocide and state-directed violence, I adopt an understanding of violence that recognizes its multifaceted nature and seeks to measure variation in its intensity.[17] I assume that the violent strategies implemented by armed groups comprise a range of behaviors that include, but are not limited, to killing. Counting the number of deaths due to violence in war is not an easy task, but capturing the dynamics of more nuanced patterns of belligerent-civilian interaction in the processes of recruitment, resource extraction, and governance poses an even more difficult challenge. Making sense of patterns of abuse requires a combination of methods of analysis: the counting of combat deaths, the coding of human rights violations and atrocities, and qualitative analysis of in-depth interviews with noncombatants about their experiences of war. In adopting multiple methods, I conceptualize variation in the intensity of violence as being reflected in both the character and the level of violence committed against civilians. While variation in levels of violence is relatively easy to assess, differences in the character of violence are reflected in its selectivity and brutality. Violence is selective if it targets individuals or groups that threaten to undermine a rebel organization; selective violence has a tactical purpose for the group. When violence is used selectively, civilians can be relatively certain that cooperation can be exchanged for the right to survive. Indiscriminate violence makes no distinction among potential victims, neither protecting supporters nor punishing defectors. Brutality refers to behaviors, including amputation, rape, abduction, and pillaging, that often accompany rebel attacks but are above and beyond what is required to send a signal of the costs of defection.[18] A major goal of this study is thus to

---

[17] See, for example, Barbara Harff, "No Lessons Learned from the Holocaust: Assessing Risks of Genocide and Mass Political Murder Since 1945," *American Political Science Review* 97 (2003): 57–73; and Benjamin Valentino, Paul Huth, and Dylan Balch-Lindsay, "Draining the Sea: Mass Killing and Guerrilla Warfare," *International Organization* 58 (2004): 375–407.

[18] This study departs from other recent explorations of violence in its exclusive focus on insurgent behavior. In contrast, Kalyvas looks at how the use of violence varies across groups within a conflict, testing theories of violence on geographic and temporal patterns of coercion by both insurgent and government actors. See *Logic of Violence*.

introduce a way of thinking about rebellion that provides analytical leverage in making sense of different patterns of warfare perpetrated by nonstate actors, with obvious implications for both conflict prevention and conflict resolution.

A final way in which this book differs from current treatments of civil war is in the primacy it ascribes to the issue of how violence is organized. "Organization" here refers to the internal characteristics of a movement: its membership, policies, structures, and culture. Studies explaining why some countries experience civil wars and others do not or why some civil wars last so much longer than others have taken organization as a given. Such research typically links macro-level factors, such as a country's wealth, ethnic diversity, or regime type, to the onset or duration of violence without being specific about the micro-level processes through which war is actually carried out. Most analysis in this area begins with an economic theory of rebellion in which groups in some way trade off the costs and benefits of mounting resistance, but few studies attempt to document an empirical basis for linking the factors that affect the viability of insurgency to the recruitment of insurgents, the building of organizations, or the implementation of violence. With a careful study of the internal dynamics of rebellion, this book aims to fill the gap.

In doing so, it seeks to move the discussion of insurgent organization beyond a weak typology of "new" and "old" civil wars that has recently gained favor in academic and policy circles toward an understanding of different rebel behaviors that is rooted in a theory of how groups form.[19] Many are right to point out variation in the characteristics of civil war and its perpetrators, but to explain this variation in terms of Cold War and post–Cold War dynamics is simplistic, theoretically unsatisfying, and empirically wrong.[20] Following the lead of scholars such as Roger Petersen, Elisabeth Wood, and Stathis Kalyvas, this book instead grapples with variation in the conduct of warfare by looking inside insurgent organizations at how they

---

[19] Descriptions of "new civil wars" first gained widespread prominence due to the work of Robert Kaplan. See "The Coming Anarchy: How Scarcity, Crime, Overpopulation, and Disease Are Rapidly Destroying the Social Fabric of Our Planet," *Atlantic Monthly* 44, February 1994. Academic scholars picked up on the distinction in subsequent work. See David Keen, *The Economic Functions of Violence in Civil Wars*, Adelphi Paper 320 (New York: Oxford University Press for the International Institute for Strategic Studies, 1998); and Mary Kaldor, *New and Old Wars: Organized Violence in a Global Era* (Stanford: Stanford University Press, 1999).

[20] For a powerful critique of the distinction between new and old civil wars, see Stathis Kalyvas, "New and Old Civil Wars: A Valid Distinction?" *World Politics* 54 (2001): 99–118.

form.[21] It identifies a set of common organizational challenges that rebel leaders confront. Making sense of the incentives that motivate participation in insurgency, the strategies groups pursue in ensuring that combatants follow orders, and the challenges they face in establishing territorial control puts a premium on uncovering the choices and strategies of – and the constraints facing – those who participate in violence. It is at this level that theorists can begin to develop logically coherent and testable theories to account for the variation in behavior observed in conflict. This book thus draws inspiration and insight from studies of organizational design in literatures that explore social movements, criminal organizations, political parties, and competitive firms. At the same time, it builds on the tradition of scholarship on insurgency and peasant organization that, in studying the dynamics of communist movements in Southeast Asia, first drew attention to the internal characteristics of rebellions that account for their emergence, growth, and effectiveness.[22]

Structure and Agency

I account for variation in the internal structures of rebel organizations by examining the initial conditions leaders confront. My argument about the determinants of violence builds from the idea that different organizational types evolve depending on the viability of insurgency; factors that heighten or lessen the barriers to organization receive primary attention. This approach is well accepted in literature on the political economy of rebellion. Where I challenge conventional views about the determinants of strategy more directly is in my contention that patterns of violence are a direct consequence of the endowments leaders have at their disposal as they organize. I argue that groups commit high levels of abuse not because of ethnic hatred or because it benefits them strategically but instead because their membership renders group leaders unable to discipline and restrain the use of force – and membership is determined in important ways by the endowments leaders have at their disposal at the start of a rebellion.

[21] Roger Petersen, *Resistance and Rebellion: Lessons from Eastern Europe* (New York: Cambridge University Press, 2001); Elisabeth Wood, *Insurgent Collective Action in El Salvador* (New York: Cambridge University Press, 2004); Kalyvas, *Logic of Violence*.

[22] See, for example, Paul Berman, *Revolutionary Organization: Institution-Building within the People's Liberation Armed Forces* (Lexington, MA: Lexington Books, 1974). This followed on earlier work by Lucian Pye (*Guerrilla Communism in Malaya* [Princeton: Princeton University Press 1956]) and Phillip Selznick (*The Organizational Weapon: A Study of Bolshevik Strategy and Tactics* [Santa Monica, CA: RAND Corporation, 1952]).

Conceptualizing strategy in this way divorces it from agency. Decisions about recruitment, organization, and violence cease to be driven by the actions of individuals and become, instead, choices made under binding constraints imposed by the resources a group has at its disposal and the membership it has attracted to participate. Leadership, skill, and ideology all take a backseat to broader, macro-level factors that structure the universe of possibilities individual rebels confront. Rebel organizations are transformed, at least in theory, from groups defined by the personalities and ideologies of their leaders to teams of would-be rebels shaped by conditions that affect the viability of challenging the state. Violence becomes the natural outcome of a path of organizational evolution rather than a strategic choice made in response to changing conditions on the ground.

Some readers may question this approach. They will point to the powerful influence of ideologies in conditioning individual behavior, arguing that variation in the content and character of political appeals must be central to explaining violence. They will highlight the critical role played by leaders of various insurgent groups in obtaining outside support, crafting opposition coalitions, and militarily outwitting the enemy as evidence of the centrality of leadership. They will point to the idiosyncratic character of warfare itself, with substantial change taking place over time in the strength of the enemy, the depth of the support base, and the role of external actors – all of which militate against an argument that implies substantial path dependence in behavior. While recognizing that the endowments leaders have at their disposal certainly shape their strategies, they will emphasize that such endowments are neither fixed nor exogenous and that leaders play a role in generating material resources and fostering social ties. These are important challenges to my argument, and I wish to offer an initial response.

When I highlight the importance of structure over agency, I am not denying that leadership, charisma, and skill affect the strategies rebel groups adopt in civil war. Nor am I suggesting that strong, coherent ideological platforms have no impact on the decisions leaders make about who to recruit and how to do it, what types of training to require of participants, and which strategies of mobilization to implement among civilian populations. Fighting wars (at least, fighting them successfully) requires leadership. Organizers must motivate and challenge untrained peasants to take up arms and engage enormous risks in fighting for a cause. The ability to inspire and lead must be a part of the story of group formation and survival. In the same vein, rebel organizations actively promote strong ideological positions, and from communist insurgencies to fundamentalist religious movements to groups organized around ethnic ties, these ideological foundations are evident in the strategies groups use to recruit and the structures they build to govern their movements. Nonetheless, my point in focusing attention primarily on the ways in which resource endowments shape the strategies leaders have at their disposal is simply that crucial explanatory variables such as leadership and strong ideologies are themselves endogenous to the process of group formation. A convincing explanation of rebel behavior must be able to account for the emergence of strong leadership in some contexts and not in others, and it must enable us to explain why some groups with strong ideological foundations form at some times in some places but not at other times in other places. This book's focus on factors that affect the viability of insurgency – in particular, on the economic and social endowments that can be activated by insurgent leaders – helps to make sense of the conditions under which leadership and group solidarity are observed. In developing the argument in subsequent chapters, I take seriously the idea that rebel leaders can sometimes shape the endowments accessible to them in organizing violence but show that differences in the viability of insurgency can account too for the leaders that come to the fore and the endowments they have at their disposal.

Looking Ahead

This book is organized into three parts. Part I, comprising Chapters 1 through 4, focuses on the structure of rebel organizations. It shows how the initial conditions rebel leaders confront shape the strategies they choose in recruiting participants and managing a growing insurgent organization.

Chapter 1 introduces in more detail a basic economic framework for understanding rebel organizations. It locates this book's focus on organizational structure in the context of two previous approaches to studying the dynamics of rebellion: those that view rebel groups as social movements and those that view them as states. Chapter 2 describes the four rebel groups that form the basis for comparative analysis. It provides the reader with a concise summary of the three civil wars, reviewing the conditions that contributed to the rise of the insurgency and introducing the key players involved in the process of organizational design.

Chapters 3 and 4 then address the factors that account for variation in the internal structures of rebel organizations. Chapter 3 explores the challenge posed by recruitment, as rebel leaders seek to overcome free rider problems that impede collective action while also motivating potential participants who are likely to be committed to the organization. The model shows how variation in the initial conditions rebel leaders confront gives rise to varying strategies of recruitment, shaping the membership (and trajectory) of each rebel organization. Chapter 4 focuses on the training and management strategies of rebel groups. It highlights the difficulty of maintaining organizational control as groups decentralize their operations during wartime, and it explores the strategies groups employ to ensure discipline among their forces. This chapter shows how investments in training and decisions about organizational hierarchy depend in important ways on the nature of the membership a group has recruited.

Once the factors that explain variation in the internal structures of rebel groups have been established, Part II tackles the central question of this book: Why are rebel groups abusive toward civilians in some contexts and not in others? Chapter 5 explores the nature of the political structures that groups build to mobilize civilian support and extract the resources necessary to maintain the organization. It identifies a central problem that groups face in gaining civilian compliance: how to credibly commit to extract only what is necessary for the sustenance of the movement. Drawing on evidence from interviews with combatants and civilians in rebel-held zones, the chapter shows how the characteristics of insurgent organizations constrain the range of governance structures they can employ in areas of civilian control.

Chapter 6 presents evidence on how rebel groups use coercion as a tool to maintain civilian support and build their militaries. Drawing on new quantitative data from Uganda, Mozambique, and Peru, it charts differences in the intensity and character of violence across the four rebel organizations. Taken together, Chapters 5 and 6 show how differences in the internal structures of groups, linked to the resources they have at their disposal, can account for variation in patterns of violence across civil wars.

The model linking resources and group structures to patterns of violence implies substantial path dependence. Chapter 7 explores the power of the argument by examining the evolution of rebel groups over time. It explores key instances of combat success and failure in each conflict, highlighting the ways in which groups sought to hold their organizations together by reinforcing rather than reforming internal structures and practices established in the earliest stage of the conflict.

In presenting the argument, this book proceeds in a fashion atypical of social science research. Rather than outlining a theory at the outset and walking the reader through four extended case studies, I instead move

23

from one step in the process of organizational evolution to the next. In each chapter, narrative description mixes with analysis as the stories of the National Resistance Army, Renamo, and the two factions of the Shining Path motivate and reinforce the theoretical arguments I advance.

In Part III, Chapter 8 takes the argument beyond the initial set of cases to explore its explanatory power in other contexts. It first tests the insight linking resources to recruitment in the cases of Sierra Leone and Nepal. The chapter then turns to quantitative data on the level and character of violence across civil wars for cross-national evidence linking variation in the costs of organizing insurgency to patterns of civilian abuse. The book's final chapter relaxes the assumption that rebel leaders begin with access to a fixed set of endowments and presents evidence that groups built around social endowments get crowded out in countries where the barriers to organization are low. It then concludes with a discussion of the policy implications of differences in the structure of rebel groups for policy makers who seek to influence and restrain the behavior of nonstate actors in civil war.

PART I

The Structure of Rebel Organizations

1

The Industrial Organization of Violence

Journalists grappling with how to explain the atrocities committed in civil war often turn first to motivation, as when they attribute the extreme violence of Uganda's Lord's Resistance Army to the messianic religious beliefs of its leader or the massacres in eastern Congo to the tribal battles between the Hema and Lendu ethnic groups. Likewise, most studies of revolution and civil war begin with the question of who is willing to fight. They draw attention to the motivations of combatant groups and their members. Explanations for the onset, duration, and dynamics of violence highlight such factors as economic inequality, ethnic antagonism, and political repression. These root causes of violence are believed to be crucial to making sense of who participates in rebellion: repression drives those excluded from the political system to embrace violent means to obtain power, policies shaped by ethnic favoritism force groups facing discrimination to organize, and economic inequality pits members of one social class against another. Taking motivation as the starting point in building explanations for the level and character of violence within civil war is a natural extension of existing approaches.

This book is focused, however, squarely on the processes through which organizations produce violence. Violence emerges as a strategy in different contexts and to different degrees as a consequence of the interaction between rebels and governments battling for control of the state on the one hand and civilians who choose to offer or withhold support from the competing parties on the other. In this back and forth, dimensions of organization – including resources, membership, authority structures, and internal rules – move to the fore as explanations for the distinct strategies groups pursue. The research question is thus framed as a problem of institutional choice. The theory emphasizes how broad factors that affect the viability of insurgency demarcate the parameters within which questions about the choices, strategies, and structures of rebel groups must be answered.

This chapter begins by exploring previous approaches to the study of rebellion. While the approach pursued by practitioners of guerrilla war, like my own, dedicates substantial attention to question of how groups form, organization takes a backseat to broader structural factors in traditional studies of revolution, which treat groups alternatively as social movements or as states. I then describe my own approach to understanding why groups turn to coercion. In conceptualizing strategy as a problem of institutional choice, I first explain the distinct set of organizational challenges rebel leaders confront and then turn to the factors that shape how individuals respond in the process of organizing violence. The chapter concludes by explaining how and why I use the cases of the National Resistance Army, Renamo, and two factions of the Shining Path to illustrate my argument.

Organizers of Revolution

The primacy given to issues of organization in this study resonates with the writings of revolutionaries themselves, who have debated intensely the various organizational forms they might deploy in rebellion. Two facts are striking when one considers the diverse blueprints of rebel organization advanced by practitioners in the twentieth century. First, there has been a remarkable convergence around a set of core beliefs about how insurgency should be organized, and these strategies – what Charles Tilly would call "repertoires of contention" – have diffused widely across territories and across groups with different motivations. At the same time, these organizational strategies have been implemented unevenly, with varied success in different contexts. This suggests the existence of variation in the organizational capacity of different insurgencies – variation that is essential to understanding how groups behave, yet is poorly accounted for in traditional studies of revolution and civil conflict.

Common Principles

Tactics of guerrilla warfare are a common feature of modern combat. Nearly three-quarters of states that have faced a civil war since 1945 have confronted a rebel organization employing primarily guerrilla tactics.[1] Guerrilla war may be distinguished from other types of combat by four main characteristics: First, groups employing guerrilla tactics rely on irregular forces organized in small and highly mobile units without heavy weaponry. Second, strategies of guerilla warfare emphasize extended campaigns of assassination, sabotage, and hit-and-run attacks designed to impose significant costs on the enemy, rather than traditional battles that seek to defeat the opposition outright. Third, guerilla forces typically operate in territories that are under the control of their military opponents. And guerilla armies, finally, turn directly to local populations for the resources needed to sustain insurgency, including food, shelter, supplies, and intelligence.[2] These unique characteristics of guerrilla warfare define the environment for which practitioners have sought to develop effective rebel organizations.

In writing about the challenges of organizing a guerrilla campaign, two of history's more influential strategists, Mao Tse-tung and Che Guevara, offered clear prescriptions to would-be rebels about how to succeed militarily while generating significant support from the masses for their campaigns. Many of their insights speak directly to the organizational challenges that occupy our attention in this book.

On recruitment, Mao underscored the importance of selecting the most committed civilians for participation in the struggle. He wrote: "Upon the arrival of the enemy army to oppress and slaughter the people, their leaders call upon them to resist. They assemble the most valorous elements, arm them with old rifles or bird guns, and thus a guerrilla unit begins."[3] In addition to valor, Guevara highlighted other desirable qualities in an insurgent, suggesting that insurgents' character matters not only for their success as fighters but also for how their organization is viewed by outsiders: "The guerrilla fighter, as a person conscious of a role in the vanguard of the people, must have a moral conduct that shows him to be a true priest of the reform to which he aspires. To the stoicism imposed by the difficult conditions of warfare should be added an austerity born of rigid self-control that will prevent a single excess, a single slip, whatever the circumstances."[4]

Writing about organization, Mao made the issue of discipline paramount. While organizations can employ techniques for monitoring

---

[1] Benjamin Valentino, Paul Huth, and Dylan Balch-Lindsay, "Draining the Sea: Mass Killing and Guerrilla Warfare," *International Organization* 58 (2004): 386.
[2] Ibid., pp. 375–407.
[3] Mao Tse-tung, *On Guerrilla Warfare* (New York: Praeger, 1961), p. 72.
[4] Che Guevara, *Guerrilla Warfare* (Lincoln: University of Nebraska Press, 1998), p. 39.

the behavior of their fighters, Mao emphasized the need for discipline to flow from a set of internal beliefs: "In all armies, obedience of the subordinates to their superiors must be exacted. This is true in the case of guerrilla discipline, but the basis for guerrilla discipline must be the individual conscience.... This [discipline] must be self-imposed, because only when it is, is the soldier able to understand completely why he fights and why he must obey."[5] Recognizing that such internal conviction sometimes wavers, Guevara highlighted the need for groups to punish indiscipline harshly as a means of controlling individual behavior and establishing coherent patterns of operation within the group: "[Discipline] should spring from a carefully reasoned internal conviction; this produces an individual with internal discipline. When this discipline is violated, it is necessary always to punish the offender, whatever his rank, and to punish him drastically in a way that hurts."[6]

When it came to the issue of how insurgents should treat civilians, both Mao and Guevara were unequivocal in linking the fate of a guerrilla band to its relationship with noncombatant populations. Guevara pointed to the difficult dilemma that groups face in maintaining a chain of supplies from civilians without extracting so much that they generate resentment: "A good supply system is of basic importance to the guerrilla band. A group of men in contact with the soil must live from the products of this soil and at the same time, must see that the livelihood continues of those who provide the supplies."[7] Mao emphasized the need for rebel organizations to engage politically with civilians who live in their areas of control and influence not simply by using political propaganda but also through the creation of formal political structures. "The political goal must be clearly and precisely indicated to the inhabitants of guerrilla zones and their national consciousness awakened," he explained. "A concrete explanation of the political systems used is important not only to guerrilla troops," Mao continued, "but also to all those who are concerned with the realization of our political goal."[8]

Guevara spoke directly to the issue of how violence is used in the context of war, warning that using violence against civilians, while in some cases an important strategy, poses significant risks to insurgent organizations if it is used indiscriminately. "It is necessary to distinguish clearly," he asserted,

[5] Mao, *On Guerrilla Warfare*, p. 91.
[6] Guevara, *Guerrilla Warfare*, p. 113.
[7] Ibid., p. 80.
[8] Mao, *On Guerrilla Warfare*, p. 43.

"between sabotage, a revolutionary and highly effective method of warfare, and terrorism, a measure that is generally ineffective and indiscriminate in its results, since it often makes victims of innocent people." He continued: "Terrorism should be considered a valuable tactic when it is used to put to death some noted leader of the oppressing forces, well known for his cruelty.... But the killing of persons of small importance is never advisable."[9]

Of course, Mao and Guevara were only two practitioners in a long line of theorists who have debated how best to organize revolution. Early small war theorists such as de Jeney and Andreas Emmerich grappled with the unique qualities of partisan armies, the Bolshevik and Menshevik factions fought over how much to centralize authority in a communist party bent on revolution, and Vo Nguyen Giap, Frantz Fanon, and Amilcar Cabral adapted theories of people's war to the local contexts they encountered.[10] The strategies advanced by Mao and Guevara receive disproportionate attention from scholars owing to the Cold War–driven fascination with communist insurgencies and the uniquely articulate spokesmen who graced the rebellions in China and Cuba.

Nontheless, I choose to begin with the common principles of guerrilla warfare proposed by Mao and Guevara because their blueprints for rebellion have emerged as general conventions of collective action across conflicts in the developing world. Tilly argues that people cannot employ strategies of organization and mobilization of which they are not aware; leaders draw on forms of action that are familiar to them and to their opponents because these forms of action have been practiced in the leaders' own societies or in others.[11] The diffusion of information through the media and the formal and informal networks that increasingly link actors in one country to those in another mean that the same strategies of guerrilla warfare practiced in one part of the world in the 1940s are now being replicated across the globe more than 60 years later. Of course, some of this diffusion was intentional, as Soviet and Cuban-inspired revolutionaries benefited from the direct guidance of their guerrilla forbearers. Much of the spread of the doctrine of people's war has been more indirect, however: would-be insurgent leaders studied together at the University of Dar es Salaam in the 1960s, for

[9] Guevara, *Guerrilla Warfare*, p. 22.
[10] For a comprehensive review of the literature, see Walter Laqueur, *Guerrilla Warfare: A Historical and Critical Study* (New Brunswick, NJ: Transaction, 1998).
[11] Charles Tilly, *From Mobilization to Revolution* (New York: McGraw-Hill, 1978).

example, before launching rebellions in Sudan, Uganda, and Mozambique, and rebel leaders have borrowed liberally from Mao and Guevara in writing their own manifestos.

Divergent Practices

The empirical record suggests that although strategies of organization pioneered by people's war theorists are openly recognized and adopted by modern insurgencies, they are implemented unevenly and with varied success in different contexts. Consider the example of Nepal: Comrade Prachanda, who founded the Communist Party of Nepal and organized its insurgent campaigns, explicitly attempted to put Maoist theories of guerrilla warfare into practice.[12] His "Problems and Prospects of Revolution in Nepal" quotes Chairman Mao extensively, and Comrade Prachanda's own contributions employ the language of Maoist thought. Prachanda proclaims to his followers, for example, that "the main task of the People's Army in the 21st century should be to accomplish the historical responsibility of developing conscious armed masses capable to use their right to rebel." He outlines the principal conditions for the success of guerrilla war: "Guerrilla war can be developed only if it is conducted for the masses and by the masses"; "Guerrilla war does not develop without a continuous process of awakening and organizing more and more people through faster and better methods"; and "Without the concrete goal of building base areas and without developing them, it is not possible to develop guerrilla [war]." Journalists report that the Maoists in Nepal have put this philosophy into practice, following in the footsteps of Peru's Shining Path by mobilizing civilians for political education campaigns, building new organs of power at the community level, and cleansing the countryside of supporters of the state.[13]

Compare this to the case of Sierra Leone. "Footpaths to Democracy," the manifesto of Sierra Leone's Revolutionary United Front (RUF), implores its followers to embrace three ideals: "arms to the people," "power to the people," and "wealth to the people."[14] Its language is also reminiscent of

---

[12] A series of writings by Prachanda and other key leaders in the Communist Party of Nepal are included in an online volume, "Problems and Prospects of Revolution in Nepal," http://www.cpnm.org/new/collected_articles/cover.htm.

[13] "Nepal's Maoists Follow Peru's Shining Path Game Plan," *Agence France Presse*, August 19, 2004; David Rohde, "Youth Ensnared in Nepal's War with Maoists," *New York Times*, December 9, 2004, p. A1.

[14] The Revolutionary United Front's manifesto, "Footpaths to Democracy: Toward a New Sierra Leone," is available at http://www.sierra-leone.org/footpaths.html.

the treatises on people's war. "It is an organized and informed people who constitute the motive force of any political and economical revolution," the manifesto declares. The organization expresses its "abiding faith in the necessity of democratic empowerment of the people" and its conviction that "political power can only stand the test of time when it originates from the people themselves." "Wealth to the people," according to the manifesto, "means that the people should empower themselves in order to harness their resources and use them for their own survival and development." Translated into practice, however, this ideology of democratic empowerment, self-reliance, and social mobilization took the form of amputation, mutilation, rape, and abduction. Efforts to mobilize civilians became campaigns of forced recruitment. Democratic empowerment in rebel-governed villages involved the appointment of civilian collaborators as "commanders" of rebel zones. Injunctions to respect the property of noncombatants were ignored in favor of widespread looting.[15]

As these examples illustrate, similar philosophies of rebel organization adopted in diverse contexts give rise to a variety of organizational forms. The proponents of people's war as a strategy for rebel organization discovered this truth for themselves in attempting to transplant the Cuban model to other contexts. Che Guevara led an international contingent of more than 100 Cuban fighters into eastern Congo in 1965 to support and build a movement against Western imperialism in Africa.[16] Because the leadership of the Congolese liberation struggle was based in exile, Guevara and his colleagues were given significant latitude in shaping and commanding the guerrilla force. Yet Guevara's effort to mold Congolese fighters in the image of Cuban revolutionaries was a disaster. He departed after less than a year, leaving Congo in the clutches of Mobutu Sese Seko, who then ruled for more than 30 years.

Examining Guevara's reflections on the struggles he encountered in Congo is instructive, as it offers insight into why rebel strategies diverge so much in practice. Guevara concluded that the rebellion had failed to select "revolutionaries" to fight. He recalled: "It was a lottery whether or not you would find [among the recruits] any real revolutionaries.... They had a very high opinion of themselves, a very highly developed concept of the personal obligation to take care of cadres [themselves] and the idea

---

[15] Ibrahim Abdullah, "Bush Path to Destruction: The Origin and Character of the Revolutionary United Front," *Journal of Modern African Studies* 36 (1998): 203–35.

[16] William Gálvez, *Che in Africa: Che Guevara's Congo Diary* (Melbourne: Ocean Press, 1999).

that the revolution owed them a lot."[17] Guevara also criticized the movement for failing to create cohesion among the cadres. Cuban participants saw themselves as "foreigners" and "superior beings" who knew how the revolution should be run. They responded to the undisciplined, uncommitted nature of the Congolese recruits by reinforcing a hierarchy within the organization. Lacking a common identity or even a shared language, the new revolutionary organization struggled to survive the hardships of war. Despite having an ideal tutor, the rebellion in Congo fizzled; its combatants turned to drinking and looting rather than face the risky proposition of launching guerrilla attacks.

The writings of Guevara and other revolutionaries point to the importance of the internal character of movements, while the empirical record suggests that differences in organizational practice may be critical to understanding how rebellions unfold. But practitioners of revolution do not offer a theoretical account of the emergence of different types of movements. We turn our attention next to scholars of rebellion in search of insight into organizational design and its effects.

Theories of Rebellion: The Puzzling Absence of Organization

The two dominant models that explain where rebellion takes place say surprisingly little about how it is organized. One approach treats rebel organizations as social movements; the other treats rebel groups as if they were states. Both take organization as a given, focusing instead on the structural conditions that pave the way for rebellion to unfold. Such approaches may be useful for understanding the onset of civil war, but a more micro-level perspective on how violence is organized is required to make sense of the strategies groups pursue.

The first model conceptualizes rebel organizations as social movements that use violence. It is argued that such movements form as a consequence of rapid structural changes in a society and their differential impact on groups in the population. In some accounts, economic change gives rise to social discontent: the specific pathway is psychological, as individuals experience a discrepancy between what they think they should have and what they can actually attain.[18] The resulting discontent, when politicized,

---

[17] Ibid., p. 288.

[18] Ted Gurr, *Why Men Rebel* (Princeton: Princeton University Press, 1970), p. 13. Gurr's book followed earlier work by James Davies that pioneered a theory of psychological response

leads to organized violence. Economic change may also result in violence if it is more detrimental to some social groups than to others. Accounts that focus on peasant subsistence crises,[19] the favoring of one region over another,[20] and the pitting of social classes against each other[21] all make arguments about the strains introduced by economic change. Scholars of ethnic violence argue that social and economic change generates "status concerns" as ethnic groups compete for control over access to wealth and political power.[22] Crucially, rapid structural changes may also weaken the state's administrative, policing, and military organizations, creating conditions favorable to organized revolts.[23] Given that grievances are a constant in many transitional societies, the opportunity for rebellion is shaped in important ways by the actions of the state.

Models that treat rebel organizations as social movements conceptualize rebellion itself as the explosion of discontent from an aggrieved group. Making sense of it thus requires a theory of what causes discontent and the conditions under which it can be acted upon. The focus is on what might be called the *demand side* of rebellion. Grievances, which motivate the masses to participate, and opportunity, which is related to state capacity and the density of social networks, emerge as critical variables in the analysis. Theories of the onset of rebellion leave much unexplained, however. They tie collective action too directly to motivation. Where peasants suffer

---

to structural change. Davies argued that political stability requires a "state of mind" or a "mood" in society and that rapid structural changes disrupt that state of mind, thereby giving rise to violence. In particular, he suggested that social changes may create a phenomenon of rising expectations that ultimately cannot be attained, leading to conflict. See "Toward a Theory of Revolution," *American Sociological Review* 27 (1962): 5–19.

[19] James Scott, *The Moral Economy of the Peasant: Rebellion and Subsistence in Southeast Asia* (New Haven: Yale University Press, 1976).

[20] Eric Wolf, *Peasant Wars of the Twentieth Century* (New York: Harper and Row, 1969).

[21] Jeffrey Paige, *Agrarian Revolution: Social Movements and Export Agriculture in the Underdeveloped World* (New York: Free Press, 1975).

[22] A classic in this literature is Donald Horowitz, *Ethnic Groups in Conflict* (Berkeley: University of California Press, 1985). For a good review of the literature on ethnic conflict, see Daniel Byman, *Keeping the Peace: Lasting Solutions to Ethnic Conflicts* (Baltimore: Johns Hopkins University Press, 2002), pp. 13–44.

[23] Theda Skocpol, *States and Social Revolutions: A Comparative Analysis of France, Russia, and China* (Cambridge, MA: Harvard University Press, 1979). Skocpol draws her conclusions based on an analysis of revolutions in France, Russia, China, Japan, and Germany. Today, these revolutions appear far removed from modern civil wars in the developing world. Skocpol took her findings on the key role of state structure and weakness, however, and applied them to the study of modern conflicts as well. See *Social Revolutions in the Modern World* (Cambridge: Cambridge University Press, 1994).

disproportionately during times of economic change, it is argued that they will rebel. Where one region is looted by the central government for the benefit of others, that region will take up arms to seek independence. The model makes implicit claims that all peasants or all residents of an aggrieved region will want to participate, will be invited to participate, and will mobilize to act on their collectively held grievances when the opportunity exists. From the perspective of the present analysis, these theories are not wrong, but they offer little that helps to make sense of why insurgent groups adopt different organizational forms and practices. Ethnic groups excluded from access to the state's coffers may organize a disciplined movement to capture power, as the Banyankole and Baganda did in Uganda, or an undisciplined campaign of violence, as the Ndau and Sena did in Mozambique. Groups living under a weakened central state may mobilize large numbers of civilians in a movement for change, as the Shining Path did across most of Peru, or, in the region where state control is the weakest, they may take advantage of that weakness to invest heavily in the drug trade, as did the Shining Path's regional committee in the Upper Huallaga Valley. These examples draw attention to the *supply side* of rebellion – to the nature of the group that emerges to capitalize on grievance and opportunity. If motivation and opportunity can be taken as a given, other factors must be considered to explain why group strategies diverge so much in practice.

The second model treats rebel organizations as states or states in the making. Applying arguments developed initially for the study of interstate war, some scholars have argued that rebellion is the result of a security dilemma.[24] Following the collapse of a central authority, domestic groups compete for control so they can protect their own interests. Like states in the international system, rebel organizations form in an environment characterized by anarchy. Unable to count on the protection of the state, they take actions to improve their own security. These actions, in turn, make others feel less secure, so they respond in kind, and the environment

---

[24] Barry Posen was one of the first scholars to specifically apply the tenets of neorealism to the study of ethnic conflict. See "The Security Dilemma and Ethnic Conflict," in *Ethnic Conflict and International Security*, ed. Michael Brown (Princeton: Princeton University Press, 1993), pp. 103–24. Others have followed suit, including Stephen Van Evera in "Hypotheses on Nationalism and War," *International Security* 18, no. 4 (Spring 1994): 5–39, and Robert Wagner in "The Causes of Peace," in *Stopping the Killing: How Civil Wars End*, ed. Roy Licklider (New York: New York University Press, 1993), pp. 235–68. For a good critique of this literature, see Steven David, "Internal War: Causes and Cures," *World Politics* 49, no. 4 (July 1997): 552–76.

is made less stable. When all groups go on the offensive, the result is violence.

Again, organization is largely missing from this model of rebellion. The logic of the security dilemma makes no predictions about *how* groups will organize to protect their security; it simply suggests that they *will* organize. The existence of an environment of anarchy is deemed sufficient to make sense of the participation of individuals in conflict, the mobilization of groups, and the violent strategies they employ. Rebel organizations, like states in traditional studies of interstate war, are treated like a black box.

Some accounts that see rebel groups performing statelike functions provide more traction on the issue of organization.[25] These accounts see rebel organizations as legitimate competitors for the mantle of sovereign control of territory and explain that they begin to perform the functions of government even before they take power in the capital. The key function they perform is the provision of collective goods. In order to deliver collective goods, rebel groups must be of sufficient size and strength to challenge the government for control of specific territories. This contestation gives rise to a situation of multiple sovereignty in which at least two contenders compete to be the central political authority and at least some part of the population honors the claim of the challenging group by following its directives.[26] With a credible claim to control over a specific part of the national territory, rebel groups offer their constituents collective benefits as an incentive for support, much as governments do when they provide basic education, health care, and infrastructure. The most important collective good rebel groups provide is security – in particular, they offer protection from government forces. Counterinsurgent armies are notoriously brutal, employing tactics that target civilians indiscriminately in an effort to dry up the support base for guerrilla movements. Such indiscriminate violence can drive civilians into the waiting arms of rebel groups, especially when such groups are able to mobilize their forces to protect noncombatants from further harm and abuse at the hands of the government. Extreme levels of state violence often leave civilians no other option than to join the insurgents or to live behind guerrilla lines.[27]

---

[25] Theda Skocpol, "What Makes Peasants Revolutionary?" *Comparative Politics* 14 (1982): 351–75; Jeff Goodwin and Theda Skocpol, "Explaining Revolutions in the Contemporary Third World," *Politics and Society* 17 (1989): 489–509.

[26] Tilly, *From Mobilization to Revolution*, pp. 135, 191–93.

[27] Jeff Goodwin analyzes the role of state violence as a motivation for the organization of insurgency, but the logic of the argument holds in wartime as well. See *No Other Way Out:*

Security is not the only collective good offered by rebel groups acting as states. Some groups begin to deliver on their political platforms long before taking power at the national level. Rebels have been known to offer land to their constituents, to reshape market relationships and interaction in the communities they control, to implement campaigns to improve public health, and to attempt to address the social ills that plague the areas in which they operate.[28]

The view of rebel organizations as providers of goods figures prominently in the chapters that follow. It rests on a compact between the rulers and the ruled, even in zones of contested sovereignty: collective goods are offered in exchange for the consent to be governed. This is an essential building block of governance. Yet while the conception of rebel groups as statelike entities provides a useful frame, it does not touch on the question of variation. It does not predict under what conditions rebel organizations will take on the tasks of governance or what types of institutions they will build, nor does it explain why some groups refrain from taking on a state-building role.

A coherent theory of why rebel groups choose the strategies they do depends, I argue, on a clear understanding of the micropolitics of rebellion, which is achieved by focusing on how groups organize violence – on the choices rebel leaders make about how to recruit soldiers, groups' decisions about whether to centralize or decentralize command, and the structures movements set in place to ensure that foot soldiers act in accordance with objectives. Engaging civilians on the outside of a rebel group is a fundamental aspect of the micropolitics of rebellion, and thus the decisions leaders make about how to extract the resources they need to maintain their organizations, govern civilians who live in their areas of control, and discipline traitors who defect or attempt to defect to the side of the enemy all figure prominently in the study of how violence is organized.

Each of these steps in an organization's development points to broader questions of institutional choice. From an array of possible strategies, rebel leaders select those they believe will best serve their organizational goals. It is in exploring how leaders weigh the costs and benefits of particular

---

States and Revolutionary Movements, 1945–91 (Cambridge: Cambridge University Press, 2001).

[28] Timothy Wickham Crowley, *Guerrillas and Revolutions in Latin America: A Comparative Study of Insurgents and Regimes since 1956* (Princeton: Princeton University Press, 1991).

organizational strategies that the macro-level factors identified in previous studies of rebellion resurface. These factors condition the choices that rebel leaders make and constrain the set of strategies they can employ. A focus on the formation and evolution of rebel groups thereby links the micropolitics of recruitment and organization to the macropolitics of rebellion and, as I will show, provides substantial leverage for understanding variation in the behaviors exhibited by groups in conflict.

In choosing to look inside rebel groups at how they are structured, I join ranks with a group of scholars whose pioneering research on the varied appeals of communism and the formation of communist groups laid a foundation for my research.[29] Lucian Pye's study of the Malayan Communist Party, for example, highlighted the centrality of organizational structure in the party's success. Pye concluded: "A particular group was 'well-organized' and thus had influence, because those who belonged to it knew how they stood with each other; they could have confidence in the stability of their relationships and outsiders would be aware of that fact."[30] His research brought aspects of organization such as indoctrination, hierarchy, and discipline – previously ignored in studies of collective action – to the fore. Philip Selznick's study of Bolshevism identified its genius as the ability to transform a voluntary association into a managerial structure.[31] Understanding strategy meant making sense of how groups turn individuals into agents capable of subsuming their individual interests for the benefit of the group. Following such scholars, I make how groups organize a question that requires explanation. But by looking beyond communist insurgencies, I draw attention to differences in the internal structures of groups that could not have been captured in previous studies.

Organizing Violence

In this section, I outline an economic approach to the study of rebel organization. The building blocks I discuss here are used in subsequent chapters to trace how groups form, why they choose the structures they do, and

---

[29] Gabriel Almond, *The Appeals of Communism* (Princeton: Princeton University Press, 1954); Lucian Pye, *Guerrilla Communism in Malaya* (Princeton: Princeton University Press, 1956); Philip Selznick, *The Organizational Weapon: A Study of Bolshevik Tactics and Strategy* (New York: McGraw Hill, 1952).

[30] Pye, *Guerrilla Communism in Malaya*, p. 190.

[31] Selznick, *The Organizational Weapon*.

why their strategies diverge so widely in practice. The framework has two main elements. The first part identifies the central organizational challenges rebel leaders face, while the second highlights politically salient variation in the initial conditions leaders confront as they organize, demonstrating how macro-level conditions constrain micro-level decisions. Choices about how to organize, made in different ways by different groups, thus become the puzzle that requires explanation. Comparing and contrasting these choices across groups depends on a recognition that leaders face similar challenges; that regardless of context, processes of organizational formation and growth can be usefully analyzed as a set of distinct choices leaders make; and that broader structural factors can be interpreted as a set of constraints that shape the organizational strategies groups pursue.

My starting point is the economics of organization.[32] I begin with the assumption that individuals are rational and that their actions reflect deliberate decisions designed to maximize payoffs. Economists traditionally think of these payoffs as material rewards, and I find that a useful starting point in thinking about how individuals weigh the costs and benefits of participating in rebellion. But these payoffs need not be material: studies of participation in high-risk collective action in diverse contexts point to nonmaterial benefits as well, such as prestige, acceptance, and the opportunity to exercise agency.[33] Reviewing the literature on the economics of organization, Terry Moe suggests that organizations can be understood in terms of the "transaction costs inherent in a system of exchange relationships among rational individuals."[34] Formalizing what can be considered contractual relationships between individuals, organizations arrange individuals hierarchically in a relationship of authority and coordinate their decisions in order to

---

[32] The use of economic tools to understand organizational design began with the work of Ronald Coase, who identified a role for entrepreneurs to structure a hierarchy in an effort to reduce transaction costs. See "The Nature of the Firm," *Economica* 4 (1937): 386–405. Subsequent work has focused on the design and impact of institutions on market exchange. See, for example, Oliver Williamson, *Markets and Hierarchies* (New York: Free Press, 1975), and Douglass North, *Institutions, Institutional Change, and Economic Performance* (New York: Cambridge University Press, 1990).

[33] Doug McAdam, *Political Process and the Development of Black Insurgency, 1930–1970* (Chicago: University of Chicago Press, 1982); Elisabeth Wood, *Insurgent Collective Action in El Salvador* (New York: Cambridge University Press, 2004).

[34] A widely cited review of the literature on institutional economics and its relevance for politics is Terry Moe, "The New Economics of Organization," *American Journal of Political Science* 28 (1984): 739–77.

reduce the transaction costs that are generated in a decentralized or voluntary system of exchange.

Employing this language to make sense of organization in the context of rebellion is not too large a leap. Individuals who share the goal of overthrowing an existing regime contract with one another to invest their time, energy, and resources in a military campaign. Mounting an effort requires negotiating access to ammunition, food, shelter, and intelligence from a host of outside parties. Organizing hierarchically reduces the costs of establishing all of these relationships to maintain the group. Hierarchy also offers a means to coordinate the decisions and investments made by individuals interested in contributing to the organization.

Taking this economic approach draws attention to the importance of incentives in motivating behavior. Contracts – and organization more generally – matter because they help to mitigate some of the inefficiencies that result when individuals act according to their self-interest. One inefficiency at the heart of organizational economics is adverse selection.[35] Problems arise from the fact that information about the skills, beliefs, and values of others is often unobservable. Consider the situation in which an employer wishes to hire someone to fill a position in a firm. Although he would like to attract qualified and motivated applicants with excellent work habits, he cannot know the true capabilities and intentions of a given applicant. Instead, he proceeds on the basis of rough indicators, such as an applicant's education or job experience. The wage he offers to potential employees is thus a statistical average: it reflects the employer's estimate of how these rough indicators translate into improved productivity and how productivity is likely to vary across all individuals who meet the nominal qualifications. Applicants offered the position know their true capabilities and intentions and evaluate the offered wage in reference to what they consider their true economic value to be. Highly skilled and committed applicants find that the wage offer is too low; less desirable applicants who nonetheless meet the formal proxy requirements find the opportunity more enticing. The result is that an employer attracts a disproportionate number of low-quality applicants and hires them, even though he wants to attract the best, and the best want to be hired. The asymmetry of information selects for less desirable employees.

---

[35] A. Michael Spence offers the classic statement of adverse selection in the employment market. See *Market Signaling: Informational Transfer in Hiring and Related Screening Processes* (Cambridge, MA: Harvard University Press, 1974).

A second concept, moral hazard, addresses how the unobservability of employees' behavior reduces the productivity of an organization.[36] Here, the problem occurs because an individual's contribution to the overall productivity of a firm cannot be directly measured, and employers must rely on proxies to evaluate the effort put forward by their staff. Employees have an incentive to redirect their efforts toward the proxy measures rather than the broader goals of the organization or to substitute leisure for effort, since their actual contributions are unobservable. Shirking behavior thus results from information asymmetries that exist in an ex post contracting situation.

The economic analysis of organizations identifies problems inherent in the contracting relationship, such as the informational asymmetries described earlier; asks why these problems exist; outlines how they affect the performance of firms; and explores how their consequences can be mitigated. In pursuit of this final goal, economists design structures and strategies of organization that properly align incentives so that individual self-interest is harnessed for the broader goals of the organization. The emergence of different organizational structures and practices can be usefully viewed as a response to the incentive problems inherent in contracting relationships.

Five Challenges of Rebel Organization

Incentive problems in the context of private firms may seem a bit removed from the organizations at the center of this book, but the contractual relationships at the heart of organized violent resistance can be reframed easily in terms first developed by theorists of the economics of organization. Thinking about the challenges rebel leaders confront as incentive problems they need to resolve helps to clarify the distinct strategies they can pursue.

Recruitment is the classic challenge of rebel organization and one to which the tools of economic analysis have already been applied. Mancur Olson's influential statement of the dilemma inherent in collective action has shaped subsequent studies of organization in areas as diverse as party formation, union mobilization, and rebellion.[37] Olson argues that organizations seeking to provide a collective good from which nonparticipants

---

[36] For a discussion of moral hazard in the context of a firm, see Gary Miller, *Managerial Dilemmas: The Political Economy of Hierarchy* (New York: Cambridge University Press, 1992), Chapter 6.

[37] Mancur Olson, *The Logic of Collective Action: Public Goods and the Theory of Groups* (Cambridge, MA: Harvard University Press, 1965).

cannot realistically be excluded face a free rider problem: only those individuals who have the strongest interest in the collective good will contribute time and effort; others will benefit from the organization's success but shirk from making their own contributions. As organizations grow in size, the free rider problem worsens. Collective action itself is threatened by the individual's pursuit of self-interest.

Studies of rebellion have recognized the incentive problems inherent in the contractual relationship between leaders of a rebellion and potential foot soldiers, and a generation of scholars has identified the range of strategies groups pursue to mitigate this problem. These include providing selective incentives to participants, activating reciprocity norms in tightly knit communities, appealing to nonmaterial interests such as ideology and social acceptance, and employing sanctions, including violence, to police defection.[38] The ways in which informational asymmetries shape the contracting dilemma in rebel recruitment have not been part of the story, however. Like employers in a private firm, rebel leaders also wish to attract qualified, committed, and able recruits interested in the long-term goals of the organization. Rebellions face a challenge of adverse selection similar to that plaguing firms: the strategies rebel leaders pursue in overcoming collective action problems (that is, the appeals they make to potential recruits) shape the profile of the members they attract. The first organizational challenge this book tackles is thus recruitment: I wish to identify the strategies rebel leaders pursue in building a membership and to explain how the strategies they choose affect the profile of the members they attract.

A second challenge of *control* emerges when rebel leaders turn from the task of recruiting members to managing their behavior. An organization's success depends on its ability to motivate its members to behave in ways consistent with its broader goals and objectives. A lack of discipline among the rank and file wastes resources, alienates potential supporters, and may undermine military efforts. Moral hazard is a particular problem for rebel

[38] On selective incentives, see Samuel Popkin, *The Rational Peasant: The Political Economy of Rural Society in Vietnam* (Berkeley: University of California Press, 1979), and Mark Lichbach, "What Makes Rational Peasants Revolutionary? Dilemma, Paradox, and Irony in Peasant Collective Action," *World Politics* 46 (1994): 383–418. On leadership, see Norman Frolich, Joseph Oppenheimer, and Oran Young, *Political Leadership and Collective Goods* (Princeton: Princeton University Press, 1971). On norms and solidarity, see Michael Taylor, "Rationality and Revolutionary Collective Action," in *Rationality and Revolution*, ed. Michael Taylor (New York: Cambridge University Press, 1988), pp. 63–97; and Michael Hechter, *Principles of Group Solidarity* (Berkeley: University of California Press, 1987).

organizations, as monitoring the behavior of combatants is difficult and costly. The imperative to decentralize by assigning tasks and authority to lower-level commanders and units for military purposes worsens the incentive problems already inherent in the principal–agent relationship. Choices leaders make in this context are about how to shape, manage, and control the behavior of their foot soldiers. In analyzing how rebel leaders control their soldiers, I consider what sorts of investments are made in political and military training, to what extent command authority is centralized, and what kinds of rules and codes are formalized to guide behavior and punish indiscipline.

Incentive problems also condition the strategies of *governance* leaders choose in their relationships with noncombatants. Rebel groups are in a bind when it comes to governing the civilians who live in their zones of influence and control. Leaders want to extract what they need from noncombatants in order to sustain their movements, but they must try to avoid extracting so much that civilians become alienated and defect to the opposition. From the perspective of civilians, rebel groups have a credibility problem: they have to prove that they can take resources without taking too much. Rebel leaders must make choices about the structure of the governments they build in liberated zones, deciding how much power should be shared with noncombatants, what lines should be drawn between military and nonmilitary spheres of the movement, and who should be the face of the group in interactions with civilians.

A similar challenge presents itself when groups consider how to use *violence*. Force is a powerful tool for influencing civilians and disciplining potential defectors. Used selectively, violence sends clear signals about the costs of supporting the other side. Like governance, however, violence can also alienate supporters and generate active resistance from noncombatants. Rebel leaders have imperfect information about who is likely to defect to the other side, and they face monitoring problems when it comes to implementing orders to use force. Rebel leaders' choices about when and how to use violence are thus shaped by the nature of their interactions with potential defectors and the structure of the organizations they manage.

A final organizational challenge relates to expansion and recovery: rebel organizations must demonstrate *resilience* in the changing circumstances they confront without alienating their members and supporters. All contractual relationships depend on the formalization of a set of expectations about who will do what for whom and when. But war is a dynamic process. At times, rebel groups experience enormous successes. At other times, they suffer significant setbacks. The challenge for rebel leaders is to manage changing expectations over time – to convince their core supporters that they will not be forgotten when the march to victory is complete and to maintain a base of supporters when defeat is on the horizon.

This is not the first study to tackle issues of rebellion from an organizational perspective or to draw on the insights of new institutional economics in making sense of violence. Following such scholars as Samuel Popkin, Michael Taylor, Mark Lichbach, Roger Petersen, and Elisabeth Wood, I begin with the puzzle of collective action.[39] Addressing the question of why individuals accept enormous risks to participate in violence is a necessary first step in the study of civil war. Building on the insights of Stathis Kalyvas, I conceptualize the use of violence as the outcome of an interaction in which rebel groups act strategically in seeking support from noncombatants.[40] Where the analysis in this book departs from these works is in exploring how the strategies a group employs in the recruitment process affect its internal structure and the strategies it can ultimately pursue. This approach identifies differences in the organization of rebel groups as something fundamental to understanding why some civil wars are characterized by high levels of indiscriminate violence and others are not.

Constraints on Strategy

Choices rebel leaders make about how to respond to the five organizational challenges I described in the preceding section have important consequences for the patterns of violence observed in conflict. Before turning to the empirical evidence, we need hypotheses about politically salient variation in the initial conditions leaders confront that may influence how they address these incentive problems in different environments. In its focus on the conditions that support and impede particular forms of collective

---

[39] Popkin, *The Rational Peasant*; Taylor, "Rationality and Revolutionary Collective Action"; Mark Lichbach, *The Rebel's Dilemma* (Ann Arbor: University of Michigan Press, 1994); Roger Petersen, *Resistance and Rebellion: Lessons from Eastern Europe* (New York: Cambridge University Press, 2001); Wood, *Insurgent Collective Action*.

[40] Stathis Kalyvas, *The Logic of Violence in Civil War* (New York: Cambridge University Press, 2006).

action, the social movement literature offers a window into the factors that shape strategy.

One dominant, albeit controversial, claim in this literature is that social movements form in response to political opportunities.[41] Opportunities help to translate the potential for action into a movement. In the words of the most prominent advocate of this theory, political opportunity structures are "consistent dimensions of the political environment which either encourage or discourage people from using collective action."[42] Political opportunity theorists identify resources external to groups – such as changes in access to power, shifts in ruling alignments, the emergence of potential allies, or cleavages among elites – that lower the costs of collective action and point political entrepreneurs toward vulnerabilities among elites that can be exploited. Scholars like Theda Skocpol who embrace a focus on political opportunities emphasize how changes within states provide openings for the mobilization of revolution.[43] But variation in dimensions of political opportunity cannot explain the different ways in which rebel groups use violence, at least for the four rebel groups discussed in this study. Each of these groups emerged in an environment where the conditions were ripe for rebellion. Those excluded from the political system voiced legitimate grievances, and weaknesses in the national political structure opened the door to the mobilization of violence. The convenient explanation that groups turn to violence when no political opportunities exist for rebellion simply does not hold.

I turn instead to the insights of an older line of inquiry in social movement scholarship: the theory of resource mobilization.[44] It begins with the idea that the dynamics of a movement depend in important ways on its resources and organization. The focus is on movement entrepreneurs, whose success

---

[41] Jeff Goodwin and James Jasper warn that the concept of political opportunity structure suffers from conceptual overstretching, making it at times "tautological, trivial, and inadequate" to the task of providing a model of social movements. See "Caught in a Winding, Snarling Vine: The Structural Bias of Political Process Theory," *Sociological Forum* 14 (1999): 27–54, and the responses that follow.

[42] Sidney Tarrow, *Power in Movement* (New York: Cambridge University Press, 1998), p. 18.

[43] Skocpol, *States and Social Revolutions*. Economists working on civil war have also identified changes in the opportunities for rebellion as a key determinant of onset, far more important empirically, they argue, than measures of discrimination and grievance. See Paul Collier and Anke Hoeffler, "Greed and Grievance in Civil War," *Oxford Economic Papers* 56 (2004): 663–95.

[44] For a review of this literature, see J. Craig Jenkins, "Resource Mobilization Theory and the Study of Social Movements," *Annual Review of Sociology* 9 (1983): 527–53.

is determined by the availability of resources.[45] In sharp contrast to the literature focused on the grievances that motivate collective action, two of the foremost proponents of resource mobilization theory claim that "the definition of grievances will expand to meet the funds and support personnel available."[46]

There is significant variation in the resources to which potential rebel leaders have access. I will be arguing that variation in these initial endowments affects the strategies they pursue in organizing violence. Yet the social movement literature has not arrived at any consensus regarding how to classify the different resources groups utilize in the process of organizing. The most useful distinction was offered by Jo Freeman, who distinguished between tangible assets, such as money and facilities, and intangible assets, such as the skills and commitments of movement participants.[47] I propose my own classificatory scheme, distinguishing between *economic* endowments on the one hand and *social* endowments on the other.

"Economic endowments" refer to resources that can be mobilized to finance the start-up and maintenance of a rebel organization. Like tangible assets, economic endowments are concrete: they can be utilized directly and immediately to purchase supplies and pay participants. They ease the organization of rebellion, putting incipient rebel groups in a better position to challenge the government. Access to economic endowments allows rebel groups to offer salaries to attract potential participants. Financial resources also permit rebel groups to equip soldiers with guns and ammunition from the beginning instead of relying on risky attacks to generate arms. And money minimizes the supply problems that typically plague guerrilla armies, from accessing food to obtaining medicine to treat wounded soldiers.

Such financing can come from many sources. Some groups are able to organize the extraction of natural resources, including timber, valuable gemstones, and other minerals. Others rely on the taxation of local production or the conduct of criminal business, including the drug trade. Still others receive donations from supporters in the diaspora or contributions from external patrons. These diverse sources of funds share a common

---

[45] John McCarthy and Mayer Zald, *The Trend of Social Movements* (Morristown, NJ: General Learning, 1973); John McCarthy and Mayer Zald, "Resource Mobilization and Social Movements," *American Journal of Sociology* 82 (1977): 1212–41.

[46] McCarthy and Zald, *Trend of Social Movements*, p. 13.

[47] Jo Freeman, "Resource Mobilization and Strategy," in *The Dynamics of Social Movements*, eds. Mayer Zald and John McCarthy (Cambridge, MA: Winthrop, 1979), pp. 167–89.

characteristic: the resources are not mobilized as voluntary contributions from the direct beneficiaries of the rebellion. Just as resource mobilization theory draws attention to the ways in which social movement organizations become more professional as a consequence of outside funding, this book explores the impact of resource wealth on the membership profile and structure of rebel organizations.

Of course, economic endowments vary in the ease with which they can be mobilized, as the case of natural resources makes clear. Michael Ross differentiates resources by the extent to which they are lootable and obstructable.[48] "Lootability" refers to the ease with which a resource can be extracted and transported by a small group of individuals. Drugs, diamonds, and agricultural commodities are highly lootable; other types of minerals, oil, and gas cannot be looted without significant investment. A resource is "obstructable" if its transport can be easily blocked by small groups of people with guns; it is difficult to obstruct if it requires large numbers of people with heavy weaponry to disrupt its transport. Resources like gemstones and illegal drugs are difficult to obstruct, as they can be easily ferreted out of remote locations by air. Oil, gas, and timber, by contrast, typically move by road or in above ground pipelines and can be intercepted or disrupted by small, armed groups. Similarly, support from external patrons can come in many forms. Outside actors may offer cash, armaments, or training, and they may do so with or without imposing conditions or their own agenda on the conflict. The nature of the economic endowments to which groups have access, along with how much they have, shapes the recruitment, organizational, and governance tactics rebels employ.

"Social endowments" refer to distinctive identities and dense interpersonal networks that can be readily mobilized in support of collective action.[49] Identities and networks provide sources of solidarity and moral commitment, enabling groups to draw on internalized values and sentiments, as well as calculations of self-interest, in motivating participation. References in the literature on revolution to the importance of "peasant solidarity" or "strong communal traditions" suggest the role of social

---

[48] Michael Ross, "Oil, Drugs, and Diamonds: How Do Natural Resources Vary in Their Impact on Civil War?" in *Beyond Greed and Grievance: The Political Economy of Armed Conflict*, eds. Karen Ballentine and Jake Sherman (Boulder, CO: Lynne Rienner, 2003), pp. 47–70. For a similar set of arguments, see Philippe Le Billon, "The Political Ecology of War: Natural Resources and Armed Conflict," *Political Geography* 20 (2001): 561–84.

[49] Tilly, *From Mobilization to Revolution*.

endowments in making rebellion possible; here, I uncover their impact on how violence is organized.[50] Social endowments help groups to overcome the barriers to organization by activating norms of generalized reciprocity among leaders and their followers, making it possible for individuals to commit time and energy to a movement in the short term in return for only the promise of rewards in the future. Feelings of solidarity and moral commitments also help to fuse personal and collective interests, providing rebel leaders with the tools they need to attract soldiers and manage their behavior in accordance with the goals of the group.

Like economic endowments, social endowments flow from diverse sources. The focus of the social movement literature on "mobilizing structures" underscores the importance as an organizational resource of social networks, which tie small groups of committed individuals to one another in contexts of repeated interaction.[51] Networks may be formed on the basis of common interests or identities, and preexisting networks can ease the process of identifying, recruiting, and managing the foot soldiers of a rebellion. "Social endowments" also refers to beliefs and norms of reciprocity that lower transaction costs and facilitate cooperation. The operation of norms and the emergence of shared beliefs is often facilitated by social networks that connect individuals to one another through horizontal ties, where each person is on an equal footing. Such horizontal linkages exist among coethnics along the lines of kinship ties, among neighbors who share the same community, and between recruits to an ideological movement who come together as they accept new beliefs and practices. My approach to thinking about social endowments is not far removed from Robert Putnam's emphasis on social capital. In his study of why some Italian regional governments were more effective than others, he found that the form and effectiveness of institutions depended on the degree to which different regions had networks of civic engagement and norms of reciprocity forged hundreds of years earlier.[52]

---

[50] Skocpol, *States and Social Revolutions*; Scott, *Moral Economy*.

[51] Doug McAdam's work on the Freedom Summer campaign drew attention to the importance of social networks for understanding participation in collective action. See "Recruitment to High Risk Activism: The Case of Freedom Summer," *American Journal of Sociology* 92 (1986): 64–90, and *Freedom Summer* (New York: Oxford University Press, 1988). See also Tarrow, *Power in Movement*.

[52] Robert Putnam, *Making Democracy Work: Civic Traditions in Modern Italy* (Princeton: Princeton University Press, 1993). For an argument about the importance of social mechanisms

The social movement literature eventually abandoned its focus on the deterministic influence of organizational resources; this book adopts a dynamic approach to their role. Endowments shape and constrain the range of strategies leaders can employ as they organize violence. Endowments are not fate, yet they play a powerful role because they affect the cost-benefit calculations leaders make while evaluating distinct approaches to resolving the organizational challenges described earlier. Of course, in practice, no group has access to or uses only economic or social endowments. Rebel organizations fall along a continuum that captures the extent to which leaders mix these resources as they build their organizations. It is useful for the purpose of drawing out different strategies, however, to explore how access to more of one endowment than another conditions the choices leaders make, the nature of the membership they attract, and the type of organization that emerges.

The Origins of Constraints

My approach may generate some controversy with its contention that an initial stock of economic and social endowments can be thought of as fixed and exogenous, but there are some very good reasons for adopting this position as a starting point. Many of the endowments I describe are determined exogenously. Whether a movement can finance itself with the proceeds of illicit coca production or diamond smuggling, for example, is primarily a function of geography. Other endowments are both difficult and slow to change. The willingness of external patrons to finance insurgency is as much a product of external factors as it is determined by the desires or strategies of an insurgent leader. The geographic distribution and relative size of ethnic, religious, or cultural groups is something that can evolve, but changing identities is difficult, and it takes concerted investment and time. But perhaps most important, treating endowments as fixed provides an enormous amount of analytical leverage for understanding the different strategies groups pursue. It might be surprising to some just how much variation in the membership, structure, and practices of rebel organizations can be accounted for simply by looking at their initial endowments.

for resolving collective action problems in economics, see North, *Institutions, Institutional Change.* A recent review of the relevance of social capital to the politics of developing countries can be found in Michael Woolcock and Deepa Narayan, "Social Capital: Implications for Development Theory, Research, and Policy," *World Bank Research Observer* 15, no. 2 (August 2000): 225–49.

Just as social movement scholars have come to recognize that many of the factors they think of as structural are in fact the result of a process shaped by culture, this book also takes seriously the argument that a group's economic and social endowments may be themselves a function of its leadership, ideology, and strategy. Particular rebel leaders may be in a better position than others to employ material resources in the recruitment of combatants or to make concerted investments in the cultivation of social networks to motivate participation. If there are potential long-term costs to building a strategy around material resources, there may be strong incentives for insurgent leaders to save economic endowments and take the time to invest in social mobilization. A satisfactory, convincing analysis of why rebel groups behave as they do must therefore offer an explanation of the origins of a rebel group's endowments. Recognizing that potential rebel leaders plot revolution at various points in time and across different geographic regions, a major challenge is to account for the nature of the groups that emerge – that cross a minimum threshold of organization – with sufficient strength to challenge the state and to explain why they have the endowments they do.

Rebel organizations reflect the voluntary and purposive behavior of their leaders: organizers mobilize initial recruits, define the agenda of the movement, and have some latitude to determine the structure and approach of the guerrilla army.[53] But insurgencies, like other political movements, are also constrained by the setting in which they operate and their need to undertake the most basic tasks of organization, including recruitment. Leadership is a critical factor, but the emergence of a cadre of rebel organizers capable of building a successful movement is shaped by a set of factors similar to those that affect a group's membership.

The story begins with a competition between a host of potential revolutionaries, all intent on upending the existing regime but none yet in possession of the organization required to wage a war. Being the first mover in this environment offers a number of advantages. The first rebel organization out of the gate gains credibility among civilian populations for its perceived strength in challenging the government. It grabs public attention, obtaining the opportunity to shape how people think about the war that will unfold. It has the first shot at recruiting those individuals most willing to engage in high-risk collective action. And its leaders can make choices about the coalitions they build and the areas in which they organize without

---

[53] Christopher Clapham, ed., *African Guerrillas* (Oxford: James Currey, 1998).

needing to consider the activities of another preexisting group. Prospective rebel leaders are thus in a race to form the dominant rebel group, which can largely dictate the terms of the rebellion and the expectations of the civilian population about who is likely to win.

In this environment, potential revolutionaries weigh the costs and benefits of different organizational strategies in light of the advantages they can achieve by moving first. Because speed is of the essence, it is no surprise that where economic endowments can be mobilized, rebel leaders who utilize them are likely to emerge as the dominant players. Appeals to identity and ideology take much longer to develop and refine. The construction of ideological movements often involves years of popular education and belief formation. Efforts to mobilize recruits on the basis of identity requires activating ethnic or religious networks, developing a compelling rationale for participation, and soliciting the initial voluntary contributions required to jump-start the organization. Leaders who seek to build groups around social endowments jockey for position in this race, but such organizations often fail to develop fully before another group successfully launches its challenge against the government. Where economic resources are available to meet the start-up costs of rebellion, the extended process of shaping identities, mobilizing networks, and building ideologies is often cut short. Even when groups built around social endowments do manage to emerge in resource-rich environments, they face an uphill battle in confronting more powerful organizations that have track records as guerrilla armies.

Analytically, this is similar to the "Dutch disease" problem, in which natural resource booms cause the collapse of manufacturing industries.[54] This generally happens because sectors experiencing a resource boom draw capital and labor away from other sectors. Substantively, it means that where resources permit, opportunistic rebel leaders crowd out activists. Because rebel groups can organize quickly in resource-rich environments, collective action rooted in identities, beliefs, and norms never takes hold. Potential recruits go elsewhere or stay away when one group becomes dominant.

One implication of this argument is disturbing and counterintuitive. Consider an environment where the barriers to insurgency are very

---

[54] On the consequences of natural resource booms for development, see J. R. Lewis, "Natural Resources and Development," in *Handbook of Development Economics*, eds. Hollis Chenery and T. R. Srinivasan (Amsterdam, NY: North Holland, 1989). On the political consequences of natural resource wealth, see Terry Karl, *The Paradox of Plenty: Oil Booms and Petro-States* (Berkeley: University of California Press, 1997); Michael Ross, *Timber Booms and Institutional Breakdown in Southeast Asia* (Cambridge: Cambridge University Press, 2002).

low – where government is corrupt, detached from the public interest, inflated by natural resource rents, and unable to control its territory. These are the conditions likely to generate grievances of the sort privileged by studies of revolution and social movements more broadly. Yet these are also the conditions under which opportunistic rebellion is most attractive. The environments we might expect to foster revolutionary change are, it seems, the most prone to the emergence of destructive, violent, and state-destroying rebel organizations.

Subsequent chapters develop my theory of how groups organize in more detail and trace the emergence of opportunistic and activist rebellions to the initial endowments available to their leaders. The concluding chapter returns to this broader issue of where a group's initial endowments come from and examines a number of predictions that follow from the preceding analysis, some of which are amenable to empirical testing.

Research Design and Data

To examine how resource endowments affect the organizational strategies and behaviors of rebel groups, this book employs the comparative method.[55] The careful and systematic use of a small number of cases allows for the generation of hypotheses about the sources of rebel behavior and the tracing of relevant causal mechanisms. For the project of uncovering the politics of rebel group formation, this method has several advantages. My dependent variable – the character and level of violence perpetrated by rebel groups against civilians – is difficult to measure. Multiple methods, both quantitative and qualitative, are required to capture the multifaceted interactions between insurgent groups and noncombatants. This book proposes new ways of thinking about how rebels behave and advances a number of strategies for systematically measuring violence and comparing it across contexts. Its approach must be evaluated and tested on other cases before we can be confident of its validity. Even though my independent variable, social and economic endowments, can be measured, the causal mechanisms described

---

[55] On the comparative method, see David Collier, "The Comparative Method," in *Political Science: The State of the Discipline*, ed. Ada Finifter (Washington, DC: American Political Science Association, 1993), pp. 105–20; Alexander George and Timothy McKeown, "Case Studies and Theories of Organizational Decision Making," in *Advances in Information Processing in Organizations*, vol. 2 (Greenwich, CT: JAI Press, 1985), pp. 21–58; and Arend Lijphart, "Comparative Politics and the Comparative Method," *American Political Science Review* 65 (September 1971): 682–93.

in this study (a set of organizational practices and structures) also pose challenges of measurement. It is through the careful selection of cases that this study generates a set of theoretical claims, specifies causal mechanisms, and explores evidence at the micro level of the observable implications of the argument.

In developing my argument, I draw on three complementary methods of qualitative analysis. Through controlled comparisons, this book identifies the factors that shape rebel behavior across civil wars. Following John Stuart Mill's method of difference, the selected cases maximize variation in the behavior of rebel groups but are drawn from a sample of civil wars that exhibit similar general characteristics. Differences in the characteristics of the chosen organizations, most notably the resources at their disposal, are candidate explanations for the variation in strategy that is observed. I also draw on congruence procedures in exploring how rebel behavior varies within each case, over time, and across different geographic regions. To test my argument about path dependence in the nature of rebel group formation, a microcomparative research design is essential. As I demonstrate in Chapter 6, this approach also provides evidence that speaks to alternative explanations of rebel behavior linked to the relative strength of the insurgents and the extent of the warring parties' territorial control. Only systematic within-case comparisons can deal effectively with such arguments.

Because the book seeks to identify the ways in which macro-level factors shape the micropolitics of rebellion, I employ process tracing. The study compares choices and decisions made under constraints rather than simply examining outcomes. The goal is to account for variation in the dependent variable while also demonstrating how variation in the independent variables of interest map on to the distinct choices rebel leaders make at each step in an organization's evolution. This book is thus built around five challenges of rebel organization rather than the stories of the four groups themselves. Analytic tools frame the empirical evidence in terms of the incentive problems leaders confront in building an organization. Thick description, as Robert Bates and his colleagues suggest, helps to highlight the actors' "preferences, their perceptions, their evaluation of alternatives, the information they posses, the expectations they form, the strategies they adopt, and the constraints that limit their action."[56]

---

[56] Robert Bates, Avner Greif, Margaret Levi, and Jean-Laurent Rosenthal, *Analytic Narratives* (Princeton: Princeton University Press, 1998), p. 11.

The National Resistance Army, Renamo, and Sendero Luminoso

The conflicts in Uganda, Mozambique, and Peru gave rise to four distinct rebel organizations. The National Resistance Army was victorious after a six-year campaign characterized by tremendous political mobilization, the refashioning of democratic governing structures during the conflict, and an uncharacteristic restraint in the use of violence. In Mozambique, Renamo agreed to a settlement with the government after sixteen years of war. High levels of indiscipline, indiscriminate violence, and authoritarian rule characterized its organizational strategies. In Peru, Sendero Luminoso adopted one strategy across much of the country, while its regional committee in the Upper Huallaga Valley followed a different path: the national movement invested in ideological formation and carefully orchestrated the use of revolutionary violence to accomplish its political objectives. In the jungle, on the other hand, Sendero abandoned its ideological fervor, became invested in the drug trade, and abandoned the organizational control exhibited in the highlands in favor of rampant corruption and violence.

Despite these differences, three similarities across the cases give us confidence that we are comparing like with like. First, all four groups faced a state apparatus sufficiently strong to finance a military more powerful than the incipient rebellion. Government forces had thousands of men under arms, supplies of armaments and ammunition, and formal organizational structures designed for warfare. This represents a classical situation of asymmetric conflict, but it excludes environments in which the state had ceased to function. The groups also shared a similar objective: all sought to capture control of the central state and its resources. This assumption is critical to how I conceptualize the challenges of rebel organization. A desire to govern disciplines the behavior of the rebel leadership and heightens the importance of developing sustainable mechanisms to supply an army and establishing constructive relationships with civilian populations.

Perhaps most importantly, all four rebel groups emerged at a time of widening political opportunity. Changes in the political and economic environment helped to increase the potential benefits of collective action while decreasing the associated costs. All four groups were organized in environments of extreme rural poverty where economic mismanagement at the national level was reflected in a bias against providing public goods and investments in the very regions from which the rebellions emerged. The bias against the Banyankole and Baganda in Uganda had been enshrined by a succession of political leaders from northern ethnic groups, each of whom resented the favoritism experienced by southern groups under the colonial regime of the British. In Mozambique, it was a bias in favor of southern ethnic groups with its roots in colonial times and its latest incarnation in devastating fractures in the anticolonial movement. A disastrous series of socialist economic policies hit the rural economy hard, but its most significant effects were felt in central and northern Mozambique – areas that felt unrepresented by the government. For indigenous Peruvians, most of whom lived in the highlands and lowland rainforests, the economic development characteristic of the coastal regions of the country was strictly the province of white elites who had little interest in promoting economic growth inland.

Across Uganda, Mozambique, and Peru, the rebel organizations also challenged governments with a limited capacity to monitor, control, and establish effective sovereignty over their territories. In Uganda, this was a consequence of economic mismanagement under Idi Amin, which starved the government of revenue and weakened the army considerably. In Mozambique, weak state capacity was the result of the country's expansive geography, the government's inexperience, and the recent implementation of socialist economic policies with negative returns. Mainly through neglect and disinterest, Peru's governments had failed to establish a strong foothold in the highlands and rainforest regions, which are populated largely by indigenous peasants, so the state's presence was often negligible in the areas where the Shining Path organized.

Finally, the four rebel groups emerged at times of political transition in their respective countries. For Ugandans, the collapse of the Amin regime was a welcome development, but the unstable transition period resulted in a contested election that plunged the country back into insecurity. The NRA was able to take advantage of allegations of electoral corruption to undermine the new government and make the argument that only guerrilla warfare could bring peace and stability to the country. Similarly, Renamo capitalized on the early missteps of the government of newly independent Mozambique. The government's massive reeducation camps, rejection of traditional authority structures, and collectivization policies in the rural countryside provided Renamo's leaders and external supporters with the political ammunition they needed to justify the use of violence. In Peru, the Shining Path launched its official military campaign following the country's first democratic election in more than a decade. Abimael Guzmán had taken advantage of increasing political liberalization under the military dictators of the 1970s to begin organizing in the highlands – areas that were of little interest to the national government based on the coast.

Where the four groups differ from one another most directly is with respect to the resources they could access in organizing rebellion. The National Resistance Army launched its first attack as an extremely vulnerable organization. Its leader, Yoweri Museveni, had been unable to attract external financing for the organization, and Uganda's geography provided little in the way of illegal or legal trade to fund it. What Museveni and his twenty-six comrades shared, however, was an ethnic Banyankole heritage. Most of the initial recruits were from the same set of communities in western Uganda; their parents knew one another; they had attended church, school, and in some cases university together; and many had fought with Museveni in an earlier insurgency launched against the regime of Idi Amin. At its inception, the NRA had a committed and culturally homogenous core of members, but it lacked the economic resources needed to fight a war.

Renamo, by contrast, launched a civil war against the Mozambican government with the full financial and military backing of the neighboring Rhodesian regime. When the Rhodesian government fell to nationalist guerrillas in 1979, South Africa stepped forward and took over the financing and logistical support of Renamo until the late 1980s. The early rebels, most in exile following the collapse of the Portuguese colonial government, came from diverse ethnic groups from central and northern Mozambique. Many had fought for the Portuguese army after being pressed into military service and had fled Mozambique to avoid persecution by the new government. The Rhodesian government brought them together to build a fighting force as part of Rhodesia's counterinsurgency campaign against guerrillas operating across the Mozambican border. Renamo was resource-rich, but it lacked cohesion.

Sendero Luminoso began its campaign against the Peruvian government in 1980. An offshoot of the Peruvian Communist Party, the Shining Path had begun organizing in the rural communities of Ayacucho nearly 10 years earlier. Its leader, Abimael Guzmán, a professor at the regional university, had encouraged his students to teach the movement's emerging Marxist philosophy to members of their own communities. By the end of the 1970s, Sendero had built a strong cadre of committed believers in a network of rural communities. The Shining Path lacked economic resources as it sought to construct its military, however. Without access to external support, the movement focused on building its local committees from local resources, in line with Maoist guerrilla philosophy. As a result, the militants struggled to survive and relied on attacks on government outposts and contributions from civilians to maintain the movement.

One regional committee of Sendero Luminoso emerged deep in the Amazonian jungle. The geography in this region permitted the production of coca, and a coca boom had been well under way in Upper Huallaga Valley since the 1970s. When Sendero sent its formed militants there to begin organizing between 1980 and 1982, the new regional committee found itself navigating the complex web of relations between coca farmers, drug traffickers, and the Peruvian military. Over time, the committee became deeply involved in the drug trade. Ideological purity became far less important to this regional committee, even as the national movement urged it to change its ways. Thus, a comparison of behavior across regions of Peru provides a unique window into the impact of resource endowments on the membership and structure of two factions of the same insurgent organization.

The Data

This book undertakes an ambitious task: to present ethnographies of four rebel organizations. The data required for such an exercise is extensive and difficult to obtain. It requires understanding how leaders made choices about how to organize, tracking the life stories of individuals who became soldiers, and learning how civilians experienced periods of violence. It involves asking tough questions about who fought for one side or another, who perished for defection, and who supported or refused to support the insurgents. It requires finding a way to enter the rebel organizations and examine them from the inside out at a time when they no longer exist as fighting movements.

The principal strategy I employ in developing and building my argument is the analysis of participant accounts. Over the course of sixteen months of fieldwork in three countries, I conducted interviews with nearly two hundred rebel commanders, combatants, civilian supporters, and members of the government forces (for full details, see Appendix A). Interviews ranged in duration from less than an hour to a number of days as individuals shared their life stories with me, taking me back to before the war and walking me through until it had come to an end. I draw on this interview data in reconstructing the four rebel organizations, making sense of their membership, and trying to understand the strategies they pursued. But in contrast to many other accounts of war and violence, I treat the interviews strictly as data. This book does not allow the perpetrators and victims of violence in Uganda, Mozambique, and Peru to tell their complete stories as they were relayed to me. The task of social science – one I take seriously in this book – is to explore such stories for patterns of commonality and difference, patterns that can help us make sense of the atrocities that too many of my interviewees experienced.

This study also draws on social histories of the violence in two formerly rebel-held communities within each country. In choosing these sets of communities, I selected one that had experienced almost unchallenged rebel control and one whose control was contested. These within-country comparisons of violence provide valuable information about the extent to which rebel groups and their strategies varied in different regions and at different points in time. Constructing them took me into different parts of the war zones, where I worked with local leaders, civilians, and former combatants to reconstruct a timeline of what happened, when, and to whom in each community.

Quantitative information on the level and character of violence within each conflict provides a third source of data. I utilize three new datasets on patterns of rebel and government violence in Uganda, Mozambique, and Peru (for full details, see Appendix B). They record all reported violent incidents perpetrated in the context of each civil war, including acts of killing, theft, abduction, and the destruction of property. Collecting these data involved reading through every issue of government and opposition newspapers in each of the countries for their respective periods of conflict; this adds up to over forty-four years of newspaper coverage. The resulting information, which captures who did what to whom, when, where, and how often, allow for systematic comparison of patterns in the character and level of violence across the four cases.

The data provided by this intensive fieldwork are rich. They offer a set of unique perspectives on how civil war unfolded in four countries. Hearing the stories was often painful, and for many the process of remembering the conflict brought forth a range of emotions, from fear and sadness to pride and exultation. Brought together, the stories provide valuable insight into how rebel organizations form, function, and survive. Doing justice to these stories is a monumental task. Each conflict deserves its own social history, one that captures the lives combatants and civilians have lived in their own words. In the chapters that follow, I recount what they told me about how they came to join, whom they found inside the movement, what skills they

gained by participating, how they interacted with the villagers they protected, how they treated villagers who resisted, and so on. Although I place
these accounts in a comparative context and tie them to an analysis of what
group leaders were trying to accomplish, I believe my presentation remains
true to the experiences that were shared with me over sixteen intensive
months among the war-affected populations of Uganda, Mozambique, and
Peru.

2

Four Rebel Organizations

During the Cold War, as the United States and the Soviet Union battled for influence in the developing world, violent civil conflict erupted in Uganda, Mozambique, and Peru. The war in Uganda, which began in 1981, followed the overthrow of Idi Amin and a flawed election that put Milton Obote, a disgraced former president, back in office. Violence came to Mozambique in 1976, less than a year after the Frente de Libertação de Moçambique (Front for the Liberation of Mozambique, or Frelimo) succeeded in ejecting the Portuguese colonialists and just as it began to implement its radical socialist transformation in the countryside. Peru's more than decade-long civil war started quietly in the rural highlands in 1980, soon after the country's first democratic election in many years returned political parties dominated by coastal elites to power.

This chapter introduces the four rebel organizations that emerged to fight these conflicts. It describes the political environments where these groups formed, which were characterized by the exclusion of southern ethnic groups in Uganda, of central and northern groups in Mozambique, and of the rural peasantry in Peru. It shows how the presence of the state and its role as a provider of public goods was limited in the regions that provided shelter to the rebel organizations. And it highlights the barriers that each group faced as it considered launching a violent campaign. Four groups that began on similar footings eventually took very different paths. With a clearer understanding of the conditions that gave rise to insurgency in Uganda, Mozambique, and Peru, we can turn in subsequent chapters to the particular choices combatants made as they organized violence.

The National Resistance Army: 27 Young Men

On February 6, 1981, a group of twenty-seven armed men attacked the Kabamba Training Wing of the Uganda National Liberation Army (UNLA). They targeted Kabamba for its armory, believing that a successful attack on the isolated garrison would send a strong signal to the government and yield a substantial cache of weapons. In many ways, the plan was ill-advised. Yoweri Museveni, the group's leader, had only been able to marshal a small number of fighters and arms for the attack. Most of the group's supporters were spread throughout the country and could not be informed in advance of the impending insurgency. And the Kabamba Wing housed nearly fifteen hundred men, of whom more than one hundred were trained Tanzanian soldiers serving as instructors and guards.

The attack did not go according to plan. As soon as the group infiltrated the training wing, a Tanzanian soldier lodged himself inside the armory and kept the rebels at bay with his machine gun. Museveni and his comrades collected a few guns from other parts of the base and took eight vehicles before fleeing the camp. They retreated into a local village, where they regrouped. Many of the members were dejected, viewing the first attack as a failure. But Museveni urged them to see it as a success: they had attacked a major military unit, captured a small number of guns, and retreated without taking any casualties. Some members of the group nonetheless decided to quit on the spot. Museveni gave them money for transportation, and they were allowed to leave. The rest followed Museveni into the Luwero Triangle, an area of thick vegetation and plentiful food that became the operational base of the new rebel movement.

According to Museveni, it was the 1980 presidential election that "sparked off the rebellion."[1] Designed to return the country to democratic rule following the brutal military dictatorship of Idi Amin, the elections were marred by allegations of rigging. Supporters of the Uganda People's Congress (UPC) and its leader, Milton Obote, dominated the Electoral Commission and denied representation to members of other political parties. As a result, the UPC exercised undue influence over the demarcation of constituencies, the registration of voters, the nomination of candidates, and the appointment of local officials to monitor the voting. Pushing it one step further, the acting head of government, Paulo Muwanga,

---

[1] Yoweri Museveni, "Theoretical Justification of the NRM Struggle," in *Mission to Freedom: Uganda Resistance News, 1981–85* (Kampala: Directorate of Information and Mass Mobilization, NRM Secretariat, 1990).

usurped the power of the Electoral Commission following the election, requiring that all returns be submitted to him personally. Violations of this decree were punishable by a US$70,000 fine. Two days after the election, Muwanga announced Obote's victory to the nation. Obote became president of Uganda for a second time; Muwanga was appointed vice president and minister of defense.

Museveni contested for the presidency in the 1980 election as a member of the Uganda Patriotic Movement, a new political party. Realizing that the UPC was prepared to steal the election, Museveni promised throughout his campaign to "meet intimidation with intimidation, violence with violence," and to launch an insurgency if the election was rigged.[2] In his opinion, however, the ills that plagued Uganda in 1980 went beyond the election, with deep roots in both colonial and postcolonial history. Obote's tampering with the election was a symptom of fundamental problems rather than the problem itself.

Between independence in 1962 and the start of the civil war, Uganda had been plagued by unconstitutional and violent transitions in power.[3] The only peaceful transition took place at independence itself, when the British governor-general handed over power to an alliance of two parties: Obote's UPC and the Kabaka Yekka movement. It was critical for Obote to involve the Kabaka Yekka movement as he sought to control Uganda at independence. Kabaka Yekka was the party of the kabaka – the king of Buganda – and Buganda was the most prosperous region in Uganda. It had a long history of centralized government under the monarchy. To exclude the kabaka, who was worshiped like a deity by the Baganda tribe (which made up 16 percent of Uganda at independence), would have been the death knell for Obote and the UPC. Under the arrangement that Obote worked out, the kabaka, Sir Edward Mutesa II, was made president of Uganda, while Obote became the prime minister.

But the UPC–Kabaka Yekka alliance did not last long. In 1966, Obote beat back rising opposition within his own party and moved to take control of the state. He arrested five ministers from the UPC and accused them

---

[2] Ondoga Ori Amaza, *Museveni's Long March from Guerrilla to Statesman* (Kampala: Fountain, 1998), p. 18.

[3] The history provided in this section draws on a number of sources on Uganda's political history: Tarsis Bazana Kabwegyere, *People's Choice, People's Power: Challenges and Prospects of Democracy in Uganda* (Kampala: Fountain, 2000); Onyango Odongo, *A Political History of Uganda: The Origin of Museveni's Referendum 2000* (Kampala: Monitor, 2000); and Samwiri Karugire, *Roots of Instability in Uganda* (1988; Kampala: Fountain, 1996).

63

of trying to subvert the state; then he announced that Mutesa had been linked to the conspiracy. After consolidating his support in the military, he abolished the offices of the president and vice president, assuming all executive powers. Despite appealing to the United Nations for assistance, Mutesa was forced into exile, forever turning the people of Buganda against Obote. Obote forced the National Assembly to abrogate the 1962 constitution and pass a new one that members had not even seen. Under it, all powers were invested in an executive president, and the previous authority delegated to tribal chiefs and local authorities was strictly curtailed. In the ensuing four years, Obote used the military to assert his control over Uganda. Military bases were built in every district, and Buganda was put under a semipermanent state of emergency, enabling Obote and his lieutenants to systematically punish Baganda peasants for their support of the kabaka and their disproportionate wealth.

With the military receiving increased resources and power throughout the late 1960s, Idi Amin, a young commander, was able to build a base of support in the army and take power from Obote in a bloody coup in 1971. Between 50,000 and 300,000 people were killed during Amin's eight-year dictatorship.[4] He strengthened the military even further by eliminating his opponents and constructed a set of repressive state intelligence and security organs to maintain his power. Amin suspended all political institutions at the national and local levels and ruled by decree. While the economy collapsed around him, he printed money to grease the wheels of his growing government and military bureaucracy.

Amin's regime came to an end only after he made the mistake of occupying a swath of Tanzanian territory in 1979. The invasion spurred Tanzania's president, Julius Nyerere, to urge Ugandan exiles to unite as the Uganda National Liberation Front (UNLF) and to deploy Tanzanian troops and resources in support of it. The UNLF incorporated two major opposition groups already armed and ready to invade Uganda: Kikoosi Maluum (Special Unit), led by Milton Obote, and the Front for National Salvation (FRONASA), led by Yoweri Museveni. Yusuf Lule was elected chairman, and he became president of Uganda when the combined forces defeated Amin in April 1979.

The UNLF had the unenviable task of setting in place a process to return Uganda to democratic rule. The odds were stacked against it. Light arms flooded the countryside, and the transitional government had little control

---

[4] A. B. K. Kasozi, *The Social Origins of Violence in Uganda* (Kampala: Fountain, 1999), p. 104.

over the armed elements in the country. Internal political forces rushed to compete for authority in the planning process, fighting over membership in transitional committees and commissions that would undoubtedly shape the future direction of the country. The combined military forces were badly divided and highly politicized. Battles over political control were being fought both in the transitional government and in the military. The result was political chaos. Lule was overthrown after 68 days in office. His successor, Godfrey Binaisa, lasted less than a year. A military commission led by pro-Obote forces took power and set in place a plan for national elections in 1980. The stage was set again for an illegal seizure of power, mirroring nearly two decades of undemocratic and authoritarian rule.

Uganda's postindependence history of political chaos and violence set the stage for armed struggle. Access to political power became the key source of wealth, and violence was the foundation of power. Concurrently, over two decades, ethnic identities became highly politicized. Ethnicity provided the key dividing lines between individuals, shaping membership in political parties, determining access to government jobs, and influencing military recruitment. Sectarian politics was the norm, and political power, whether achieved peacefully or violently, was a fundamental means of economic redistribution to marginal ethnic groups. This state of affairs had deep roots: ethnic discrimination had been promoted extensively by the colonial regime.[5] At independence, demarcation lines between districts coincided with "tribal" boundaries. Social historians argue that Uganda could be conceived of as a series of concentric rings, with Buganda at the center; Busoga, Bugishu, Teso, Toro, and Ankole as the semiperiphery; Kigezi, West Nile, Bunyoro, Lango, and Acholi as the periphery; and Karamoja as the furthest outlier.[6] Buganda was highly developed under its precolonial monarchy, with a common language, territory, and system of centralized control. As a consequence, the British colonial authorities favored Buganda and gave its people special privileges, including the rights to individual land tenure, to elect their own leaders, and to reject colonial taxes. Buganda and Busoga were anointed as areas of cash crop production, while the peripheral regions were designated to provide cheap labor. Economic inequality between the center and the periphery, or, geographically, between the South and the

---

[5] An important source on ethnic and religious conflict in Uganda is Dan Mudoola, *Religion, Ethnicity, and Politics in Uganda* (Kampala: Fountain, 1996).

[6] Kasozi, *Social Origins of Violence*, p. 48.

North, increased. To maintain control, the colonial power armed recruits from the peripheral regions (the North) to balance the power of the privileged Baganda. At independence, 61 percent of the military was of northern origin, although northerners made up only 19 percent of the national population.[7]

Ethnic politics became even more contentious after independence. Political parties were organized entirely around ethnic identities. The Uganda People's Congress was founded to counter Baganda dominance in an independent Uganda. Uniting the ethnic groups of the North, the UPC leadership sought to rectify the uneven development of colonial times by privileging groups from northern Uganda. The Kabaka Yekka movement, on the other hand, represented the people of Buganda, particularly those of the Protestant faith. Importantly, under each passing postindependence regime, a new ethnic group had its opportunity to benefit from government patronage. Under the first Obote regime, government jobs were systematically taken away from the Baganda; their share of high-level jobs dropped from 47 percent to 36 percent in six years.[8] After his coup in 1966, Obote dismissed twenty-five army officers who were mainly Baganda, signaling his commitment to northern dominance of the military. This process continued under Idi Amin, who favored Sudanic army recruits from his own West Nile region. Anxious to consolidate his power, Amin decided that other northern groups could not be trusted and eliminated large numbers of Acholi and Langi recruits who had supported Milton Obote.[9]

Thus, before Museveni launched his rebel movement, Uganda was caught in the midst of a cyclical power struggle between ethnic groups. Without democratic institutions to mediate the disputes and distribute economic resources, the only avenue to development was military force. Northern ethnic groups capitalized on their colonial-era dominance of the military to keep the people of Buganda out of political power. By continuing a process of recruitment biased in favor of the North, political leaders created new battles for control among northerners, leading to Amin's coup and Obote's resurgence as part of the UNLF.

Unconstitutional transfers of power and contentious ethnic politics both helped to precipitate Uganda's civil war. A third factor was the inevitable economic decline that occurred as a consequence of Uganda's political

---

[7] Ibid., p. 54.
[8] Ibid., p. 74.
[9] Ibid., p. 111.

mismanagement in the 1960s and 1970s. A large literature has developed that links poor African economic performance to the policies of colonial administrations. There is no doubt that such policies, including those that prevented the advancement of Africans into high-level commercial and industrial positions, harmed Uganda's growth prospects. Uganda was well placed to take advantage of its independence, however, having never endured a liberation struggle and possessing significant cash-crop industries to sustain economic growth. The decline began later, as Ugandan politicians battled for power through extraconstitutional channels and used economic policies to redistribute national wealth to their own ethnic groups. Without significant economic development in the industrial or agricultural sectors, taxes were an insufficient source of revenue. The main sources of wealth for redistribution were generated from the nationalization of industries, the use of marketing boards to tax the agricultural sector, the expulsion of Uganda's Asian communities (and the seizing of their property), and the direction of public funds to expand the public sector and the military with members of marginal ethnic groups. Between 1972 and 1980, gross domestic product (GDP) declined dramatically except in the coffee boom years of 1976–77. In 1979, as Amin's reign came to an end, gross domestic product fell by nearly 12 percent.

It was in this context of political mismanagement, sectarian politics, and economic decline that Museveni decided to launch the National Resistance Army. He had first emerged as a political leader during the Amin regime, forming the Front for National Salvation in Tanzania. (Table 2.1 provides a chronology of Museveni and the NRA beginning with the founding of FRONASA.) Over the course of six years, Museveni recruited students and recent graduates to come to Tanzania for military training and further education in politics, revolutionary theory, and the history of liberation struggles in Africa and around the world. Most of his recruits were from western Uganda, were of Banyankole heritage, and knew Museveni or his family personally. Military training was organized in concert with guerrillas from the Front for the Liberation of Mozambique, which welcomed Ugandans into its units and trained them in the techniques of insurgency. Museveni largely kept these cadres in Tanzania, waiting for an opportune moment to reenter Uganda and begin a protracted guerrilla struggle.

When the Tanzanians expressed their willingness to assist Ugandan exiles in defeating Idi Amin, FRONASA joined hands with Kikoosi Maluum, Obote's armed movement, as part of the UNLF. Museveni was committed to working within the framework of the UNLF, and he inducted his cadres

Table 2.1. *Chronology of the National Resistance Army*

Year	Event	Regions of Operation	No. Rebel Soldiers
1972	Museveni creates FRONASA in Tanzania and begins training recruits to overthrow the Amin regime.	Largely external	53
1979	FRONASA joins with the Tanzanians to overthrow the Amin regime, recruiting heavily as it advances on Kampala.	Western Uganda	9,000
1980	Museveni's political party loses the national election; Obote and his party (UPC) claim victory in what was later called a rigged election.		None
1981	Museveni organizes the NRA and attacks the Kabamba Military Training Wing.	South-central Uganda	27
1982–83	The NRA establishes a liberated zone in the Luwero Triangle, governing close to 200,000 civilians.	South-central Uganda	4,000
1983	The NRA evacuates the liberated zone following a major operation by Obote and the UNLA.		
1984	The NRA is forced to evacuate all civilians from its areas of control; its operations are restricted to mobile warfare.	South-central Uganda	4,000–11,000
1985	The NRA moves a large number of its soldiers to western Uganda, opens a two-front war, and builds a government administration to run the western districts.	South-central and western Uganda	21,000
1986	The NRA takes Kampala and consolidates control over western and central Uganda.	South-central and western Uganda	21,000
1986–89	The NRA moves into eastern and northern Uganda to establish control.		80,000

into the new liberation army. As they marched into Uganda, FRONASA cadres led the western flank, recruiting new Banyankole members along the way, while Kikoosi Maluum entered from the east, building its forces with Acholi and Langi as it moved into northern Uganda. The unified liberation army was riven by ethnic factionalism, however; FRONASA followed orders from Museveni, and Kikoosi Maluum was under the leadership of Obote's commander, Oyite Ojok. When Lule was installed as president, Museveni encouraged his followers to fully commit to the transitional government by turning in their arms and pledging their allegiance to the UNLA.

After the rigging of the 1980 elections, Museveni believed he had no choice but to return to the armed struggle. Envisioning a "protracted people's war," he gathered his closest colleagues to plan their first attack on Kabamba. Most of his FRONASA cadres, now members of the UNLA, had been dispersed throughout the country to isolated military postings; Museveni could only draw on those cadres who were still near the capital. This group of twenty-seven would make up the first members of the new rebel movement. Those present at the initial meetings remember that the planning process was short-term in nature: the group decided to attack Kabamba and retreat into Buganda, where Museveni had a local contact. No further plans were made. The force did not even have a name.

On retreating from Kabamba, Museveni's rebels organized into four sections and began a series of hit-and-run operations in the Luwero Triangle.[10] They gave their movement a name – the Popular Resistance Army – and set out to capture additional weapons to support the campaign. Weeks later, after making contact with their supporters in Kampala, the National Resistance Council (NRC) was formed. The NRC's central mission was to organize civilian support committees in the Popular Resistance Army's areas of operation and in the capital and to supply the army with food, clothing, medicines, and other resources. During a three-month period of total concealment in the Triangle, the insurgents set out to organize civilians in support of the cause, building resistance councils (RCs) and recruiting new militants for the army. Because it had little external assistance, the provision of resources by civilians was absolutely essential to the movement's survival.

By late 1981, the Luwero Triangle had become a no-go area for government forces. The rebels were moving freely among the civilian population, mobilizing the masses, and administering life in the region. During this period, the Popular Resistance Army became the National Resistance Army. On a trip outside of the country to build external support, Museveni joined forces with former president Yusuf Lule and his external political movement. The NRA became the armed wing of the National Resistance

---

[10] Written sources on the war itself are the Resistance News publications found in *Mission to Freedom* and Odongo, *Political History of Uganda*. See also Yoweri Museveni, *Sowing the Mustard Seed: The Struggle for Freedom and Democracy in Uganda* (London: Macmillan, 1997), and Pascal Ngoga, "Guerrilla Insurgency and Conflict Resolution in Africa: A Case Study of Uganda," Ph.D. thesis, Lancaster University, December 1997.

Movement (NRM), with Lule as chairman and Museveni as the leader of the NRA.

The Ten-Point Programme, a platform of political reform used to mobilize external assistance and build domestic support, was at the center of the NRM. Recruits were required to understand the political agenda and share it with civilian populations. The program included a commitment to restore Ugandan democracy and security, a pledge to promote national unity and to end sectarian politics, a plan to consolidate national independence and build an integrated, self-sustaining economy, and a commitment to eliminate corruption and the misuse of power.

The NRA governed the Luwero Triangle until January 1983, when the Obote regime launched the Grand Offensive. Up to this point, the UNLA had been unable to flush the guerrillas out of the Triangle. The military was plagued by corruption and indiscipline, and with each operation against the guerrillas the government sent scores of civilians fleeing into the arms of the NRA for security and protection. The Triangle was littered with the skulls of massacred civilians. UNLA soldiers looted private property, and much of the Triangle's infrastructure was destroyed.

The UNLA was further handicapped by the necessity of fighting other insurgent movements throughout the country. The Uganda Freedom Movement opposed Museveni's plan for a protracted war and instead sought to defeat the Obote regime through quick terror tactics in urban areas. Its attacks on the national radio, the post office, a major prison, and military installations rattled the Obote government. The Uganda National Rescue Front was active in the far north of the country in West Nile, where it scored major victories against government forces. By 1982, it held most of the district. In western Uganda, another group, the UNLF Anti-Dictatorship, was also organizing civilians in resistance. Overstretched, the UNLA lacked the resources to combat all of these insurgent forces successfully.

With the Grand Offensive, Obote committed himself to breaking up the NRA's dominance of the Triangle. He organized more than 75 percent of his military to participate in a four-month offensive. The NRA was forced to retreat into the plains of Singo with more than 1.5 million civilians in tow. The loss of the liberated zone was a major defeat for the NRA. It struggled to meet its subsistence needs in a less fertile zone and faced a constant barrage of UNLA attacks in the following months. Knowing full well that it was unable to protect and feed civilians on the plains, the NRA encouraged them to return to areas of government control.

Over nearly two years in Singo, the NRA gradually rebuilt its strength. By April 1985, the rebels had sufficient strength and resources to open a second front in western Uganda, Museveni's home area. Within months, they had established a new liberated zone, set in place a full-scale government administration, and prepared to attack the capital. The Obote regime fell three months later to a military coup led by two army officials, Tito and Basilio Okello. The Okellos encouraged Museveni to participate in peace talks in Nairobi to create a plan for a full transition in Uganda. The NRA backed out of the Nairobi talks, however, when it became clear that the Okellos were not interested in fundamentally transforming the political system. Months later, the NRA attacked Kampala from two sides and defeated the UNLA forces in dramatic fashion. Six years after the attack on Kabamba, in January 1986, Museveni was sworn in as president of Uganda.

The war had a devastating impact on the civilian population. It is estimated that between 300,000 and one million people died during the civil war, most at the hands of Obote's government forces. The UNLA also demolished much of the infrastructure in central and western Uganda. Across Luwero, Mpigi, and Mubende districts, it destroyed 148 schools, putting at least 25,000 children out of the classroom. Many health centers were decimated as the combatants sought medicines and health personnel fled for their safety. Springs, wells, dams, and roads were damaged in the fighting, making transportation and basic survival difficult.

Nonetheless, the NRA succeeded in capturing power from a formidable opponent without any material resources at its disposal. Its campaign was characterized by political mobilization, local organization, and discipline. It suffered major defeats, yet it did not collapse. By 1986, the National Resistance Army had grown to more than twenty thousand troops and was strong enough to take power. In the subsequent chapters, I will consider what held this rebellion together, why political mobilization was so central to its mission, and how it succeeded in maintaining discipline even as it faced failure.

Renamo: The Gift of External Patronage

It is hard to date the launch of the Resistência Nacional Moçambicana. Only limited details are available about the first years of the

organization.[11] Civilians often point to radio broadcasts as their first rec-
ollection of the rebel movement in postindependence Mozambique. The
broadcasts, called *Voz da Africa Livre (Voice of a Free Africa)*, were sponsored
by the Rhodesian government. Daily sixty-minute transmissions began in
July 1976 and were broadcast in English, Portuguese, Swahili, and the
main native languages of Mozambique. The broadcasts were designed by
Orlando Cristina, a former Portuguese military officer in Mozambique who
had joined forces with a number of Mozambican exiles living in Rhodesia.
Together, they rejected the policies of the new Mozambican government
under Frelimo, which had successfully defeated the Portuguese colonial
army after more than a decade of conflict. The Rhodesians jumped on
board as part of an effort to destabilize the Frelimo government, which
was providing safe haven to guerrillas from the Zimbabwe Africa National
Union.

With the defection to Rhodesia in 1976 of André Matsangaissa, a former independence fighter, the radio station began its gradual transformation into a full-fledged rebel movement. Matsangaissa urged Cristina to
think more broadly about what it would take to overthrow the Mozambican government. Radio broadcasts, he asserted, could only encourage
civilian uprisings. An armed movement capable of defeating Frelimo's military would also have to be organized if the dissidents were to take control
of the country.

The Rhodesian Central Intelligence Organization (CIO) was already in
the process of organizing a commando unit of Mozambicans to operate
against Zimbabwean guerrillas across the border. With the goals of gathering intelligence and launching selective attacks on Mozambican institutions, the CIO and the Rhodesian armed forces offered their financial and
logistical support to the nascent Mozambican insurgency. Seeking to transform the operation into a resistance movement, Matsangaissa encouraged
the Rhodesians to recruit disaffected Mozambican exiles living in Rhodesia. In 1977, after a successful attack on a Frelimo reeducation camp in
Sacuzi, Mozambique, that yielded a large number of new recruits, Matsangaissa was able to gain CIO support for ongoing investment in an emerging
Mozambican resistance movement.

---

[11] Some of the most detailed stories are captured in a recent book by a former Renamo member. See João Cabrita, *Mozambique: The Torturous Road to Democracy* (New York: Palgrave,
2000). Another key source is a detailed study of South African military operations under the
apartheid regime. See Peter Stiff, *The Silent War: South African Recce Operations, 1969–1994*
(Alberton, RSA: Galago, 1999).

Renamo's rise came as a surprise to many outside observers.[12] In 1974, the new Mozambican nation was seemingly united behind Frelimo, a liberation movement that had successfully defeated the strong colonial army of the Portuguese. Based first in Cabo Delgado and Niassa provinces in the far northern parts of Mozambique, Frelimo later extended its bases into Tete, Manica, and Sofala before the war was brought to an end by a coup in Portugal. The Frelimo guerrillas were renowned in Africa for the strength of their ideology, the rigor of their training and political education, and their efforts to build educational and health care institutions in liberated zones. Further, Frelimo sought as part of its central mission to build a deep sense of national unity among the ethnically and linguistically diverse Mozambican population.

Yet internal divisions had wracked the liberation movement from its inception. In founding Frelimo, Eduardo Mondlane had sought to unify a number of distinct independence movements with their own geographic and ethnic bases. Mondlane believed that a united front was the only effective way to fight the Portuguese. Bringing the different movements together, however, generated stiff competition for leadership and fierce disagreements about the path to take after independence. After Mondlane was assassinated under suspicious circumstances in 1968, the new leadership of Frelimo endorsed a platform advocating socialist strategies of development for Mozambique. This direction was met with resistance by many of the founding members, who were then forced out by the new leadership. The divisions in the liberation movement had a regional dimension: some argued publicly that the shift in strategy was an indication of southern dominance in Frelimo, as a strong core of educated southerners within the movement had consistently advocated socialist policies.[13] Mozambicans from the Center and the North of the country gradually left

---

[12] The brief history I offer here draws on Margaret Hall and Tom Young, *Confronting Leviathan: Mozambique since Independence* (Athens: Ohio University Press, 1997); William Minter, *Apartheid's Contras: An Inquiry into the Roots of War in Angola and Mozambique* (London: Zed Books, 1995); and David Hoile, *Mozambique, Resistance and Freedom: A Case for Reassessment* (London: Mozambique Institute, 1994). See also Mark Chingono, *The State, Violence and Development* (Aldershot: Avebury, 1996); William Finnegan, *A Complicated War: The Harrowing of Mozambique* (Berkeley: University of California Press, 1993); and Carolyn Nordstrom, *A Different Kind of War Story* (Philadelphia: University of Pennsylvania Press, 1997). For colonial and precolonial history, see Malyn Newitt, *A History of Mozambique* (Bloomington: Indiana University Press, 1995).

[13] For a description of the splits within Frelimo, see Alex Vines, *Renamo: Terrorism in Mozambique* (Bloomington: Indiana University Press, 1991).

Frelimo and joined other independence movements based in Zambia and Kenya.

The regional divisions went deeper than simple power struggles within Frelimo. In part, the differences were ethnic and linguistic. The Tsonga and related groups dominated southern Mozambique but accounted for only 23 percent of the national population. In central and northern Mozambique, the Macua and Lomwe tribes were predominant, although they coexisted with a broad range of other groups. Central Mozambique, in particular, was home to the Shona-speaking tribes (Manayika, Ndau, and Teve) with a historical connection to the people of Zimbabwe. Nationally, the Macua and Lomwe populations constituted the largest linguistic grouping (47 percent of the population), yet they never came to control Mozambican politics.

This is because regional divisions mirrored economic inequality in colonial Mozambique. The colonial state administered the southernmost provinces directly, investing significantly in the development and infrastructure of the region. By contrast, territories in central and northern Mozambique were divided among various Portuguese companies, which received concessions to develop agricultural industries. The South became the major income-earning region of the colony, while companies forced peasants in central and northern Mozambique to work on private farms as indigenous slave laborers. Southerners were richer and better educated. Mozambicans in the Center and the North were poor, and their opportunities for advancement were limited. As a result, when political disagreements came to the fore in Frelimo during its struggle, educated southerners rose to direct the movement. Mozambicans from the Center and the North often felt disenfranchised and discriminated against during the guerrilla war. Many left for other movements, others participated reluctantly in support of the guerrillas, and some were forced to fight for the Portuguese army against the insurgent forces.

Regional divisions only worsened after Frelimo took control of the government. Its agenda was radical and included a set of programs designed to transform social, political, and economic life in Mozambique. Traditional leaders were forced to give way to party secretaries, subsistence agriculture to collective farming, and traditional settlement patterns to state-mandated communal villages. These programs were part of a Marxist-Leninist agenda that Frelimo implemented with the full support of the Soviet bloc. As part of its campaign to refashion social relations, political freedoms were curtailed. Oppositionists – soldiers and civilians alike – were carted off to reeducation

74

camps.[14] Singled out for special harassment were members of Frelimo splinter groups and veterans of service in the Portuguese colonial military and police services, many of whom were from central and northern Mozambique. While some were captured by Frelimo's security forces, others fled to Rhodesia, South Africa, and Portugal, fearing for their lives. Frelimo's repression took on a regional cast that fed the flames of national division: southerners had gained control of Mozambique's postindependence trajectory, and discontent began to grow among people in the central and northern provinces and those in exile.

The emergence of Renamo cannot be understood completely, however, without reference to the geopolitical context.[15] When Frelimo came to power in 1975, Mozambique was bordered by the white-settler regimes of Rhodesia and South Africa, both of which were struggling against insurgencies. Frelimo actively supported African liberation movements, including those in Rhodesia and South Africa. It further magnified the threat faced by the Rhodesians when it joined the United Nations–sponsored sanctions regime and prevented Ian Smith's government from accessing oil through the Beira pipeline or from using Mozambique's ports to export Rhodesian products. The Rhodesian government interpreted these acts as a declaration of war.

Moreover, Mozambique achieved its independence from Portugal at the height of the Cold War. At the time, the United States and the Soviet Union were engaged in a competition for influence and control in Africa and other parts of the developing world. By throwing its support behind African liberation movements and launching its own socialist development program, Frelimo established itself as a state allied to the Eastern bloc. South Africa and Rhodesia, on the other hand, were key bulwarks against communism in the region. They benefited from tacit – and often direct – support from the United States and other European powers. In short, Frelimo's two principled stands – in favor of African liberation and socialist development – made it an avowed enemy of the major military powers in the region.

---

[14] The government established reeducation camps in seven of Mozambique's ten provinces, with nearly 75 percent of them in the central and northern regions. Interestingly, Frelimo's stronghold of Gaza province did not have a single reeducation camp. Cabrita, *Mozambique*, p. 97.

[15] Key works on Rhodesian and South African strategies in southern Africa include Paul Moorcraft, *Africa Nemesis: War and Revolution in Southern Africa, 1945–2010* (London: Brasseys, 1994), and Gavin Cawthra, *Brutal Force: The Apartheid War Machine* (London: International Defence Aid Fund, 1986).

In 1976, the Rhodesians attacked Mapai in Mozambique's southern Gaza Province. This was the first direct attack on Mozambique following its independence. The Rhodesians operated largely from the air with helicopters and airplanes, attempting to destroy the bases of anti-Rhodesian rebels based in Mozambique. But such actions were indiscriminate and often ineffective; the Rhodesian leadership knew that a small combat force prepared to do battle in Mozambique would be a more effective tool in the fight against the insurgency.[16] This environment provided fertile ground for André Matsangaissa to organize the Mozambican resistance movement. The CIO and Matsangaissa worked together to recruit discontented Mozambicans, including colonial army veterans and ex-Frelimo guerrillas, for the new insurgent force. In subsequent years, the Rhodesian army and its Mozambican subsidiaries targeted areas of discontent within Mozambique. Rhodesia financed the rebellion, paying for salaries, weapons, food, and clothing. And Renamo, as the insurgent force came to be called, resurrected claims of Frelimo's "southern bias" as it recruited new members from central and northern Mozambique. Table 2.2 provides a chronology of Renamo's history.

The year 1979 marked a watershed for the new insurgency. Prior to this point, Renamo had no internal base. The Rhodesians largely dictated the movement's strategy, and Renamo guerrillas had little flexibility to shape their own direction: the movement was hostage to the interests of its sponsors. In 1979, however, the Rhodesian government fell, and Zimbabwe achieved its independence through the Lancaster House Agreements. At almost the same moment, government forces killed Matsangaissa in a battle inside Mozambique. The line of succession and the future direction of Renamo were far from clear. The organization's entire force (numbering less than 2,000) gathered in the mountains of central Mozambique. Aphonso Dhlakama rose to the leadership in a bloody succession battle and consolidated control over the movement.[17] South Africa stepped in as the major financial backer of Renamo as part of its grand strategy to defeat the African National Congress in southern Africa. The South Africans committed to provide training, financial resources, and logistical support to

[16] Ken Flower, the former head of the CIO, claims credit for the organization of Renamo. See *Serving Secretly: An Intelligence Chief on Record, Rhodesia into Zimbabwe, 1964–1981* (London: John Murray, 1987).

[17] These claims are advanced in Cabrita, *Mozambique*. An interview with a combatant present at the meeting in Sitatonga supports stories about Dhlakama's use of force. Interview, Maríngue District, Sofala Province, May 24(B), 2001.

Table 2.2. *Chronology of Renamo*

Year	Event	Regions of Operation	No. Rebel Soldiers
1975	Frelimo takes control of Mozambique after an extended guerrilla war against the Portuguese.		
1976	The Rhodesians recruit the first members of Renamo and begin to incorporate them into activities against Zimbabwe Africa National Union in the border provinces.	Central	200–400
1979	André Matsangaissa, the first leader of Renamo, is killed in Mozambique during rebel operations.	Central	2,000–2,500
1979	South Africa agrees to finance and train Renamo; the senior leadership of Renamo is transferred from Rhodesia to a base in South Africa.	Central	
1980	Rhodesia falls as Mugabe takes control of Zimbabwe.		
1980–81	Aphonso Dhlakama gathers the entire rebel army in Sitatonga, assumes the leadership of the movement, and redeploys soldiers in southern and central Mozambique	Central and southern	6,000–10,000
1984	South Africa and Mozambique sign a nonaggression pact, supposedly ending South Africa's financial and logistical support for Renamo. It does not actually end.		
1984	Renamo moves into northern Mozambique.	Southern, central, and northern	20,000
1985	Renamo establishes liberated zones in central and northern Mozambique and begins to build an administrative structure.	Southern, central, and northern	20,000
1986	Renamo establishes a presence nationwide and begins to mount attacks in urban areas and along the coast.	Southern, central, and northern	20,000
1987–88	Frelimo begins a major offensive against Renamo, building on the assistance of external troops from Zimbabwe, Tanzania, and Malawi.	Southern, central, and northern	20,000
1988–90	Negotiations begin in secret, encouraged by the Catholic Church and involving presidents Moi and Mugabe. The war is at a stalemate.		
1990–92	A full-fledged peace process begins in Italy.		
1992	Both parties sign a General Peace Agreement, and the war ends.	Southern, central, and northern	20,000

Renamo, but they also encouraged the insurgents to expand their internal operations and their domestic social base.

Right-wing backers in Europe and the United States assisted Renamo in developing a clear political agenda that advocated a capitalist approach to development and a transition to multiparty democracy. A program of action drafted in 1981 called for the establishment of a government of national unity with Frelimo to pacify the country and plot a transition to democratic rule. As a requirement for peace, though, Frelimo was called upon to abandon a centralized economy and open the way to the private sector.[18] But Frelimo was not interested in negotiating with Renamo. The government saw the insurgency as nothing more than a puppet of external forces bent on the destruction of Mozambique. Instead, Frelimo continued to implement a complete socialist transformation, and the policies it set in motion left the peasantry reeling. Efforts to promote collective farming and centralize production left peasants unable to survive on the meager produce they grew on plots of land in their free time.[19] Governmental controls on the sale of products ushered in an era of scarcity in which peasants were unable to get even the most basic household goods. Political repression at the local level resulted in the replacement of traditional leaders (*régulos*) who had managed social relations since before colonial times. Finally, in an effort to improve the delivery of services and to maintain security, peasants were forced to abandon their dispersed patterns of settlement and move into communal villages (*aldeias communais*), where they had to participate in party activities under constant watch.[20] As Renamo began to build its internal operations, then, peasants were suffering at the hands of the new regime, particularly in central and northern Mozambique.

---

[18] Cabrita, *Mozambique*, p. 186.

[19] There is a vast literature addressing the economic crisis of the peasantry in Mozambique following the implementation of Frelimo's socialist policies. Good places to start include C. Geffray, *A causa das armas: Anthropologia da guerra contemporanea em Moçambique* (Porto, Portugal: Ediçoes Afrontamento, 1991); M. Bowen, "Peasant Agriculture in Mozambique: The Case of Chokwe, Gaza," *Canadian Journal of African Studies* 23, no. 3 (1989): 355–79; and A. Pitcher, "Disruption without Transformation: Agrarian Relations and Livelihoods in Nampula Province, 1975–1995," *Journal of Southern African Studies* 24, no. 1 (1998): 115–40. In interviews, civilians in central and northern Mozambique described how the structure of collective production monopolized their labor, leaving little time for efforts to develop their own agricultural fields.

[20] On communal villages, see J. P. Borges Coelho, "State Resettlement Policies in Post-Colonial Rural Mozambique: The Impact of the Communal Village Program on Tete Province, 1977–82," *Journal of Southern African Studies* 24, no. 1 (1998): 61–91.

Frelimo was hard pressed to stop Renamo's growth. The government focused its diplomatic efforts on cutting off South African support to the guerrillas. This policy was a failure, as the apartheid regime repeatedly violated its commitments. The South African military stepped back only as the apartheid government neared its final days. Military efforts within the country were constrained by Mozambique's precarious financial situation. The economy collapsed, with GDP decreasing by nearly 5 percent in 1975, 1980, and 1985. Just as the colonial government had been unable to extend its authority throughout rural Mozambique, which has over 2,000 kilometers of coastline and borders with four countries, the socialist state suffered the same fate.[21] Mozambique's geography gave Renamo significant latitude as it plotted its expansion. The guerrillas consistently moved into areas with low settlement density where government presence was weak and where poor roads limited the military's advance. By 1986, Renamo was operating in every province in Mozambique. Its headquarters were in the central province of Sofala, but it also had major regional operations in southern and northern Mozambique. Renamo had grown significantly, and Dhlakama commanded an army of nearly 20,000 soldiers. The guerrillas controlled most rural areas outside of the southern provinces, while government forces were confined to urban centers and populated outposts in the countryside.

Renamo's methods were brutal and authoritarian yet effective. Participation was largely coerced, even in areas likely to be supportive of Renamo's cause. Killings were widespread, and insurgent forces participated in the war's largest massacres. Renamo augmented its financial base – hedging against a South African withdrawal – by systematically looting household property, trading in illegal goods, and extorting payments from private enterprise in exchange for protection. And in the communities it controlled, Renamo governed with an iron fist, using traditional authorities to maintain a consistent supply of food, abducting new members from local schools and homes, and taking women as "wives" for the soldiers in the conflict.

---

[21] The territory that came under Frelimo's control in 1975 was truly immense. When Frelimo abandoned systems of traditional leadership and banned religion, the territory was left weak and exposed in the countryside, as local leaders and priests had been the critical sources of governmental authority under the colonial regime. See I. B. Lundin and F.J. Machava, eds., *Autoridade e poder tradicional*, vol. 1 (Maputo, Mozambique: Ministerio da Administração Estatal, 1995).

Renamo's campaign to defeat Frelimo began to weaken only when the government called for the assistance of outside forces. Welcoming troops from Zimbabwe, Malawi, and Tanzania, Frelimo shifted the burden of combating Renamo away from its own military, whose soldiers were disenchanted with their own failures and struggling to survive without major new government investment. At the same time, Frelimo renounced socialism, signing an agreement with the International Monetary Fund and the World Bank to rejuvenate the economy. With these new resources, Frelimo pushed Renamo back from the urban centers and sent the war into a stalemate that would continue until peace negotiations began in the late 1980s.

Ideological divisions had melted away as the Mozambican war continued. The apartheid government fell. The Soviet Union collapsed. Frelimo embraced a program of capitalist reform and set the stage for a new, democratic constitution. In this context, international pressure to end the conflict mounted, and major investments by external actors pushed Renamo and Frelimo to the negotiating table. Between 1990 and 1992, the warring parties finally hashed out a transition plan that guaranteed the demobilization of both forces; the construction of a new, unified national army; and the implementation of a system of democratic government in which members of both movements could participate. The war officially ended in October 1992 with the signing of the General Peace Agreement. Neither party was a victor in the conflict, and the Mozambican population was the clear loser. By 1985 (only halfway through the war), 25 percent of the nation's health facilities had been destroyed, 40 percent of primary schools had been ruined or abandoned, and more than 20 percent of students had been forced from school. At that same point in the conflict, reports estimated that more than 100,000 people had already been killed in the fighting, with at least 100,000 more lost to famine.[22] It is widely accepted that Renamo was responsible for much of this destruction and violence.

Yet Renamo nearly succeeded in capturing power. Launched and sustained by external investment, it grew into a powerful military force that credibly threatened to defeat the Frelimo government. Although it lacked a coherent political agenda and rarely bothered to mobilize noncombatant populations around its political aims, it nevertheless prospered. Renamo's organization presents a stark contrast to the National Resistance Army in

---

[22] UNICEF, *Children on the Front Line: The Impact of Apartheid, Destabilization, and Warfare on Children in Southern and South Africa* (New York: United Nations Children's Fund, 1987), pp. 18–19.

Uganda. Explaining why Renamo took the route of coercion and violence and why the NRA did not is a key goal of this study.

Sendero Luminoso Nacional: A Decade of Preparation

The Shining Path launched its military struggle the night before Peru's first democratic presidential election in seventeen years. On May 17, 1980, at around two o'clock in the morning, a group of five hooded men entered the voter registration office in Chuschi, tied up the registrar, and then burned the ballot boxes and the registry. The attack was short, lasting less than thirty minutes, and no one was injured. The registrar untied himself and alerted the local authorities. Within hours, four young men were captured just outside of town. It was easy to identify the attackers: they were the same youths who had consistently threatened the registrar over the previous week. Only one, a teacher from another town who had organized the attack, managed to escape.

The attack on Chuschi was largely symbolic. It targeted electoral symbols to make a statement about the upcoming election. But what had been taking place in the years leading up to the attack in Chuschi had also been happening in rural communities throughout Ayacucho. Beginning in the early 1970s, Abimael Guzmán, a professor at the regional university in Ayacucho, sent his students into various communities to jump-start the process of "popular education."[23] As teachers in local elementary schools and high schools, they became active in the communities where they lived. Guzmán's protégés gathered community members together, asked them about the challenges they faced, and began to introduce peasants to the ideas of Marx, Mao, and Professor Guzmán. By 1980, when the ballot box attack was launched, Sendero Luminoso had constructed an extensive network of cadres in rural communities throughout Ayacucho.

The Sendero military campaign began just as Peru was undergoing a political transition. In 1968, General Juan Velasco Alvarado had overthrown the elected president, Fernando Belaúnde, in a military coup and embarked on a reformist campaign to establish a "fully participatory social democracy." Major economic and political reforms were launched during the twelve years of military rule under Velasco and his successor (after another coup), General Francisco Morales Bermúdez. In response to a rising tide

---

[23] Billie Jean Isbell, "Shining Path and Peasant Responses in Rural Ayacucho," in *Shining Path of Peru*, ed. David Scott Palmer (New York: St. Martins, 1992), pp. 76–99.

of social unrest in 1977, the military government announced a transition to democracy. A Constituent Assembly was elected to write a new constitution for the country, and democratic elections followed two years later. They were widely seen as free and fair, with parties of all stripes and ideologies participating. Belaúnde was elected for a second time. As in Uganda and Mozambique, then, Peru's civil war began as the nation's government experienced a major political transition. Surprisingly, though, it was a transition to democracy – a democracy that would fail to stem the growth of Sendero Luminoso throughout the 1980s.

The foundation of the Shining Path was laid in response to a protracted period of economic decline that hit peasants particularly hard. Between 1970, when Sendero began organizing in rural Ayacucho, and 1992, when the authorities captured Guzmán, Peru experienced a pronounced economic collapse. The average annual growth rate in GDP per capita dropped from 2.5 percent in the 1960s to 0.9 percent in the 1970s and then to –3.2 percent in the 1980s. By contrast, Peru's neighbors in Latin America were growing at a rate of nearly 3 percent per year on average throughout the 1960s and 1970s. During the debt crisis in the 1980s, much of Latin America did poorly, but Peru did significantly worse.

And the plight of Peru's peasants is not fully captured in macroeconomic data. During the 1970s and 1980s, the living standards of peasants in rural areas declined dramatically, creating a climate of severe poverty and hopelessness.[24] The distribution of land ownership in Peru, which in 1961 was the most unequal of fifty-four nations surveyed, grew worse over the next two decades, even as the military regime launched major agrarian reform.[25] This was primarily the result of population growth, as the expansion of haciendas had been largely curtailed. Lack of access to land on which to grow food left many peasants struggling to survive.

During this same period, persistent regional inequalities grew worse. Peasants in the southern highlands, where the Shining Path emerged, lacked access to even the most basic services provided in the rest of the country. When Sendero was beginning to penetrate rural communities, the infant

---

[24] My brief description of the economic environment in which the Shining Path emerged draws on the analysis of Cynthia McClintock, *Revolutionary Movements in Latin America: El Salvador's FMLN and Peru's Shining Path* (Washington, DC: U.S. Institute of Peace Press, 1998), Chapter 4.

[25] A 1975 survey of economically active families revealed that 87 percent of families in Ayacucho did not benefit from the agrarian reform. This was a significantly higher percentage than in the rest of the country. See ibid., p. 179.

mortality rate in Ayacucho was 128 per 1,000 births, whereas nationwide it was 92. More than 80 percent of the population of Ayacucho had no access to clean water. And there were almost 17,000 Ayacuchanos per doctor, while in the rest of the country the number was 1,255. There was a clear correlation between the rural departments with the lowest living standards and the areas of strongest support for Sendero Luminoso.

Peru's economic decline had negative effects on aspirants to the middle class, as well. Although secondary school enrollments were increasing dramatically between 1960 and 1990, employment opportunities for educated individuals were stagnant. Nor was the situation any better for university graduates: even though university enrollment grew from 19 percent of the school age population in 1970 to 40 percent in the early 1990s, one estimate put the unemployment rate for people with a high level of education at double that of the rest of the unemployed.[26] And still more graduates of secondary schools wanted to attend university than were able to find places in the national system. In 1987, close to 80 percent of secondary school graduates (nearly 250,000 young people) failed to enter a Peruvian university.[27] To peasants and educated young people, Sendero Luminoso offered hope for a better future and an opportunity to be actively involved in seeking change.

The growth of Sendero Luminoso must also be understood with reference to the national political climate.[28] The organization rejected conventional wisdom by mounting an armed struggle in opposition to a democratic regime. Even as it was organizing in the 1970s, it rejected participation in a political system that, although under military leadership, was open and reform-minded. General Velasco's government launched a campaign of economic transformation, nationalizing major foreign-owned firms and implementing an ambitious agrarian reform program. At the same time, Velasco opened up the political space, enabling leftist political groups to prosper and workers and peasants to organize. The military was not repressive; there was little torture and few disappearances. The officer corps was

---

[26] Ibid., p. 186.

[27] Gabriela Tarazona-Sevillano, "The Organization of Shining Path," in Palmer, *Shining Path of Peru*, pp. 189–208.

[28] Fuller treatments of the political context in Peru before the war can be found in Steve J. Stern, ed., *Shining and Other Paths: War and Society in Peru, 1980–1995* (Durham: Duke University Press, 1998); Gustavo Gorriti, *The Shining Path: A History of the Millenarian War in Peru* (Chapel Hill: University of North Carolina Press, 1999); and Palmer, *Shining Path of Peru*.

largely sympathetic to the demands of rural peasants and workers, with more than 50 percent of officers hailing from provincial backgrounds. Yet Guzmán prepared for armed struggle.

He did so in part because the open political climate had little or no impact on the rural highlands where Sendero was based. Peru's party leaders had never established strong networks beyond the coast. Residents of the highland regions felt that political activists, even those on the Left, had largely abandoned their cause. Guzmán castigated leaders of the leftist parties and refused to take part in the workers' strikes that eventually pushed the government to hold elections in 1978. The economic crisis also damaged state capacity severely. State authorities were unable to penetrate many rural areas to deliver education and health services or to provide order. The southern highlands and the deep jungle areas were the furthest removed from the exercise of governmental authority. Rural peasants in the jungle and the highlands, as well as the indigenous people of southern Peru (the Quechua), were basically ignored as resources became scarce. Sendero Luminoso generated interest and support by pointing to the government's economic and political failures.

During its insurgency, the Shining Path was fiercely ideological. Guzmán stuck closely to the ideas and strategies of his predecessors: Marx, Lenin, and Mao. He saw himself as the "Fourth Sword of Marxism," developing and improving on the theories created before him. Like Mao, he described the problems of Peru by making reference to its "semifeudal" and "semicolonial" character. In particular, Sendero Luminoso rejected the spread of "Yankee imperialism," which, by putting in place a system of "bureaucratic capitalism," fails to unleash the productive forces of the country and ignores the urgent needs of the people. Guzmán envisioned a rural movement led by the peasantry that would "encircle the cities from the countryside." The struggle would be protracted and would require significant investments in the building of a rural base, with educated cadres and local support structures. Thus, in spite of its authoritarian leadership, the organization was highly decentralized. Regional committees were formed throughout the country, organized on the basis of local resources, and developed with a small number of "formed" cadres from the national movement. At the local level, most new members were brought in as part of the "masses" and were forced to pass rigorous tests of ideology and commitment before advancing within the organization. Only a small number ever achieved positions within the full-time armed force that took part in armed operations outside of Sendero's bases of support.

Ideological commitment was central to membership in the movement. At first through the Communist Party and later through the armed Shining Path, Guzmán sought to build increasingly well-organized cadres with a firm understanding of his ideology. To achieve this goal, the movement employed authoritarian tactics. In Stalinist terms, "the line" decided everything, and it was therefore critical that cadres comprehended the "correct" ideas. These philosophies were generated by Guzmán himself – the "philosopher king" – and transmitted to the entire membership through written propaganda, speeches, and local meetings. Although many of Sendero's recruits were illiterate, they gained a profound understanding of political economy and history, albeit from only one perspective, and many received their basic education within the movement.

The focus of rebel activity, especially in the early days, was on political tactics: agitation, mobilization, and popular education. Shining Path cadres were sent into local communities to meet with peasants and set in place popular schools that would gradually introduce the movement. The movement would also provide benefits when it could, taking cows captured in an attack on a hacienda, for example, and distributing them to peasant supporters. At the same time, Sendero Luminoso extolled the use of revolutionary violence to accomplish its objectives. In the beginning, it used violence to establish "order" in Sendero communities. Militants would identify the most hated individuals in a village – thieves, rapists, crooks, adulterers – and assassinate them publicly as a way of implementing "popular justice." As the war progressed, the use of violence extended far more broadly and was targeted at all representatives of governmental and imperialist structures, including local officials, workers in nongovernmental organizations, owners of private enterprises, and active supporters of the government.

Sendero's expansion was plotted by its Central Committee, which, in concert with the leadership of each regional committee, monitored the progress of the conflict. While the Central Committee provided the overall direction of each military campaign (telling militants, for example, to target government officials, to build new guerrilla bases, or to increase urban actions), it was the responsibility of regional committees to decide what actions would be taken. Through successive campaigns, Sendero extended its activities into rural highland areas in central and northern Peru and into the jungle. By the end of 1985, Sendero Luminoso was a national presence. Table 2.3 provides a chronology of its development beginning in 1970.

At first, the Peruvian government had pretended that Sendero did not exist. Between 1980 and 1982, President Belaúnde believed that this new

Table 2.3. *Chronology of Sendero Luminoso Nacional*

Year	Event	Regions of Operation	No. Rebel Soldiers
1970	Abimael Guzmán forms the Partido Comunista del Perú in the department of Ayacucho.		
1980	Peru holds its first democratic election, ending twelve years of military rule.		
1980	Sendero Luminoso launches it first military attack in Ayacucho.	Southern highlands	500
1982–83	Ayacucho is declared an emergency zone, and the military begins a brutal counterinsurgency campaign.		
1984	Sendero is briefly forced out of Ayacucho and launches its Great Leap to expand operations throughout the countryside.	Southern highlands, jungle region	1,500
1986	Sendero begins a dramatic expansion of its military forces as it spreads its influence in new regions.		7,000
1988	Sendero holds its first Congress. Guzmán shifts the military emphasis to the cities.	Southern highlands, jungle region, central highlands	14,000
1989	President García supports the establishment of peasant self-defense patrols (*rondas*) to combat Sendero. Human rights abuses by the military increase.		
1990	Sendero succeeds in organizing large support networks in the slums around Lima. Terrorist attacks in the city increase.	Southern highlands, jungle region, central highlands, shantytowns in Lima	10,000
1992	President Fujimori disbands the Congress and abrogates the Constitution in an *autogolpe*.		
1992	Guzmán is captured by the counterterrorism police in Lima.		
1993	Guzmán renounces the armed struggle and proposes a peace accord with the government.		

movement did not represent a serious challenge to the government. As a result, he did little to improve the desperate conditions in the southern highlands or to authorize the security forces to take action. This enabled the insurgency to recruit, expand, and build bases of popular support without much fear of infiltration. But by 1983, Belaúnde had shifted course entirely. He launched a brutal counterinsurgency campaign that was completely at odds with the norms of his democratic government. Ayacucho was declared an emergency zone and was flooded with the armed forces. The army briefly gained the upper hand, and Sendero militants scattered to other parts of the country. Civil rights were suspended as security personnel moved in to occupy local communities. Human rights violations skyrocketed, and the behavior of the armed forces only strengthened the resolve of many peasants to support the guerrillas. The sense that Peru's democracy was only for those in the capital and on the coast was reinforced.

After taking power in 1985, President Alan García tried to crack down on human rights violations within the military. He dismissed senior generals and sought to punish those guilty of killing innocent civilians. Also, recognizing the "destitution" and "marginalization" of the highland peasants, García made major investments in rural areas in an effort to stem the spread of Sendero. He increased public investment in Ayacucho and launched a short-term employment program to provide income to rural peasants. Without a strong military component, however, aid to the rural areas was insufficient to defeat the now-entrenched guerrillas, and the military increasingly rejected García's leadership. Officers refused to send their soldiers into battle and opted not to participate in his efforts to expose human rights violations. In 1988, realizing his predicament, García allowed the military to reassert control over the counterinsurgency, and the brutality returned.

In 1988, Guzmán made a critical decision. During the Shining Path's first Congress, he called for a prioritization of the war in the cities. This represented a departure from his rural mobilization strategy, but it also indicated his sense that Sendero was on the verge of taking power from the government. The Lima Metropolitan Committee increased its presence in the slums around the capital, building rear bases of support (just as in the countryside) into which Sendero cadres could disappear after launching terrorist attacks in the capital. A number of major attacks followed in the early 1990s. Launched in the center of the capital city and in residential areas, they were designed to sow fear among the populace of Lima. The most significant event was a truck bomb in middle-class Miraflores that killed 22 people, injured 250, and destroyed over 400 homes in 1992.

By the early 1990s, Sendero Luminoso was nearing victory. Attacks were constant in both urban and rural areas. The Peruvian state seemed unable to defeat the insurgency. Rates of desertion in the military were very high, and

87

the government was fiscally incapacitated after years of high inflation and poor growth. Peru's ten-year experiment with democracy, severely weakened by years of brutal counterinsurgency tactics, was crushed by President Alberto Fujimori's self-coup (*autogolpe*) in 1992, with which he disbanded Congress and the Constitution. Nothing seemed capable of stopping the movement's ascent.

In September of 1992, however, Abimael Guzmán was captured by the Special Intelligence Group of the Peruvian police force. Beginning in 1988, García and Fujimori had made sustained investments in the intelligence capacity of the police, and they paid off as Shining Path leaders were captured one by one in the ensuing years. These attacks on the center of Sendero's organization were critical. As the authoritarian leadership of the movement fell, the sense of its invincible progress toward victory went with it. With the Central Committee largely imprisoned, those leaders who were left behind proved unable to maintain the organization, to prevent the defection of peasant cadres, or to sustain control of Peru's highland and jungle areas. By the mid-1990s, the Shining Path had been defeated throughout most of Peru.

Sendero Luminoso has traditionally been seen as an outlier, examined as an isolated case, and deemed incomparable to other revolutionary movements. But like the National Resistance Army and Renamo, it emerged during a political transition in a country characterized by extreme poverty. Brutal counterinsurgency campaigns and increasingly authoritarian leadership aided its growth. Like the NRA and unlike Renamo, the Shining Path was a highly disciplined force. Ideology rather than ethnicity or religion was at its center. The group was able to use ideology, even without significant economic resources, to grow and extend its power nationally. Yet Sendero Luminoso also promoted the use of violence. Between 1980 and 1992, Sendero killed religious workers, foreign development workers, grassroots leaders, businessmen, teachers, students, workers, political officials, urban residents, and peasants – in sum, Peru's Truth and Reconciliation Commission has held the Shining Path responsible for 54 percent of the killings and human rights violations committed during the war.[29] Were these killings a reflection of Sendero's discipline or its inability to maintain control? Was the Shining Path invested in social mobilization or social control?

---

[29] Comisión de la Verdad y Reconciliación, *Informe Final: Peru, 1980–2000, Tomo I* (Lima: Pontificia Universidad Católica del Peru y Universidad Nacional Mayor de San Marcos, 2003), p. 89.

Comparative analysis enables us to explore the determinants and dynamics of the Shining Path's strategies and to understand them in a broader context.

Sendero Luminoso–Huallaga: On the Other Side of the Mountains

Deep in the Amazonian jungle, far from the plight of Peru's highland peasants, Sendero's Comité Regional del Alto Huallaga (Regional Committee of Alto Huallaga, or CRH) began its work in the early 1980s. Owing to the Shining Path's highly decentralized structure, the Central Committee sent only a small number of formed militants from Ayacucho to launch the CRH. They first arrived in 1980, but the buildup of the organization really did not begin until two years later.

In 1984, the mayor of Tingo María, the provincial capital in the Upper Huallaga Valley, was assassinated. Mayor Tito Jaime was a coca farmer who had founded an organization of growers, the Defense and Development Front of Leoncio Prado Province, which sought to represent the interests of farmers. Although no one knows for sure who killed Jaime, two factors led observers to believe that Sendero was responsible.[30] First, the CRH was interested in controlling the coca trade. The government had discovered coca paste laboratories along the banks of the Huallaga River in areas the Shining Path had begun to infiltrate. Jaime's organization represented a threat to the regional committee's supremacy over coca farmers. Second, Jaime was a government official, and by 1984 Sendero had begun to target local politicians for assassination. Jaime had leadership ambitions, was a representative of state institutions, and was actively resisting Sendero's infiltration of the region. His assassination created a climate of fear in Tingo María.

Other assassinations followed, and within a year the fear of Sendero in the province was so great that the Provincial Council struggled to name an official replacement. In July 1984, the Peruvian government placed the Huallaga Valley under a state of emergency. Armed forces moved into Tingo María and began to patrol the valley in search of CRH militants. A debate raged within the military over whether to focus on combating the guerrillas or continuing its antidrug operations. Already, the connections between the Shining Path and the drug traffickers were becoming visible. The army

---

[30] José Gonzales, "Guerrillas and Coca in the Upper Huallaga Valley," in Palmer, *Shining Path of Peru*, p. 125.

worried that by trying to prevent coca production it would send peasants fleeing into the arms of the rebels. Allowing drug production to continue, however, created significant problems of corruption within the army's own ranks, as poorly paid soldiers sought wealth through drug trafficking; such corruption threatened external support for Peru's war on the Shining Path. This debate was a constant theme in the UHV throughout the 1980s and the 1990s, and it remains a live issue even today.

The CRH developed and behaved as a unit apart from Sendero Luminoso Nacional.[31] The decentralized structure of the movement enabled regional committees to organize without much direction from the top. They had to raise resources, recruit members, build bases of support, and plan military actions on their own. Only a small number of formed cadres from the highlands decamped to Huallaga to initiate the regional committee, moreover; the vast majority of CRH members were locally recruited and trained. While the Central Committee provided ideological direction, authority rested with the local organizations. Monitoring came in the form of regular reports to the Central Committee, and feedback on those reports was transmitted to the local membership, but actual sanctions were limited. Only the senior leadership of each committee interacted personally with members of the Central Committee, and only they could be monitored and punished. The compartmentalized system of organization meant that, for most recruits in the Huallaga Valley, connections to the rest of the organization were quite attenuated.

The CRH also evolved in a distinct context. Tingo María was a Peruvian backwater for much of the twentieth century. The first one-lane highway reached the UHV in 1937. Passage to the inner reaches of the jungle was only possible by means of long boat journeys or by traversing dense jungle paths. These constraints made it very difficult for the state to establish an effective presence and authority in the Amazonian jungle. It was the coca boom of the 1970s that transformed Tingo María. The Upper Huallaga Valley quickly became one of the most prosperous regions of Peru outside of the urban, coastal areas. Owing to the perfect climatic conditions and a flood of migration from the poor highland areas, coca plantings grew sixfold in ten years. Peasants came from all over the country to take part in the coca trade

---

[31] The Truth and Reconciliation Commission describes Alto Huallaga as a region in which local commanders had significant autonomy. Comisión de la Verdad y Reconciliación, *Informe Final: Peru, 1980–2000, Tomo IV* (Lima: Pontificia Universidad Católica del Peru y Universidad Nacional Mayor de San Marcos, 2003), p. 318.

as small farmers, seasonal laborers on the coca plantations, and workers in the cocaine-producing laboratories. In 1987, a UHV government official estimated that more than 95 percent of the local economy was based on illegal activity.[32]

The coca boom brought criminality as well as prosperity. Colombian traffickers came quickly to the region to take advantage of the extensive supply. They set up plantations, laboratories, and runways, and they brought their own security with them. The Peruvian state was powerless to stop them. By 1980, the UHV was characterized by lawlessness, corruption, and violence. Traffickers controlled leaf production by force, and their armed security guards ruled the valley, stealing, raping, and killing almost at will.[33] Peasants were unhappy with this arrangement but could do little about it. Traffickers provided peasants with their income; without the Colombians, the peasants knew, they would return to lives of miserable poverty.

As a result, when Sendero Luminoso began to organize in the UHV, the regional committee faced an environment far different than the one that prevailed in the southern highlands. Like their comrades in Ayacucho, the initial members of the CRH were formed militants – committed to the ideology of Guzmán, indoctrinated within the movement, and aware of the strict authoritarian structure of the organization. When they arrived in Tingo María, however, they had to organize in the midst of a drug war between traffickers, the military, and the peasants. Importantly, territorial control in Huallaga meant access to a consistent flow of resources from the drug trade that could be used to finance growth, operations, and personal enrichment. In theoretical terms, the CRH had access to both social and economic endowments.

After the attack on Mayor Jaime, the military responded with surprisingly effective counter-guerrilla patrols in the valley. By ignoring the problem of coca production, it was able to disperse the columns of militants and reduce the threat for a significant period of time. By 1986, however, members of the CRH had returned to political organizing, extending their influence and control throughout the valley. A chronology of the history of the CRH appears in Table 2.4.

The committee's mobilization strategies enabled it to build bases of support up and down the Huallaga River. Typically, the militants would attract

---

[32] Gonzales, "Guerrillas and Coca," p. 124.
[33] Gordon McCormick, *The Shining Path and the Future of Peru* (Washington, DC: Rand, 1990), p. 23.

Table 2.4. *Chronology of Sendero Luminoso–Huallaga*

Year	Event
1970–80	The coca boom begins in the Upper Huallaga Valley. Coca plantings increase at least sixfold, and the region is flooded with migrants.
1980–82	The first Sendero militants arrive in the UHV and begin organizing the regional committee.
1984	The UHV is designated an emergency zone after the mayor of Tingo María is assassinated. Army actions successfully disperse Sendero militants.
1986–87	The Sendero Central Committee targets the UHV as a key area for growth in the next campaign.
1988	The regional committee establishes near complete control over the UHV outside of Tingo María.
1989	The United States throws its weight behind a drug interdiction initiative in the UHV. Civilians organize in resistance to drug eradication efforts. Sendero suffers a series of setbacks.
1992–94	Sendero's national organization collapses. Coca prices fall, and crop production gradually shifts to Colombia to escape active Peruvian/U.S. counternarcotics operations.
1992–present	The UHV regional committee survives and maintains its involvement in the coca trade. Coca prices begin to increase again in the late 1990s, and drug production returns to the UHV.

support first by administering revolutionary justice in a village. They would promise order and assist the local civilians by killing those thieves, rapists, and traffickers who had made life most difficult for peasants during the coca boom. Such exercises of summary justice were welcomed by most villagers after years of living under the traffickers' control. The militants would then set in place popular committees to manage local villages and organize the civilians to assist the guerrillas.

As it expanded its territorial authority, the CRH was better able to monitor the trade in coca leaves and paste, and it began extending its control over the coca trade in the zones it "liberated." At first, the committee focused on the taxation of drug traffickers who sought to do business in their areas. Controlling access to runways, Sendero members charged a landing fee and a "licensing" fee to Colombians who wanted to purchase crops. The CRH then began to organize markets for the selling of leaves and to tax anything produced in its zone. It also took control of abandoned land, on which it cultivated coca to increase the revenues flowing into its coffers. Although peasants had to pay a tax to the militants, they now had an advocate as they bargained with traffickers for higher prices and a "government" that would eliminate the criminality that plagued their villages.

As early as 1983, the Central Committee was expressing its objections to the involvement of the CRH in the coca trade, arguing that the militants should direct the peasants to plant other crops. The Central Committee worried that if Sendero Luminoso did not prevent the growing of coca, it would be publicly linked to the traffickers – a situation the committee found highly undesirable.[34] Three years later, commenting on the challenges they would face in 1986, the senior leadership of the Shining Path argued that the CRH should begin a campaign to introduce new crops in the valley. Knowing that its doing so could cause a rupture with the peasants, the committee encouraged the CRH to "educate" the peasants and show them that the "delinquency" of the drug traffickers could be eliminated.[35] In 1989, the Central Committee commented to its membership on a Rand Corporation study that linked Sendero to the drug trade. Accused of using drug revenues to finance arms purchases, the Central Committee insisted that it had mounted a "front" against drug trafficking. It claimed that Sendero's main source of arms was the enemy, and it mocked the assertion that the Shining Path could even purchase arms on the international market, isolated as it was inside the Peruvian jungle and in the highlands.[36] The Central Committee's claim that Sendero Luminoso did not benefit from the drug trade was largely true: much of the money generated from the coca trade (estimated at between $20 and $30 million a year) stayed in the CRH.[37]

As the CRH gained financial strength, it also began to launch more frequent attacks on police stations and military installations. By the late 1980s, the movement controlled most of the major towns and villages in

---

[34] These comments were made in "Iniciar el Gran Salto," captured Sendero document, 1983, DINCOTE Sendero collection, Lima, Peru.

[35] Summary of the fourth national conference in August, September, and October 1986, captured Sendero document, 1986, DINCOTE Sendero collection, Lima, Peru.

[36] "Informe Sobre Las Concreciones Politicas," captured Sendero document, November 1989, DINCOTE Sendero collection, Lima, Peru.

[37] This point is controversial. It has been assumed that these resources were used to fund the national organization. See McClintock, *Revolutionary Movements*, and Gonzales, "Guerrillas and Coca." Recently uncovered documentation and interviews on the ground in the Huallaga Valley suggest, however, that much of the revenue stayed in the regional committee. In interviews, senior members of the police and intelligence forces, including Benedicto Jiménez, the former head of the counterterrorism police, confirm that the funds remained in the CRH. Interview with Benedicto Jiménez, Lima, October 2001.

the valley. Sendero and its supporters also blew up the two bridges that provided an entrance to the Huallaga Valley and dug ditches in the highways running through the region, limiting the military's access to the liberated zones. New counternarcotics operations by the García administration and later by Fujimori and his U.S. allies only reinforced peasant support for the CRH. With financial and logistical support from abroad, the Peruvian government dealt a series of setbacks to the guerrillas as they battled the insurgency and drug trafficking simultaneously. The regional committee responded with a pledge to protect the rights of the peasants to grow coca and actively prevented the infiltration of forces advocating eradication and interdiction in guerrilla zones.

The fall of Abimael Guzmán in 1992 coincided with a major decrease in the price of coca and a production surplus in the UHV. Eradication and interdiction efforts in both Colombia and Peru decreased the frequency of flights between the two countries, leaving much of the coca and paste stuck in Peru. For the first time, crop substitution became a real possibility for Peruvian peasants, who saw the returns from illegal crop production decrease dramatically.

Over the last decade, however, the Peruvian government has been unable to defeat the CRH. While the national Shining Path organization crumbled between 1992 and 1994, the regional committee in the UHV continued its operations, maintaining a column of militants in the jungle and continuing to control coca production and trafficking in the liberated zones. Terrorism decreased in the rest of the country, but attacks on police posts and military installations in the valley remained consistent. They were met with brutal counterinsurgency operations by the military in 1994 that threatened international support for Fujimori and the Peruvian regime.[38] By the late 1990s, as interdiction efforts improved in Colombia, drug production had shifted back to the UHV, giving rise to a renewed regional committee. Drug profits increased, and the guerrillas began to introduce new crops, including poppies.

That the CRH did not collapse when Sendero Luminoso fell is an interesting puzzle that deserves explanation. But an examination of the regional committee in Huallaga proves important as well for the broader puzzle that is the subject of this book. Over time, ideology came to play a minor role in the CRH's efforts to organize peasants. Stories of corrupt behavior by

---

[38] See Coordenadora de Los Derechos Humanos, *Los sucesos del Alto Huallaga* (Lima: Coordenadora de Los Derechos Humanos, 1994).

Sendero cadres in the UHV were rampant, and little was done to prevent it. Anecdotal evidence suggests that killings were often unconnected to the political aims of the movement. These are striking differences from the behavior of the Shining Path militants in the highlands.

Examining Rebels' Choices

The National Resistance Army, Renamo, Sendero Luminoso, and its regional committee in the Upper Huallaga Valley launched their insurgencies in similar contexts. All four groups emerged at a time of widening political opportunity. Each faced a regime in transition that was struggling to build its legitimacy among rural populations. In all four cases, the rebels grew stronger as the national military cracked down on peasants in response to the insurgency. And, like the insurgents led by Mao and Guevara, the rebel groups began as small, vulnerable movements with the dream of capturing state control.

Two of the movements were resource-rich, one supported by external forces and another sitting on a veritable gold mine of illicit wealth. The other two were resource-poor, forced to capture weapons from the government and totally dependent on the civilian population for survival. In this context, one group turned to ethnicity and religion, the other to ideology. Both survived to wage a war, but neither ever managed to gain access to substantial financial resources.

It is important to ask whether these differences in initial endowments matter, how they shape the choices rebel leaders make as they organize, and in what ways they are linked to the different behaviors of rebel groups. The remainder of this book addresses these questions by looking comparatively at the key challenges of rebel organization: recruitment, management and organizational control, governance, the use of violence, and resilience in the face of rapid change. I begin by considering the first step in group formation: how to recruit men and women to fight.

3

Recruitment

The National Resistance Army recruited educated university students, many with previous political involvement, through a clandestine urban network; ethnic appeals were among its most crucial tactics. Renamo enlisted discontented Mozambican exiles living in Rhodesia, most of whom had fought with the Portuguese against the liberation movement. Salaries were offered to sweeten the pot. The Shining Path mobilized rural communities in the Andean highlands and drew its recruits from schools of popular education that indoctrinated rural peasants in a new ideology. Its regional committee in the Upper Huallaga Valley, on the other hand, forged an alliance with farmers of coca and accepted all who wished to participate in Sendero's jungle campaigns.

This chapter asks why rebel groups, when faced with the similar challenge of building a military organization, adopt such different strategies of recruitment. It considers why some groups appeal to combatants' short-term, material interests and why others activate ethnic, religious, or ideological identities to motivate participation, as well as why some groups use preexisting social networks to screen potential recruits, while others open the doors to all who wish to join. It then shows how different recruitment strategies shape the characteristics of the membership that groups are able to attract. In exploring this process, I begin with the set of factors that shape how rebel groups recruit before turning to the consequences of these strategies. I conclude by examining the cases of Uganda, Mozambique, and Peru for evidence of how a group's recruitment strategy affects the qualities of the participants it is able to mobilize.

Participation in Rebellion

Rebellion occurs only when individuals acting in isolation or in groups decide to run mortal risks by challenging the government. Participation encompasses multiple roles.[1] Some individuals are merely sympathizers. They support a group in private and, perhaps, advocate its strategies and aims among a small network of relatives, friends, and neighbors. Others provide material support to a rebellion. They choose to share some of the food they grow, make their houses available as shelter for combatants on the move, or provide labor on an informal basis. Still others engage as militants, investing all of their energies and resources in a group's activities. The question of why some take these steps while others do not has preoccupied scholars of political violence for decades.

One answer, discussed in Chapter 1, is that rebel groups act as if they are states, offering peasants collective benefits. They make promises about the political agendas they will implement if they succeed in capturing power. They pledge to dedicate funds to education and health care, commit to make political institutions more participatory, promise to redistribute land from wealthy landowners to the rural poor, and offer protection from repressive government forces. In short, rebellion offers potential recruits a pathway to a different, and perhaps better, future. But how the promise of collective benefits itself motivates individuals to take enormous risks is not clear. Social transformation potentially benefits all peasants, not simply those who choose to invest in the rebellion. These collective benefits are important, but they are a consistent feature of rebel organization, and thus they cannot account on their own for why some individuals participate and others remain on the sidelines.

This represents the essence of Mancur Olson's challenge to theorists of revolution.[2] He argued that forms of collective action that are costly to individuals can only be sustained if cooperation is coerced or motivated by providing selective incentives only to those who participate. This simple insight, which shifted the focus from the macro to the micro, challenged scholars to understand the calculations individuals make about whether to

---

[1] For a discussion of multiple roles, see Mark Lichbach, *The Rebel's Dilemma* (Ann Arbor: University of Michigan Press, 1994), p. 17, and Roger Petersen, *Resistance and Rebellion: Lessons from Eastern Europe* (New York: Cambridge University Press, 2001), pp. 8–9.

[2] Mancur Olson, *The Logic of Collective Action: Public Goods and the Theory of Groups* (Cambridge, MA: Harvard University Press, 1965).

support, collaborate, or participate in violent resistance. This classic starting point for discussions of rebellion prompts us to ask what strategies groups pursue to respond to the dilemma of collective action.

Although controversial, Olson's own answer to this question has occupied the bulk of scholarly attention. It inspired controversy at first because the idea that dissidents might be motivated by material self-interest cut against the grain of traditional approaches to understanding rebellion. Empirical evidence dampened these criticisms. Samuel Popkin first extended Olson's argument to the case of peasant resistance.[3] Drawing on the testimony of peasants in Vietnam, he argued that revolutionary leaders offer material incentives to potential supporters and soldiers contingent on their participation. For example, one of his interviewees commented: "[Before joining,] I thought about my grandmother. I worried that she would live in misery if I went off and joined the army because no one would be left to look after her. I brought these apprehensions up with the cadres and they said that they were certain that the village authorities would take care of my grandmother. After I left, my grandmother was given 0.6 hectare of rice field."[4]

More recently, Mark Lichbach catalogued examples of how selective incentives operate in a wide variety of contexts, from organized and unorganized rural protests to strikes, riots, and rebellion. He identified a range of possible private goods that might be offered to rebel recruits, from money, loot, and land to protection and positions of authority.[5] Acceptance of the role of selective incentives in motivating participation is now widespread, leading Jeffrey Goodwin and Theda Skocpol to conclude that "it is the on-going provision of such collective and selective goods, not ideological conversion in the abstract, that has played the principal role in solidifying social support for guerrilla armies."[6]

While it is clear that selective incentives help groups to overcome free rider problems, offering them is not the only strategy that rebel groups have employed, nor is it one that all groups can utilize to equal effect. Another line of scholarship emphasizes the actions rebel leaders take to activate

---

[3] Samuel Popkin, *The Rational Peasant: The Political Economy of Rural Society in Vietnam* (Berkeley: University of California Press, 1979).
[4] Ibid., p. 240.
[5] Lichbach, *Rebel's Dilemma*, pp. 217–26.
[6] Jeffrey Goodwin and Theda Skocpol, "Explaining Revolutions in the Contemporary Third World," *Politics and Society* 17 (1989): 489–509.

particular beliefs and norms by appealing to ethnic, religious, cultural, and ideological identities. Identities are important because they link individuals to one another. In an informal sense, shared identities provide a set of common practices, understandings, and reference points. Formally, identities are often accompanied by preexisting networks that tie people together through kinship, religious groups, geographic proximity, or formal associations. Shared identities and social ties help to resolve the dilemma of collective action by providing for reciprocity.[7] The fact that participants have been and believe they will continue to be engaged in repeated interaction with others from the group makes it important for them to cooperate today in order that others will cooperate with them in the future. In other words, a future orientation is paramount among members who share a particular identity. In groups mobilized on the basis of identity, strong norms of cooperation often develop, and group members take responsibility for imposing costs on nonparticipants. Often, but not always, reciprocity tends to operate in more homogenous settings where members share similar backgrounds and experiences. A similarity of outlook, interests, and preferences reduces the costs of organizing cooperation and punishing nonparticipation.

One source of shared norms is a strong community. Roger Petersen argues, for example, that participation in the Lithuanian resistance to Soviet occupation, and in particular in the decisions individuals made to move from being sympathizers to being active militants, is best explained by reference to the strength of their community structures.[8] Specifically, strong communities enable collective action by elevating the value of status rewards, activating norms of reciprocity, encouraging people to seek "safety in numbers," and allowing for the better monitoring and punishment of informants.

Rebel leaders also utilize a third approach in recruiting soldiers. Instead of activating norms of reciprocity, leaders sometimes draw on community norms to activate a process orientation rather than one focused on potential ends. Here, the act of participation is a reward in itself: it contributes to a greater sense of personal efficacy, it is enjoyable to the participant, and, for members of the community, it is as important as any victory that might be achieved. Elisabeth Wood saw this process orientation at work in motivating

---

[7] Michael Taylor, "Rationality and Revolutionary Collective Action," in *Rationality and Revolution*, ed. Michael Taylor (New York: Cambridge University Press, 1988), pp. 63–97.
[8] Petersen, *Resistance and Rebellion*.

participation in El Salvador's civil war.[9] She argues that revolutionaries in El Salvador were distinguished by a belief in the value of participation per se, a refusal to acquiesce to the government, and a "pleasure in agency" related to their role in the struggle. She quotes an elderly man who collaborated with the insurgency: "To live through this war was something very hard, but also a great source of pride: to have stood up to it all. We have achieved quite a lot even though we lost family members."[10] A process orientation resolves the dilemma of collective action by reshaping people's preferences: community norms that predate the war or, as in the case of El Salvador, are created in the process of mobilization for war make participation as important to individuals as any material rewards they might receive.

Given the common challenges of recruitment and the various established methods for motivating participation, we must ask why groups adopt such different recruitment strategies, consider the factors that account for the use of ethnic or ideological appeals rather than the offer of material rewards, and investigate whether the choice of strategy shapes the nature of who is attracted to participate. Of course, groups may use multiple strategies in practice, and how they recruit can vary over time within a conflict or even across different regions. I wish to draw attention, however, to overriding patterns of recruitment that vary across contexts. We turn now to some of the factors that may account for this variation.

Endowments, Information, and Recruitment

To explain why rebel groups pursue different recruitment strategies, I focus on two factors: the mix of endowments that different rebel leaders have at their disposal to attract new recruits and the informational asymmetries that exist between leaders and prospective soldiers. While previous research on rebel recruitment has identified various ways in which rebel groups mobilize participants and overcome collective action problems, far less attention has been given to variation in initial endowments which conditions leaders' choice of strategy. By adding a new focus on the role of information in the recruitment process, moreover, I move beyond an important limitation of existing research: the assumption that all potential recruits are of the same value to a rebel group.

---

[9] Elisabeth Wood, *Insurgent Collective Action in El Salvador* (New York: Cambridge University Press, 2004).

[10] Ibid., p. 205.

I proposed in Chapter 1 that rebel leaders encounter different initial conditions as they organize a strategy for recruiting new members. In some contexts, rebel leaders initiate a conflict with access to substantial economic resources. In others, they lack access to economic resources but may draw on a set of social endowments. The initial mix of resources affects the feasibility and effectiveness of the different types of appeals rebel leaders might make.

Economic endowments can be used to fund salaries, uniforms, food, and other supplies, all of which can be distributed to supporters contingent on their participation. Because wealth makes it possible to deliver such benefits immediately, the use of economic endowments minimizes the importance of trust in the unofficial contract between rebel leaders and recruits. Economic endowments also reduce the potential costs of participation by enabling groups to purchase arms and ammunition, to organize transport for rebel detachments, and to continually replenish their forces. Finally, wealth improves the relative position of the insurgency vis-à-vis the government forces.

Where economic endowments are in short supply, promises must substitute for immediate payoffs as rebel leaders anticipate the private rewards they will be able to deliver at later points in the conflict.[11] Such promises put a premium on the credibility of the rebel leadership, and it is the presence of social endowments that makes rebel leaders' promises of future rewards credible.[12] The presence of social endowments also favors the use of nonmaterial recruitment strategies. Norms of reciprocity emerge and are reinforced in contexts where people have interacted with one another repeatedly over time and where they have common expectations about how others will behave, as in ethnic and religious networks, formal associations,

---

[11] It might be possible for a group without economic endowments to offer immediate payoffs to recruits by allowing its soldiers to loot as soon as they join. Groups that choose this strategy rarely if ever manage to generate combat sufficient for a civil war, however; instead, they remain as bandit and criminal groups. As a result, for the analysis in this chapter, I assume that rebel groups can only offer payoffs in the near term that come from a taxing capacity, resource extraction, or external support.

[12] Ethnic and religious linkages help make contracts enforceable because membership in these informal and formal networks facilitates trust and makes the threat of sanction credible. Where ideology provides the social bond across individuals, tight groups are also created, but they do not tend to predate the conflict itself. In this context, ideology often serves to make the leaders appear trustworthy to the combatants. It specifies goals, objectives, and codes of behavior against which leaders can be measured. It also leads recruits to think that success is more likely (because "history is on our side") and that, as insiders, they are the people most likely to benefit from success.

and tight-knit communities. Appeals based on a process orientation also depend in an important way on social endowments. Valuing participation in itself, seeing its costs as benefits, requires placing a value on action that may be held or developed within a social group. Importantly, in the absence of economic endowments, recruitment strategies privilege patience and a future orientation.

Such high-commitment recruits, dedicated to the cause of the organization and willing to make costly investments today with the promise of receiving rewards in the future, are *investors*. Low-commitment individuals are *consumers*, seeking short-term gains from participation. Low-commitment individuals are less productive for an organization, as they require a continual expenditure of resources in the short term. In practical terms, we can think of the level of commitment as a discount rate. It is an indication of an individual's patience.

The problem for rebel leaders is that while recruits are aware of their level of commitment to the organization, the rebel leadership is not. Whether a recruit is an investor or a consumer is private information, and individuals have a strong incentive to misrepresent their level of commitment.[13] Selective incentives further magnify this challenge for rebel leaders. By offering short-term rewards that are higher than the opportunity cost of participation, rebel leaders can create a steady stream of potential recruits; in this context, distinguishing between high- and low-quality recruits is of paramount importance. But rebel leaders are unable to choose recruits on the basis of an individual's type. Unless the recruits or the rebel organization take strategic actions, the market for recruits will suffer from adverse selection.[14] Unable to distribute selective, private rewards linked to the actual productivity of insurgent forces, rebel leaders may find their organizations flooded with low-commitment individuals. The recruitment process can thus be viewed as a set of strategic actions by recruits and rebel leaders designed to overcome the constraint of collective action and avoid the pitfall of adverse selection.

[13] Lichbach calls this the problem of "preference falsification." He writes: "Dissidents will support a side in which they do not believe, remain neutral, support both sides, switch sides, switch among opposition groups, and take sides only after the conflict is over." *Rebel's Dilemma*, p. 284. See also Timur Kuran, *Private Truths, Public Lies: The Social Consequences of Preference Falsification* (Cambridge, MA: Harvard University Press, 1998).

[14] This challenge of industrial organization is well covered in standard economics textbooks. The seminal paper developing the concept is Michael Spence, "Job Market Signaling," *Quarterly Journal of Economics* 87, no. 3 (August 1973): 355–74.

A Theory of Rebel Recruitment

This section integrates the resource mix available to rebel leaders and the informational problems they confront into a theory of how rebel leaders recruit. The story begins with an offer. Finding themselves in competition with other groups for the affection, energy, and investment of civilians, rebel leaders issue an appeal for support. They can adopt a variety of strategies to overcome the participation constraint, but their options are constrained in turn by the endowments they can access. As we have seen, economic endowments lend themselves to appeals rooted in the offer of selective incentives: resource-rich groups offer payoffs to motivate potential recruits. Social endowments, on the other hand, favor appeals rooted in a longer-term orientation: the promises of private rewards in the future and appeals to the cooperative norms characteristic of some social networks are feasible for groups rich in social endowments. Either approach is sufficient to motivate individual participation, but the strategies employed have very different ramifications when it comes to adverse selection.

Potential recruits send signals of their level of commitment to the leaders of rebel organizations when they make decisions about the offers they receive.[15] High-commitment individuals signal their quality by responding to appeals that emphasize a long-term orientation and staying away from organizations that rely on short-term, material rewards. The signal of quality is credible because it is more costly for low-commitment individuals to accept deferred benefits: rebel organizations can infer that an individual's willingness to make investments in the short term without concomitant private rewards is an indication of sincere commitment to the organization. Of course, committed individuals would be better off if they did not have to bear the cost of deferring rewards to the future, but their willingness to absorb that cost protects organizations from a flood of opportunistic joiners. Conditional on resource endowments, then, recruitment sorts

---

[15] The concept of signaling was initially developed in economics. Political scientists have also explored the role of signaling in addressing informational asymmetries in political interaction. James Fearon, for example, explores the role of two types of signals, "tying hands" and "sinking costs," in helping political leaders make credible threats of force in the international arena. See "Signaling Foreign Policy Interests: Tying Hands versus Sinking Costs," *Journal of Conflict Resolution* 41, no. 1 (February 1997): 68–90. More recently, Alan Krueger and Jitka Maleckova have suggested that high levels of education may signal to terrorist groups a potential recruit's sincere commitment to the cause. See "Education, Poverty, and Terrorism: Is There a Causal Connection?" *Journal of Economic Perspectives* 17, no. 4 (Autumn 2003): 119–44.

high-commitment and low-commitment individuals into groups that make different types of appeals. Resource-rich rebel groups are overwhelmed by opportunistic joiners, while those waging war with limited economic endowments attract committed soldiers by appealing to a long-term orientation.[16]

Importantly, the sorting process unleashed by a group's appeals is not sufficient on its own for groups that are intent on keeping out opportunists. Rebel leaders often take strategic actions to reduce their informational disadvantage. The key to any such strategy is its selectivity: rebel organizations develop recruitment methods that attempt to identify and exclude potential recruits who might be joining with little interest in the group's overall objectives.[17]

Rebel leaders rely on three methods in particular to overcome their informational handicap. The first requires that rebel organizations actively *gather information* about the past behavior of interested individuals. Previous practice is a strong indication of the likely performance of potential recruits. To gather such information, rebel groups must establish or draw on preexisting links with the communities in which they operate that enable them to collect information about potential members. Community leaders are likely to have information about the reliability and trustworthiness of community members that precedes the beginning of the rebel movement.

For information gathering to provide useful signals about a recruit's level of commitment, potential members must care about their reputations, as well. In attempting to join, recruits make assertions about their level of commitment. Groups with access to information-gathering networks have the capacity to authenticate these pledges. Where reputation matters and groups are able to gather information, those recruits with a demonstrated incapacity for honest and committed behavior will avoid the movement or, when they try to join, will be stopped at the door.

---

[16] Resource-rich groups seem to be unable to preserve their wealth and invest it in the organization. They tend to be unable to recruit on the basis of promises because they lack the shared ethnic, religious, or political identities that make promises credible and allow for effective screening. In resource-rich contexts, groups that organize around social linkages are crowded out as opportunistic insurgencies emerge quickly and gain the dominant position. This process is described in greater detail in the conclusion.

[17] One analyst of civil war has argued that screening mechanisms such as those described here can be used to select for psychopaths and criminals rather than committed individuals if leaders are motivated to plunder and kill rather than capture control of the state. See John Mueller, "The Banality of Ethnic War," *International Security* 25, no. 1 (Summer 2000): 42–70.

A second strategy also requires that reputation matter. Instead of look-ing to actors outside of the movement to authenticate the pledges of new recruits, however, it relies on the credibility and commitment of current members. This screening mechanism is called *vouching*. Potential members must be invited to join by current rebel soldiers, and while the new recruit is considered for membership, the current soldier must vouch for his hon-esty and commitment. If a new recruit fails to live up to his pledge, both the recruit and the current soldier bear the costs of his failure. As long as rebel soldiers seek to protect their reputations within the organization, vouching is an effective strategy for screening out opportunists. Since the private benefits that are used to overcome collective action problems can be withheld, rebel soldiers will seek to protect their own positions within the organization as long as they remain a part of it.

The final method used to screen recruits is *costly induction*. Rebel organi-zations set in place processes for evaluating potential recruits' level of com-mitment. In order to be effective, these processes must be more costly for some individuals than others, creating a disincentive for low-commitment recruits to join. Two examples of costly induction demonstrate how it works. The first is a required period of political indoctrination for new recruits to the rebel movement. This might include the sustained study of the ideol-ogy and political messages of the rebel group followed by oral or written examinations. As a screening mechanism, the process introduces a number of additional costs for disinterested recruits: the time delay in access to a gun and the authority of being a rebel, the time wasted in study, and the reputational costs likely to accrue if the recruit fails his examinations. A sec-ond example is a required period of rebel apprenticeship in which recruits participate actively in attacks without the use of a gun. This method clearly elevates the level of risk involved to a level that would be unmanageable for low-commitment individuals.

A clean test of the implications of my argument about recruitment would involve revealing the true types of recruits attracted to various rebel groups: groups that offer payoffs should be found to have significantly higher pro-portions of low-commitment individuals among their ranks. But the level of individual commitment is private information, and it cannot be discerned directly from outward markers.

The theory suggests a number of other patterns to look for across rebel organizations that allow it to be assessed. First, the logic suggests that groups that are unable to overcome the participation constraint by employing short-term, material appeals instead turn to alternative strategies, including promises of deferred gratification and the activation of norms of reciprocity. Such strategies depend on the credibility of the rebel leadership to be effective. Credibility in this context may flow from the fact that rebel leaders and combatants are embedded in preexisting social networks formed around ethnic, religious, cultural, or other identities. Groups employing these alternative appeals thus tend to exhibit homogeneity of identities or beliefs among their members that facilitates their leaders' recruitment strategies. Rebel organizations that launch appeals based on payoffs, on the other hand, tend to exhibit heterogeneity of identities or beliefs within their membership.

Second, potential recruits may signal their level of commitment by showing a willingness to defer private rewards into the future or to make investments without any promise of remuneration. Such actions are indicative of an individual's patience, or future orientation. Although educational opportunities are limited in many of the developing countries that experience conflict, a small percentage of citizens manage to receive places in the national university system. While education is too restricted in its supply to serve as an accurate signal of commitment across all individuals, an individual's level of education is likely to be negatively correlated with his or her discount rate.[18] People who place a higher value on rewards they might receive in the future are far more likely to absorb the costs of investing in education. One implication of this logic is that the level of advanced education in groups that recruit using payoffs should be much lower than in groups that employ alternative approaches.

The final empirical implication is that strategies of information gathering, vouching, and costly induction are more likely to be used by rebel organizations that rely on social endowments. Information gathering requires groups to be embedded in particular communities from which the rebel leadership can obtain reliable information about the quality of potential

---

[18] Because discount rates are not directly observable, scholars have identified a variety of instruments for time preference, including, most notably, whether someone smokes cigarettes. See Victor Fuchs, ed., *Economic Aspects of Health* (Chicago: University of Chicago Press, 1982). Smoking is negatively correlated with a whole series of future-oriented activities, including investments in health, educational attainment, and the choice of careers with a steeper wage profile. On wages, see Lalith Munasinghe and Nachum Sicherman, "Why Do Dancers Smoke? Time Preference, Occupational Choice, and Wage Growth" (NBER Working Paper no. 7542, National Bureau of Economic Research, Cambridge, MA, February 2000).

recruits. Vouching is only as effective as the members who have already joined the group; high-commitment individuals are more likely to protect their reputations by inviting only other committed recruits to join. Finally, costly induction generally necessitates the presence of a coherent set of political beliefs or ideological leanings that help to structure the training period required of rebel recruits.[19]

In sum, ethnic, religious, and political mobilization emerge as critical tools that enable rebel organizations to recruit committed soldiers to their movements. This mobilization takes particular forms, including information gathering, vouching, and costly induction, that effectively screen out opportunistic joiners. And importantly, these methods of recruitment can be employed only by groups rooted in shared identities or belief systems with networks that connect them to the civilian population. The alternative approach to recruitment, which uses payoffs to attract recruits and does not screen new members, is also an efficient strategy, but it is important to recognize the ways in which it shapes group membership. Resource-rich groups are overwhelmed by opportunistic joiners. The recruitment process thus leaves a legacy that shapes how these groups respond to organizational challenges at later points in their evolution.

Recruitment in Practice

When we examine the recruitment strategies of the National Resistance Army, Renamo, Sendero Nacional, and Sendero–Huallaga, we seek to discover whether groups that recruit on the basis of promises alone seem to draw on social sources of credibility to overcome collective action problems, whether methods of ethnic mobilization and political indoctrination appear to be linked to the challenge of identifying committed members, whether such methods attract older and more educated members, and whether groups that recruit on the basis of short-term rewards lack social bases in their membership.

---

[19] A period of rebel apprenticeship does not on the surface seem out of reach to resource-rich groups. But low-commitment individuals would need to be compensated with greater private rewards to make it worth their while to absorb initiation costs. Because even resource-rich rebel groups face budget constraints, they are poorly equipped to make joining more difficult unless they can defer some payments to participants into the future.

Ethnic Appeals and Community Ties: The NRA

When one student arrived at an NRA camp not more than two months after the war commenced, he found himself surrounded by people from similar backgrounds.[20] Recruited by a clandestine network in Kampala, the new soldiers were educated university students who were willing to interrupt their studies to participate. Many had worked with Yoweri Museveni and the Uganda Patriotic Movement in its campaign to defeat Milton Obote's Uganda People's Congress in the 1980 election. Some had fought previously with Museveni in the 1970s, when he organized FRONASA in exile. The vast majority were ethnically Banyankole, from western Uganda. The recruits also knew one another well: many had grown up in neighboring villages, attended the same schools, and gone to church together. A substantial segment had been raised as born-again Christians, and this strong religious influence shaped their childhoods. They had been encouraged to eschew alcohol and embrace education and had been channeled into professional rather than agricultural careers as a way of improving the economic and social conditions of their communities.

The membership of the National Resistance Council, the political wing of the NRA, at the moment of the NRA's victory reflects a similar ethnic and religious composition. The NRC included most of the senior leaders of the NRA along with some civilian collaborators. When we examine the characteristics of only those who joined during the bush war (the so-called historical members), the predominance of the Banyankole is evident: of forty members, twenty-five (62.5 percent) were Banyankole. Moreover, although born-again Christians made up only 15 percent of the leadership core in the NRC (six members), they included the leader of the movement, the head of the rebel army, and other senior members of the political and military establishment.[21]

The NRA's reliance on social rather than economic endowments made its path more difficult in the early years, and the movement struggled to survive throughout 1981.[22] Government forces backed by Tanzanian soldiers were

[20] The characteristics of early NRA recruits are drawn from interviews with senior NRA commanders in Kampala on October 20(A), November 2(A,B), and November 6(A,B), 2000, and January 24(A) and July 15(A), 2001.

[21] An NRA commander provided information about the ethnic and religious makeup of the National Resistance Council, November 12(A), 2000.

[22] For a detailed description of the early days of the NRA's campaign, see Yoweri Museveni, *Sowing the Mustard Seed: The Struggle for Freedom and Democracy in Uganda* (London: Macmillan, 1997), pp. 121–37.

present throughout the Luwero Triangle. The rebels, who numbered not much more than one hundred soldiers in all and lacked sufficient guns to go around, were forced to hide during the day. There were no resources with which to pay them.[23] The NRA relied entirely on contributions from urban supporters and rural contacts to survive.

While Museveni had initially targeted his recruitment efforts at coethnics based in Kampala and the West, this approach was insufficient to meet the group's recruitment targets. The Banyankole were a relatively small ethnic group, and it was difficult for them to move from western Uganda and Kampala to the Luwero Triangle without being discovered. Within the first year of the conflict, the NRA began to look to the Baganda, who dominated the Luwero Triangle, for potential recruits. Although many Baganda harbored tremendous resentment toward the Obote regime, they were not easily convinced of the necessity to join the NRA's struggle because they viewed the group's Banyankole leadership as ethnic outsiders.[24]

Museveni initially turned to local contacts in the Triangle – Baganda with whom he had built relationships before the struggle began.[25] They provided the NRA's initial cadres with food, shelter, and local guides to help them through the unfamiliar terrain. But he needed a broader network of civilian supporters, one tied to the NRA by political rather than ethnic allegiances. Operating from hidden rebel camps in the Triangle, the NRA began to build networks of civilian contacts.[26] It relied on its local supporters to select others from their villages to form small clandestine committees, which provided the rebels with food, guides, information, and recruits. The NRA paid special attention to respected elders within the villages (the *bataka*) and those who were wealthy.[27]

---

[23] Interview with senior NRA official, Kampala, September 20(A), 2000.

[24] Surprisingly, the leadership of the NRA never made a strategic decision to base itself in the Luwero Triangle. Such a decision might have made sense given the Baganda's strong opposition to the Obote regime. One senior commander present at the organizing meetings before the NRA launched its first attack admitted, however, that they plotted an exit strategy from their first target that took them into Luwero, but they did not discuss long-term plans for remaining in the area. Interview, Kampala, November 10(A), 2000.

[25] Museveni, *Sowing the Mustard Seed*, p. 128.

[26] Interviews with civilian collaborators, Semuto, November 14(B), 15(A,C), 16(A,B), 2000.

[27] Ibid., November 18(A,B), 22(A), 2000. It is worth noting that after its victory in 1986 the NRA established a compensation commission to distribute benefits directly to those in the Luwero Triangle who supported the war in its infancy. Detailed lists of names and corresponding contributions had been kept during the war, and the tangible rewards that

Central to this process of generating broader support was the articulation of a political agenda that linked the historical experiences of the Baganda to those of the Banyankole. Using language he first employed during the election campaigns in 1980, Museveni pointed to a shared experience of persecution at the hands of President Obote and a realistic fear of continued northern dominance of the military. In mobilizing supporters, the rebels explained their political cause, emphasized their desire to defeat the Obote regime, and promised to end ethnic tribalism in Uganda.[28] Museveni and the rebel leadership also made promises about the future, the shape of the new regime they would install, the benefits that would come to Buganda (including the return of the kabaka), and the compensation that those who contributed to the rebellion would receive. At the same time, the NRA took public steps to incorporate Baganda into leadership positions.[29]

The local networks established in the Triangle were the basis for recruitment over much of the next two years. Members of the clandestine committees were asked to deliver "disciplined" recruits to NRA camps.[30] In particular, Museveni encouraged the bataka to volunteer their sons for the cause.[31] After these young men were brought into the military units, Museveni remained in close contact with the bataka. The new recruits were thus in a position of needing to protect their reputations with the NRA and with their families. Furthermore, the NRA instituted a rigorous period of military and political training that had to be completed before a recruit could participate in operations. Political commissars were appointed from within the rebel force and given responsibility for the political training. Lectures included topics from the history of Uganda to political economy and strategies of guerrilla warfare. When possible, recruits were encouraged to read the books the NRA had on hand, including works by Mao and Fanon.[32] Before recruits could participate in any

---

had been promised were delivered back to Luwero in the years immediately following the conflict.

[28] I will return to issues of political mobilization and civilian organization in more detail in Chapter 5.

[29] Interviews with civilian collaborators, Semuto, November 15(A,B), 17(A), 2000.

[30] Ibid., November 15(A), 17(C), 2000; interviews with NRA commanders, Kampala, September 27(A), October 22(A), 2000.

[31] Interviews with civilian collaborators, Semuto, November 15(B,C), 16(A,B), 22(A,B), 2000.

[32] Interviews with senior NRA commanders, Kampala, October 22(A), 24(B), 25(B), 2000.

operations, the NRA required them to understand and digest the political aims of the movement as well as the strategies of guerrilla warfare the NRA sought to use. Consistent with the theory, then, the NRA activated social networks to overcome collective action problems, generated cross-ethnic group appeals as the ranks of Banyankole grew thin, and sorted activists from opportunists as it sought to overcome its resource handicap in building its guerrilla army.

From Voluntarism to Violence: Renamo

With André Matsangaissa at the helm, Renamo grew quickly. Between 1976 and 1979, the force increased its ranks from a few hundred to nearly two thousand.[33] In seeking recruits, it turned first to the discontented Mozambican population living in Rhodesia. Orlando Cristina, a former operative with the Portuguese intelligence services in Mozambique, assisted the rebel leaders in identifying and recruiting former *flechas* to participate in the insurgency.[34] Forced out of Mozambique when Frelimo took power, these individuals had perfected their military skills as part of the Portuguese effort to retain control of its colony. New recruits were taken to a guerrilla camp at Odzi organized by the Rhodesian Central Intelligence Organization.[35] Former Rhodesian soldiers and CIO operatives served as the instructors, preparing the recruits for internal operations in Mozambique. The Rhodesians provided them with weapons and uniforms, food, and comfortable shelter in the guerrilla training base. And of course, the rebels received money, too: Matsangaissa was paid Rh$75 a month; Dhlakama, his deputy, received Rh$65; and the rest of the infantry was rewarded with salaries of Rh$20 a month.[36]

Renamo also sought to recruit soldiers from inside Mozambique. The Rhodesian-funded *Voz da Africa Livre* broadcast anti-Frelimo propaganda

---

[33] William Minter, *Apartheid's Contras: An Inquiry into the Roots of War in Angola and Mozambique* (London: Zed Books, 1995), p. 33.

[34] Cristina had fled to Rhodesia with detailed files on the membership of the Portuguese special forces in the anticolonial struggle. He had been involved previously with the CIO in the 1960s, aiding its efforts to gather intelligence on the Frelimo guerrillas in Tete Province. See Margaret Hall and Tom Young, *Confronting Leviathan: Mozambique since Independence* (Athens: Ohio University Press, 1997), p. 117.

[35] Peter Stiff, *The Silent War: South African Recce Operations, 1969–1994* (Alberton, RSA: Galago, 1999), p. 159.

[36] Ibid., p. 160.

and provided information about the fate of Mozambican detainees in the hands of Frelimo. Renamo's first military operations included attacks on reeducation camps to free forcibly detained "students" and other antigovernment operatives. The prisoners released in each attack were invited to return to Rhodesia with Renamo. Like the flechas from Rhodesia, former prisoners were welcomed to the base and provided with new uniforms, training, weapons, and salaries. Many embraced the opportunity to fight against a government that had imprisoned them and taken away their rights, particularly if they could do so while operating from a safe base outside of the country.

These recruitment strategies yielded a membership without preexisting social or ethnic ties. One can get a rough idea of the diversity of Renamo's social base by looking at its first National Council, established in 1981 and largely composed of early joiners (see Table 3.1).[37] The leadership structure encompassed a broad range of ethnic groups, including the Macua, Lomwe, Ndau, Manyika, Sena, Shangaan, Chope, Yao, and Ronga tribes. Many of the key leaders were from the center of the country, but they lacked the close-knit ties that shared ethnic identity and language can bring to a group.[38] Most of these early joiners had no education beyond primary school.

In late 1979, Renamo moved the vast majority of its forces into Mozambique.[39] It established areas of operation around Gorongosa, Mabate, and Sitatonga – all in the central provinces of the country. At this same moment, Rhodesia collapsed, leaving Renamo without a source of economic and logistical support. South Africa stepped forward to fill the gap. Importantly, South Africa's commitment to Renamo included logistical support, military supplies, and training, but the flow of salaries and food that kept Renamo comfortable in Rhodesia came to an end.[40]

---

[37] João Cabrita, *Mozambique: The Torturous Road to Democracy* (New York: Palgrave, 2000), p. 184.

[38] The bias in the senior leadership toward people from the center of Mozambique is the result of a number of coinciding factors. Clearly, groups in the Center and the North felt excluded from Frelimo, which had a southern bias. In addition, the Portuguese army was recruiting quite heavily in the Center and North during the independence struggle, since Frelimo guerrilla bases were largely in these regions. The Portuguese invested their resources in training Mozambicans for special forces operations and selected individuals who knew the areas and spoke the local languages. As a result, a large percentage of flechas and other special forces were from the Center.

[39] Stiff, *Silent War*, p. 177.

[40] Alex Vines, *Renamo: Terrorism in Mozambique* (London: James Currey, 1991), p. 17.

112

Table 3.1. *Ethnic and Regional Makeup of Renamo's National Council, 1981*

Name	Position	Ethnic Group	Region of Origin
Aphonso Dhlakama	Commander-in-chief, president	Ndau	Center
João Macia Fombe	Deputy commander-in-chief	Manyika	Center
Vareia Manje Languane	Commander, Second Battalion	Sena	Center
José Domingos Cunai Calção	Secretary, Defense Department	Manyika	Center
José Luís João	Commander, Ninth Battalion	Sena	Center
Raúl Manuel Domingos	Secretary, Defense Department	Sena	Center
José Marques Francisco	Head, Training Department	Sena	Center
José Manuel Alfinete	Head, Telecommunications Battalion	Lomwe	Center
Mário Franque	Commander, Third Battalion	Manyika	Center
Joaquim Rui de Figueiredo Paulo	Deputy battalion commander	Shangaan	South
Henriques Ernesto Samuel	Deputy battalion commander	Chope	South
Ossufo Momade	Deputy battalion commander	Macua	North
Olímpio Osório Caisse Cambona	Head, Telecommunications Department	Yao	North
Albino Chavago	Head, Health Department	Ronga	South

Source: João Cabrita, *Mozambique: The Torturous Road to Democracy* (New York: Palgrave, 2000).

From their new internal base, the rebels began a recruitment drive to expand their forces dramatically in order to challenge Frelimo for control of the state. Without salaries to offer new recruits, however, Renamo's appeals for support took on a new shape. An example is instructive: recall from the introduction Renamo's arrival in the small town of Marínguè in the waning months of 1979. After destroying a number of Frelimo structures and killing seven people in the center of the village, Renamo's operatives abducted a number of youths from the community.[41] From 1979 until the end of the war, Renamo recruited heavily by force. Children were abducted on their way to school, homes were raided and young men taken away, villages were destroyed, and those fleeing were corralled by Renamo troops and taken to rebel bases.[42] Forceful abduction was used even in the areas

---

[41] Interview with civilian, Marínguè, May 23(B), 2001.
[42] Interviews with former Renamo combatants and civilian supporters, Nampula, March 30(A,B,C,D), April 1(A), 3(A,B), 4(A), 2001; interviews, Marínguè, May 18(A,B), 24(A,B), 2001.

Table 3.2. *Age at Recruitment of Soldiers in Mozambique's Civil War*

	No. Demobilized Soldiers	No. Recruited before Age 18 (%)
Government	70,902	16,553 (23.3)
Renamo	21,979	8,945 (40.7)
TOTAL	92,881	25,498 (27.4)

Source: Ton Pardoel, *Socio-Economic Profile of Demobilized Soldiers in Mozambique* (Maputo: UNDP, 1994).

where Renamo's cause was the most popular.[43] While some of the Renamo rank and file in the 1980s joined voluntarily, it is generally estimated that close to 90 percent were recruited by force.[44]

Coercive recruitment reinforced the absence of any coherent social bonds in the rebel movement. Recruits represented the diversity of Mozambique's entire ethnic and religious population. Little effort was made to politicize them, and no attempt was made to screen out opportunistic join-ers.[45] This more coercive approach was successful: Renamo expanded dramatically. By 1985, the rebel group had more than 20,000 soldiers under arms.[46]

Tables 3.2 and 3.3 point to the characteristics of Renamo's growing force. Over 40 percent of Renamo's recruits were younger than 18, abducted before they could receive any advanced education.

The following data on the population of Mozambican demobilized soldiers, including both government soldiers and rebels, indicate that less than 3 percent had a high school education or better.

---

[43] Supportive régulos who were working with Renamo in the areas they controlled were not even asked to volunteer members of their communities for military service. Interviews, Marínguè, May 21(A,D), 2001.

[44] William Minter, *The Mozambican National Resistance (Renamo) as Described by Ex-Participants* (Washington, DC: Report Submitted to the Ford Foundation, 1989), p. 5.

[45] Interviews, Marínguè, May 19(B,C), 2001. Although overall patterns suggest little in the way of political socialization and a predominance of forced recruitment as the war progressed, some combatants, nonetheless, described their participation in terms of "an element of political conviction that was not insignificant." See Jessica Schaeffer, "Guerrillas and Violence in the War in Mozambique: De-Socialization or Re-Socialization," *African Affairs* 100 (2001): 215–37.

[46] Vines, *Renamo.*

Table 3.3. *Soldiers under 18 in Mozambique's Civil War*

Age	No. in Government (%)	No. in Renamo (%)	Total No. (%)
10	289 (1.75)	791 (8.84)	1,080 (4.24)
11	222 (1.34)	529 (5.91)	751 (2.95)
12	401 (2.42)	742 (8.3)	1,143 (4.48)
13	709 (4.28)	1,004 (11.22)	1,713 (6.72)
14	1,452 (8.77)	1,268 (14.18)	2,720 (10.67)
15	2,558 (15.45)	1,551 (17.34)	4,109 (16.11)
16	4,279 (25.85)	1,556 (17.4)	5,835 (22.88)
17	6,643 (40.13)	1,504 (16.81)	8,147 (31.95)
TOTAL	16,533	8,945	25,498

Source: Ton Pardoel, *Socio-Economic Profile of Demobilized Soldiers in Mozambique* (Maputo: UNDP, 1994).

Level of Education	No. Demobilized Soldiers (%)
None	26,434 (28.46)
Primary	25,381 (27.33)
Middle School	23,754 (25.57)
Secondary	2,197 (0.29)
University	271 (0.20)[47]

Even if all the university-educated demobilized soldiers had been members of Renamo, they would have represented only 1 percent of the group, an educational profile demonstrably different from that of the NRA.

The leaders of Renamo had little choice but to shift their recruitment strategy from offering salaries to abduction. With the group's move into the harsher climate of war-torn Mozambique and the loss of its main external patron, the incentives Renamo could offer potential recruits changed dramatically. Brought together by opportunity rather than conviction, Renamo's core membership lacked a set of social ties that could be activated and mobilized to draw volunteers into the army. Without a strong ethnic identity, Renamo had no home base in which to organize. And lacking a coherent political agenda, Renamo was hard-pressed to motivate to action civilians who preferred to stay on the sidelines. The situation worsened

---

[47] Ton Pardoel, *Socio-Economic Profile of Demobilized Soldiers in Mozambique* (Maputo: UNDP, 1994).

for Renamo as the government's counterinsurgency campaign herded civilians into communal villages, preventing them from interacting with rebels.

Most surprising to many outside observers is the fact that new recruits tended to stay in the movement. Coercion is part of the reason, as Renamo wielded force against those who attempted to escape. But given that Renamo had over twenty thousand members dispersed throughout the country, coercion cannot be the entire explanation. As the organization grew in size and strength, it resurrected its ability to provide short-term material rewards to motivate continued support and participation. Payoffs to participants resumed after Renamo began permitting its soldiers to capture public and private property when they attacked civilian areas.[48] Looting was a direct mechanism through which soldiers could improve their personal economic situations.[49] Because of the dramatic wartime shortage of consumer goods, looted items could be traded in areas of Renamo control for almost anything.[50] In addition, Renamo became involved in the cross-border trade in ivory, which yielded it US$13 million in 1988 alone.[51] Renamo also obtained funds by extorting them from multinational corporations in exchange for security guarantees.[52] In short, following the fall of Rhodesia, coercion became a necessary strategy because Renamo lacked the social resources to adopt an alternative; it was a feasible strategy because Renamo's leaders ensured that payoffs for participation returned. Unlike in the NRA, between economic incentives and coercion, Renamo's recruitment strategies yielded an uneducated membership, lacking social bonds, and without the mechanisms needed to distinguish those committed to the insurgency from those interested only in short-term gains.

Spreading Ideology: Sendero Luminoso Nacional

In a process initiated long before the first attack on Chuschi, Sendero Luminoso successfully recruited militants in the rural areas around the

---

[48] Interview, Maríngue, May 18(A), 2001.

[49] Former combatants described how the commander distributed loot to the rebel soldiers after an attack. Interview, Nampula, April 4(A), 2001; interviews, Maríngue, May 21(E), 24(C), 2001.

[50] Ibid.

[51] Vines reports in *Renamo* that government raids on Renamo bases in 1988 produced over 19,700 elephant tusks, p. 89.

[52] Alex Vines, "The Business of Peace: 'Tiny' Rowland, Financial Incentives, and the Mozambican Settlement," in *The Mozambican Peace Process in Perspective* (Maputo: Accord, 1998).

Universidad Nacional de San Cristobal de Huamanga, where Abimael Guzmán was a professor. By 1981, Sendero claimed to have almost five hundred armed rebels.[53] The strategy of building a movement of university students and sending them back to their home communities to mobilize their families and the next generation of young people generated a steady flow of new recruits. These young teachers invested in mobilization by setting up popular schools to educate people about the Shining Path's vision of liberation and reform in Peru. They owed their success to strong preexisting networks of trust that connected them to the local peasant communities.

Young people flocked to take part in the movement. Sendero offered students a life of intellectual growth and sustained action as well as the promise of opportunities for leadership, authority, and improved living standards. Given that most secondary school students had little hope of entering Peru's university system, the Shining Path provided an attractive alternative.[54] Importantly, those drawn to Sendero did not come from one ethnic group. The Shining Path reflected Peru's diversity, with new militants coming from white families as well as indigenous groups. Although some scholars initially saw the movement as an organization of Peruvian Indians, this view was largely discredited as more information emerged about the makeup of the guerrilla group.[55]

There were few opportunities within Sendero Luminoso for immediate material gain. The Shining Path began with limited economic resources and did little to improve its economic position. Guzmán saw the movement in Maoist terms as an organization that sought to base itself within the civilian population and to use the resources it could generate through popular participation. With the government's military presence in Ayacucho growing by 1982, the risks of participating in Sendero were high, while the immediate benefits to rebels were few.

Nonetheless, it was not easy to become a member of the Shining Path. Three mechanisms were in place to keep out those who were not truly

[53] Noted in "Desplegar la guerra de Guerrillas," captured Sendero document, May 1981, DINCOTE Sendero collection, Lima, Peru.

[54] In 1987, for example, of 217,679 students applying to public university, only 36,369 (16.7 percent) were accepted. One can easily imagine that rural students, in particular, were at a disadvantage in applying for those spots, given the poor quality of their schools and their limited resources. See Gabriela Tarazona-Sevillano, "The Organization of Shining Path," in *Shining Path of Peru*, ed. David Scott Palmer (New York: St. Martins Press, 1992), p. 198.

[55] This view was best articulated by Cynthia McClintock in "Why Peasants Rebel: The Case of Peru's Sendero Luminoso," *World Politics* 37, no. 1 (October 1984): 48–84.

committed. First, members already inside the organization almost always brought in new recruits. This was particularly true in the earliest stages, when the popular schools served as the main source of new militants. Even as the war progressed and the movement required larger numbers of rebels, however, current members still had to vouch for the commitment of potential recruits.[56] Sendero rebels were careful not to propose just anyone for membership in the movement.

Second, the Shining Path required new members to undergo a period of intense political indoctrination. The first "military school" of the rebel movement provides a good example. For seventeen intense days in April 1980, combatants in the new guerrilla force were put through their basic training for the movement. This was no ordinary military school, however: the students learned almost no technical military skills. Instead, the goal was to "relate and overlap ideology with its military manifestations at every level."[57] Rebels came out of the training not with the know-how to build weapons and plan assaults but instead with notebooks full of ideological positions, political arguments, and a distinct interpretation of Peruvian history.[58] They were required to analyze what was presented, to write and speak publicly, and to accept criticism from their comrades.

And political indoctrination was only the beginning. Throughout the conflict, political meetings provided Senderistas with substantive ideological information that they were required to digest. This was supplemented with extensive written documentation from the Central Committee that amplified and extended points made in oral presentations. Sendero's soldiers were forced to read and write, regardless of their previous level of education. It was inside of the rebel organization that many members first learned these skills.[59]

If sitting through extended periods of political education was not trying enough, the rebels were also forced to undergo a process called *crítica y autocrítica* (criticism and self-criticism). Based on a mechanism developed during Lenin's time to control groups and individuals, this process required rebels to publicly accept criticism of their beliefs and behaviors, to

---

[56] Interview with former Sendero commander, Lima, November 5(A), 2001.
[57] Gustavo Gorritti, *The Shining Path: A History of the Millenarian War in Peru* (Chapel Hill: University of North Carolina Press, 1999), p. 29.
[58] Notes from seventeen days of Sendero military training, captured Sendero document, 1980, DINCOTE Sendero collection, Lima, Peru.
[59] Interviews with former Sendero combatants, Lima, November 6(A,B,C), 2001.

outline the ways in which they would improve and change, and to beg for forgiveness from their comrades in the movement. As a mode of testing the level of a rebel's commitment to the movement, its operation hinged on the belief that one could be objectively guilty while subjectively believing that one was acting correctly. Given this possibility, "a party cadre's honesty [was] measured by the degree to which, once an 'objective' responsibility [was] pointed out, the cadre cooperate[d] with the party in picking apart conduct, in discovering the elusive roots of failure or treachery."[60]

Finally, membership in Sendero could be achieved only after a number of steps were completed. New recruits would likely begin as part of the *fuerza base* (the local guerrillas), who would remain in the village living as peasants, gathering intelligence, and sometimes participating in attacks at night. The second level was the *fuerza regional* (regional force), whose members were better trained than the local guerrillas, given access to armaments, and authorized to participate in attacks in other provinces. The final level was the *fuerza principal* (principal force), which was the main group of rebel combatants. These insurgents were experienced, trained, armed, and possessed significant authority. Moving from one level to another was a slow process, and it required Senderistas to demonstrate their knowledge and understanding of the ideological and political lines of the movement. As a result, even if one joined the movement as a way to obtain a position of authority, the opportunity to hold a gun and wield real power was far down the road.

Data on the socioeconomic characteristics of rebels captured and imprisoned between 1983 and 1986 reflect Sendero's sorting mechanism at work (see Tables 3.4 and 3.5). When compared to criminals incarcerated for simple assault and robbery, rebels exhibited significantly higher levels of education. More than 63.4 percent of rebels captured in this period had completed their secondary education or a university or postgraduate degree. By contrast, only 26.9 percent of the common criminals had a similarly advanced education. Sendero attracted young men; moreover, most remained inside the movement. Among the captured rebels, 77.6 percent were between the ages of 21 and 35, while 64.8 percent of common criminals fell in this age group. More than 20 percent of those imprisoned for assault or robbery were younger than 20.

[60] Gorritti, *Shining Path*, p. 30.

Table 3.4. *Education of Captured Sendero Luminoso Rebels, 1983–1986*

Level of Education	Captured Rebels, %	Criminals, % [a]
No formal education	1.1	0.0
Some primary	16.4	23.4
Some secondary	16.9	46.3
Complete secondary	26.8	24.4
Advanced education (nonuniversity)	1.1	0.0
Some university	29.5	2.5
University degree	1.1	0.0
Postgraduate degree	4.9	0.0
No information	2.2	3.4
TOTAL NO.	183	205

Note: [a]These criminals were incarcerated for assault or for robbery.
Source: Dennis Chávez de Paz, *Juventud y terrorismo: Características sociales de los condenados por terrorismo y otros delitos* (Lima: Instituto de Estudios Peruanos, 1989).

Table 3.5. *Age of Captured Sendero Luminoso Rebels, 1983–1986*

Age	Captured Rebels, %	Criminals, % [a]
18 to 20	14.2	21.5
21 to 25	43.2	39.5
26 to 30	22.4	16.1
31 to 35	12.0	10.2
36 to 40	2.7	6.8
41 to 45	3.3	2.9
46 to 50	1.7	2.0
51 to 55	0.5	0.5
56 to 60	0.0	0.5
Older than 60	0.0	0.0
TOTAL NO.	183	205

Note: [a]These criminals were incarcerated for assault or for robbery.
Source: Dennis Chávez de Paz, *Juventud y terrorismo: Características sociales de los condenados por terrorismo y otros delitos* (Lima: Instituto de Estudios Peruanos, 1989).

Although the Shining Path's recruitment strategies emphasized ideological appeals reinforced by ties to the rural peasant communities, it is important to recognize that these approaches were not uniformly successful, even within Ayacucho, the province where Sendero had its strongest base of support. Quechua-speaking Indians populated the highlands, and their children had limited access to education above the primary school level. With its base in universities and secondary schools, the Shining Path's network in highland areas was severely constrained.[61] In these areas, Sendero arrived making promises about how it could improve the lives of the often-ignored Quechua peasants. At people's assemblies, the rebels railed against a government that had left highlanders without access to health care, education, transportation, or sufficient food to survive in the rough climate. Peasants initially welcomed the Senderistas and their promises about the future as a possible avenue of escape from the struggles of their daily lives.[62] But since many of the rebels who came to mobilize the population were outsiders (non–Quechua speaking and white), friction soon developed between highland locals and the rebel leadership. In the absence of an immediate sense of shared identity, the process of political indoctrination became more complex. Even though the cause was perceived as just and its goals reflected the desires of many peasants, the mounting risks to participants created divisions within the highland communities, making Sendero's job much more difficult. Recruitment strategies in the high Andean areas thus sometimes relied more heavily on fear and coercion than they did elsewhere in Peru.[63] Abduction of the sort witnessed in Mozambique was not widespread, but where inroads were most difficult because of government pressure and civilian division, Sendero's militants sometimes complemented their ideological appeals with threats. Processes of indoctrination took time, and education sometimes commenced only after individuals had joined the movement out of fear. Once they began participating, though, political indoctrination was a powerful socializing force. For many, new identities forged within the movement trumped old allegiances, generating a desire to remain part of the rebellion. Thus recruits to the Shining Path, like those who joined the NRA, came via a process of indoctrination and socialization, initiated through social networks, which helped rebel leaders identify the most committed participants for the struggle ahead.

---

[61] Interviews with displaced civilians from the highlands, Huanta, December 2(A), 3(A,E), 2001.

[62] Ibid., December 3(A), 4(B), 2001. See also Ponciano Del Pino, "Family, Culture, and 'Revolution': Everyday Life with Sendero Luminoso," in *Shining and Other Paths*, ed. Steve J. Stern (Durham: Duke University Press, 1998), p. 170.

[63] Interviews, Huanta, December 2(A), 3(C,D,E), 5(A), 2001. See also Del Pino, "Family, Culture, and 'Revolution,'" pp. 166, 171.

Table 3.6. *Characteristics of the Migrants to Alto Huallaga, 1981*

Characteristics of the Head of Household	Tingo María, %	Aucayacu, %	Uchiza, %	Total, %
Years of residence				
More than 20	52.3	18.3	14.3	22.9
11–20	26.2	57.2	25.3	37.1
6–10	7.7	13.5	39.0	23.8
Fewer than 5	13.8	11.0	21.4	16.2
Reason for migration				
For land	41.0	53.6	57.0	52.8
For work	39.7	33.7	28.2	32.4
Join relatives	18.0	11.4	10.7	12.3
For state help	1.3	1.2	4.1	2.5
Age at arrival				
Younger than 15	13.8	8.7	6.5	9.0
15–19	21.5	12.7	9.1	13.0
20–29	29.2	39.7	39.0	37.0
30–39	20.0	28.5	22.7	24.0
Older than 40	15.5	10.3	22.7	17.0

Source: Fundación para el Desarrollo Nacional, *Plan de ejecución del proyecto de desarrollo rural integral del Alto Huallaga* (Lima: Fundación para el Desarrollo Nacional, May 1981).

A Coalition of Cocaleros: Sendero–Huallaga

The Regional Committee of Alto Huallaga utilized a set of recruitment strategies different from those of the rest of Sendero Luminoso. Although its initial forays in the coca-growing zones in the early 1980s included the same emphasis on cultivating local contacts, establishing popular schools, and mobilizing peasants along political and ideological lines, the committee that emerged as Sendero grew in size appeared driven by a different logic.

In part, the demographics of the local population shaped the membership of the regional committee. The areas around Tingo María, the provincial capital, had experienced a dramatic inward migration in the 1970s as coca production boomed in the Huallaga Valley. Between 1972 and 1981, more than 42,363 new migrants arrived in Tingo María, settling in surrounding areas. By 1981, ninety of every one hundred families in the region had recently arrived from other areas.[64] Table 3.6 provides some additional

[64] Fundación para el Desarrollo Nacional, *Plan de ejecución del proyecto de desarrollo rural integral del Alto Huallaga* (Lima: Fundación para el Desarrollo Nacional, May 1981).

Table 3.7. *Labor Returns in Alto Huallaga, 1992*

Region of Origin	Principal Activity	Annual Returns, $US
Highlands	Coca production (avg. 2 hectares)	2,000
	Agricultural worker, coca farm	1,500
	Cocaine production	5,400
	Teacher	1,200
Coast	Agricultural worker, coca farm	1,500
	Government employee (professional)	2,400
	Government employee (nonprofessional)	1,600
	Short-term laborer	2,000
Jungle	Coca production (avg. 1 hectare)	1,000
	Production of food crops	700
	Teacher	1,200
	Agricultural worker, coca farm	1,200
	Small-scale business owner	900

Source: Information gathered from local researcher in Tingo María, November 13, 2001. Data reported in Fundación para el Desarrollo Nacional, *Plan de ejecución del proyecto de desarrollo rural integral del Alto Huallaga* (Lima: Fundación para el Desarrollo Nacional, May 1981).

detail about the characteristics of the population in the Huallaga Valley in 1981, just before Sendero began to operate in the region. In the areas where the Shining Path would assume almost total sovereignty six years later (Aucayacu and Uchiza), between 25 and 60 percent of the residents arrived after 1970 following the coca boom. The majority were young (younger than 29), and most came in search of land to grow coca.

People came in spite of the fact that coca production was illegal. In part, this was because the economic returns from growing coca and producing *pasta básica* (basic paste) far outweighed what the peasants could generate from agriculture in their home communities. The results of a small study completed in 1992 – after the coca boom ended and coca prices had fallen – demonstrates how profitable coca cultivation remained relative to other occupations in the region (see Table 3.7).

Sendero began its organizing in the early 1980s, just as the government initiated its political and military campaign against coca production. State repression of coca producers, including arbitrary arrests, looting, and other abuses, drove cocaleros to the streets in an eleven-day general strike in Tingo María in 1982. Although professors at the local agricultural college had begun to conduct political work in the years before the strike, testimonials given to the Truth and Reconciliation Commission describe a process by which enraged cocaleros actively sought the assistance and support of the Shining Path following the strike as government pressure increased.[65] The Senderistas who arrived from the highlands partnered with local coca farmers to construct liberated zones. They received clear guidance from the Central Committee to encourage peasants to move away from coca production, though the committee did worry that such a move would inspire the anger of the traffickers.[66] But the leadership of the regional committee largely ignored the directions of the Central Committee. From its very first actions in the region, the CRH staked its claim as a defender of the peasants. One of its first attacks, in late 1983, was on the local office of the coca eradication project in Tingo María proper.[67] In practice, defending the peasantry meant protecting coca farmers both from the military, which sought to destroy their land, and from the traffickers, who did not want to pay a fair price for coca leaves. It was a far different task than that faced by Sendero in the highlands.

Over the course of the late 1980s, the regional committee became deeply involved in coca production, taxing peasants in the market, producing coca on its own appropriated territory, requiring payments from traffickers who wished to buy in areas of Sendero control, and demanding money for the flow of goods and services in liberated zones. Most of the funds the CRH collected stayed in the regional committee, shared among its members, as the Central Committee rejected involvement in the coca trade.[68] The local organization was rich, and individuals joined it in pursuit of wealth and for the protection needed to continue the production of coca.[69]

The organization was exceedingly popular among coca farmers, and few constraints were put on membership as the regional committee built its liberated areas.[70] Political indoctrination was deemphasized in the region, and the process of vouching for new members largely disappeared.[71] Criticism and self-criticism was still present in the regional committee

---

[65] Comisión de la Verdad y Reconciliación, *Informe Final: Peru, 1980–2000, Tomo IV* (Lima: Pontificia Universidad Católica del Peru y Universidad Nacional Mayor de San Marcos, 2003), p. 341.

[66] Noted in "Iniciar el Gran Salto," captured Sendero document, 1984, DINCOTE Sendero collection, Lima, Peru.

[67] Interview, Tingo María, November 13(A), 2001.

[68] Interviews with the former chief of DINCOTE, Lima, October 24(A), 2001, and a former Sendero commander, Lima, November 5(A), 2001.

[69] Interviews with civilian, Tingo María, November 19(B,D), 2001.

[70] Ibid., November 13(A), 14(A,B) 2001.

[71] Interview with former Sendero commander, Lima, November 5(A), 2001.

because of its links to the Central Committee; however, members of Sendero at the lower levels escaped many of the screening mechanisms that existed in the rest of the country. In Huallaga, the movement recruited almost entirely from a population of coca farmers, offered them an opportunity to enrich themselves further by carrying a gun, and made little effort to screen out those who were not interested in the group's political aims. The result, of course, was a very different Sendero Luminoso.

Conclusion

It is clear that the National Resistance Army, Renamo, Sendero Nacional, and Sendero–Huallaga began their guerrilla campaigns on very different footings. While the rebels in Mozambique and the Huallaga Valley in Peru had access to a wealth of economic resources to fund their insurgencies, the guerrilla leadership in Uganda and in the highlands of Peru had to find other ways to meet the costs of organization. In Uganda, Museveni turned to identity politics, building a coalition of ethnic groups opposed to Obote's regime. In Peru, Guzmán built an all-encompassing ideology from scratch, sharing it gradually with broader groups of people through a network of university and secondary school students in Ayacucho, Peru. Differences in the four groups' initial economic and social endowments constrained their recruitment strategies and ultimately shaped the characteristics of their members. Figuring out who was actually involved in each movement is a critical step toward making sense of the organizational choices and strategies used by the rebel leadership in the course of the civil wars in Uganda, Mozambique, and Peru.

I have demonstrated that rebel organizations take on distinct shapes as soon as they begin to recruit members. Recruitment sets in motion a process of sorting, as different types of people are attracted to different opportunities. An alternative argument might emphasize that even if individuals are drawn from the same population of potential recruits, it is participation in the organization itself that shapes their preferences, values, and norms. Some of this shaping is explicit, as it is in the political and ideological training characteristic of the NRA and the Shining Path. Other influences are less formal: expectations are shaped by the behavior of commanders and other combatants. As I will show in the next chapter, the evidence strongly supports the idea that organizations reinforce different sets of expectations among combatants. But this alternative view cannot account for the origins of the different norms internal to each group.

I adopt a different starting point. Society is composed of different types of people with different preferences. Some people are embedded in communities that place a higher value on investment; others come from environments in which consumption is prioritized. I argue that variation in the opportunity that rebellion presents to potential recruits acts as a sorting mechanism. Some groups become overpopulated with recruits seeking short-term gains. Others manage to screen out opportunists and identify only those individuals most committed to the long-term goals of the organization. Whether a group is filled with activists or opportunists then constrains the choices leaders make as they organize military operations, govern civilian areas, and struggle to retain their members in the course of conflict.

From the earliest moments of organization, moreover, it is clear that in some groups rebels share linkages that go beyond purely material interests. Identities, beliefs, and shared community ties enable groups to elicit long-term investments and to identify committed recruits. Without them, groups are constrained as they try to build strong organizations. The extent to which these links connect recruited members to the leadership becomes even more important as we examine the choices groups make down the road.

4

Control

James Q. Wilson observed that "war is the greatest test of a bureaucratic organization."[1] The fact that poorly paid men, recruited by a government and sent to some distant land to fight against an unknown foe, manage to hold their positions, stay in their units, and march on toward battle is a testament to the power of organization. In exploring the organization of insurgency, it is necessary to ask why rebels stay and fight – or, more to the point, how rebel leaders resolve problems of management and organizational control.

Troops in the National Resistance Army risked serious punishment for any acts that contravened the formal code of conduct adopted by its High Command, but they had tremendous autonomy when it came to the organization of operations. Renamo's rebels, on the other hand, were part of a highly centralized military structure but faced few sanctions from the leadership for indiscipline. Militants fighting on behalf of the Shining Path found their actions in and out of battle dissected and analyzed by their local comrades in public sessions, the results of which were then relayed to the movement's senior leadership. But combatants in the Upper Huallaga Valley, although they operated under the same rules, experienced only arbitrary and uneven punishment for misdeeds that would have brought about expulsion in other regions of Peru.

This chapter focuses on the organizational structures of rebel groups. It documents their leaders' efforts to set in place mechanisms to shape and control the behavior of combatants so that they could effectively compete against government forces. In particular, it explores three central tools groups utilize to prevent defection: investments in training, organizational

---

[1] James Q. Wilson, *Bureaucracy* (New York: Basic, 1989), p. 45.

culture, and structures of hierarchy and delegation. In exploring why some groups develop rigorous training programs in political education while others emphasize military techniques, why some organizations formalize codes of conduct while others allow practices to develop informally, and why some groups centralize power while others share authority with local commanders, this chapter highlights a key determinant of rebel groups' internal structure. The nature of a group's membership both affects the magnitude of the challenge of maintaining control and constrains the set of tools leaders can employ in response, but its effects become visible only as rebel leaders move from the challenge of recruitment to that of organization.

The Rationale for Organization

Across the four rebel groups in this study, the initial core of rebel leaders was small. When there were fewer than thirty members in each group, communication was easy. Decisions were made on the basis of consultation. Leaders outlined plans and assigned specific roles to each individual. And there was little doubt that behavior would conform to expectations: in all four contexts, the initial leaders knew one another and had a basis for trust.

But the rebel organizations did not remain small for long. Within a year of beginning to organize, the membership of each had ballooned from tens into hundreds and even thousands of members. Some of these new recruits were family members or personal contacts; the majority, however, were unknown to the rebel leadership. And in each case, the rebel leaders had to entrust the new combatants with the movement's limited resources and its secret information. Any one of these recruits could have defected to the government's side and brought the fledgling movement to an end.

So why grow at all? The simple answer is that growth creates economies of scale. The most efficient organizational form for committing crime may be that of a small, tight-knit mafia family, for a number of reasons. A crime family has the capability to run its local operations while protecting the safety of its members. Its small size facilitates its secret operations: members' defection can be credibly punished by death. Thus, to survive and avoid police infiltration, crime families must stay small and maintain a capacity to control their members.[2] A rebel group's adversary, however, is typically a state military endowed with significant resources and large numbers of

---

[2] Diego Gambetta, *The Sicilian Mafia: The Business of Private Protection* (Cambridge, MA: Harvard University Press, 1996).

soldiers. Even though groups may be able to hide out for long periods of time without being overrun by the government, any organization that seeks to control the state must grow to a size sufficient to compete with the government's forces. Up to a certain point, moreover, increases in the size of a rebel movement result in more than proportionate improvements in its capacity to initiate and succeed in attacks on government forces and to operate across the national territory.

But it is not simply a rebel group's size that determines its effectiveness. Rebel organizations perform better when members coordinate their actions; like other types of organizations, they benefit from cooperation and specialization. If the rebels assigned to reconnoiter a government target gather detailed information about the behavior of the government's security patrols, for example, the unit planning the operation will be better able to pinpoint the weaknesses of the target and launch a successful operation without taking casualties. The production function of rebellion is thus highly interactive: the more effort an individual rebel puts in, the more productive other members of the group will be. Economists call this property of production a "team production function."[3]

To achieve the higher level of output possible in a team production environment, organizations take on a hierarchical form. Members task supervisors with responsibility for monitoring their productive efforts. Supervisors then apportion rewards on the basis of individual performance. Monitoring enables groups of people to realign the incentive system to reward members for greater effort and punish them for shirking. Rebel groups build large organizations, then, to create a supply of labor sufficient to compete with government forces and to realize the benefits of cooperation. The need for sufficient size and cooperation, however, also points to a serious challenge for rebel leaders that plagues organizations of all forms.

The Structure of Organization

When members of an organization do not exert themselves to achieve the goals of the organization, they are shirking. Failure to cooperate in team production is one example of shirking. More generally, shirking occurs whenever members take actions that do not contribute to the maximum efficiency of the organization. Shirking behavior includes workers extending

---

[3] Armen Alchian and Harold Demsetz, "Production, Information Costs, and Economic Organizations," *American Economic Review* 62 (December 1972): 777–95.

their lunch break when the plant manager is not around to tell them to go back to work, teachers handing out easy mimeographs to occupy their pupils instead of implementing complete lesson plans, and corporate managers cooking the accounting books to enable them to realize higher profits at the expense of the company's profitability. Shirking is common and detrimental to the functioning of any organization.

Economists call the organizational challenge posed by shirking a "principal-agent problem" because it highlights the need for a principal (that is, the owner of a firm or the leader of an organization) to set in place a system of incentives so that an agent (a worker or member of a group) will perform exactly as the principal expects.[4] The reason the principal-agent relationship creates problems is that in most cases the principal cannot directly observe and control the agent's actions. Sometimes this is because the principal cannot know for certain how the agent is likely to perform; the problem of adverse selection outlined in the previous chapter is such a situation. Alternatively, shirking may result from the unobservability of an agent's behavior after he or she has been retained. In this case, the principal cannot know for sure to what extent the individual is productive and must rely on imperfect proxies to assess his or her behavior. To the extent that monitoring mechanisms are not perfect, incentives to shirk remain strong, and the organization suffers.

For private firms, the economists' solution is to design a set of employment contracts that tie an individual's rewards to his or her productivity. Individual productivity is often hard to measure, however. It may be tied up in the behavior of others, as in the team production function, or it may be affected by factors other than the individual's level of effort, including the performance of equipment, the supply of inputs, and even the weather. An incentive structure also requires the development of monitoring systems to gather information about individual performance, and the rewards for the monitors must also be arranged so that they have the incentive to exert maximum effort in the job.

The organization of rebellion presents particular management challenges to rebel leaders. In most cases, rebel combatants take actions that cannot easily be observed and evaluated by their superiors. Imagine that a

---

[4] For a good summary of the economic approach to organizational structure, see Terry Moe, "The New Economics of Organization," *American Journal of Political Science* 28, no. 4 (1984): 739–77.

rebel unit is sent to attack a police post and it returns with no weapons. One possible explanation for the result is that the rebels attacked the police post, dispersed the government forces, and found that the weapons cache was empty. But it is also possible that the rebel unit never attacked the police post or that it attacked and, when the police returned fire, its members fled. Even though the outcome is observable, the actions taken by the rebels themselves are not. It is difficult for commanders to know for sure who did what, who exerted how much effort, and who was shirking.

Moreover, rebel combatants operate under the command of multiple principals. Operations are typically decentralized. Most rebel groups have limited access to communications technology, and to prevent detection they operate hidden from public view and dispersed throughout their operational zone. Principal-agent problems are rife throughout rebel organizations as a result. Combatants take orders from their unit commanders, units take orders from higher superiors, and each of these combatant organizations falls under the leadership of the group's senior commanders. In every case, the units that benefit from decentralization have an informational advantage relative to their superiors: they have more complete information about the extent to which they followed the commands they were given. And the commanders at every level are hard-pressed to monitor their agents and gather the information necessary to assign rewards and sanctions based on performance.

Both the difficulty of monitoring dispersed rebel forces and the complications introduced by multiple principals contribute to the third challenge of management in rebel organizations: incentives to defect are magnified by the level and immediacy of the risks combatants face. A soldier's decision to follow orders and work on behalf of the group's objectives requires him to put himself in the line of fire. It also requires him to resist the temptation to use his weapon to abuse the local population. As we saw in Chapter 3, individuals differ in their willingness to take on these risks and obligations, making principal-agent problems more difficult to resolve in some contexts than in others.

It is clear that some rebel groups set in place mechanisms for long-term cooperative behavior, while others permit (or at least suffer from) defection. By defection, I refer to actions individual combatants take that maximize their personal gains at the expense of the group's broader objectives. One might think that this difference is a result of the incentive system that rebel leaders choose – that where rebel leaders set in place the right incentive systems, they can resolve principal-agent problems. But there are always strong incentives for at least one individual (one of the principals, typically) to engage in purely self-interested behavior.[5] If agents anticipate that a principal is likely to renege on his or her commitment to the group's objectives, the whole system of control unravels.

In fact, the difference lies in the capacity of the rebel leadership to create an environment in which members expect to cooperate with their fellow combatants and commanders. The role of leaders, I argue, is to create common knowledge and expectations, a set of cooperative work norms, and, as a foundation, a system of monitoring and control that makes threats to punish defectors credible. Individuals must know how others in the group will respond when they confront various situations, but the system of cooperation I describe also depends critically on the capacity of rebel leaders to prove their own commitment to the group's objectives. Leaders must show that regardless of their position at the top of the principal-agent hierarchy, they will not renege on the commitments made to their members. Demonstrating this commitment requires rebel leaders to invest resources and authority in their agents as a way of binding their own hands.

Although some groups are unable to achieve a cooperative equilibrium, this does not mean that they are doomed to fail. As with the challenge of recruitment, there are at least two equilibria in organizational management and control. While some groups may be unable to realize the full gains of cooperation, strategies of individual defection can be profitable. Whether such organizations survive is a function of the broader environment in which they operate. Even where groups are poorly organized – where their combatants flee from combat, target civilians rather than military targets, and capture resources for themselves rather than the group – they may still prosper because the market is not capable of disciplining them. Economic theorists, drawing on theories of natural selection, have argued that firms that are well suited to the particular conditions of an environment will be selected for survival, while the rest will fail and disappear.[6] In markets, it is competition among firms that disciplines laggard organizations. In conflict, however, the actions of the government, competing rebel groups, and civilian populations have the greatest potential to shape rebel behavior.

[5] Gary Miller, *Managerial Dilemmas: The Political Economy of Hierarchy* (Cambridge: Cambridge University Press, 1992), p. 76.
[6] Armen Alchian, "Uncertainty, Evolution, and Economic Theory," *Journal of Political Economy* 58 (June 1950): 211–21.

When opposing forces are incapable of rooting out an organization characterized by defection, such a group can remain and prosper. If the government is sufficiently weak, such a group may even emerge as the victor.

How Important Is Hierarchy?

So far, we have assumed that hierarchy is a central part of organizational management and control in rebellion. While this assumption accords with what we know of how rebel groups operate, it necessarily narrows our attention to the analysis of principal-agent relationships and the incentive problems they create. An approach rooted in hierarchical structures focuses attention on the diverging interests of leaders and followers and the importance of designing incentive structures or monitoring arrangements that protect a group's objectives. But there is an alternative approach to understanding how groups achieve collective ends. It proposes a distinct set of tools organizations can use to shape individuals' choices about the level of effort they will exert. Approaches rooted in the analysis of "community governance" or "cooperatives" identify the mechanisms people use to maximize the economic returns of a group by preventing shirking.[7]

Some examples help to illuminate this approach. Samuel Bowles and Herbert Gintis point to the interactions of residents in a Chicago neighborhood who speak sternly to young people who skip school, create a disturbance, or put graffiti on the wall. In this case, the problem is an insufficient provision of local police enforcement; monitoring by members of the community can help to redress the problem. Bowles and Gintis also describe the internal workings of cooperatives, such as one created by plywood workers in Oregon and Washington who bound themselves together in a "firm" by electing a group of managers from among themselves and requiring all participants to own a share in the joint enterprise. The group saved significant resources in monitoring and supervision costs while at the same time achieving high levels of work commitment. These two examples suggest that even without hierarchy, communities possess a number of properties that support specialization and address the incentive problems described earlier. In particular, communities have crucial information about the needs, capacities,

---

[7] For a fuller treatment of peer monitoring mechanisms and a discussion of experimental results suggesting their efficacy, see Samuel Bowles and Herbert Gintis, "Social Capital and Community Governance," *Economic Journal* 112 (2002): F419–36.

and behavior of their members. They use that information in a multilateral manner to uphold shared norms, binding individuals together for a common purpose. And communities actively hold violators accountable by using tools that are sometimes not available to more formal organizations, including solidarity, reputation, personal pride, and retribution.

Yet in practice, rebel groups seem to employ hierarchical structures rather than peer monitoring mechanisms to manage their organizations, for three reasons. First, rebel organizations are shaped in powerful ways by first movers, the initial core of leaders who set the rebellion in motion. These individuals have a great deal at stake and often demand significant control over the trajectory of the organization, including control over the selection of members. They are often willing to bind their hands in order to elicit higher levels of effort from their followers, but they will not relinquish control over the direction of the group in favor of a more decentralized form of coordination.

Second, the scale and scope of activity in rebellion makes peer monitoring less efficient than hierarchy. In coordinating the activities of multiple agents, clear lines of hierarchical control help leaders to operate effectively in environments of uncertainty and limited information. Top-down leadership allows a group to control multiple arms working in unison toward common objectives. Peer monitoring mechanisms work most effectively in small, homogenous communities, but rebel groups are constantly shifting in size and membership, making it more difficult for patterns of decentralized cooperation to take root on their own.

Third, rebel organizations face a government adversary that is highly resourced, centralized, and coordinated. While one could imagine that an organization without hierarchy might be difficult for a government to defeat, a fully decentralized structure would also make it more difficult for rebels to take on the tasks of governance fundamental to guerrilla warfare and the effective rule of the state should they succeed in battle.

This is not to say, however, that the underlying mechanisms that make community governance effective – solidarity, trust, reciprocity, and retribution – are not at work in contexts of rebellion. Indeed, as the case studies will suggest, rebel leaders actively cultivate shared norms and expectations within their organizations to reduce the resources that must be expended on managerial monitoring and supervision. These norms and expectations, forged among networks that predate the conflict, are also often critical in overcoming the constraints on individual participation, which makes them fundamental to the operation of activist rebellions.

Rebel Strategies

In building their organizations, rebel leaders face principal-agent problems in two distinct realms.[8] The first is the field of battle: Commanders issue orders to rebel combatants to ambush government patrols, attack military outposts, and maintain territorial sovereignty over liberated zones. In most cases, these orders are implemented outside of the commanders' immediate purview. In battle, soldiers operate in the midst of confusion and mayhem, and commanders are fortunate if they know where their units are at any point in time. Knowing exactly what they are doing and who is doing what within each unit is nearly impossible. But commanders do discover how successful their units have been in battle. It is clear when the fighting is over whether the unit has achieved its goal or whether it has sustained significant casualties in defeat. Rebel organizations, then, fall into the category that James Q. Wilson refers to as "craft organizations": they consist of agents whose actions are hard to observe but whose outcomes can be more easily evaluated.[9] But it is not enough for managers to simply focus on measuring outcomes; such an approach allows defection to take place within units and can lead to the unraveling of an organization. It also matters how units and groups achieve particular outcomes. Since procedures cannot be observed, leaders who wish to prevent defection within units must create and rely on an internalized set of professional norms to guide the behavior of a group's members.

The second place where principal-agent problems arise for rebel groups is in zones of rebel control. Soldiers interact with noncombatant populations in the organization of resources, the gathering of intelligence information, and the recruitment of supporters. Combatants often move freely among civilian populations, encountering opportunities for indiscipline and misbehavior. Within their zones of control, rebel groups operate as "procedural organizations." Commanders are able to observe (or gather information about) most of the activities of their combatants. Rebel soldiers can be monitored during training, their conduct with noncombatants is visible to other soldiers, and commanders can easily pinpoint the misbehavior of particular individuals. In this context, however, it is difficult to link the behavior of rebel combatants to the ultimate outcomes of the war.

---

[8] In this chapter, I focus on challenges of management and organizational control with respect to rebel soldiers. In subsequent sections, I explore rebel strategies that assign authority to noncombatant populations.

[9] Wilson, *Bureaucracy*, pp. 157–71.

Commanders cannot know for sure whether soldiers are internalizing the lessons of training, whether their comportment with civilians is strengthening or damaging the group's causes, and whether a soldier's use of the group's resources is a worthwhile investment. None of this can be tested until soldiers are put into action in battle. For procedural organizations, Wilson argues, the best management style is one that focuses on how agents go about their jobs rather than on whether those actions produce the desired outcomes. Encouraging an environment of professionalism with its concordant norms of behavior and conduct should be leaders' overriding goal. Since agents can be observed, the danger is that principals will watch them all the time and that continual supervision will weaken the organization by threatening morale and leading individuals to conform to procedures that, in the end, have little relevance with respect to outcomes.

Unlike professional armies, rebel groups regularly shift back and forth from craft to procedural organizations as they move in and out of battle. Thus, in rebel organizations, Wilson's two solutions – the monitoring of procedures and the creation of internalized norms – operate in tandem. Rebel leaders can regulate soldiers' comportment, put procedures to the test in battle, and regularly evaluate the success of their organizational structures on the basis of battlefield performance. The creation of an organizational culture is central to group performance, and it comes from leaders' strategic efforts both inside and outside of military actions.

Rebel leaders develop three critical strategies to create an environment of sustained cooperation among combatants and commanders. The first requires that rebel groups make investments in the training of new combatants. Training is used to impart a set of skills to prepare soldiers for combat. It can also be used to shape individual behaviors and beliefs around a shared set of expectations about how the organization will operate. One avenue for creating expectations is political education – a mode of indoctrination used in many rebel organizations. Political education is used to create a shared sense of mission, purpose, and duty. The substance may come in part from the social practices and beliefs of the individuals who make up an insurgent organization, especially if they are drawn largely from the same ethnic or religious groups. Alternatively, political training may be rooted in an ideology that provides a set of beliefs and behaviors to all new adherents. Wilson sees the establishment of a sense of mission as a way of introducing nonmaterial rewards for cooperation.[10] Gary Miller suggests that the

[10] Ibid., p. 157.

belief in a common purpose creates a willingness to make sacrifices for that purpose.[11] Both explanations suggest that shared beliefs made possible by political education are an important source of sustained cooperation.

Training also demonstrates the commitment of the principals to the agents. When leaders expend time and resources on military and political training, combatants realize that their labor is not expendable. If they were worthless and could be replaced at a minimal cost, there would be little incentive for commanders to set aside time and effort to train them. Such investments signal that the relationship between combatants and commanders will be durable. The prospect of repeated interaction is a key source of cooperation in groups.

A second strategy involves building an organizational environment that reflects the shared expectations and norms of conduct taught to new combatants. Making sure that the codes and expectations are understood and, in some cases, formalized is the first step in this effort. Codes of conduct, rules, and procedural guidelines – all characteristic of formal organizations – also appear in rebel groups as tools to guide combatant behavior. But these shared behaviors must be enforced to be effective. Leaders set in place mechanisms for monitoring combatants' behavior. When rewards and punishments are disbursed, groups evaluate combatants on the basis of their performances vis-à-vis the group's code of conduct. To the extent that leaders show favoritism and bias in distributing rewards and punishment, they weaken efforts to set in place shared expectations about behavior. By making both continued membership in the group and promotion to higher ranks within it uncertain, leaders create a desire for status that can be used to shape combatants' actions.

Cooperative efforts, even when supported by powerful organizational cultures, inevitably fail when mechanisms are not set in place to bind the hands of the principals. If rank-and-file combatants see that their commanders are rewarded despite violations of the code of conduct, there is little incentive for them to continue cooperating. Constraining the actions of leaders is typically the hardest part of management and organizational control, but rebel leaders' third strategy of control is to reinforce shared expectations by ensuring that they, too, behave responsibly and cooperate to realize common objectives.

Leaders may share decision-making power with combatants by creating forums in which soldiers can participate in discussions about the direction of

[11] Miller, *Managerial Dilemmas*, p. 197.

the movement. These forums also allow combatants to criticize the behavior of their superiors, holding them accountable for their actions. Rebel commanders may also place constraints on their own capacity to supervise other members of the group as a demonstration of their trust in the norms of behavior. By decentralizing power and resources, rebel leaders place real authority in the hands of their agents to mount operations, organize their troops, and work on behalf of the group's objectives. This serves as a costly signal of the leadership's belief in the capacity and trustworthiness of its combatants – costly because decentralization is a risky strategy. To make it work, commanders and combatants must share an understanding of how they will respond to the various situations they encounter. Decentralization makes it possible to achieve higher levels of productivity only when subunits act coherently to advance the long-term goals of the organization.

These three institutional choices about how to structure training, what kind of organizational culture to build, and how to distribute authority and power shape the decisions group members make about whether to invest their efforts toward the group's objectives or to act for their own personal benefit. Leaders play a fundamental role in forming organizations' internal environments. They influence combatants' expectations about what life will be like in the organization, how others will behave, and to what extent particular types of behavior will be rewarded or punished. They use their pulpit to communicate these expectations and their actions to reinforce shared beliefs, structuring the rebel hierarchy to reflect their own commitment to sustained cooperation toward long-term objectives.

Investments in human capital (through training), the establishment of norms and shared expectations for cooperation, and irreversible commitments to shared decision making and authority all contribute to the creation of an environment in which combatants and commanders alike are willing to make costly investments in the short run in exchange for the promise of long-term benefits. Armed with the belief that others will cooperate today and in every period in the future, members have the right incentives to invest in the organization, cooperate, and resist the urge to defect for short-term gains.[12] The prospect of large payoffs in the future, reinforced by a culture of cooperation, enables groups to avoid problems of defection.

---

[12] For a game-theoretic treatment of the importance of repeated play for cooperation, see Robert Axelrod, *The Evolution of Cooperation* (Princeton: Princeton University Press, 1994).

Leaders of organizations founded on social endowments are better equipped to institutionalize the long-term commitments of their members by building a cooperative environment. Chapter 3 demonstrated that resource-poor groups tend to attract only the most committed activists to rebel. Members join with the expectation that the road will be difficult and that they are unlikely to benefit from their participation until success is achieved. Strong ethnic, religious, or political identities make participation in these groups rational because these informal networks, which often predate the rebel organization, provide a group's members with shared beliefs about the purpose and conduct of the war, a tool for ensuring selectivity in the recruitment process, and institutional arrangements that facilitate the sanctioning of defectors within the group. Resource-poor groups attract members willing to cooperate and capable of cooperating for the long term. As a result, in these organizations, combatants are more likely to follow the orders of their commanders, take on military targets, and exhibit discipline and control in liberated zones.

Where rebel organizations are unable to put in place mechanisms to restrain the behavior of combatants and commanders, soldiers avoid military engagements, attack civilian targets, and show indiscipline in zones of rebel control. When rebel commanders and combatants share a short-term orientation, this result becomes more likely. Chapter 3 showed how resource-rich groups tend to attract members on the basis of short-term rewards. These groups offer immediate payoffs and relatively low risks to potential recruits. Such actions in turn create a membership bias in favor of recruits with short time horizons and a low level of commitment to the organization's long-term objectives. Their leaders struggle to set in place institutional mechanisms to promote cooperation. Lacking a membership base constructed around a shared identity, leaders have no basis on which to create common expectations. The dearth of informal mechanisms for selecting high-commitment recruits and sanctioning defectors contributes to the group's short-term orientation. And when commanders or combatants act in ways that reflect the group's defection mentality, they weaken the prospects for sustained cooperation.

When leaders cannot constrain the actions of their members with internal checks on behavior, their groups operate on the basis of consistent defection, becoming oriented toward maintaining the flow of rewards to their leaders and members. They avoid engagement with the opposing military force and use attacks on civilian populations, which tend to carry much lower risks, to capture the resources they need to sustain the organization.

In this context, only external checks – government force or civilian resistance – can discipline a group's behavior.[13]

Organizational Control in Practice

In considering the four case studies in this section, I explore how rebel organizations handle principal-agent problems, whether groups built around social identities or political ideologies are better able to set in place systems of shared norms and expectations, and whether organizations that recruit on the basis of short-term payoffs suffer from more serious problems of defection.

Formal and Informal Codes of Conduct: The NRA

A former commanding officer of the NRA reflected on the organizational structure of the movement: "It was based on discipline, 'need to know,' open communication, and free criticism. One could even see a meeting of commanders and combatants in which soldiers criticized the commanders for drinking and going after women, things that threatened the security of the camp."[14] The NRA constructed an organization that gave power and authority to lower-level commanders and combatants. It entrusted them with the limited resources of the movement in part because the senior leadership believed that NRA members shared a set of beliefs about how the war should be conducted and how they should behave.

Sustained investments in political education fortified these beliefs. Commanders required all new combatants to attend lectures and discussion sessions as part of their training. At first, Yoweri Museveni taught the courses

---

[13] Where government forces have the resources and capacity to identify and target insurgent groups, they can break up movements organized around defection. Unwilling to face the opposing force, combatants will flee in multiple directions when attacked, fracturing the rebel organization. If the government is incapable of breaking up a movement, organized civilian resistance can also be leveraged to expel it or force its combatants to change their behavior. But in most developing countries where civil wars take place, externally imposed discipline is difficult to mobilize. Governments face insurgencies largely because they are incapable of controlling their territory and mounting effective counterinsurgencies. Civilian populations fear organizing against insurgents because they lack access to weapons or resources and consequently face the prospect of increased rebel brutality and violence in response to their actions. I return to the important role of external checks in Chapter 7, where I explore the impact of rebel success and failure on organizational control.

[14] Interview, Kampala, November 2(A), 2000.

140

himself; later, other commanders and combatants took charge of the political education program.[15] Topics included the pre- and postcolonial history of Uganda, political economy, and specific instruction in how revolutions are carried out.[16] Sometimes, there were debates. Recruits were encouraged, for example, to learn about and carefully consider alternative approaches to defeating the Obote regime. Although Museveni endorsed the idea of a "protracted people's war," recruits also analyzed the costs and benefits of assassination, a coup, and urban insurrection.[17]

The focus of political training was not only on the great issues of the day; commanders also used the opportunity to shape the expectations and behaviors of the new recruits. One recalled that "the focus of political education was also on the building of interpersonal relationships."[18] He remembered that the commanders were trying to build a "cohesive" group. Another explained that the NRA's leaders were concerned with protecting the civilian population, and they felt that combatants needed to share the same beliefs about how civilians should be treated. He recalled being told, "You must go out of your way to help and support the local population" by providing physical protection, water, food, and any other assistance local people required.[19]

To reinforce these political messages, the NRA built a system of political commissars into the army structure. Combatants who rotated into the position of commissar were responsible for sharing the NRA's political aims and goals with the civilian population. Rebels needed to understand the NRA's purpose not only for themselves, but also because their commanders might require them to pass the message on to others. A former commander described the leadership's philosophy: "Political education sought to enable every soldier to know why he was fighting and to be able to explain it to civilians."[20]

Political education comprised only one part of a larger NRA investment in training. Museveni organized a special training group, the Nkrumah Unit, and based it in an area outside the immediate reach of UNLA troops. The leadership sent all new recruits to Nkrumah for training regardless of their previous military experience or education. Training lasted from one to

[15] Ibid., September 27(A), 2000.
[16] Ibid., October 27(A), November 6(B), 2000.
[17] Ibid., October 25(B), 2000.
[18] Ibid., October 25(A), 2000.
[19] Ibid., October 25(B), 2000.
[20] Ibid., November 7(A), 2000.

three months, depending on the needs of the army and the performance of the recruits. The Nkrumah Unit developed a formalized program of training, with half of each day dedicated to military field craft and the other half to political education.[21] The training covered weapons handling, guerrilla war tactics, and strategy. But it, too, focused on how rebels should behave during combat. A former commander said: "The main issue was teaching respect for the civilian population. An army is meant to be controlled by the people, the ones who pay the taxes to feed and clothe it, not to rape and loot from the people."[22] Soldiers were evaluated on the basis of their performance before passing into the NRA's combat units. It was clear that the leadership valued the recruits and sought to equip them with necessary skills before putting them to work on behalf of the movement.

Over the course of the war, the NRA found that simply teaching recruits about the purpose of the movement and providing guidelines about appropriate behavior was not sufficient to create an environment of sustained cooperation. "Comradeship" was essential to the movement, and one former commander with whom I spoke believed that political education efforts worked to foster it. He explained: "[Comradeship] represents a relationship where one is willing to die or sacrifice for the common good ... where the individual is not above the interests of the majority."[23] But these relationships needed support from formal structures and guidelines to which commanders and combatants could refer when uncertainties arose.

Efforts to formalize commander-combatant and combatant-combatant relations took on great urgency during the period of Museveni's first trip outside of the country to raise external support for the movement. Between June and December of 1981, Museveni left Sam Magara, a close comrade, in charge of the NRA. With the war in its earliest stages and the key commander outside of the country, conflicts among NRA soldiers threatened the movement. The largest schism was between ethnic Banyankole and ethnic Baganda recruits. The Baganda began to demand greater representation in the hierarchy of the movement.[24] A second struggle arose between educated and uneducated recruits.[25] The educated recruits typically lacked military experience, but they sought influence and power because of their academic backgrounds. Tensions came to a head when Magara ordered the execution

[21] Ibid., October 22(A), 2000.
[22] Ibid., October 24(A), 2000.
[23] Ibid., October 21(A), 2000.
[24] Ibid., November 2(A), 2000.
[25] Ibid., January 24(A), 2001.

of a young recruit, Shaban, who had returned to the encampment after disappearing for a short period. Magara accused him of collaborating with the government; others claimed he had simply gone into town for a leave.[26]

The execution damaged relationships that were already fraught with tension. One commander recalled that at the time, the rebels "were few, and all from the same area," but the execution and the mistrust it generated began to destroy the movement.[27] The problem, one officer explained, was that rules about conduct and procedure had not been formalized. There was no common knowledge about how things would be handled.[28]

When Museveni returned at the end of December, he took two major steps that solidified the structure of the NRA for the duration of the civil war. In fact, his innovations continue to guide the NRA's successor, the Ugandan People's Defence Force, even today. First, Museveni circulated a draft Code of Conduct that he had been working on during his visit to London. It put in writing the norms of interaction that were taught in political education about how combatants should treat one another, their commanders, and the civilian population.[29] It prohibited abuses of the civilian population and clarified the hierarchical structure of the army. Moreover, it spelled out the punishments that would be ordered for various types of indiscipline and outlined the processes that would be followed to adjudicate cases when necessary. An abridged version of the Code of Conduct appears in Appendix C.

As part of this reform, Museveni made membership and promotion in the NRA entirely an issue of merit and performance. While favoritism had previously been shown in allocating responsibility, the new structures of the movement sought to ensure fairness to all commanders and combatants.[30] One former officer explained that after the reorganization, "no one would complain about being treated unfairly because the standards of behavior were clear as well as the rules for punishment."[31]

In establishing formal guidelines and punishment mechanisms, Museveni also initiated a democratization of the rebel movement. The High Command, which included Museveni and other senior officers, responded to the tensions apparent during Museveni's absence with a sustained effort to solicit the concerns and advice of combatants at all levels. Its members

[26] Ibid., October 25(A), 2000; January 24(A), July 15(A), 2001.
[27] Ibid., January 24(A), 2001.
[28] Ibid., October 25(A), 2000.
[29] Ibid., September 27(A), 2000.
[30] Ibid., July 15(A), 2001.
[31] Ibid., October 25(A), 2001.

met with each unit and allowed for the free expression of criticism as they sought to "come to consensus and clear up mistrust and suspicion."[32] The leadership encouraged combatants to tell the truth about how the army was being run. This "democratic climate" became a hallmark of the NRA's organizational structure throughout the rest of the conflict.

Museveni also initiated a decentralization of power in the movement in line with his philosophy of "democratic centralism." He sought to combine an emphasis on democratic participation with centralized command. While the High Command plotted the strategic direction of the movement, local commanders had significant autonomy to mount operations.[33] Each unit had a Policy and Administrative Committee, composed of the commanding officer and other members of the unit, to aid in administration and command. It acted as a critical check on both the officer of the unit and the High Command. When limited monetary resources became available during the war, they were transferred to the individual units to enable them to purchase food and other resources from the civilian population.[34]

Efforts to democratize and decentralize the movement afforded an opportunity for constant discussion and dialogue. A former commander referred to the conflict as a "war of meetings."[35] Rank-and-file soldiers were empowered to criticize their commanders and to participate in shaping the direction of the group. Commanders were held in check by administrative and disciplinary structures that clearly spelled out the behaviors that were allowed and those that were prohibited. Political education provided guidance and focused members of the NRA on its guiding ideas and beliefs. The system of administration provided a foundation that made continued adherence to the movement's guidelines possible. A former leader in the NRA's political education efforts explained: "I had to ensure that soldiers operated with conscious discipline rather than mechanical discipline. Mechanical discipline is enforced by sanctions alone. But conscious discipline comes about when you explain to soldiers the value of things like not stealing property from civilians, not raping women, not injuring prisoners of war."[36] "Political education was important," one former officer told me, adding, "but so was punishment."[37]

[32] Ibid., January 24(A), 2001.
[33] Ibid., July 15(A), 2001.
[34] Ibid., November 2(A), 2000.
[35] Ibid., November 11(A), 2000.
[36] Ibid., November 7(A), 2000.
[37] Ibid., July 15(A), 2001.

The NRA's disciplinary procedures reinforced efforts to guide the behavior of combatants and commanders through political education. Commanders and combatants alike were put on trial for violations of the Code of Conduct. The NRA held public trials to determine their guilt or innocence and administered punishment brutally and quickly to underscore the seriousness of indiscipline. NRA soldiers, as well as civilians in rebel-held zones, came to expect certain behaviors from members of the movement. And by holding the line through mechanical discipline as well, members and supporters could trust that if they behaved, others would follow suit. These efforts contributed to the NRA's reputation for cooperation, cohesion, and trust.

Centralization and Distrust: Renamo

While the NRA invested power and authority in local commanders and rank-and-file combatants, Renamo centralized control in its Estado Maior General (Military Headquarters) in the center of Mozambique. One might have expected the opposite result: based entirely in a small geographic zone, the NRA could have consolidated total control in the hands of Museveni and his most senior commanders; Renamo, on the other hand, stretched its operations over a country more than two thousand miles in length, so a decentralized structure might have been optimal. Instead, ultimate authority for all decisions rested with Renamo's military commander, Aphonso Dhlakama, and his senior officers in Gorongosa and Maríngue. Commanders and combatants in Renamo did not trust one another; the organizational structure of the movement reflected this lack of cohesion.

As Chapter 3 explains, Renamo's organizational culture lacked a basis for cooperation from its earliest days. As the ranks increasingly filled with abducted recruits, the potential for cooperation eroded further, and recruits quickly learned that even though Renamo sought to take over the country and transform its political and social structure, participation was equally about survival and enrichment. Defection became the dominant norm of rebel conduct.

The Renamo leadership did not use political education as a tool to set in place shared beliefs about the purpose of the war and the way in which it should be conducted. Most former combatants remembered that their abductors said little about the purposes of the war. One described how her captors "explained that they were fighting a war against Frelimo, but not

145

much else."[38] When new recruits arrived at Renamo bases and began military training, efforts to share political messages and purposes did not go much deeper. None of the former combatants whom I interviewed referred to regular political meetings, discussions, or training. There was no formal process for indoctrinating new recruits and no consistent messages shared across bases and units. Moreover, Renamo combatants played no role in explaining the purposes of the conflict to civilians living in rebel-held zones.

When political education did take place, it varied in its depth and duration. One soldier described undergoing a full week of political education prior to three months of military training. He recalled the commander saying that "Renamo wanted to form a popular government and start elections."[39] Another described how his abductors told him informally that they were taking him because "people were living in fear of the regime, the population didn't have clothes and other products, and they needed to build a democracy."[40] One former combatant described a formal system of political commissars who trained new recruits and interacted with civilians,[41] but other former Renamo soldiers did not support his claims, and where civilians recalled hearing about the war from Renamo, it was only through interactions between local leaders and senior Renamo commanders.[42] Rank-and-file combatants were not involved in educating the local population.

The dearth of political education stands in stark contrast to Renamo's investments in military training. Building on the expertise of their Rhodesian and South African supporters, Renamo recruits participated in fairly extensive training exercises that focused on weapons handling.[43] Often, after completing basic training, recruits were encouraged by their commanders to specialize. Some focused on communications and radio operation, others on artillery and antiaircraft, and still others on education and first aid in order to supply Renamo's hospitals and schools. A small number of

---

[38] Interview, Ribáuè, Nampula Province, April 3(A), 2001.
[39] Ibid., March 27(A), 2001.
[40] Ibid., March 30(D), 2001.
[41] Interview, Marínguè, Sofala Province, May 18(B), 2001.
[42] Interviews, Ribáuè, Nampula Province, March 31(A,C), April 1(B), 2001; interview, Marínguè, Sofala Province, May 19(A), 2001.
[43] Interviews, Ribáuè, Nampula Province, March 27(A), 30(D), 2001. See also William Minter, *The Mozambican National Resistance (Renamo) as Described by Ex-Participants* (Washington, DC: Report Submitted to the Ford Foundation, 1989), p. 6.

recruits transferred to South Africa to receive additional training in military intelligence and special operations.[44]

These investments in military training at the expense of political indoctrination contributed to the impression among Renamo recruits that they were part of an army rather than a political movement – an impression shared by civilians.[45] Commanders thrust soldiers into battle situations as soon as they completed training, and each recruit was armed with an AK-47, but investments in training did not provide recruits with the message that they were valued members of Renamo's force. Because abduction could be used to refill the ranks at any time and in practically any place, Renamo's combatants understood that the leadership saw them as expendable. As a result, they sought to make the best of a difficult situation: they avoided direct contact with government forces and attempted to gain wealth and power through attacks on noncombatant populations.

Systems of control designed to punish and reward combatants did little to stem the tide of defection within the movement. There was no clear, specified code of conduct for Renamo's members. Moreover, there was no established process for determining the guilt or innocence of combatants who abused civilian populations or fled from battle. The authority to make these choices rested entirely with local commanders. In consequence, favoritism predominated in commander-combatant relationships, and decisions about whether and how to punish indiscipline were entirely arbitrary. Renamo's combatants did not share expectations about how they should behave, which behaviors were permitted and which prohibited, or how punishments would be administered.

Renamo combatants described a haphazard system of enforcing rules. One soldier said that there were rules, but they were never written down.[46] Others countered that commanders never explained the system of discipline to them.[47] Interviews with former combatants and civilians made it clear that near-total authority for the administration of justice within units rested with the local commanders.[48] For serious crimes, such as rape or murder, the commander might execute a soldier, but only one former combatant could remember such an execution.[49] Civilians, for their part, never knew

[44] Interview, Marínguè, Sofala Province, May 18(B), 2001.
[45] Minter, *Mozambican National Resistance*, p. 7.
[46] Interview, Ribáuè, Nampula Province, March 30(D), 2001.
[47] Ibid., April 3(B), 4(A), 2001.
[48] Ibid., March 27(A), 2001; interviews, Marínguè, Sofala Province, May 18(A), 24(B), 2001.
[49] Interview, Marínguè, Sofala Province, May 18(A), 2001.

whether soldiers were punished when they abused the local population because commanders adjudicated most cases in the privacy of the rebel base.[50]

Adding to civilians' confusion, there was little regulation of combatant-civilian interaction. Although authorities insist to this day that combatants were prohibited from having relationships with women outside of the base, former soldiers tell a different story. One told me that in 1987, when his Renamo unit was suffering from a number of desertions, the commander allowed the insurgents to begin keeping wives on the base. "If a soldier liked a woman, he would marry her just the same [whether she had a husband or not]," he added.[51] Combatants were also allowed to take goods from the local population during attacks and even from civilians within areas of rebel control. Often, the goal of an attack was to loot a village and then to divide up the take among the commanders and combatants.[52] One former soldier who stayed behind at a Renamo base said, "To eat, we would wait for the guerrillas to return with the loot."[53] A civilian explained that "whatever they asked for, a person was required to give."[54]

Renamo's hierarchical structure reinforced combatants' belief that the movement did not have a long-term orientation. Although the commanders stressed a desire for democratic change, on the ground, units were enriching themselves, attacking local populations, and avoiding extended contact with the government's forces. Dhlakama and his commanders, who had no basis to trust their local counterparts, maintained strict control over the strategic direction of the movement. The Estado Maior General coordinated the movement of troops, arranged for the establishment of new bases and fronts, and made decisions about when and where to launch attacks. Communications operators routed all information through the national command up to four times a day so that strategic planning could be conducted with up-to-date local information.[55] If a local commander wished to launch an attack, he or she first needed to receive clearance from the top.[56] Even after an attack was launched, decisions to vacate an occupied village or

---

[50] Interviews, Ribáuè, Nampula Province, April 1(B), 2001; interviews, Marínguè, Sofala Province, May 20(C), 21(A), 2001.
[51] Interview, Ribáuè, Nampula Province, April 2(B), 2001.
[52] Ibid.
[53] Ibid., March 31(B), 2001.
[54] Interview, Marínguè, Sofala Province, May 23(B), 2001.
[55] Interviews, Ribáuè, Nampula Province, March 27(A), 30(D), 31(A); April 4(A), 5(A), 2001.
[56] Ibid., April 4(A), 5(A), 2001.

town were made by the national command. Senior Renamo commanders did not invest any power or authority in local commanders or rank-and-file soldiers.

This climate of defection created the conditions for major fractures within the movement. In fact, a senior Renamo commander, Gimo Phiri, broke away from the group with 500 men in 1988.[57] But centralization nonetheless worked because the subsidiary units were dependent on the central command for the flow of military equipment and other resources. Too frightened to attack government outposts in search of guns, local units accepted their position within the hierarchy because the central command ensured that South African military supplies would be dropped to them on a regular basis. They could continue to loot and survive as relatively privileged authorities in the rural areas while the national movement continued to reap significant profits from cross-border trade in looted goods, the extortion of private companies, and South African assistance.

In Mozambique, Renamo created an internal culture in which commanders and combatants alike sought to realize immediate rewards in the short term from their participation. Defection became the norm, and few efforts were made to counter this pattern of behavior. It was an organizational structure that worked, but only due to the government's incapacity to root out the rebels effectively. Members of Renamo rewarded themselves for nearly sixteen years before the conflict came to an end.

Decentralization and the Guiding Line: Sendero Luminoso Nacional

In comparing the organizational trajectories of the NRA and Renamo, one might wonder if it is possible to create a climate of cooperation and shared authority in a large organization that operates across a vast swath of territory. The NRA's success at decentralizing power to its local commanders and members may have been simply a function of the close proximity in which its units operated, and perhaps the Renamo leadership chose centralization because it was the only feasible mechanism of control for a truly national organization.

The case of Sendero Nacional suggests, however, that the capacity to create an environment characterized by cooperation and shared decision making does not depend on the geographic spread of a conflict. The Shining Path operated in every corner of Peru during its twelve years of

---

[57] Alex Vines, *Renamo: Terrorism in Mozambique* (London: James Currey, 1991), p. 70.

struggle against the government. In building an organization, Abimael Guzmán and other leaders devolved significant power to local committees to organize their own resources, plan actions, and maintain discipline. The Central Committee provided strategic direction, ideological substance, and rigorous guidelines regarding how members should behave; nevertheless, Sendero Nacional entrusted its members with decision-making power and operational authority – a strategy only possible in a climate of shared expectations about where the movement was headed and how it planned to get there.

The Shining Path placed political indoctrination at the center of its recruitment and training efforts. Guzmán was a teacher by trade, and as he laid the groundwork for the movement during the 1970s he used his lectures and discussions with students in Ayacucho to generate the ideological backbone of the struggle. As these ideologically committed students moved into the rural areas, popular schools provided the mechanism through which they recruited new members and engaged the civilian population.[58] Their message attracted peasants as they spoke about the suffering of rural people and the need for dramatic reform. Who among the poor peasants in Peru's highlands could object to the goal one militant shared as the rationale for his participation: "In reality, the movement sought to take from the rich to give to the poor and the needy"?[59]

But it was not so much the message itself that ensured the shared commitments and expectations of Sendero members. The process of continually learning and updating one's understandings of the ideological directions of the movement reinforced the evolution of a single set of beliefs. The Central Committee held regular party meetings to evaluate the progress of the struggle, point political and military work in new directions, and challenge the masses to work toward the party's goals. The content of each of these meetings was dutifully recorded and copied for members of Sendero Luminoso at all levels to absorb. These documents reproduced the thematic structure of each and every debate and enabled the movement to involve all of its members in its strategic trajectory.

Like the political commissars of the NRA, Sendero militants constantly shared these new developments with the local population. Political

---

[58] Interviews, Huanta, Ayacucho, December 1(D), 3(A,E), 4(A), 2001.
[59] Sendero militant quoted in Cynthia McClintock, *Revolutionary Movements in Latin America: El Salvador's FMLN and Peru's Shining Path* (Washington, DC: United States Institute of Peace Press, 1998), p. 278.

education was at the center of the recruitment process, and the existence of consistent meetings was part of what separated "guerrilla zones" from areas in which Sendero had only limited influence. One civilian described the pattern of life in rebel-controlled areas in this way: "Sendero was active [in the community].... they invited me to a meeting.... The meetings were continuous."[60]

Sendero militants were challenged, moreover, to articulate the political importance of their military actions to one another and to peasant populations. Senderistas mobilized peasants to dispense "revolutionary justice" to wealthy landowners in their communities.[61] Those who had benefited at the expense of the peasant masses were stripped of their wealth, which was later distributed to militants and their supporters. But these attacks were organized and were not characterized by pillaging. Militants carefully explained the importance of such actions to the greater cause of the struggle.

Leaders of the movement underscored the importance of Sendero's set of political and ideological beliefs by making entrance into the party and promotion within the party and the military fully dependent on mastery of the material.[62] Sendero members had to prove their worth at lower rungs of the organization before advancing. Much time was spent as a member of the masses before one could hope to become an active member of the military wing. Understanding the purpose of the movement and its ideological leanings was an essential criterion for promotion. A Rand Corporation analyst described the significance of this organizational character as follows: "Sendero is said to take three years to vet a prospective recruit before he or she is assigned to an operating cell. Only an organization with the confidence and patience to take the long view could afford to carry out such a lengthy process of recruitment and observation before a new member is given the 'secret handshake' and absorbed into its day-to-day routine."[63]

New recruits were thus encouraged to think of their efforts as an investment in the movement. Rewards were not immediate, and success depended on a willingness to wait, demonstrate one's worth, and show a commitment

---

[60] Ibid., p. 277.
[61] Gustavo Gorritti describes the pattern of Sendero actions in the earliest years of the conflict. See *The Shining Path: A History of the Millenarian War in Peru* (Chapel Hill: University of North Carolina Press, 1999), p. 60.
[62] Interview, Lima, November 5(A), 2001.
[63] Gordon McCormick, *The Shining Path and the Future of Peru* (Santa Monica, CA: Rand, 1990), p. 12.

to the ideological directions and organizational structure of the Shining Path. Actual military training was secondary to political indoctrination, as evidenced by the stories from Sendero's first military school described in Chapter 3. Guzmán believed that participation was the best preparation for a protracted guerrilla struggle. Technical skills would come with time; the leaders were more concerned with ensuring that new cadres were willing to die for the cause of the movement.[64]

As in the NRA, the creation of a "conscious discipline" in the cadres required continual repetition of the beliefs and codes of behavior that guided the Shining Path. Often, these codes of behavior were put down on paper. At Sendero Luminoso's second national conference (April 21–June 6, 1982), the Central Committee endorsed a report outlining the eleven norms of behavior of a local commander.[65] These norms are listed in Appendix D. The report was based on an analysis of the behavior of two model Shining Path commanders, Rommel and Patton.

Sendero Luminoso also set in place a system of guidelines for how members of the mass of supporters should behave. The eight principles that the militants outlined included: do not steal, do not help the police or the military, return what you borrow, be faithful to your partner, do not lie or insult others, do not mistreat prisoners, respect the property of farmers, and maintain good moral conduct.[66]

But respect for these principles and sustained cooperation also required the establishment of institutional mechanisms to ensure that militants who violated the expectations of others would be punished. Such structures are essential to allow a cooperative equilibrium to continue. Leaders relied on two key monitoring mechanisms. The first was the process of crítica y autocrítica described in Chapter 3: rebels were regularly subjected to examination by their peers and commanders with respect to their understanding of the ideology, their behavior within the movement, and their willingness to sacrifice for the cause. They would present themselves to a gathered assembly or be called to participate, and they would face harsh questioning and analysis. If they failed to satisfy others and accept their own shortcomings, commanders could administer punishment. Sanctions

---

[64] Gorritti, *Shining Path*, p. 86.
[65] Report of the second national conference April 21–June 6, 1982, captured Sendero document, 1982, DINCOTE Sendero collection, Lima, Peru.
[66] Reported in Fundación para el Desarrollo Nacional, *Plan de ejecución del Proyecto de Desarrollo Rural Integral del Alto Huallaga* (Lima: Fundación para el Desarrollo Nacional, May 1981), p. 31.

included demotion within the ranks of the party and the military, expulsion, and, in extreme cases, death. Particularly brutal treatment was reserved for militants who strayed from the party line and sacrificed the group's objectives to their own personal interests. The constant threat of examination and punishment provided the Shining Path with an important measure of mechanical control over the behavior of its militants.

The movement also set in place a second monitoring mechanism to control the conduct of militants during military attacks. Units submitted a *plano operativo táctico* (operational tactical plan) in advance of every military action. The plan outlined the reconnaissance work that had been completed, the tactical plan of attack, the weapons to be used, and the political rationale for going after the target. Most important, it assigned responsibilities to named individuals for specific parts of the operation. Local commanders evaluated the performance of units and their members on the basis of the operational tactical plans. After each action, militants provided an evaluation of the attack, and they were encouraged to point the finger at those who had failed to fulfill their commitments. These reports were reviewed by local commanders and then forwarded to the party leadership.

Captured party documents show how this mechanism worked in practice. The Shining Path planned a major prison break of captured militants in Ayacucho for February 28, 1982. It was timed to coincide with a series of other prison breaks around the country. Militants inside the prison were sent word of the attack and told to begin a revolt at 10:10 p.m. But when the appointed time arrived, "there were no weapons," and the organization also "had other problems."[67] Four militants were killed, and five were badly wounded. The written evaluation pointed the finger at the leadership of the regional committee. In particular, it targeted the committee's political chief, César, who it claimed "[did] not concern himself with the operation," but "only want[ed] the glory, to be a great general." César and four other members endured extensive criticism and self-criticism for their actions. They were forced to repudiate their own behavior and pledge their absolute commitment to abide by the decisions of the party leadership regarding their punishment. The debate over their actions was broadcast through documentation to militants throughout the country, and when a decision was finally reached, the militants were kicked out of their leadership positions and forced to return to the lowest level of the party hierarchy. Guzmán

[67] Captured documents reported in Gorritti, *Shining Path*, p. 178.

argued, "We must impose discipline with rigor no matter what the cost; the slightest weakness means death and hunger."[68]

Although evaluations of operational tactical plans rarely received the attention of the party's highest officers, the process of reflection created an environment in which behavior was monitored and sanctioned. As one former militant described it: "I especially liked the military organization.... Everything was carefully calculated, and you couldn't make a mistake; the directives they gave us had to be executed precisely, because if not, you exposed your *compañeros* and endangered the success of the mission."[69]

The Shining Path also created an environment in which militants committed themselves to the movement by sharing authority and decision-making power with regional committees, local commanders, and rank-and-file militants. Sendero, like the NRA, was guided by a theory of democratic centralism. The Central Committee reserved the power to provide the movement with a "guiding line" in terms of ideological direction and strategic actions, while regional and local committees received significant latitude to choose their targets, organize activities, recruit new members, and reward and sanction their own militants.[70] The Central Committee oversaw these activities by requiring regular reports and providing detailed advice and criticism about the directions taken in each region. By decentralizing operations, it demonstrated its faith in the abilities and commitments of Sendero members. At the same time, decentralization enabled local commanders to check the authority of the senior leadership.[71] One captured militant explained this system of checks and balances by saying, "We were directed by the leaders, and they by us."[72]

Its decentralized structure enabled the Shining Path to better respond to local conditions and to execute its military operations succesfully. It was difficult for the Peruvian intelligence services to penetrate and disrupt the movement because of its multiple centers of power. Militants were highly committed to the goals of the group, and when one committee was

---

[68] Ibid, p. 180.

[69] Quoted in McClintock, *Revolutionary Movements*, p. 278.

[70] Gabriela Tarazona-Sevillano, "The Organization of Shining Path," in *Shining Path of Peru*, ed. David Scott Palmer (New York: St. Martins, 1992), p. 190.

[71] It should be noted that Guzmán himself was never the subject of criticism and self-criticism, according to Gorritti. But he focused his efforts almost entirely on providing ideological direction to the movement. Decentralization enabled local commanders to check the authority of other national-level officials who could have used their positions in the leadership to profit personally.

[72] Interview, Lima, November 7(A), 2001.

infiltrated, the others took up the slack, often from the other end of the country.

The leaders of the Shining Path used political education to put in place a set of shared beliefs about the purposes of the movement and the ways in which its members should behave. They used monitoring mechanisms and organizational structures to reinforce these messages and ensure that behavior was consistent across regional committees and local groups. In doing so, Sendero Nacional created an environment in which militants were willing to invest in the organization in return for only the prospect of rewards in the future. Cooperative behaviors triumphed over widespread defection.

The Consequences of Autonomy: Sendero–Huallaga

The Shining Path's national structure, however, did not ensure that an environment of cooperation would emerge in every subsidiary committee. Even single incidents of defection can damage the prospects of long-term cooperation, and when defection goes unpunished, members can no longer trust that their actions will be reciprocated. The only rational response in such a situation is to defect as well. The leadership of Sendero Luminoso constructed a national organization that overcame significant barriers to success largely by virtue of the sheer effort it invested in building a committed cadre of followers and coordinating their actions, but the devolution of power could be abused, especially in environments where the shared set of beliefs and behaviors characteristic of the movement were routinely violated.

In the coca-growing zones, the Comité Regional del Alto Huallaga began as a mirror image of other regional committees. The political aims of the movement dominated its military components, and membership status was reserved for the very few. Early in its evolution, however, its leadership transformed the committee's organizational structure by beginning to accept nearly all interested participants, militarizing most cadres, and allowing immoral behaviors to go unpunished. The CRH became an organization defined by its capacity to provide short-term rewards; the movement's long-term objectives gradually faded from view.

The resulting committee looked far different than Sendero organizations in the rest of the country. One analyst explained, "there are strong indications that...the military component of Sendero [in Huallaga] has been overshadowing the political and...the columns themselves are not very well coordinated."[73] The CRH's units were large – between 60 and 120 soldiers – and unlike the forces in the highlands, they carried heavy weaponry. A former Upper Huallaga Valley combatant reports that Sendero–Huallaga units were heavily militarized; they traveled in military clothing, while Senderistas in Ayacucho dressed as peasants; and there were much clearer distinctions made between military cadres and peasants.[74]

By focusing its efforts around the protection of the drug trade rather than the shared ideology of the movement, the CRH also eliminated the role of the rank and file in spreading the political messages of Sendero to civilian populations. Instead of promoting the movement's long-term vision of societal transformation, CRH leaders encouraged civilians to support the rebels for the short-term rewards they could gain. Sendero promised civilians higher prices for their coca products and protection for their families. There was no hint of the sacrifices that were necessary for social revolution. Another analyst states that "[Sendero's] support among the general population was based more on local concern for protecting and expanding coca crop and coca paste production than on the political cause of orthodox Maoism that Shining Path offered."[75]

The CRH reinforced an environment of opportunism by rejecting in practice the codes of conduct set in place by the national organization. The rules dictated respect for the property of noncombatant populations and total adherence to the goals of the party at the expense of personal gains. Yet in the Upper Huallaga Valley, combatants followed the lead of their commanders, many of whom benefited directly from the coca trade instead of providing those resources to the party coffers.[76] A civilian who lived in the coca-growing zone explained that senior Senderistas in the committee would desert the movement, fleeing soon after collecting taxes on the coca trade.[77] Importantly, this pattern of personal enrichment went largely unpunished because most members of the CRH were also benefiting. Civilians complained that their neighbors were punished by the CRH for the same activities that militants were allowed to get away with.[78]

---

[73] Tom Marks, "Making Revolution with Shining Path," in Palmer, *Shining Path of Peru*, p. 218.

[74] Interview, Lima, November 7(A), 2001.

[75] José Gonzales, "Guerrillas and Coca in the Upper Huallaga Valley," in Palmer, *Shining Path of Peru*, p. 129.

[76] Interviews, Lima, November 7(A), 2001; interview, Tingo María, November 17, 2001.

[77] Interviews, Tingo María, November 17(B), 19(D), 2001.

[78] Ibid., November 19(B,C,D), 2001.

As a result, the leaders of the CRH did not seek to protect the status of Senderistas as political and ideological revolutionaries. Status derived purely from access to the wealth of the coca trade. Individuals could join and advance without demonstrating their commitment to the goals of the movement. Rebels could remain in the organization even as they violated its supposed codes of conduct. Defection for personal gain was the modus operandi of most participants.

The decentralized structure of the national movement enabled this climate to develop. The devolution of authority also allowed the CRH to resist any efforts by the national movement to constrain its behavior. Although Sendero–Huallaga often participated in nationally coordinated activities to demonstrate its commitment to the movement, it was rife with corruption at the local level.[79] The CRH provided the required regular updates to the Central Committee, but when the senior leadership rejected its efforts to continue building relationships with the cocaleros, the CRH ignored the Central Committee's complaints.[80] Among the counterterrorism police's captured documents, very few include pointed critiques of the CRH, but the documents demonstrate that the Central Committee regularly evaluated and repudiated the behavior of other regional committees.[81] One can speculate that the senior leadership allowed the CRH additional authority in exchange for a flow of resources from the coca trade, but the police have not been able to uncover evidence of this money in the national party coffers. It seems, rather, that the CRH truly operated outside of the control of the national leadership and that, due to the decentralized structure of the movement, little could be done to restrain its behavior.

Regardless, it is clear that the organizational culture of Sendero–Huallaga differed from that of the movement's other committees. The CRH created an environment in which combatants and commanders benefited on an ongoing basis from the coca trade. Membership in Sendero–Huallaga was prestigious not because it was a sign of political and ideological

---

[79] Ibid., November 14(A,B), 2001.

[80] Noted in Sendero report of August–October 1986, captured Sendero document, 1986, DINCOTE Sendero collection, Lima, Peru; Sendero report of November 1989, captured Sendero document, 1989, DINCOTE Sendero collection, Lima, Peru.

[81] This could be simply a function of the sample of documents that were captured. Given the number of documents and the random events that led to their capture, however, one would imagine that they represent a fair sample of Sendero's secret material. If the CRH had been regularly corrected as much as the other committees were, it should be apparent from these documents.

commitment but instead because it provided access to profits from the coca business. The national leadership was unable to prevent defection by the committee, and the committee's leadership made no visible efforts to break the cycle of opportunism that came to characterize its local operations in the Huallaga Valley.

Conclusion

To be successful in combat, groups must ensure that their members will confront the enemy's forces. To survive in the midst of civilian populations and stem the tide of civilian resistance, moreover, rebel groups must show consistency in their behavior. Ensuring that combatants follow orders is no small challenge for rebel leaders. Combatants face significant risks, and most organizations lack the formal structures and territorial control required to make threats of punishment credible.

This chapter demonstrates that rebel leaders tend to resolve problems of management and organizational control in two ways. Some create an environment in which members can expect that their comrades and commanders share the same long-term goals for the movement. Efforts to build on shared identities or beliefs make these expectations common knowledge. Mechanisms of monitoring, control, and shared decision making provide guarantees that cooperative behavior will be reciprocated. Power can be devolved to subunits without threatening the success of the movement.

Alternatively, groups develop an internal set of relationships organized around short-term rewards. Sustained cooperation among group members is not required for each individual to realize his or her personal objectives. Such groups make limited investments in efforts to coordinate expectations and behaviors, and they show arbitrariness in establishing mechanisms of monitoring and control. Without shared identities or beliefs, there is no basis for shared authority or decision making. The resulting hierarchical structure is either centralized or extremely decentralized.

The membership profile of a rebel group plays a large part in shaping the organizational path that it follows. Principal-agent problems pose a far greater challenge to groups that have been unable to successfully screen out opportunistic joiners. Organizations constructed around long-term goals and those that draw on identities or beliefs to make commitments credible are better placed to establish cooperative norms of interaction.

This argument has the counterintuitive implication that structures of decentralization in rebel organization are associated with more coherent patterns of behavior and more effective levels of internal discipline. By contrast, centralization is a characteristic of (and perhaps a response to) higher levels of indiscipline. In spite of efforts to wield power from the center, centralized organizations exhibit much higher levels of incoherence and inconsistency in the behavior of their combatants.

With a clear understanding of the membership and structure of insurgent movements, I now turn to their interaction with noncombatant populations. I begin in the next chapter by exploring how the diverse organizational cultures established in the earliest stages of conflict affect how rebel groups govern and then focus on how they use force against civilians.

PART II

The Strategies of Rebel Groups

5

Governance

Rebel groups, it is held, depend on civilian populations for their survival. Mao Tse-tung famously asserted that "because guerilla warfare basically derives from the masses and is supported by them, it can neither exist nor flourish if it separates itself from their sympathies and cooperation."[1] Civilians are thought to be central players in insurgency: access to food, shelter, labor, and information depends on their compliance. For this reason, rebel groups often build governing structures that mobilize political support from noncombatants and enable the extraction of key resources.

Institutions for governing civilians emerge as rebel groups begin to hold territory. Territorial control allows rebels to move freely rather than remain in hiding, offers the prospect of regularized interaction with civilians, and sends a strong signal of rebel strength. The control of territory and civilian populations also creates a new organizational challenge for rebel leaders. Civilians are strategic actors, and as such they have the capacity to provide or withhold their participation and support. Noncombatant populations can assist rebel groups by providing the resources groups desire, they can ignore rebel groups, or they can actively resist them by fighting back on their own or by assisting the government. In managing civilians, rebel groups must take into account their desire for security, their need for food and shelter, and their incentives to choose one side over the other.

The National Resistance Army invested in institutions of grassroots democracy. It placed authority and influence in the hands of elected local officials in the communities it governed. The Shining Path also shared power with noncombatants through popular committees that represented civilians' interests to the national movement. Yet in other contexts,

---

[1] Mao Tse-tung, *On Guerrilla Warfare* (Chicago: University of Illinois Press, 1961), p. 44.

structures of governance take on a different character: Renamo resurrected traditional authorities that had been largely discredited in the postcolonial period, while the regional committee in the Upper Huallaga Valley formed a centralized, authoritarian administration that was in many ways reflective of the interests of its constituents.

This chapter focuses on the structures rebel groups create to manage their relationships with civilian populations. It begins by describing variation in the character of rebel governments in practice, drawing attention to two dimensions of difference – the extent of power sharing and the degree of inclusiveness – that merit explanation. It then identifies the incentives that exist for rebel groups to organize governments during conflict and explores how these conditions vary across contexts. In particular, it asks to what extent rebel groups need to bargain with civilians in order to survive and documents the nature of the bargains that groups must strike to solicit compliance in different contexts. Finally, I turn to the cases and explore the construction of governments in rebel-held zones, looking closely at the organization of a food supply, the management of resource extraction, and the formation of a political apparatus. Diverging experiences of civilian control in the four cases help to clarify the causal mechanisms linking group endowments and organizational structures to patterns of governance during civil war.

Variations in Rebel Governance

To capture the diversity of structures of civilian control, I begin with a simple definition of a rebel government. A rebel government exists when and where (1) a rebel group exercises control over territory,[2] (2) it establishes institutions within or outside of its military to manage relations with the civilian population, and (3) these institutions set in place a series of formal or informal rules that define a hierarchy of decision making and a system of taxation.

The interesting variation in rebel governments, it seems, is in their character, and particularly in the extent to which structures of civilian control exhibit the characteristics of democracy. I follow Robert Dahl in thinking about the democratic character of a rebel government in terms of how

---

[2] By "control," I mean that the rebel group has a monopoly on the use of force. It may be that the government can infiltrate the area, but the strongest player is the rebel group.

responsive it is to the preferences of its citizens.[3] Responsiveness, in his formulation, requires that citizens have the necessary freedoms to formulate their preferences, signal them to fellow citizens and the government, and have them weighed equally by the government without reference to their source or content.

Some who have grappled with the definition of democracy point to a series of other basic characteristics that must be satisfied. Philippe Schmitter and Terry Karl argue that although the specific institutions of each democracy may be unique, democracy itself depends on the accountability of rulers to their citizens through a process of contestation and competition. They suggest, moreover, that because the very idea of citizenship is central to democracy, formal and informal restrictions on citizenship are antidemocratic.[4]

Even with simplified definitions of democracy, it is not an easy task to say that one rebel group governs democratically while another employs autocratic means of control. Among forms of governance, there exist innumerable shades of gray. In his classic book, Dahl proposes that regimes be arrayed along two dimensions to assess their democratic character: opposition and participation. Adapting his basic structure to fit the dynamics of rebel governance, I focus on two distinct but not unrelated dimensions of civilian control. The first is the extent of *power sharing*. The two key actors in a rebel-held zone are the rebel army and the civilian population. The rebel army arrives with a preexisting structure of hierarchy and control. The civilian population may also have its own leadership defined by communal structures, ethnic or religious traditions, or the state. In the governments that rebel groups build, a key issue is the extent to which power is shared between the rebel military and the civilian population. A power sharing structure creates a system of checks and balances that enables the civilian population to express its preferences and shape the behavior of the rebel army. Fundamentally, power sharing, or comanagement, is reflective of how responsive the rebels are to the preferences of the citizens they oversee. When power is shared, rebel groups in effect sanction nonviolent contestation and opposition to the policies they set in place.

---

[3] Robert Dahl, *Polyarchy: Participation and Opposition* (New Haven: Yale University Press, 1971).

[4] Philippe Schmitter and Terry Karl, "What Democracy Is...and Is Not," in *The Global Resurgence of Democracy*, eds. Larry Diamond and Marc Plattner (Baltimore: Johns Hopkins University Press, 1993), pp. 49–62.

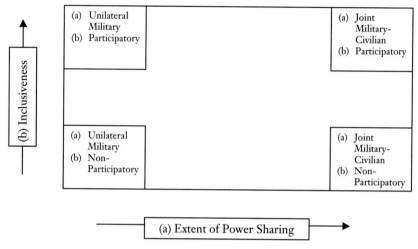

Figure 5.1. Variation in Structures of Civilian Governance

A second dimension is the *inclusiveness* of the rebel government. Just like states, rebel governments vary in the proportion of the population they entitle to participate in political deliberation and contestation regarding the conduct of government. In examining formal state structures, inclusiveness can be measured by looking at how broadly basic rights – including the right to vote, to organize, to hold public meetings, and to participate in the political structure by holding office – are extended to the citizenry. In rebel governments, one can look for similar, more informal indicators by asking if the structure empowers various levels of the civilian population beyond the elite and whether the burdens and benefits of the governing structure are spread widely across the population. While power sharing is a measure of the responsiveness of rebel governments, inclusiveness identifies to whose preferences the government responds. Inclusiveness is obviously more meaningful where power sharing is permitted, but it does not automatically follow. Indeed, governments may represent the preferences of a broad cross section of citizens even as they actively restrict power sharing and contestation.

With these two dimensions, we can sketch out a range of rebel regime types. Figure 5.1 presents the possibilities. On the first dimension – the extent of power sharing – rebel governments vary between those that rule unilaterally and those that put in place structures of joint rule with the civilian population. In terms of inclusiveness, we can think of a range from engaging a small civilian elite to soliciting the broad participation of civilians of all types. Of course, a rebel government might be located anywhere in the space bounded by these dimensions, so the proposed typology only captures ideal types.

These forms of government parallel the ideal types suggested by Dahl. In the lower left corner, where rebel groups rule unilaterally and severely restrict the rights of participation, we have a form of "closed hegemony," or autocratic rule. In the upper right-hand corner, by contrast, where rebel groups comanage geographic zones with civilian partners and extend rights to a broad range of citizens, we find polyarchy, or democracy. These two forms of government are most common, but one also finds rebel groups that severely restrict rights while allowing some contestation among civilian elites (competitive oligarchies) and others that represent a broad array of preferences while ruling unilaterally (inclusive hegemonies). Understanding the conditions under which these various forms of government are likely to develop and exist is the purpose of this chapter.

The Challenges of Rebel Governance

The relationship between rebel groups and civilians parallels that between rulers and constituents in the modern state. Insurgents choose to share power with civilians in some contexts and not in others, to extend participation to large numbers of civilians in some cases, and to restrict involvement to the elite in others. As rebel groups bargain with constituents over the design of political institutions, their incentives to share power and be inclusive vary in important ways.

Douglass North and Barry Weingast argue that constitutions, and political institutions more generally, place restrictions on the state that provide the appropriate incentives for long-term growth and development.[5] Simply put, if a constituent can trust the ruler not to confiscate all the wealth he accumulates, both will be better off. If the constituent believes that the ruler will act in the ruler's self-interest and tax his wealth out of existence, however, he has no incentive to invest in productive activity. North and Weingast show that for productive activity to proceed, "the government must not merely establish the relevant set of rights, but must make a credible commitment to them."[6]

---

[5] Douglass North and Barry Weingast, "Constitutions and Commitment: The Evolution of Institutions Governing Public Choice in Seventeenth-Century England," *Journal of Economic History* 49, no. 4 (December 1989): 803–32.

[6] Ibid., p. 803.

Their example can be generalized to a more fundamental problem of political organization: the state has a comparative advantage in coercion, so what prevents political organizations from using force to extract the entire surplus? Institutions do. Institutions develop because rulers are conscious that greater rewards can be reaped in the long term if they constrain their behavior today. By providing the population with some security, the state can increase its revenue if it strikes a bargain with the population to accept slightly less of the surplus in the short term. Under such conditions, the population will invest its energy in the most productive activities.

Creating Trust

The central problem for rulers seeking to maximize their take is that while political organizations and their constituents have strong incentives to strike a bargain, political leaders often face new incentives after the fact that are incompatible with maintaining the agreement. If constituents are aware of the ex post incentives of political leaders, they will choose not to invest in productive activity.

North and Weingast argue that the primary political problem for a ruler in this context is to find a way to make a credible commitment not to violate the citizen's trust and seize his wealth. Solutions to this problem come in two forms. The first sets a "precedent of responsible behavior" in that the ruler's actions demonstrate his commitment to a set of rules that will be consistently enforced. This solution assumes that the interaction between the ruler and his constituents is repeated. Repetition provides incentives for the ruler to stick by his binding commitments in the short term in order to realize gains in the future. North and Weingast downplay the significance of this solution, arguing that the "pressures and continual strain of fiscal necessity" eventually lead the ruler to violate his agreements with his constituents. Further, repeat play fails to prevent reneging when the ruler heavily discounts the future. One could argue that this exact situation prevails in the context of rebel organizations. I am more sanguine, however, about the prospects of reputational mechanisms, even on their own, for resolving the rebel's challenge.

A second solution is the construction of political institutions. Rulers can knowingly establish and commit to a set of institutions that constrain them to obey a set of rules, with costs applied when those rules are violated. These "constitutions" arise from bargaining between the ruler and his constituents and must be *self-enforcing* in the sense that the parties have an incentive to abide by the agreement after it is made. Institutions act as a constraint on the behavior of the ruler when reputation is insufficient to prevent opportunistic behavior.

What Rebel Groups Do

Rebel groups are not unlike the rulers described by North and Weingast. Like rulers, they exercise a monopoly over the use of the force. They control territory – becoming "stationary bandits" – because repeated interaction offers the promise of far greater rewards.[7] Rebel groups also face incentives to renege on the pledges they make to civilian populations. As a consequence, the organization of cooperative relations requires bargaining and credible agreements between rebel groups and civilian populations.

To realize the long-term rewards that can come from cooperation, rebel leaders participate in the formation of political institutions designed to constrain their self-interested actions, some of which could come at the expense of the civilian population. They set in place structures for the constitutional representation of civilian interests in the governance of a geographic territory. To provide a credible commitment of restraint on the part of the government and participation on the part of civilians, these institutions must have a number of key qualities.

The first is that they establish a structure for joint governance, involving the rebel military and civilians in the process of rule making, resource management, and the provision of public goods. Structures of joint control weaken the ability of the rebel army to unilaterally mandate civilian behavior. They create a check on rebel power and make it more difficult for the rebel leadership to change course in a direction contrary to the interests of the civilian population. Formal or informal rules governing exchange and interaction become more difficult to revise in a context of shared power.

A second quality of the arrangements is that they provide a continued incentive for the rebel government to show restraint in the extraction of

---

[7] Distinguishing between "roving bandits" and "stationary bandits," Mancur Olson makes the case that groups prefer to be stationary if they can exercise a monopoly on force because regular taxation (as opposed to theft) provides the opportunity to realize much greater rewards in the long term. A rational, stationary bandit will take only part of his constituents' income in taxes because over time he will be able to extract a larger total amount. See "Dictatorship, Democracy, and Development," *American Political Science Review* 87 (1993): 567–76.

resources. This incentive is strengthened by a commitment on the part of civilians to make the necessary contributions from their own resources to enable the rebel group to prosper and survive. Regularized yet manageable contribution schedules, like taxes, reinforce the rebel group's expectation that it will be supported. The rebel government is held in check, moreover, by the capacity of civilians to flee, leaving the rebel group without resources.

The commitment of civilians is also reinforced by making governance structures as inclusive as possible so that civilian preferences play a role in shaping choices about how to distribute the burden of contributions and in whom to vest political power in the community. Mechanisms to ensure the buy-in of civilians provide a foundation for cooperation: rebel groups show their commitment by enabling checks and balances to exist, and civilians demonstrate their willingness to participate through broad-based, regular involvement.

Mechanistic designs in the form of political institutions are only the formal component holding up the bargain that rebel groups and civilians strike in designing governments. Informally, cooperation is reinforced through shared beliefs and repeated interaction. I have already established that a critical distinguishing feature of rebel organizations is whether their leadership and membership share beliefs, expectations, and codes of behavior. These foundations of trust emerge from both identity groups and social networks. Where groups are organized around social endowments, the basis for a precedent of responsible behavior already exists in the shared expectations that hold the group together. In building relationships with civilian populations, rebel groups often draw on these norms and beliefs to structure their interactions. Investments in political education or appeals to ethnic, religious, or community symbols are used to draw attention to the preexisting bonds that make trust possible.

The credibility provided by formal institutions is also strengthened over time through repeated interactions in which members of both parties live up to one another's expectations. Accordingly, the rebel group's internal systems of monitoring and control play a critical role in reinforcing the formal institutions of government. When violations of either the formal arrangements or the unstated codes of behavior are committed by rebel leaders or their members, civilians expect that these violations will be punished. In order to preserve a precedent of responsible behavior, the punishment must be consistently applied, and civilians must have knowledge of its application. Where internal systems of control function, credible commitments made by rebel organizations hold, and civilians invest their resources and energies in organizational maintenance.

Why Don't All Groups Strike a Bargain?

Given that formal structures of governance provide the prospect of greater rewards for rebel leaders over the longer term, why do some groups choose not to put in place constitutional arrangements that promote the highest levels of productivity? One possible answer is that governance presents significant costs that some groups are unwilling to bear. Participatory governance, for example, imposes logistical constraints on the operations of a still-emerging insurgency. Rebel commanders find themselves responsible not only for the needs and safety of their units but also for those of civilians, who present their own demands to the rebel leadership, possibly threatening the flexibility of rebel leaders to make strategic choices important to their organizations' survival. Shared governance implies a partial loss of command and control, moreover, making rebel decisions subject to the influence of civilians.

I argue, however, that rebel group strategies have deeper origins: they are shaped by the conditions present at the organization's inception and the types of members who are attracted to participate. Some groups have no choice but to take on the risks posed by shared governance, while other rebel organizations have few incentives to democratize their rebel-civilian relationships. Three factors shape the incentive of groups to strike a bargain with civilians: their stake in the productivity of the civilian population, the time horizons of their members, and their capacity to credibly commit to an agreement with noncombatants.

Some rebel groups have the ability to prosper even when civilians withhold contributions and support.[8] These groups are typically constructed around economic endowments. Because their survival is not fundamentally dependent on civilian support, such groups behave in a more predatory fashion, unconcerned about the reactions of the population.[9] Civilians, aware

---

[8] Oil-rich states in the Middle East and North Africa are in this situation. A large literature on resource-rich states has reinforced the finding that states endowed with access to minerals and oil are more likely to be autocratic and much less likely to share power with the population and create space for political opposition. See Michael Ross, "Does Oil Hinder Democracy?" *World Politics* 53 (2001): 325–61.

[9] Robert Bates, Avner Greif, and Smita Singh make a similar argument in their examination of the factors that lead governments to become predatory rather than to invest in the

of the fact that they cannot pay a bribe large enough to convince the rebel group to restrain itself, have fewer incentives to participate and are more likely to withhold support or even resist. This situation leads to the creation of a governance structure rooted in military control that employs coercion to maintain a semblance of stability and to prevent defection in rebel-controlled zones.

A second factor that affects the incentive of a rebel group to build cooperative governmental structures is the time horizons of its membership. While a rebel group may be organized with the ultimate goal of capturing the state, the interests of its members shape its behavior. Rebel groups differ in the degree to which their members are willing to make short-term investments in the hope of realizing long-term gains. Where rebel participants join to realize short-term gains, groups are less concerned about future losses that may mount in the absence of the development of cooperative governance structures.

The capacity of a rebel group to make a credible commitment also shapes the likelihood of a bargain being reached between rebels and civilians. Because of the short time horizons that predominate in resource-rich rebellions, resource-rich rebel groups have a difficult time selling their membership on the need to trade off restraint for long-term gains. They also face a challenging task in trying to constrain the behavior of individual members, as we saw in the previous chapter. Where defection and inconsistency in behavior characterize organizations, civilians learn quickly that commitments are not credible and promises cannot be trusted. Such groups are more likely to encounter resistance or the withholding of support. The bargaining required to set in place long-term mechanisms of cooperation may never even begin.

Making Government Inclusive

Explaining why rebel governments extend the franchise requires investigating what incentives they have to represent the broadest range of civilian participants in structures of rebel governance. I have already argued that inclusiveness, when combined with formal structures of joint military and civilian control, strengthens the credibility of rebels' commitments to

long-term growth of their societies. See "Organizing Violence," *Journal of Conflict Resolution* 46 (2002): 599–628.

restrain their behavior. Broad-based participation creates opportunities for large numbers of civilians to express their preferences and to challenge the choices made by their own leadership and by that of the rebels. An extended franchise also makes it more difficult for rebel groups to change course without lobbying for the support of civilians as part of the decision-making process. As rebel groups seek to set in place democratic structures of control, comanagement and inclusiveness tend to move together. But inclusiveness – the breadth of the citizenry represented by the government – also appears as a characteristic of groups that do not employ joint structures of governance. Where groups are constructed around economic endowments, they may not face the same incentives to share power, but may still require broad-based participation for their survival. The extent to which groups of this type extend participation depends on the nature of the resource being extracted from the population.

As I discussed in Chapter 1, economic endowments come in many shapes and sizes. External support provides cash and weaponry that can be immediately put to use in rebels' operations. Revenues realized from natural resources require labor for extraction, an investment in transportation and export, and a time lag before financial rewards can be channeled into the organization. Economic gains from agricultural products also require labor, depend on the climate and harvest, and are subject to shocks from droughts and market price fluctuations. One dimension on which economic endowments differ, then, is the extent of civilian labor required for their extraction or production. Civilian populations must be organized to some extent in order to realize the gains from the extraction or production of a particular resource. Resources generated from external patrons require little if any civilian labor, so groups with such support remain largely independent of civilian populations for their survival. But where the realization of revenues from economic endowments requires civilian labor, rebel groups tend to build structures that are more broadly participatory, even if they lack mechanisms for sharing significant power.

A participatory structure of governance in which power is not shared is inherently contradictory. Large numbers of citizens are involved in maintaining the rebel government, but joint control is severely restricted. Rather than a partnership, it is a symbiotic relationship in which civilians have their interests represented by the government but have little direct leverage over the policies it sets in place. This may be a highly unstable form of governance in the long term, but as the case of the CRH makes clear, rebel groups *can* advocate for the interests of the broader citizenry, providing them with opportunities to be engaged, while they simultaneously prevent citizens from actively comanaging the rebellion.

Organizing the Food Supply

While it is important to challenge the assumption that rebel groups are uniformly dependent on civilian populations for their survival and to show the ways in which this dependence varies across contexts, it is fair to say that most rebel organizations rely on the population for the provision of food. But the need to extract food is not sufficient to provide incentives for all rebel groups to construct power sharing and participatory arrangements with civilians. The question is why.

The organization of a food supply is often the first motivation for interacting with civilian populations in civil war. From the very beginning, rebel groups need sources of sustenance because they abandon their farms and homesteads to join the rebellion. But the production of food for survival creates a different set of incentives than those present with respect to the production of agricultural goods for export, the extraction of resources, or labor investments in the movement itself.

While rebel leaders organize power in a way that allows them to maximize what they net through the taxation of civilians, the provision of food for survival depends only on a minimal level of contribution. Because agricultural products used for subsistence do not tend to provide revenue for rebel movements, leaders show little concern to create the conditions for the sustained, productive cultivation of food. Groups want to be sure that they can collect the food they need to survive on a day-to-day basis, but this only requires that the burden on civilians be manageable.

Civilians, too, are conscious of the need for food production. If they did not grow their own crops, there would be no source of subsistence for most of the rural peasants embroiled in civil war. Consequently, withholding labor from food production is not realistically an option of resistance. The only threat that civilians can mount is that of flight. By extricating themselves from rebel-controlled zones, they can leave rebel groups in the position of needing to produce their own food.

The resulting bargain between rebel groups and civilians – regardless of their initial endowments – balances the subsistence needs of the rebel group against those of the civilian population. Civilians play a role in shaping the food collection system where formal political institutions provide them with an opportunity to affect policy. But where no such system exists, civilians continue to provide food as long as their own subsistence is protected. The need to gather food is not a sufficient incentive, in most cases, to restrain the behavior of rebel groups.

Rebel Governments in Practice

To explore how rebel governments manage civilian populations in practice, we return to the stories of the four rebel organizations around which this book is built. Each rebel group confronted the challenge of building a government with different tools at its disposal – distinct endowments, differing memberships, and unique organizational structures – and these differences shaped the processes of governance they put in place.

Mobilizing a Grassroots Democracy: The NRA

Like other rebel leaders in Africa and beyond, Yoweri Museveni articulated the conventional wisdom about the link between the NRA and the population. Writing in the *Uganda Resistance News* during the war, Museveni explained:

> The population is the one which gives us food, shelter, and intelligence information about the movement of enemy troops. We are both educating our soldiers in practical and every day examples that it is the people who matter in this exercise. The NRA has learnt that without the support of the people, it cannot carry out the struggle alone, and successfully. At the same time, the population knows that without the effective defence from [the] NRA the enemy would harass [them], rape their womenfolk, destroy their property with impunity, kill them and eventually make their struggle a failure.[10]

It is striking that the leader of the NRA made the connection between his own movement's dependence on civilian support and its need to provide security to maintain continued cooperation with noncombatants. Only by presenting a different face than that of the government and protecting the population from the government's crimes could the NRA build a movement with its roots in the civilian population. In fact, the NRA, in discussing the importance of political education, argued that civilians must understand

---

[10] *Mission to Freedom: Uganda Resistance News, 1981–1985* (Kampala: Directorate of Information and Mass Mobilisation, NRM Secretariat, 1990), p. 151.

"the aims and objectives of the Movement, the cause of the struggle, what we expect the people to do for the struggle, the dangers involved in accepting to join the Movement, and the material weakness of the Movement, i.e. [its] lack of adequate supplies of arms and ammunition, money, and uniforms, etc."[11] Little effort was made to hide the movement's weakness from the population. No false promises were made. Risks were shared openly, needs were identified, and the population came to understand what participation would entail and what benefits might be realized in the longer term. To reinforce the expectations of mutual exchange between the rebel army and the civilian population, the NRA instituted a formal democratization of local government that enshrined power sharing arrangements with noncombatants. These new forms of local government, later called resistance councils, transformed local hierarchies and fundamentally altered the balance of power between rulers and the masses.

The Baganda of the Luwero Triangle had been governed by a highly centralized system of chieftainships first instituted by the Baganda Kingdom and later reinforced by British colonial rule. A hierarchy of chiefs governed each community: a county chief, a sub–county chief, and a parish chief. Below this formal hierarchy, a number of unofficial minor chiefs – the *batongole* – dedicated their energies to maintaining order and ensuring productivity at the community level. The batongole were not officially appointed from the center like the other chiefs but instead were remunerated in kind at the local level by the peasants under their jurisdiction.[12]

Within the Baganda Kingdom and under colonial rule, this system of administration offered little opportunity for people to participate in the management of their affairs. Orders devolved from above down the chain of command from the center to the chiefs. Chiefs could report concerns to the centralized administration, but most did not see themselves as advocates for their constituents. Mahmood Mamdani captures the sentiments of the peasants in describing the system of taxation: "If you were a peasant in a village and it was taxation time, the chief is the person who assessed your property. The chief decided how much tax you would pay. If you thought you had been unfairly assessed, you appealed to the chief. The chief decided on that appeal."[13]

---

[11] The National Resistance Movement, *The 6th of February* 1, February 1987, p. 13.

[12] S. R. Karugire, *The Roots of Instability in Uganda* (Kampala: New Vision, 1988), p. 14.

[13] Mahmood Mamdani, "The Politics of Democratic Reform in Uganda," *Africa World Review*, May–September 1994, p. 41.

Although efforts were made to democratize the chieftainship structure after independence, much of its dictatorial character remained. After coming to power in 1980, the Uganda People's Congress enjoined local chiefs in a campaign of intimidation in the Luwero Triangle. Aided by party officials and by members of the UPC's Youth Wing, chiefs harassed the local population, trying to identify supporters of the rebels and threatening to kill those who resisted. By the time the NRA arrived in the Triangle, the hierarchical structure of chiefs already faced a crisis of legitimacy.

In this context, the NRA set in place a structure of local government that put power squarely in the hands of the civilian population. The resistance council structure was a revolutionary reconfiguration of local power. Each community was to be governed by a locally elected committee of members. The committees included a chairman, vice chairman, secretary, mobilizer, and a person in charge of defense.[14] The RCs thus empowered civilians to make decisions about their own communities, replacing the institution of the chiefs. Elections ensured that committees were representative, and the population had the power to recall the RC members if they were dissatisfied.

The NRA's Ten-Point Programme described the functions of the RC system:

The Committees could deal with law-breakers in cooperation with the chiefs and police, take part in discussing local development projects with government officials but, above all, they would be political forums to discuss relevant issues concerning the whole country and act as forums against the corruption and misuse of office by chief government officials.... they would be a channel of communication between top and bottom.[15]

Even though the RC system was designed as a check on the power of a hierarchical structure, at its inception it faced the threat of capture by holders of power in the previous system. The NRA's approach to the construction of these institutions, however, ensured that the new RCs would be representative. From the beginning, the rebel army approached the baton-gole chiefs and other elders around them, as they were the one level of the hierarchy that credibly operated with civilian consent.[16] A former guerrilla explained that secret committees in the area were chaired by opinion leaders, people with networks that could form the foundation of a power base in

---

[14] Interview, Semuto, November 15(A), 18(B), 2000.
[15] Yoweri Museveni, *Selected Articles on the Uganda Resistance War* (Kampala: NRM Publications, 1986), pp. 50–51.
[16] Interview, Semuto, November 18(B), 2000.

the community.[17] The NRA constructed these committees secretly at first, fearing their infiltration by the UPC in the Triangle. A soldier, preferably one from the local community, would be charged with approaching relatives and friends in the village one by one. These initial contacts were encouraged to identify "others of good character" and to invite them to join the movement.[18] Political education was central to these first interactions, with the guerrillas explaining the reasons for the war and outlining the ways in which they would need assistance. As soon as the NRA established effective control of the Triangle, the secret committees were made public. Elections were held out in the open, often by asking community members to line up behind their candidate of choice.[19] Although anonymity was not preserved using this method, there was no doubt about the identity of the victor.

The committees were used first and foremost to organize the provision of food for the nascent insurgency. Hiding in the bush, the rebels had little capacity to produce their own food and were wholly dependent on the contributions of the civilian population. As long as the money gathered before the insurgency lasted, the rebels sought to pay directly for their food. The NRA "paid for everything," Museveni explained, "because [its members] did not want to use 'voluntary contributions' from the peasants for fear of the system being abused."[20] The NRA's monetary resources were depleted quickly, however, and the rebels turned to the civilian population for support.

Here, the structure of the committees became important. Because they were composed of opinion leaders, often those with access to land and resources, the RCs faced little resistance in gathering contributions from the villagers. Typically, those with surplus food tended to give; villagers who struggled to meet their subsistence needs were not forced to contribute.[21] Wealthy individuals became regular sources of food and other goods, and the rebels recorded their contributions diligently, promising to compensate them at the end of the war.[22] Most wealthy peasants gave willingly. The RC structure enabled the NRA to keep the military out of food collection.[23]

---

[17] Ibid., November 23(A), 2000.
[18] Ibid., November 17(B,C), 20(B), 21(A), 2000.
[19] Ibid., November 21(A,C), 22(A), 24(B); interview, Kampala, November 2(A), 2000.
[20] Yoweri Museveni, *Sowing the Mustard Seed: The Struggle for Freedom and Democracy in Uganda* (London: Macmillan, 1997), p. 132.
[21] Interview, Semuto, November 18(B), 2000.
[22] Ibid., November 17(C), 19(C), 20(B).
[23] Ibid., November 15(A), 2000.

Soldiers never wandered into the village or stopped at civilians' houses in search of food. This system reduced the potential for corruption and ensured that the demand for food was not unmanageable either for the community or for any individual household.

While resistance committees broadened civilian participation in governance, they also created a power sharing structure that involved the rebel military and the civilian population jointly in the control of territory. RCs could have been created simply as a tool of propaganda to take power away from the coercive system of chiefs, but the NRA purposefully gave the RCs political power to create a check on the military's control of civilian life. The RCs provided a forum for political dialogue and debate about the progress of the war and issues that arose in the management of the Luwero Triangle. Political commissars from the NRA called together the leaders of multiple RCs on a regular basis in the form of an overall committee to share reports of military progress and solicit the perspective of the NRA's civilian supporters.[24] But fundamentally, "the committees oversaw the administration of the civilians, not the soldiers."[25]

Beyond creating a space for the expression of preferences, the RC system was also designed to check formally the power of the military. RCs were organized as the grassroots arms of the National Resistance Council, the overarching political leadership of the movement, which was composed of both military and civilian members. Leaders of the RC system, clandestine political supporters in Kampala, and prominent political intellectuals formed the foundation of the NRC. Its membership was 60 percent civilian and 40 percent military leaders from the NRA. During the war, the NRC sat jointly with the Army Council in planning strategy and focusing on the governance of rebel territories.[26]

At the local level, political commissars served as the link between the military wing of the NRA and the RC system. Commissars invested their energies in organizing community meetings, at which they shared the political goals of the movement and helped the civilians to organize effective committees. Commissars channeled the concerns of the civilian population to the military leadership. But civilians also felt comfortable taking their concerns directly to the military leadership when necessary.[27] As we

---

[24] Ibid., November 17(B,C), 19(A), 20(B), 2000.

[25] Ibid., November 14(A), 2000.

[26] Ondoga Ori Amaza, *Museveni's Long March from Guerrilla to Statesman* (Kampala: Fountain, 1998), p. 47.

[27] Interview, Semuto, November 15(A), 2000.

learned in the last chapter, the military leadership quickly and consistently addressed civilians' concerns about rebel misbehavior. At the high point of security in the liberated zone in 1983, a senior army official estimated that the NRA governed through 2,000 to 3,000 RCs, each representing 40 homes.[28]

Fundamentally, the NRA maintained civilian support by providing public goods in exchange for civilian contributions. Civilians recalled two types of goods. The first was security. The NRA used the RC system to set in place a network of local militias to warn villages of approaching UNLA soldiers. Although the militias were not armed and therefore rarely engaged UNLA soldiers directly, they alerted villagers and the rebels about impending attacks, enabling civilians to flee to safety and the rebels to organize a counterattack. The NRA encouraged the development of militias by taking defense representatives of the RCs to camps for military training and then by assisting them in the organization of observation points around the villages.[29]

The NRA also delivered a basic set of health care services to its constituents in the Triangle. Doctors in the NRA became concerned that serious health problems, including malaria, intestinal worms, tuberculosis, venereal diseases, and dysentery, were developing in the liberated zones because lack of security had made the resupply of health posts impossible. The senior leadership of the NRA organized a training program to create a cadre of medical aides to work in the liberated communities. Aides focused on basic skills, including first aid, sanitation, and how to identify emergency medical conditions. The NRA also attacked government health posts and stores to provide the resources for this health campaign. Importantly, in the provision of health care, no distinction was made between civilians and soldiers. The coordinator of the campaign recalled that "the peasants were amazed, and many thought that if the NRA could work these miracles in the bush, they would be a good government."[30] Such investments in the health of civilians under its control demonstrated the NRA's sustained interest in the welfare of the civilian population. In terms of improved security and health care, civilians realized returns on their contributions to the movement.

[28] Interview, Kampala, November 7(A), 2000.
[29] Interviews, Semuto, November 17(B,C), 19(A,B,C), 2000.
[30] Interview, Kampala, October 27(A), 2000.

Resurrecting Traditional Authorities: Renamo

While the NRA democratized local systems of governance in rebel-held zones, Renamo reestablished structures of hierarchical control in villages by returning power to the colonial and precolonial régulos, community-level chiefs who were much more like traditional authorities than administrators. Based on Renamo's propaganda, one would have expected an alternative strategy of local governance. Rejecting Frelimo's attempts to force peasants into party committees and communal villages, Renamo called openly for the advent of multiparty democracy, free and fair elections, and a broad range of freedoms for civilians. But at the local level, Renamo leaders spoke little of such matters. Instead, they placed régulos firmly in control.

Some have characterized this approach to governance as a political appeal. Frelimo, in implementing a plan for socialist transformation in the countryside, had rejected the preexisting arrangements that governed peasant life. The party excluded traditional authorities from power, ceding control to outsiders; forced peasants to leave their land and to live in communal villages; and strictly limited the opportunities that were available to peasants to produce and market their products, buy consumer goods, and move freely from place to place. Many civilians felt that régulos were wrongly stereotyped as discredited collaborators with the colonial regime. Some analysts believe that Renamo responded to this political situation by reasserting the rights of régulos and the peasantry: by putting the régulos back in power, Renamo capitalized on peasant discontent with the policies of villagization and the imposition of rules from above.[31] Régulos represented a return to freedom and tradition in the eyes of many peasants.

There is little debate that Renamo relied heavily on traditional structures to govern civilian populations. Villagers described how Renamo would arrive in a community and explain to people that it was "reestablishing the old structure, that people no longer had to live in villages, or participate in the party."[32] When the new Renamo general arrived in Ribáuè, a civilian recalled that he asked, "Who was in charge here in colonial times?"[33] He was directed to a man named Metaveia, a traditional leader in the area.

[31] Christian Geffray, *La cause des armes: Anthropologie de la guerre contemporaine au Mozambique* (Paris: Karthala, 1990).

[32] Interviews, Marínguè, Sofala Province, May 18(B), 21(A), 2001; interviews, Ribáuè, Nampula Province, April 1(B), 4(B), 2001.

[33] Interview, Ribáuè, Nampula Province, April 1(B), 2001.

The general and other Renamo leaders explained their cause and requested Metaveia's support and his traditional blessings to operate in the region. This same approach was used in community after community.[34]

But Renamo coupled this reinforcing of traditional structures with a stated aim to "form a popular government, not implemented by force, negotiated with the people, and through elections."[35] This is how civilians remember its platform. "The country needed to be democratic, that people should have rights and freedoms, they should not be intimidated," one former combatant explained.[36]

This apparent contradiction is less troubling if we look beneath the surface. Democracy, at least at the local level, was not really a goal of Renamo's rebel army. Nor was strengthening and working through traditional structures. Although the reappointment of régulos was an effective political appeal, it was also a strategy aimed at centralizing political control in a hierarchical structure and limiting both the participation of civilians and their capacity to shape the trajectory of the organization.

A variety of evidence supports this theory. First, across rural communities, Renamo sought to appoint rebel-friendly régulos. Many traditional leaders, out of fear or opportunism, had joined Frelimo's local party organizations, realizing that the only alternative was the loss of political power. Frelimo allowed this to happen, seeing it as a way to boost its credibility in the villages. As a result, in many villages, régulos did not immediately welcome the arrival of Renamo. In establishing local structures of governance, Renamo worked only with cooperative régulos, and it appointed new régulos where it encountered resistance.[37]

The traditional administration also provided a ready-made structure of authority that civilians could easily understand and would respect. Villages under the authority of régulos were further subdivided into smaller units and managed by the régulos' deputies, the *cabos de terra* and *chefes de povacão*. With this basic administrative structure, Renamo could control the

---

[34] Interview, Marínguè, Sofala Province, May 19(A), 2001.

[35] Interview, Ribáuè, Nampula Province, March 27(A), 2001.

[36] Ibid., March 30(A), 2001.

[37] I was told of examples of this behavior in each of the communities in which I conducted field research. In Ribáuè, Metaveia was appointed chief régulo because Tarrua was not a supporter of the rebels. Metaveia had only been a low-level chefe de povacão previously (ibid., April 4(B), 2001). The same situation presented itself in Marínguè, where Biasooni was appointed régulo because the son of the previous leader was not interested in supporting Renamo (interview, Marínguè, Sofala Province, May 25(A), 2001).

population, direct its movement, organize the collection of resources, and punish defection, all without expending the energy and labor of the rebel army.

Third, Renamo made a show of cultivating support from the régulos, but their consent and assistance were not required for Renamo's governance system to function. When régulos were not supportive, they were simply replaced. During Renamo attacks, régulos, cabos, and chefes sometimes found their spouses abducted, their houses looted, and themselves forcibly displaced.[38] As I will argue in the next chapter, Renamo applied force indiscriminately, paying little attention even to the authority structures that it had helped to resurrect.

The most important evidence that a renewed traditional system of leadership was nothing more than a political appeal to villagers, however, was Renamo's unilateral approach to governance. Régulos were not given political authority; they merely received their titles in exchange for cooperation. No forum existed for constructive debate, civilian perspectives were rarely aired, and traditional leaders served at the will of the rebel army. Governance was not joint and did not involve power sharing. There was no formal check on the actions of the rebel leadership.

The central task of the régulos was to manage the life of the civilian population. Traditional leaders organized the displaced and forcibly abducted, distributing them on their arrival in Renamo zones to different plots of land.[39] They managed the collection of food on a regular basis to be provided to combatants living in the rebels' base. And they appointed *mudjibas* – local militias – to maintain order at the rebels' behest. Such militias were effectively an extension of the guerrilla army, as all the mudjibas went for military training, and they focused less on protecting the security of the population than on enforcing the rules laid down by Renamo in cooperation with the traditional leaders.[40]

Civilians had little access to the rebels. As one former combatant explained, "The people didn't live in a Renamo base; they lived a safe distance away, but under the control of the guerrillas."[41] The only people who had regular access to rebel soldiers were the régulos and the mudjibas. A full separation of the two parties might have been a sound approach to prevent

---

[38] Interview, Ribáuè, Nampula Province, March 31(C), 2001.
[39] Ibid., April 1(B), 2001.
[40] Ibid., April 5(C), 2001; interview, Marínguè, Sofala Province, May 20(A), 2001.
[41] Interview, Ribáuè, Nampula Province, March 31(A), 2001.

indiscipline and protect security, but exclusion was effectively a one-way affair. Rebels could move freely among the civilian population, and they used this freedom, as we will see in the next chapter, to demand food, take "wives," and harass the people. Renamo restricted civilian access as a way of limiting participation in and influence on the rebels' activities.

Moreover, the channels of political education and communication that played an important role in airing preferences and debating approaches in Uganda did not exist in Mozambique. While Renamo bases often had political commissars of some sort, they were typically from another part of the country, without connections in the local area. They forged relationships largely with the régulos, and rarely engaged the civilian population in conversation.[42]

Finally, unlike the National Resistance Army, Renamo did not allow for shared military-civilian governance of the movement as a whole. While the NRA relied on the National Resistance Council to articulate and represent the demands and interests of the population, Renamo generated its policy entirely within the military hierarchy. To improve its international image, Renamo held a National Political Congress during the war, but it brought together almost exclusively senior military commanders and rebel soldiers.[43] For Renamo, the governance of civilians was a military task. Régulos were given leadership positions, but they served at the will of the Renamo leadership, followed orders from the military, and had little autonomy to resist or reshape the strategies of the rebels.

These dynamics – unilateral military control and coercive governance – played out in the politics of food collection. Like most rebel armies, Renamo eventually arrived at a system for regularizing the collection of food. But it was a system characterized by what civilians perceived as an onerous burden with little flexibility, and it was subject to regular abuse by rebel soldiers. In the initial stages of the struggle, Renamo soldiers gathered food in an ad hoc manner. Sometimes, they would approach régulos and ask for assistance from the villagers.[44] On most occasions, however, Renamo combatants simply showed up at people's homes asking for food. One civilian recalled that "people were continually forced to give food to the soldiers

---

[42] Ibid., March 30(D), 2001.
[43] Alex Vines, *Renamo: Terrorism in Mozambique* (Bloomington: Indiana University Press, 1991).
[44] Interviews, Ribáuè, Nampula Province, March 27(A), April 1(B), 3(B), 2001.

who visited their houses."[45] The problem with this ad hoc system is that it did not distribute the burden of supporting the rebels evenly. One family might be visited regularly while another was ignored. Moreover, civilians had little idea of the cause to which they were contributing. They gave largely because a soldier showed up at their door with a gun.

By 1985, when the rebel army was fully operative in most of the country, the rebels were managing food collection through an organized system of *blocos*.[46] Within each bloco (an administrative unit of territory), an individual gathered a specified amount of food from each family to deliver to the rebels. Every family participated in the process. There was no option not to participate. If a family could not provide its mandated contribution one week, it would have to give double the next week.[47] "If someone didn't give, they would be taken to the soldiers by the leader of the bloco and asked if they did or did not have food," one civilian recalled. "If they insisted they did not, they would be killed."[48] Even within this organized structure, some civilians found the burden unmanageable. No effort was made to distinguish between those who could afford to contribute and those who were unable. The rebel army was sizable and concentrated, moreover, which burdened small groups of civilians with responsibility for feeding large numbers of soldiers. Sometimes, rebel bases contained more than one thousand soldiers at a single point in time.[49] The bloco system also failed to prevent abuses committed by individual soldiers. As a consequence, the transition from an ad hoc arrangement to organized collection did little to relieve the burden on particular families. One civilian explained, "If there were some people who did not get food [in the base], they would simply ask the population to provide additional food."[50]

Renamo's coercive and hierarchical system of governance enabled such exploitation to continue unimpeded. People could flee, but in doing so they risked execution. The mudjibas and rebel soldiers actively sought to

---

[45] Interview, Marínguè, Sofala Province, May 24(B), 2001.

[46] Conflicting perspectives were presented about the origins of the bloco system. Soldiers explained that it was organized by the Renamo hierarchy to ease the collection of food and was then instituted nationwide. Civilians, on the other hand, claimed that they demanded a regularized system for collecting food and that blocos were organized as a response. Ibid., May 20(A,B,C), 21(A), 24(B), 2001.

[47] Ibid., May 21(A,D,E), 23(B), 2001.

[48] Ibid., May 23(B), 2001.

[49] Interview, Ribáuè, Nampula Province, March 30(D), 2001.

[50] Ibid., March 31(B), 2001.

prevent defection to the other side. And given the coercive structure of Frelimo administration, it was not entirely clear that life was better under the government's protection. Unconstrained by the threat of exit, then, Renamo was able to prevent wholesale civilian defection in spite of its governance strategy.

In this context of unilateral governance and limited participation, Renamo did little to provide public goods in exchange for civilian labor and contributions. A Renamo civilian administration did not take shape until 1988, at which point the organization began to train teachers and medical aides to send into rebel-held communities.[51] The leadership also created a national administration with directorates for agriculture, internal administration, education, health, information, and external relations – in effect, a shadow government.[52] One might take these actions as evidence of the disciplining of the Renamo leadership. But I would assert another explanation that is more plausible in light of Renamo's strategy with regard to civilians from the beginning: The civilian administration came into being just as the international spotlight began to shine on the ongoing civil war in Mozambique. In advance of the peace talks, Renamo sought to improve its image worldwide and to gain access to promised resources from the Red Cross, which would provide food, health care, and support to civilian populations in its zones. For Renamo to make a credible claim to national leadership at the peace talks, it needed to demonstrate that it controlled territory, governed populations, and was capable of providing services. The civilian administration developed not as a consequence of civilian demands, then, but as a strategic choice by the leadership to improve Renamo's image abroad.

An Alternative to Elite Democracy: Sendero Luminoso Nacional

Observers of the insurgency in Peru often point to a puzzle that, in the context of the trajectories of rebel groups in much of the world, merits explanation: Why did Sendero Luminoso take up arms at the exact moment at which the military government handed power to democratically elected civilian officials?[53] Analysts often identify repression and closed systems of

---

[51] Interview, Maríngue, Sofala Province, May 19(D), 2001.

[52] Ibid., May 24(B), 2001.

[53] James Ron tackles this puzzle directly, arguing that the Shining Path sought during a period of increased openness to differentiate itself from other leftist groups and reinvigorate the protest movement within the country. Ron suggests, moreover, that the turn to violence would not have happened if the leadership of Sendero had not embraced a radical worldview

government as key sources of insurgency; rarely do the opposite situations of openness and democracy give rise to revolution. This puzzle has a bearing on how we think about the Shining Path's strategies of governance in rebel-held zones, as these strategies should be indicative of whether Sendero's rejection of the national elections was a rejection of broad, participatory governance.

The evidence suggests that the Shining Path sought to bring about a fundamental revolution in governance at the local level. Changes in electoral rules, the incorporation of the elite political Left, a transition from military control – none of these were sufficient transformations in the eyes of Sendero Luminoso's political leadership. In rebel-held zones, the Shining Path built structures of governance that broadened participation beyond elite intellectuals; created overlapping institutions of control where power was shared between the military, the party, and the local administration; and drew resources from the civilian population in manageable and accepted ways. In spite of its rejection of national democracy, the Shining Path brought about a democratic reorganization of political participation at the local level. Fundamental to this strategy of governance was the involvement of a broad range of civilians in each community.

The peasants of Peru were experiencing a dramatic shift in the distribution of power and wealth even prior to Sendero's emergence. The agrarian reforms implemented by the military government in the 1970s redistributed land to hundreds of thousands of peasant workers, breaking down the structure of haciendas that had come to define political power and wealth.[54] But these benefits barely reached into the highlands where Sendero put in its roots. The arid, windswept provinces where Sendero mobilized the population lacked the prosperous haciendas of the coastal areas. Most of the beneficiaries of agrarian reform were peasants who lived far from the poor Andean regions.

The Shining Path's arrival promised a social mobility that Andean peasants had not yet experienced. As one civilian described it: "They said that Ayacucho was going to be a liberated zone by 1985. A famous illusion they created among the muchachos was, way back in 1981, that by '85 there would be an independent republic. Wouldn't you like to be minister?

---

that saw armed struggle as central to political change. See "Ideology in Context: Explaining Sendero Luminoso's Tactical Escalation," *Journal of Peace Research* 38, no. 5 (September 2001): 569–92.

[54] Cynthia McClintock, *Revolutionary Movements in Latin America: El Salvador's FMLN and Peru's Shining Path* (Washington, DC: U.S. Institute of Peace Press, 1998), p. 175.

Wouldn't you like to be a military chief? Be something, no?"[55] To people who had been consistently left out of Peru's prosperity and the efforts to broaden its distribution, these promises were meaningful, and the Shining Path acted in concrete ways to demonstrate that its commitment to the peasantry went beyond promises: it empowered community members in local governance. As the movement built support within villages, the rebels established *comités populares abiertos* (open people's committees) composed entirely of people from the community.[56] These committees replaced pre-existing structures of the national administration. In many communities, the very establishment of a comité popular abierto was a sign that Sendero was providing political power to many who had previously been excluded from its exercise.[57]

The national hierarchy provided clear directions about the tasks assigned to the leadership of the open committees. The secretary general's duties – to be carried out "openly," like the duties of all other secretaries – were to direct the committee, meet with its other officers, and create "a plan for governance" in conjunction with them. The secretary of security was charged with creating "a plan of defense for the Open Committee and the vigilance of the organization," as well as with "working every day and night with men, women, and children" to "undertake the 'cleaning' of traitors and strange elements." "Planning and organizing collective planting and the distribution of seeds" fell to the secretary of production, while the secretary of justice was responsible for dealing with "injuries, litigation, and [the placement of] sanctions." Material "captured in attacks on medicine posts" was to be "turned in to the Open Committee for centralization," and the secretary of education was called on to "organize the basic schools with language, math, social science, and natural science." The secretary of popular organizations, finally, organized civilians into groups to "articulate their demands specifically to the Open Committee through the Assembly of Representatives," which met twice a month.[58] Sendero documentation makes it clear that positions on the open committees were not simply titular.

[55] Quoted in Carlos Iván Degregori, "Harvesting Storms: Peasant *Rondas* and the Defeat of Sendero Luminoso in Ayacucho," in *Shining and Other Paths: War and Society in Peru, 1980–1995*, ed. Steve J. Stern (Durham: Duke University Press, 1988), p. 130.
[56] Interviews, Huanta, Ayacucho, December 1(D), 3(A,C,E), 4(C), 5(A), 2001.
[57] Ibid., December 2(A), 2001.
[58] In "Sobre el balance de la aplicación de la primera campaña del Plan de Impulsar el Desarollo de las Bases de Apoyo," captured Sendero document, February 1990, DINCOTE Sendero collection, Lima, Peru.

Participation involved exercising leadership and authority and making a real commitment to the governance of the civilian population in line with the principles of the movement.

For the Shining Path, the broadening of participation also involved the full incorporation of civilian participants into the rebel movement. Sendero expected its civilian members to excel in political education in the popular schools, to demonstrate physical fitness in preparation for military attacks, and to strive continually to improve their political and ideological orientation. Advancement within the civilian structure of self-governance in the villages depended on merit, not on wealth or connections.

The incorporation of civilians into the governing structure, the party, and the military demonstrates the extent to which governance in rebel-held zones was a joint project of rebels and civilians. The distinction between civilian supporters and rebel soldiers that was so evident in Uganda and Mozambique was often less clear in Peru. Community members participated in popular schools, they conducted physical conditioning to prepare for the insurgency, and they organized resources to support the movement. In military terms, the civilian population was the fuerza base. But the civilian population was also seen as the supporters of Sendero's political movement and the face of its new state. In this respect, to make a sharp distinction between the rebel government and the civilian population unfairly characterizes the arrangement of life in Sendero zones.

The overlapping structure of power created by Sendero is evident in the dual responsibilities of the secretaries in the open committees. A captured party document describes their role: "The secretary of the cell is at one time the political commander of the military and the secretary general of the Open Committee; the subsecretary of the cell is at once the military commander of the military and the secretary of security of the Open Committee."[59] Individuals participated alternately as soldiers, party members, and governors in their communities. The Shining Path made it quite clear, however, that the true power lay jointly with the secretary general and the secretary of security:

The secretary general and of security are the political commander and military commander of the base force but are not militants.... To mount an armed force, we have a principle: that of two commanders.... there is a military commander who commands the military organization ... and there is also a political commander ... who

[59] "Notas sobre el Plan del 'Gran Salto,'" captured Sendero document, August–October 1986, DINCOTE Sendero collection, Lima, Peru.

monitors the orders of the Party, who ensures the politicization of the members of the military, and who manages the work of the masses, who allow for the armed apparatus in which he works.[60]

Military commanders and the needs of the military organization were subject to the directions and desires of the political leadership.[61] The Shining Path did not see the possibility of armed struggle in the absence of engagement with the civilian population. Open committees were the foundation of a popular support base. Military units – those forces actually waging the war on a day-to-day basis – traveled from one support base to another, as if operating in their own republic.[62]

Sendero's overlapping structures of power significantly eased the collection of resources required for the organization's survival. The integration of civilians into every aspect of the Shining Path meant that the dynamics of exchange – the extraction of civilian-held resources and the provision of benefits by the rebel group – was often not an issue of contention in Sendero-governed communities. The Shining Path did not require resources from civilians on a regular basis, largely because the base force that protected the rebel-held zone (and governed it) was made up entirely of community members. People produced their own food. It was unnecessary to collect it.

The open committees turned to the civilian population for contributions only when the community played host to traveling units of higher-level military forces.[63] These full-time rebel soldiers received nourishment and shelter from supportive community members as they made their way from one support base to another. This burden was eminently manageable and stands in stark contrast to the requirements of civilian populations living, for example, outside of a Renamo base with over one thousand permanent soldiers.

To the extent that the Shining Path imposed structures of resource management on the civilian population, it did so with an eye toward redistributing wealth. This was a popular approach. Sendero approached shop and factory owners, wealthy cattle herders, and rich agricultural producers demanding *cupos*, a form of revolutionary tax.[64] Of course, the payment

---

[60] "IV Conferencia Nacional," captured Sendero document, August–October 1986, DIN-COTE Sendero collection, Lima, Peru.
[61] Interview with Benedicto Jiménez, former chief of DINCOTE, Lima, October 2001.
[62] Interview, Huanta, Ayacucho, December 1(B,D), 2001.
[63] Ibid., December 1(D), 4(A,C), 5(A), 2001.
[64] Ibid., December 2(A), 3(C), 2001.

of cupos was not optional; however, paying the tax was often a guarantee of one's survival. Even in spite of this tax collection, Sendero militants lived in absolute poverty, "often asking for clothes" just to keep themselves covered.[65]

Centralized production was another aspect of resource management, although it is difficult to tell how widely it was applied in practice. Theoretically, the Central Committee charged the open committees with "[making] a classification of the land and [defining] the percentage that [its owners] should give in exchange for the labor [provided]." By giving this portion to Sendero, civilians paid "a type of tax." In exchange, Sendero "provide[d] a part to the poor peasantry, so they [could] see that the power structure serves them, and the other part stay[ed] with the armed forces." This system was described as "a mutual help, a form of cooperative."[66] Even though civilians who formerly lived in Sendero zones described the organization's emphasis on redistribution, systems of taxation and communal production were not in existence in every rebel-held community. Nonetheless, the goal of providing for the poor peasantry was one shared by open committees and the rebel leadership across communities.

In exchange for their participation and their contributions, civilians in Sendero received an education. Each community had popular schools that taught people to read and write in addition to the political and ideological line of the movement.[67] The political structure provided civilians with the opportunity to advance professionally and to be rewarded for their labor – experiences that were foreign yet valuable to many highland residents. Moreover, these structures empowered communities to govern themselves by organizing production, guarding against the infiltration of government forces, and maintaining communal order.

Somewhat surprisingly, the Shining Path did not provide security in exchange for civilian support, the most common bargain struck between rebels and civilians. But the integrated structure of the Shining Path's design meant that communities governed and protected themselves. Mobile units traveled from region to region launching military campaigns against the government. They did not entrench themselves in bases near civilian communities and guarantee protection. This situation did not create problems

---

[65] Ibid., December 2(A), 2001.
[66] "Iniciar el Gran Salto," captured Sendero document, March–May 1984, DINCOTE Sendero collection, Lima, Peru.
[67] Interviews, Huanta, Ayacucho, December 1(D), 4(B,C), 2001.

in the early stages of the war, as Sendero built structures of governance and mobilized support. When the military began to crack down on civilians, however, the base forces found themselves severely outmatched by the government, and a rupture was created with the rebel force in communities wholly exposed to the attacks of the government's armed soldiers.[68]

The Shining Path's approach to governance – of empowering civilians and sharing power almost completely with respect to the management of daily affairs – created a second channel that eventually gave rise to civilian resistance. In communities where Sendero lacked local contacts, the appointment of open committees often served to empower younger individuals, as it was an explicit rejection of the traditional administrative structures that had previously existed.[69] Because communities were left on their own to govern themselves, moreover, young *mandos* (commanders) had significant autonomy from the rebel leadership. There was room in this system for abuse, particularly in the regions where Sendero's civilian membership lacked training, indoctrination, and oversight. I will explore the implications of this structure in divergent communities in the next chapter.

Authoritarianism and Inclusion: Sendero–Huallaga

While committees in the southern highlands of Peru incorporated civilians into every aspect of rebel life – the party, the military, and the administration – leaders in the Comité Regional del Alto Huallaga saw civilians as serving a single purpose: the production of coca leaves. Sendero's desire to organize civilian labor to maximize the production of coca shaped its strategy of governance, leading the committee's leaders to establish a military hierarchy of control and a structure for the taxation of coca. The military structure of governance guaranteed that the CRH maintained unilateral control over the coca market, while the establishment of a taxation system ensured that civilians benefited sufficiently from the trade to prevent defection to the other side. The CRH's task was made easier by the fact that the population's exit option was limited: outside of the valley, one could not grow coca without risking arrest.

Unlike alluvial diamonds, timber, and other resources that a rebel army can extract efficiently with its own soldiers, coca requires extensive and sustained civilian labor. Importantly for Sendero–Huallaga, civilians, too,

---

[68] Degregori, "Harvesting Storms," p. 141.
[69] Interview, Huanta, Ayacucho, December 2(A), 2001.

cared about maximizing production. Without the rebels in the area, they were caught between drug traffickers from Colombia and government soldiers. For many, the CRH was a welcome arrival. Sendero's goal of maximizing production, its aim to control the market unilaterally, and its desire to minimize the size of the leadership that would benefit from the monopoly rents all shaped the rebel government that emerged.

To ensure that civilians invested their time and energy in the production of coca leaves, the CRH created a public market for the taxation of coca. The Senderistas published a set of rules outlining how coca would be sold.[70] Within each public market in the Huallaga Valley, coca leaves were weighed and taxed at a set price per kilogram under the watchful eye of a rebel representative. The public market allowed the rebel leadership to monitor what was bought and sold, tax it appropriately, and prevent civilians from hoarding their leaves to sell them in other settings. Civilians benefited from the public market as well, because it acted as a check on the taxation policies of the CRH. The committee set taxation rates, and civilians were able to monitor their even application. The market also guaranteed the presence of buyers, and when coca prices dropped in the later stages of the war, the CRH and civilians could use their monopoly control to raise prices artificially. To further improve productivity, the CRH took over vacated lands when civilians fled the Huallaga Valley. The rebels required that civilians work these "communal" farms in exchange for the freedom to grow coca and profit from production on their own lands.[71]

To prevent competition in the market, the CRH established structures of hierarchical military control. Sendero–Huallaga sought to ensure its supremacy to govern the production and export of coca so that no autonomous civilian organizations could emerge to compete for control. This goal necessitated investments in militarization and security to prevent encroachment from armed drug traffickers and the military.

The resulting structure of control vested power in small numbers of armed mandos in each village – leaders connected to the central structure of the CRH. These *delegados* (delegates), as some people called them, ran the villages when the armed Sendero militants were not around.[72] Unlike in Sendero Nacional, however, armed militants were the dominant force in Sendero–Huallaga. Highly militaristic, the force traveled in large groups

[70] Interviews, Tingo María, November 13(A), 14(A,B), 2001.
[71] Ibid., November 17(C), 19(B), 2001.
[72] Ibid., November 18(B,C), 19(A,B,D), 2001.

and moved regularly in and out of villages to maintain order and authority. Like régulos in Mozambique, the delegados served at the behest of the Sendero hierarchy, with a limited capacity for autonomous action. Delegados enabled the CRH to extract the maximum amount of coca with the minimum effort, and they were rewarded for it. Promotion was not based on ideological aptitude or commitment, as it was in other parts of the country.

The CRH's military strength also enabled it to control access to the zone. Sendero–Huallaga charged fees to the drug traffickers in return for allowing them to land their airplanes on CRH runways in the jungle and to purchase coca leaves and more finished products in the public marketplaces. Sendero's military capacity made the operation of an effective market possible. The rebels could guarantee to civilians that buyers would be present and ensure sellers that a high-quality product would be available.

The structure of the CRH's government, then, combined a unilateral military authority with an odd form of inclusiveness. Without reflecting the preferences of civilians to produce and sell coca, the organization could not have survived, nor could it have provided the short-term benefits that maintained its membership. Unilateral authority was necessary to ensure that no alternative sources of power emerged to compete with the rebel movement. Small numbers of armed delegados maintained control in the villages, but no additional structures were necessary. In many rebels' minds, more leaders would have meant less wealth for the CRH and its members.

The problems created by this system were apparent, however: by arming and militarizing a small, local leadership structure, the CRH laid the foundation for the corruption and desertion of its own civilian proxies. Like Renamo, the CRH was plagued by defection. Delegados would flee with the funds collected in the public markets.[73] Rebel soldiers would do the same, keeping coca profits for themselves.[74] The short time horizons that dominated the choices of the CRH's membership created a cascade of extraction in which the rebels demanded ever larger cupos from villagers, producers, trucks passing through the region, and eventually business owners living in regions that the CRH did not even control.[75]

Civilians remained in what was an ever-more-corrupt environment because they valued whatever surplus they could obtain by maintaining the right to grow coca. As long as their primary goal was to produce coca

---

[73] Ibid., November 17(B), 2001.
[74] Interviews, Lima, November 6(A,B,C), 2001.
[75] Interviews, Tingo María, November 13(A,B), 14(A,B), 19(D), 2001.

leaves, they were hostages to whoever maintained control in the region. Had the government legalized drug production, it might have undercut the influence and power of the CRH. Civilians wanted the benefits they could realize from living in Sendero zones. The CRH, capable of guaranteeing a modicum of security to residents of its areas, made it possible for civilians to reap benefits far in excess of those that could be gained in the production of legal crops.

Sendero–Huallaga's need to mobilize broad civilian participation forced the organization to develop a public marketplace that restrained its ability to extract all the wealth generated by the drug trade. At the same time, because civilians desired the benefits that could come from producing an illegal crop, they were hostage to a militarized and increasingly corrupt rebel group. The bargain struck between the rebels and the civilians was a tenuous one that could be shaken by shocks to the system – changes in coca prices, a new government strategy, or an alternative power in the zone. We turn to the impact of such developments in Chapter 7.

Conclusion

Rebel organizations must build structures to manage their relationships with civilian populations. The decision to control territory – one that emerges early on in conflict as groups seek to obtain resources and security and to demonstrate strength – necessitates the development of a strategy for governing noncombatants in the course of conflict. But governance is not an easy task. Like rebels, civilians act strategically and condition their behavior on the basis of how rebel groups behave.

Rebel governments differ from one another on two key dimensions. In some contexts, rebel leaders construct institutions that formalize power sharing arrangements with civilian populations. Their constitutional commitments create a set of incentives that discipline the behavior of the rebel group and promote the sustained commitment of civilian supporters. In other contexts, groups reject such power sharing arrangements in favor of unilateral military control, a structure that employs coercion in the organization of resources and the prevention of defection. A second key dimension is the inclusiveness of the rebel government. Rebel leaders may set in place structures that ensure the broad-based participation of the civilian population, empowering previously ignored segments of the community. Alternatively, groups may elevate small numbers of civilians to elite positions, creating a hierarchical structure of control.

In this chapter, I have argued that three factors determine the shape of governing structures. First, the resource endowments of rebel groups influence the degree to which rebel leaders need to strike a bargain with civilian populations. Where groups can survive largely independent of civilian support, little incentive exists for rebel leaders to share power with civilian populations. In situations where rebel groups are organized around social endowments, however, their very existence depends on the continued participation and support of their membership and potential membership. Strong incentives exist in these contexts to maximize civilian support and assistance.

A second factor is the degree to which the resources a rebel group wishes to obtain require civilian labor to produce. Where resources are provided externally or are of a type that requires minimal labor, groups have few reasons to ensure broad-based participation in their activities. When resources cannot be extracted without the sustained labor of large numbers of civilians, however, governing structures must be designed to promote broad participation.

The final factor is the membership and organizational structure of the rebel group building the government. Groups filled with short-term opportunists that are unable to effectively prevent and punish defection fail to build cooperative relationships with civilians even when they try. Resistance emerges as a consequence of the organization's behavior. Credible commitments become more likely, however, when the organization is capable of committing itself and its membership to a particular set of behaviors, as in the case of organizations built around social endowments.

In this chapter, ideology has not figured prominently as an explanation for the varied structures of governance in Uganda, Mozambique, and Peru. My argument departs from standard accounts of rebel behavior that emphasize the ideological predilections of movements in accounting for the character of rebel-civilian relations. Ideology no doubt plays an important role in shaping the *form* of rebel governments: Museveni's desire to reject the hierarchical system of chiefs in rural Uganda, for example, undoubtedly influenced the democratic system of governance by resistance councils that the NRA instituted in its zones of control. But ideology itself cannot explain why both the NRA and Sendero Nacional embraced power sharing while Renamo and Sendero–Huallaga rejected participatory approaches. I argue instead that resource-poor contexts give rise to ideological groups fully dependent on civilian populations for their survival, creating a need to build long-term relationships with civilians. Ideologies may shape the design of such institutions and the language groups employ in building them, but their emergence is conditioned by a group's resource constraints.

Governments, whether organized by formally elected leaders or rebel groups, face the difficult task of deciding the conditions under which they will use their coercive power against civilians. I turn to the determinants of the use of violence in the next chapter.

6

Violence

The killing of civilians is a common consequence of armed conflict. Some of this violence is the unintended result of large-scale fighting between warring parties. Some follows directly from conflict-induced famine, malnutrition, and disease. But much of the violence directed at noncombatant populations in the course of war is intended. Armed groups target civilians as they organize their militaries, solicit resources to sustain the fighting, build bases of popular support, and weaken the support networks of opposing groups. This chapter explores patterns of rebel violence in civil war, investigating whether variation in the level and character of violence can be explained by examining differences in the origins and structure of rebel movements. I argue that high levels of indiscriminate violence are committed by insurgent groups that are unable to police defection within their ranks; early missteps in the use of force generate civilian resistance and ever greater levels of coercion over time. Activist rebellions tend to have the institutions needed to choose targets carefully; as a consequence, such movements employ largely selective violence at much lower levels of intensity.

The chapter is divided into five sections. In the first, I introduce a definition of violence that captures a broad range of rebel-civilian interactions that include but are not limited to killing. In the second, I show how differences in the membership and organizational structure of rebel groups can account for variation in observed patterns of violence in civil war. Structures matter because they affect the capacity of rebel leaders to employ violence selectively without making errors; mistakes make a difference because they affect the calculations of potential civilian supporters about how to respond to rebel groups when they enter a region. I then contrast the observable implications of this model with hypotheses that

198

follow from two others, one of which focuses on the impact of contestation with government forces on rebel strategies and the other of which draws attention to how variation in the degree of control exercised by insurgents shapes patterns of violence. In the fourth section, I present quantitative evidence that rebel groups with different internal characteristics exhibit different patterns of rebel-civilian interaction. Drawing on information about incidents of violence in each of the four civil war case studies, I show how activist and opportunistic rebellions differ in the extent to which rebel groups (as compared to the government) are responsible for violence, the form that violence takes, and who is targeted. Finally, I turn to a consideration of subnational variation within each civil war, demonstrating how theories that focus on organizational capacity better explain the observed consistency in the character of rebel behavior over time and across regions than do approaches that emphasize dynamics of contestation and control.

Defining Violence in Civil War

Violence against and between civilians is a defining feature of civil war. Levels of violence are central to definitions that distinguish civil war from other forms of political instability, but analysts' attention has rarely been directed at understanding variation in the violence that accompanies civil war. Charles King describes this variation: "Episodes of social violence, whether riots or atrocities committed during civil wars, may be well patterned, but they do not occur uniformly across time or space. There are lulls and peaks. Violence comes to different cities, towns, and neighborhoods at different times."[1] Violence also takes on different forms in different contexts. Patterns of killing, rape, and pillage are not the same across all armed groups, nor are strategies of violence consistent throughout every conflict. Yet this variation is traditionally subsumed in the concept of civil war. This chapter instead engages violence at the micro level in a way that allows for systematic comparisons of violence across countries as well as assessment of patterns within countries across geographic space and over time.

I define violence broadly to include patterns of rebel-civilian interaction that involve coercion. Violent homicides in the context of war are an obvious

---

[1] Charles King, "The Micropolitics of Social Violence," *World Politics* 56 (April 2004): 431–55.

component: killings are distinct events that are relatively easy to identify and count. Rebels also perpetrate other forms of abuse that include the beating of noncombatants, the rape of women and children, abduction, forced relocation and labor, looting, and destruction.

A focus on broader patterns of rebel-civilian interaction is reflective of the range of human rights violations prohibited under the Geneva Conventions.[2] Article 3 provides the following:

In the case of an armed conflict not of an international character occurring in the territory of one of the High Contracting Parties, each Party to the conflict shall be bound to apply, as a minimum, the following provisions:

1. Persons taking no active part in the hostilities, including members of armed forces who have laid down their arms and those placed 'hors de combat' by sickness, wounds, detention, or any other cause, shall in all circumstances be treated humanely, without any adverse distinction founded on race, colour, religion, or faith, sex, birth, or wealth, or any other similar criteria. To this end, the following acts are and shall remain prohibited at any time and in any place whatsoever with respect to the above-mentioned persons:

(a) violence to life and person, in particular murder of all kinds, mutilation, cruel treatment, and torture; (b) taking of hostages; (c) outrages upon personal dignity, in particular humiliating and degrading treatment; (d) the passing of sentences and the carrying out of executions without previous judgment pronounced by a regularly constituted court, affording all the judicial guarantees which are recognized as indispensable by civilized peoples.[3]

A subsequent protocol drafted in 1977 further clarifies the protections guaranteed to noncombatant populations in internal conflicts. All persons "who do not take a direct part in the hostilities" are protected from "violence to life, health, and physical or mental well-being; collective punishments; taking of hostages; acts of terrorism; outrages upon personal dignity;

---

[2] Common Article 3 of the Geneva Conventions and Protocol II are designed to govern "non-international armed conflicts." Debates over the characteristics of internal conflicts that merit inclusion have been intense. Protocol II provides a fairly clear elaboration, stating that it concerns "all armed conflicts . . . not covered by Article I [of Protocol I] . . . which take place in the territory of a High Contracting Party between its armed forces and dissident armed forces or other organized armed groups which, under responsible command, exercise such control over a part of its territory to enable them to carry out sustained and concerted military operations and to implement [Protocol II]." The inclusion of conflicts hinges on the capacity of the insurgent group, which is debated on a case-by-case basis. The conflicts discussed in this study clearly meet the threshold for inclusion; as such, the provisions of Article III and Protocol II apply. For a fuller discussion, see Babafemi Akinrinade, "International Humanitarian Law and the Conflict in Sierra Leone," *Notre Dame Journal of Law, Ethics, and Public Policy* 15 (2001): 391–454.

[3] Article 3 Common to the 1949 Geneva Conventions.

slavery; pillage; and threats to commit any of the foregoing acts."[4] Protections extend not only to civilian life but also to "objects indispensable to the survival of the civilian population." A broad definition of violence helps us avoid the problem of focusing only on the most violent places or on atrocities that are easy to identify and measure, such as massacres.[5]

Doing research on violence requires an explicit focus on micro-level interactions. Behaviors, such as killing, abuse, and destruction, are experienced by individuals, groups, and communities. Aggregate patterns tend to obscure these local dynamics. From a more local perspective, one can quickly see that observed patterns of violence are not necessarily a reflection of group strategies. Perpetrators make decisions about assassinations they wish to carry out or government strongholds they would like to destroy. Actual killings and attacks, however, capture the results when such strategies are put into practice. Issues of organization (how groups translate strategies into actions) and interaction (how those actions are received and responded to by civilians) must be entered into the equation. The common tendency to conflate observed violence with strategy leads scholars to search only for plausible explanations of the strategic value of amputation, massacres, and rape when such behavior may or may not have been ordered by commanders at all.

An approach that emphasizes micro-level interactions also requires an understanding of the context in which violence is observed. Warfare empowers actors and structures choices in important ways. Because the nature of warfare differs across contexts, the strategic considerations of perpetrators and the resources available to them are likely to vary.[6] In irregular warfare, insurgent groups operate (at least initially) with fewer resources and less power than government forces. As the strategically weaker side, rebels avoid conventional battles in favor of tactics that emphasize stealth and surprise. They embed themselves in the civilian population, which acts a source of support and sustenance and as a shield against detection. Civil

---

[4] Protocol Additional to the Geneva Conventions and relating to the Protection of Victims of Non-International Armed Conflicts (Protocol II), 1977.

[5] Stathis Kalyvas, "Wanton and Senseless? The Logic of Massacres in Algeria," *Rationality and Society* 11 (1999): 243–85.

[6] Stathis Kalyvas distinguishes irregular war from two other contexts in which violence is committed: conventional war, in which there is a parity of high resources across the two parties, and symmetric nonconventional warfare, in which both parties are severely resource-constrained. See "Warfare in Civil Wars," in *Rethinking the Nature of War*, eds. Isabelle Duyvesteyn and Jan Angstrom (Abingdton: Frank Cass, 2005), pp. 88–108.

war violence emerges in irregular warfare from the interactions between at least two actors who compete for power and the loyalties of noncombatant populations.

Measuring violence as I define it necessitates capturing the dynamics of this interaction at the local level within and across conflicts. This is a difficult task because perpetrators have strong incentives to misrepresent their behavior during the war and rewrite history in its aftermath, and researchers must turn primarily to participant accounts, as records of violence are rarely kept. Following scholars such as Ashutosh Varshney, Steven Wilkinson, and Stathis Kalyvas, I therefore supplement participant accounts with a systematic coding of incidents of violence across the three civil wars.[7] An *event* is the unit of analysis, defined as any incident of soldier-civilian interaction that involves one of a range of forms of coercion.[8] Culled from decades of local newspaper reporting in each country, the events are coded to reveal patterns of responsibility, the range of tactics and strategies employed, and the identities of those targeted by combatant groups in the context of conflict. This approach yields information on 711 violent incidents in Uganda, 1,379 in Mozambique, 4,159 in Peru (outside of the Huallaga Valley), and 804 in the Huallaga Valley. When combined with information gleaned from hundreds of interviews with combatants and civilians, these event datasets offer a compelling picture of patterns of violence across the three countries and within each of the conflicts. They allow for two sorts of comparisons: tests of hypotheses predicting differences in the aggregate behavior of groups across conflicts and explorations of theories that suggest geographic and temporal patterns of violence within a single civil war. At the same time, such data enable the measurement of two different dimensions of violence. "Intensity" refers to the level of violence – the number of killings, attacks, and incidents of coercion. The "character" of violence, on the other hand, measures the range of violent behaviors rebel groups exhibit and the identity of their targets. These assessments of the character of violence are compared and contrasted with the participant accounts of rebel behavior that we explore in subsequent sections.

---

[7] Ashutosh Varshney, *Ethnic Conflict and Civic Life: Hindus and Muslims in India* (New Haven: Yale University Press, 2002); Steven Wilkinson, *Votes and Violence: Electoral Competition and Ethnic Riots in India* (New York: Cambridge University Press, 2004); Stathis Kalyvas, *The Logic of Violence in Civil War* (New York: Cambridge University Press, 2006).

[8] A detailed description of the structure, coding, and potential biases of events data is presented in Appendix B.

Organization and Violence

Explanations of violence against noncombatants often begin with a focus on military tactics. Because rebel groups begin as small, vulnerable military organizations, they tend to employ guerrilla warfare as a strategy against government forces. Guerrilla tactics, almost by definition, make violence against civilians more likely in civil conflict. With the absence of clear lines of battle in guerrilla war, rebel forces operate in areas of fragmented control or in regions dominated by the state. They rely on small, mobile forces to carry out hit-and-run attacks, sabotage, and assassinations. To survive, these units must be able to blend in with noncombatant populations. The result is that guerrillas and their supporters are not always easily identifiable to government forces or to each other. In many cases, they are indistinguishable from the civilian population. The blurring of the line between combatants and civilians grows more extreme when guerrilla armies themselves emerge from the populations in which they seek to hide. Civilians from war zones often become combatants in the rebel group, and local leaders assist in the organization of resources, information, and support for guerrilla armies.

Central to the story of irregular war is the interaction between rebel groups, the armed forces of the state, and civilian populations. Armed groups compete with one another for the affection and loyalties of noncombatant populations. Civilian support is important to the outcome of the conflict: noncombatants are in a position of power, able to shift their support from one side to another, to provide or withhold resources necessary for the groups' operation, and to offer information to combatants about who is supporting the opposition. From the perspective of combatant groups, the dynamics of irregular warfare put a premium on information because knowing who is friend and who is foe helps them to build support, weaken the enemy, and avoid detection. Because control over territory is fragmented, there are often strong incentives for civilians to defect to the other side, even in places where support for the rebel group (or the government) is strong. Both sides offer material and nonmaterial benefits to civilians to induce defection in the hope of shifting civilian support and gaining information that may be useful in weakening the opposition.

Because civilian defection has potentially devastating consequences for a group's survival, groups sometimes employ violence to maintain civilian support. The threat of force is *persuasive* because it sufficiently raises the costs of defection to individuals that care most about survival. To be effective, though, force must also be *selective*.[9] If collaborators cannot be sure that their participation guarantees their survival (or at least protection from attack), they have much weaker incentives to collaborate. Violence is used efficiently if it is employed to punish only those who defect (or are likely to defect): in this case, it acts as a credible signal of the actors' ability to exercise control and protect their supporters. Avoiding the indiscriminate use of violence also helps to minimize the negative consequences of using force against civilians for a group's reputation among domestic and international actors.

But selective violence is difficult to implement in practice. Information that enables groups to distinguish friend from foe must be obtained from civilians living in war zones. Potential denouncers make their own individual calculations about whether to turn a neighbor in – calculations that are often as much about personal feuds and vendettas as they are about broader issues at stake in the conflict. Rebel groups thus require institutions capable of soliciting information from noncombatants and validating denunciations. They also require structures that can translate valuable information about potential enemies into strategic actions to eliminate the threat.

Activist and opportunistic rebellions behave differently as perpetrators of violence. Activist rebellions attract individuals committed to longer-term goals and embedded in networks of repeated interaction that enable leaders to shape the incentives and interests of their followers. Organized around shared identities or ideologies, activist groups build organizational structures that decentralize power while retaining control through a system of norms and formal mechanisms of command and control. Opportunistic rebellions, on the other hand, attract participants interested only in short-term, material gains. Joined together by nothing more than their material interests, opportunistic groups are plagued by indiscipline, as combatants often sacrifice a group's objectives to their individual interests. Figure 6.1 summarizes the differences in activist and opportunistic groups' organizational control and governance structures.

These differences in the membership and structure of rebel groups are reflected in the quality of a group's institutions – its capacity to obtain information and use it to direct violence without making mistakes. Activists build organizations capable of using violence strategically. They construct relationships with noncombatant populations that yield information that enables them to punish defectors and reward collaborators. Networks of

---

[9] The understanding of selective violence I adopt here is drawn from Kalyvas, *Logic of Violence*.

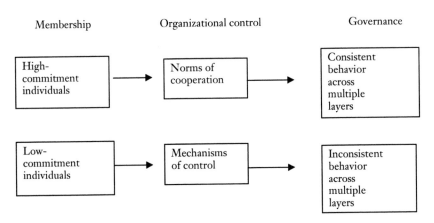

Figure 6.1. The Nature of the Perpetrator

local ties that enable recruitment, provide the resources needed to maintain the movement, and help to govern areas of influence can also be utilized in pursuit of valuable information. Activist groups also punish misbehavior by rebel combatants publicly to ensure that behavior is consistent across the organization. Beatings, looting, destruction, and other behaviors that potentially diminish civilian support are strictly controlled. The cost of losing loyalty is far too high in activist rebellions.

Opportunistic rebellions lack the social ties and connections necessary to obtain valuable information. Few resources have been invested in constructing institutions of comanagement and cooperation with local leaders that would elicit the truthful denunciations necessary to use force selectively. Moreover, the short-term-oriented behavior of combatants leads to incidents of looting, destruction, and indiscriminate killing that diminish civilian support and condition noncombatants' expectations. When these behaviors go unpunished, as they tend to do in opportunistic rebellions, a group develops a negative reputation. Commitments to restrain the use of force lose credibility. Opportunistic rebellions evolve without the formal and informal mechanisms they need to restrain the behavior of their members.

A group's institutions matter also because rebel behavior that goes unpunished early on in the conflict shapes civilians' expectations about how groups are likely to behave in the future. War involves a series of repeated interactions between combatants and civilians. In the beginning of a conflict, rebel groups often make mistakes in using violence. Because control over territory is fragmented, groups tend to have imperfect information about who is collaborating and who is defecting. Efforts to use force selectively can backfire when individuals are unjustly targeted. At the same time, new rebels are often unsure of how they are expected to behave. Acts of indiscipline are an inevitable result. Where groups punish indiscipline and apologize for mistakes, they build reputations for restraint. Where such behavior goes unpunished, a reputation for coercion is established.

A group's reputation is important because, in spite of the breakdown of institutions and physical infrastructure, information manages to flow during civil wars. From rural villages to the cities, civilians learn quickly how the rebels are behaving. Information about one attack spreads quickly, conditioning how civilians prepare for and respond to future rebel incursions. Even one incident in which a combatant kills a civilian without cause damages the reputation of the rebel group. When civilians are unsure of what to expect from insurgents or, alternatively, are convinced that rebels are likely to abuse them, they often choose to resist or flee when rebels arrive. This sets into motion a cycle of resistance followed by increasing coercion that leads violence to spiral out of control. Only sustained cooperative behavior enables rebel groups to establish a reputation that elicits civilian collaboration without recourse to coercion. Figure 6.2 depicts the two pathways of rebel action and civilian response.

It may seem puzzling that the use of high levels of indiscriminate force emerges as a rational strategy for groups to employ. Undoubtedly, groups that employ violence against noncombatants incur significant costs in consequence. Indiscriminate violence engenders discontent among civilian populations, creates higher levels of resistance to rebel advances, and damages the reputation of a rebel group both within the country and outside of it. But opportunistic rebellions are largely unable to reverse patterns of indiscriminate violence, for two reasons. Because they are held together by short-term material incentives, combatants' access to material rewards must continue if an organizational collapse is to be prevented. Groups are thus permissive, if not encouraging, of attacks on civilian populations in order to maintain their membership. And since reputations form early on in the conflict, these groups are unable to retreat from high-violence strategies precisely *because* they employ them. Once a cycle of rebel violence and civilian resistance begins, it is difficult to stop.

The logic of this model of violence suggests a number of observable implications. Its most important prediction is that the level and character of violence perpetrated by insurgent groups is likely to vary across groups and across conflicts. Some insurgent organizations will emerge with the capacity

Violence

The sequence

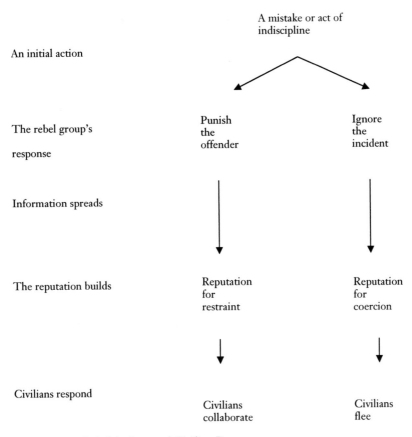

An initial action

The rebel group's

response

Information spreads

The reputation builds

Civilians respond

Figure 6.2. Rebel Actions and Civilian Response

to use violence selectively while holding other forms of coercion in check. These activist groups will tend to commit low levels of violence. Other groups will exhibit behavior akin to indiscriminate violence, interspersing killing, looting, and pillaging with more traditional military operations. The resistance such behavior generates among civilians tends to exacerbate coercive behavior over time, leading opportunistic groups to commit much higher levels of violence.

Looking within conflicts rather than across them, the argument suggests that the character of violence will remain fairly consistent across time and in different geographic regions of each conflict. That is, groups that kill

207

indiscriminately, destroy villages, and loot property are likely to do so at the beginning of the conflict as well as at the end and will tend to do so in every region in which they operate. When facing activist groups, civilians' expectations of cooperation obviate the need for coercive behavior; confronted with opportunistic insurgencies, civilian resistance leads to the persistence of indiscriminate violence. The model offers fewer insights into determinants of levels of abuse within each conflict. Levels of violence vary geographically and temporally within each conflict and are likely linked to the size of a group, the extent of its operations, and its patterns of interaction with government forces. Other theories that seek to explain how groups behave, described later, offer more traction on within-case variation in levels of violence.

Contestation and Control

Two other explanations of violence within civil war have been offered by scholars. Both begin with the assumption that violence is rational – that it is both intentional and a part of the war aims of the party that commits it. Instead of focusing on dynamics internal to the organizations that commit atrocities, these approaches both draw attention to a rebel group's external interactions, the first with opposing forces and the second with noncombatants. The theory of contestation locates the sources of anti-civilian violence in the battle between rebel forces and the government. It begins with the idea that war is the consequence of a bargaining failure between parties unable to agree on a mutually preferable negotiated settlement.[10] Even though on-the-ground military outcomes reveal information about the relative military capabilities of the warring parties, an information asymmetry exists with respect to the resolve of the competing organizations. Rebel groups send signals of their resolve by waging war against civilians.[11] Such tactics raise the price of continued fighting for the government, changing the dynamics of the bargaining process. Violence

---

[10] James Fearon, "Rationalist Explanations for War," *International Organization* 49 (1995): 379–414.

[11] David Lake first articulated an argument about the rational uses of extremist terror. See "Rational Extremism: Understanding Terrorism in the Twenty-First Century," *Dialog-IO* (2002): 15–29. More recently, Lisa Hultman drew on Lake's analysis in trying to understand the behavior of rebel groups. See "Killing Civilians to Signal Resolve: Rebel Strategies in Intrastate Conflicts" (paper presented at the annual meeting of the American Political Science Association, Washington, DC, September 3, 2005).

may impose costs on the party that perpetrates it due to the disapproval of both domestic and international audiences, but it is a strategy that is relatively easy for groups to implement. One observable implication of the contestation theory is that as rebel groups experience greater battlefield losses, they compensate by increasing their use of violence against civilians. A second implication points to the decreasing effect of this strategy as war progresses: long wars provide both parties with substantial information about the opposition, decreasing the utility of anticivilian violence as a signal of resolve. Therefore, the theory predicts variation over time in the level of violence linked to the relative military capabilities of the parties. A theory rooted in the dynamics of contestation makes no predictions about variation in the behavior of rebels across conflicts; the logic of the model is intended to be universal. A similar argument that does predict cross-case variation links strategies of violence to the signal rebel groups must send to external patrons and financiers of their commitment to the cause.[12] External support for rebellion is thus associated with anticivilian violence, although for different reasons than those outlined in the theory of organization described earlier.[13]

A second approach highlights how variation in the degree of territorial control exerted by military actors affects their interaction with noncombatants.[14] Military actors seek access to information, which enables them both to prevent civilians from taking actions that can harm the organization and to punish civilians who defect. Because defection requires access to the opposition, however, it is largely a function of control. Organizations that enjoy unrivaled power in a zone are thus unlikely to confront defection, while it is more likely in areas of contested sovereignty. Where they face defection, armed groups aim to use force selectively so as to minimize the negative costs of indiscriminate violence. This puts a premium on obtaining high-quality information about potential defectors. But denunciations are provided by civilians with their own private agendas, who weigh the benefits of informing (gratification and rewards) against the potential costs (retaliation). The likelihood of retaliation is also a function of control, as contested sovereignty makes it possible for the rival organization to exact

---

[12] Lucy Hovil and Eric Werker, "Portrait of a Failed Rebellion: An Account of Rational, Sub-Optimal Violence in Western Uganda," *Rationality and Society* 17 (2005): 5–34.

[13] The data on Renamo presented in this chapter is consistent with this version of the signaling theory of violence; however, it cannot account for why similar patterns of abuse appear in groups with other sources of finance beyond those provided by external patrons.

[14] Kalyvas, *Logic of Violence*.

retribution. This approach, which conceptualizes violence as an outcome of the interaction between combatants and civilians willing to denounce, generates predictions about the character and level of violence as a function of geography. Zones of absolute control (for one side or the other) are expected to experience the lowest levels of violence. Defection is highly unlikely in such places, and denunciations, while common, are often false. It predicts low levels of selective violence as well in areas of high contestation where defection is common but denunciation is unlikely because the threat of retaliation is high. In such areas, information is scarce, and thus violence, when used, is likely to be indiscriminate; as it is counterproductive, however, the theory suggests such strategies will not be employed. If they are used at all, indiscriminate violence will be observed only at the early stages of the conflict until actors adjust their behavior to minimize its negative consequences. Zones of intermediate contestation, where one group is relatively stronger than the other, are likely to experience the highest levels of selective violence. The theory of control thus draws attention to geographic and temporal variation in violence within conflicts. Like theories of contestation, it is believed to apply uniformly; its predictions can usefully be explored with the evidence provided by our four cases.

The Practice of Violence Across Countries

Neither the theory of contestation nor the argument about territorial control makes empirical predictions about how violence is likely to vary across conflicts in its character or intensity. One of the clearest observable implications of my theory of organizational structure, on the other hand, is that the level and character of violence will vary across rebel groups. Groups constructed around economic endowments are predicted to exhibit much higher levels of indiscriminate violence, looting, and destruction, while rebellions rooted in social endowments are expected to demonstrate restraint and discipline. In this section, I present evidence from Uganda, Mozambique, and Peru that the level and character of anticivilian abuses varies in meaningful ways across conflicts. Specifically, I show that rebel groups are sometimes responsible for much of the violence committed against civilians, but not always; that violence is sometimes accompanied by pillaging and destruction, but not in all contexts; that victims are sometimes massacred in large groups, but only in some conflicts; and that individuals targeted for violence are sometimes identifiable as key supporters of

Table 6.1. *Responsibility for Violence Committed against Noncombatant Populations*

	Uganda (1981–85)	Mozambique (1976–94)	Sendero Nacional (1980–88)	Sendero–Huallaga (1980–2000)
Government	45%	7%	4%	4%
Rebel groups	17%	82%	36%	32%
External forces	0%	4%	0%	0%
Unclear	38%	8%	60%	64%
Total no. incidents	711	1,379	4,159	804

the state (functionaries, politicians, and government workers) but at other times are largely nameless peasants.

On the first aspect of violence, responsibility, patterns of behavior varied in important ways across the conflicts in Uganda, Mozambique, and Peru. Table 6.1 summarizes the differences. In the Ugandan conflict, rebel groups, including the NRA, were responsible for only 17 percent of the total incidents recorded.[15] By contrast, government forces were identifiably linked to nearly 50 percent of the violations committed against civilians. These data accord with anecdotal reports on the conflict in which analysts characterized the violence as a government-directed genocide that led to the deaths of between 200,000 and 300,000 people. In Mozambique, rebel forces were identifiably connected to a much higher percentage of attacks on civilians: Renamo combatants were linked to over 80 percent of the incidents in a war in which estimates suggest that more than 100,000 civilians died in battle-related events.[16] In Peru, both at the national level and in the Upper Huallaga Valley, Sendero Luminoso was responsible for high levels of violence, committing at least one-third of the reported violence against

---

[15] The NRA was actually responsible for an even smaller percentage of attacks because more than one rebel group was operating in the country throughout the conflict. The dataset includes information about the activities of all rebel groups. Later in this section, I focus only on acts committed by NRA cadres; this data can be extricated by looking at only those incidents where the NRA was identified officially or attacks perpetrated in regions where the NRA operated.

[16] The actual number of deaths in the Mozambican conflict was far higher – some suggest between 200,000 and 300,000. Many of these deaths were the result of significant periods of drought rather than combat itself. Data on civilian casualties can be found in the *SIPRI Yearbook 1999* (Stockholm: Swedish International Peace Research Institute, 1999).

civilians between 1980 and 1988.[17] Government counterinsurgency campaigns, which began in late 1983 and continued throughout the war, also involved the targeting of civilian populations, and more than 60 percent of incidents in Peru could not be identifiably linked to either the rebels or the government. New data gathered by Peru's Truth and Reconciliation Commission offer some confirmation of these general trends.[18] The commission concluded that Sendero was responsible for 54 percent of the total deaths that occurred during the war. The government was blamed for 37 percent of overall deaths and disappearances reported by victims and their families, although it bore responsibility for significantly more deaths than the Shining Path in the early years of the struggle after the counterinsurgency began. In total, the Truth and Reconciliation Commission concluded that close to 70,000 civilians were killed by the warring parties, far exceeding previous estimates by the Peruvian police of just over 10,000 victims.[19]

Because violence often involves a range of tactics that include but are not limited to killing, it is important to analyze the full range of behaviors perpetrated by groups across conflicts. According to the quantitative data, which are summarized in Table 6.2, the NRA used force in a limited fashion, but when it did, nearly three-quarters of the incidents involved killing. The NRA rarely committed acts of destruction, and looting, while reported in 30 percent of incidents, tended to involve not civilian villages but rather the sacking of government stores and hospitals for supplies. Renamo combatants often killed members of the civilian population as well: they did

---

[17] Data for Sendero Luminoso's national operations covers the period 1980–88. The war continued until mid-1992, but data for that period have not been collected and coded. Data reported here therefore cover about two-thirds of the civil war. Peru's Truth and Reconciliation Commission reports an increase in Shining Path attacks in the late 1980s before a sharp decrease in the run-up to Guzmán's capture. Incidents coded for the incident dataset were only attributed to Sendero Luminoso if the written record of the violence explicitly named the Shining Path as the perpetrator. Undoubtedly, many of the attacks coded as "unclear" were also perpetrated by Sendero.

[18] See Comisión de la Verdad y Reconciliación, *Informe Final: Peru, 1980–2000, Tomo I* (Lima: Pontificia Universidad Católica del Peru y Universidad Nacional Mayor de San Marcos, 2003), Chapter 3, for a summary of the data gathered by the Commission on violence committed against civilians. A useful English summary of the report was produced by Amnesty International. See "Peru: The Truth and Reconciliation Commission – A First Step towards a Country without Injustice," September 2004.

[19] These estimates come from the police force in data provided to the author. The commonly quoted figure (before the release of the Truth and Reconciliation Commission report) of twenty thousand deaths includes members of the armed forces and presumed terrorists, in addition to civilians.

212

Table 6.2. *Types of Violence Committed against Noncombatant Populations*

	The National Resistance Army		Renamo		Sendero Nacional		Sendero–Huallaga	
	No.	%	No.	%	No.	%	No.	%
Total incidents	110		1133		1504		258	
Killing	81	74%	692	61%	344	23%	103	40%
Looting	33	30%	396	35%	170	11%	70	27%
Destruction	7	7%	471	42%	989	66%	84	33%

so in more than 60 percent of the recorded incidents. But their attacks consistently also included the destruction of civilian property and the looting of household goods. Newspaper reports of violence refer to the pillaging of villages and the theft of individual property rather than attacks on government facilities. Violence perpetrated by Sendero's national organization had its own unique character: Combatants tended to destroy large numbers of public and private buildings, while killing was part of less than 25 percent of Sendero incidents. Soldiers in the Huallaga Valley, however, employed much higher levels of violence, killing civilians in 40 percent of their attacks.

A third dimension of the character of violence relates to the extent of massacres, that is, whether individuals are singled out for execution or whether rebels kill large numbers of noncombatants at a time. Measuring the number of massacres provides a rough indication of the degree to which violence was selective or indiscriminate. Figure 6.3 summarizes the data. Attacks by the NRA and Sendero Luminoso largely resulted in the deaths of single individuals or persons in small groups. More than 80 percent of Sendero killings in its national operations and by the jungle faction caused the deaths of fewer than six individuals.[20] In Uganda, although the NRA sometimes killed in larger groups, 70 percent of its attacks involved the killing of fewer

[20] Data from the Truth and Reconciliation Commission confirm this finding. They report that violence committed by the Shining Path tended to take the form of assassinations rather than indiscriminate attacks, with 68 percent of total incidents (regardless of perpetrator) involving the deaths or disappearances of fewer than five people at a time. Much of this selective violence was committed by the Shining Path, as the government, especially in the early years of counterinsurgency, engaged in indiscriminate massacres in Sendero's rural strongholds. See Comisión de la Verdad y Reconciliación, *Informe Final*, p. 238.

214

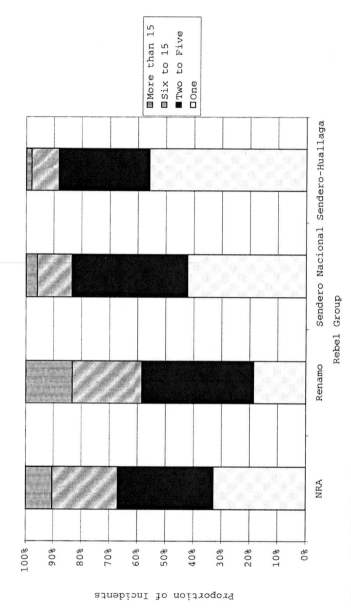

Figure 6.3. The Size of Victim Groups

than six victims. On the other hand, Renamo's actions often resulted in the deaths of many civilians in each incident. A comparatively small percentage of attacks were single-person assassinations, and more than 40 percent of incidents caused the deaths of six or more individuals.

A second way of measuring selectivity involves coding the identities of victims in rebel attacks. Newspaper reports often identify individual victims as political officials, local leaders, government workers, teachers, religious leaders, or private businessmen. Where the identities of victims are not reported, it is fair to assume that the individual was a peasant or someone of lesser stature in the community. I coded incidents in terms of whether the victims were reported to have an "affiliation," such as a partisan connection or occupation, or whether no information about the identities of those attacked was provided. Figure 6.4 compares the extent to which victims of rebel attacks could be identified. Victims of NRA and Sendero Nacional attacks had identifiable affiliations in more than 40 percent of the attacks,[21] while 75 percent of Renamo attacks were perpetrated against victims who could not be identified as anything other than a peasant. Sendero–Huallaga also tended to kill a larger number of unaffiliated victims. As I will demonstrate with evidence from local contexts, these aggregate patterns reveal a deeper dynamic: while the NRA and Sendero Luminoso targeted specific individuals for attacks, Renamo often killed civilians because its members encountered them during attacks, not because these civilians opposed the insurgents' advances.

Some additional data on the behavior of Sendero Luminoso in the Huallaga Valley reveal its divergence from the national organization more directly and point to parallels with the behavior of Renamo.[22] By 1988, Sendero–Huallaga averaged between 150 and 200 actions per year, a pattern that remained consistent until 1998. After the fall of Guzmán in 1992, actions in the jungle made up an increasingly large share of total attacks in

---

[21] Truth and Reconciliation Commission data suggest that 12 percent of Sendero's victims (or approximately 930 individuals) were government authorities. This figure does not include the large number of community leaders also targeted by the Shining Path in its attacks. See Comisión de la Verdad y Reconciliación, *Truth and Reconciliation Commission Final Report – General Conclusions* (English translation) (New York: International Center for Transitional Justice, 2003), p. 6.

[22] This section draws on statistics produced by the National Police Force in Peru and shared with the author. These data provide details about the incidence of Sendero violence by region and over time. In addition, the police database includes indicators of the identity of the victims and the nature of the attacks.

216

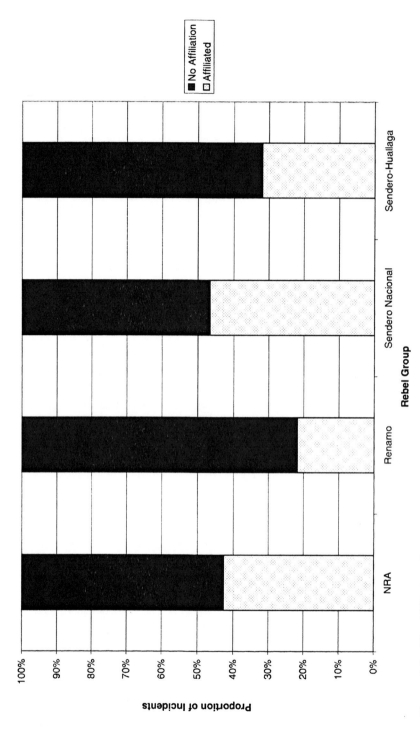

Figure 6.4. The Affiliation of Victims

the country (see Figure 6.5).[23] At the same time, Sendero's attacks in the jungle were consistently more deadly than those in other areas including the Shining Path's principal region, Ayacucho. In 1992, for example, Sendero–Huallaga was responsible for only 6 percent of the total actions launched across the country. The rebels in the jungle, however, caused more than 45 percent of the total deaths that year. Sendero–Huallaga was responsible for an ever-larger portion of total deaths throughout the 1990s.

These aggregate indicators of the level and character of rebel violence in Uganda, Mozambique, and Peru underscore a critical point: rebel groups use force in very different ways across conflicts. Some groups target victims carefully, singling out defectors and restraining the behavior of their combatants. Other groups are responsible for much higher levels of violence, often indiscriminate, and their combatants participate in the looting and destruction of civilian property. A theory of rebel violence rooted in the different organizational structures of groups helps us to make sense of cross-country variation in the character of rebel-civilian interaction. Theories of contestation, on the other hand, suggest uniform dynamics of violence across countries, even though the data used to test such arguments indicate that nearly one-third of groups used *no violence* against civilians at all.[24] Theories of control also present a model thought to operate across contexts, but the argument hinges on the capacity of rebel groups to solicit information.[25] Because differences in capacity are assumed away, theories of control cannot then account for the emergence of indiscriminate violence (and its persistence) in some contexts and not in others.

Violence within Civil War

The logic of my argument about the links between organizational structure and rebel behavior also suggests that the character of violence is likely to be consistent over time and across geographic regions within each conflict. Consistency in patterns of violence results from a process in which

---

[23] Truth and Reconciliation Commission data confirm the trend highlighted in the police force data. In 1990, violence in the province of Huanuco, which is home to Sendero–Huallaga, accounted for close to 20 percent of total deaths. By the mid-1990s, deaths in Huanuco had exceeded 50 percent of the national total. See Comisión de la Verdad y Reconciliación, *Final Report*, Chapter 3, p. 178.

[24] Hultman, "Killing Civilians," p. 22.

[25] Stathis Kalyvas, "The Logic of Violence in Civil War" (unpublished working paper, 2000), p. 11.

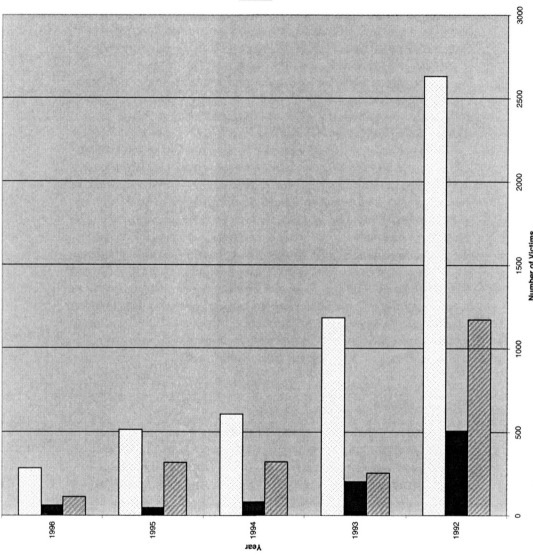

Total
Principal
Huallaga

Year

Number of Victims

1996

1995

1994

1993

1992

0   500   1000   1500   2000   2500   3000

218

civilians update their expectations about how rebels are likely to behave and respond with resistance when they believe that force will not be used selectively. Opportunistic movements find themselves trapped in a cycle of indiscriminate violence and civilian resistance, while activist groups build a reputation for restraint and discipline that eases their entry into new territories. Other explanations of anticivilian violence generate predictions of temporal and geographic variation in the level *and* character of abuse. Theories of contestation suggest that violence will increase as the rebels' relative military capabilities degrade, although no predictions are made about the form that rebel behavior will take. Theories of control focus instead on geographic variation and indicate, first, that indiscriminate violence will occur only in zones of highly contested sovereignty at early stages of the conflict and, second, that levels of selective violence will be highest in zones where one party is slightly stronger than its opponent. In this section, I present evidence that the character of violence perpetrated by the four rebel groups in this study was surprisingly persistent across regions and over time within each conflict – a result consistent with my theory of violence. I draw on two types of evidence: quantitative data that captures variation in the character of violence and short case studies of two different regions within each conflict, one near the center of rebel control (uncontested sovereignty) and one at the fringe (intermediate sovereignty).

A War of Targeted Assassinations: The NRA

Although the NRA operated in a zone that was overwhelmingly Baganda, one should not imagine that it did not encounter resistance in the Luwero Triangle. A notorious example is that of Hajji Musa Sebirumbi, the United People's Congress chairman for Luwero District.[26] Sebirumbi would gather a handful of young men, the UPC Youth Wingers, and attempt to flush the guerrillas and their supporters out of the Triangle. In trying to identify guerrilla supporters, UPC cadres often could call on the assistance of the Alur population, an ethnic group that hailed from northern Uganda. The Alur, many of whom were connected through familial ties to the northern-dominated army, supported Milton Obote in the 1980 elections and were willing to aid the UNLA in its efforts to defeat the NRA. The NRA had a clear policy for dealing with these opponents: the focus was on members of

---

[26] Interview, Semuto, November 14(A), 2000. See also Ondoga Ori Amaza, *Museveni's Long March from Guerrilla to Statesman* (Kampala: Fountain, 1998), p. 59.

the armed forces and the police. Museveni explained: "We concentrate on neutralizing armed opponents. We believe in disciplined, organized, and politically motivated violence against a system, but not individuals."[27]

But the actions of Sebirumbi and his supporters created complications for the NRA. These *vipingamizi* (enemy agents) abused the local population and raised the risk that UNLA detachments would encounter an NRA camp and strike a devastating blow to the insurgency. The NRA needed a policy for dealing with threats to its survival that came from the civilian population, as well. Museveni described the strategy: "It must be emphasized that notoriously anti-people elements who persistently undermine the struggle, especially by causing the death of civilians and our fighters, will not escape their just reward. For he who excels himself in committing anti-people crimes, turns himself into a legitimate military target and earns his death as a just retribution and deterrent."[28] NRA combatants were thus authorized to identify and target defectors and, when necessary, to use force against them. Targeted assassinations were the dominant form of NRA violence against noncombatants.

Overall patterns of violence in Uganda during the civil war underscore this picture of the restrained, disciplined behavior of NRA combatants (see Figure 6.6).[29] Throughout the conflict, rebel groups were responsible for the smallest number of incidents of violence.[30] UNLA-perpetrated violence, on the other hand, rose as the counterinsurgency campaign began in 1982 and remained consistently high until the war came to an end. The NRA committed only 17 percent of the total incidents of violence against civilians recorded during the war. NRA attacks did increase in 1983 as the UNLA made major inroads against the rebels in the Luwero Triangle. When the NRA evacuated its safe zone and moved its

---

[27] Yoweri Museveni, *Selected Articles on the Uganda Resistance War* (Kampala: NRM Publications, 1986), p. 13.

[28] Ibid.

[29] One should keep in mind that the numbers likely overstate the true level of rebel violence and systematically bias NRA behavior toward indiscriminate attacks and destructive actions. This is because governments typically assign blame for their own misdeeds to rebel forces. Thus, we can take the fact that the NRA appears disciplined and restrained even in spite of this bias as demonstration of its real behavior. I discuss this source of bias more in Appendix B.

[30] Because multiple rebel groups were operating in Uganda between 1981 and 1986, I assign responsibility to the NRA in cases where rebels are identified as the perpetrators only when actions took place in areas where the NRA was active. These areas include most of central Uganda between 1981 and 1983 and both central and western Uganda in 1984–86.

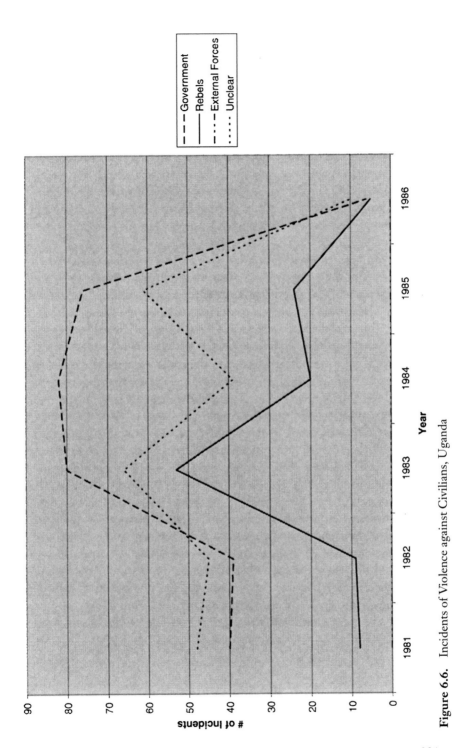

Figure 6.6. Incidents of Violence against Civilians, Uganda

operations farther north in late 1983, however, levels of violence began to decrease.

The character of NRA-perpetrated incidents is also revealing. Even though the geographic spread of the NRA's operations was limited, incident data help us to trace changes in rebel behavior as it grew from a force of hundreds into one of many thousands (see Figure 6.7). NRA cadres consistently targeted civilian victims as individuals and small groups. Although a small number of massacres took place at the hands of the rebels in 1983, the rebel army perpetrated fewer large-scale killings in 1984 and 1985 as it moved into new regions of operation and mobilized civilian support.

Semuto, the Luwero Triangle   The stories of combatants and civilians who lived under NRA control in Semuto reinforce the patterns reflected in aggregate data. "The guerrillas never killed people unjustly," a peasant insisted. "They would seek information about who was informing the government."[31] He recalled an incident in the early days of the civil war, only months after it began. Near the town, the NRA assassinated a man named Senyenya.[32] He was a strong supporter of the Uganda People's Congress – a rarity in Luwero, where most of the ethnic Baganda were opposed to the autocratic rule of Obote. The guerrillas had begun to organize in the surrounding villages, but they remained in hiding most of the time. A small number of UPC supporters in the area, Senyenya among them, began to provide information to the government's army. Senyenya gave a list of names to the UNLA indicating who was supporting the rebels. No one remembers how the NRA discovered Senyenya's crime, but many spoke of the consequences.

Senyenya was not the only informer in Kikandwa. Akuya and Adda were members of the Alur ethnic group, and from the beginning of the war they resisted the NRA's advances in the Luwero Triangle.[33] Immediately after a UNLA massacre in June 1981, Akuya and Adda scolded the people in the village for not heeding their warnings about the potential costs of supporting the rebels. At a subsequent UPC rally in Luwero town, the two kept tabs on who attended and who chose to stay home. They warned the residents of Kikandwa that those who decided not to attend "would suffer

---

[31] Interview, Semuto, November 21(A), 2000.
[32] The story of Senyenya's death was corroborated by other sources in the Luwero Triangle. See ibid., November 21(A), 23(B), 2000.
[33] Ibid., November 22(A), 2000.

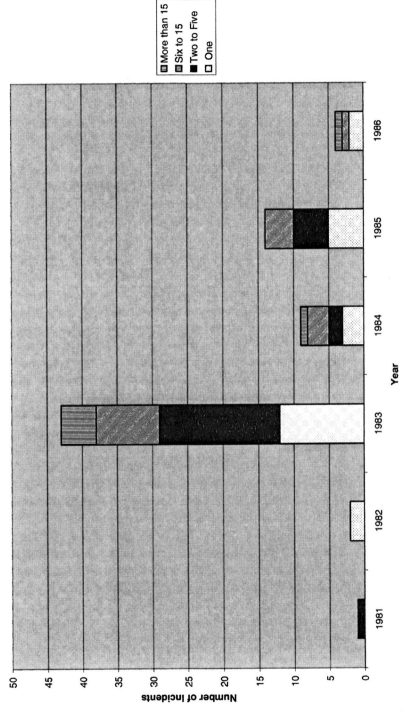

Figure 6.7. The Size of Victim Groups, NRA

223

the same fate as Lutta," a local leader who was killed by the UNLA. Almost everyone from Kikandwa went to the rally as a result. Soon after the guerrillas began to move freely and control the zone, Adda fled from the area, taking his belongings and his family. No one knows exactly what happened to Akuya, but he and another informer, Josua, are believed to have been killed about a month after the UNLA incursion. Although my respondents could not definitively attribute responsibility to the NRA for their deaths, one civilian remembered a speech Museveni gave in the village of Kikandwa soon after the UNLA massacre in which he said that "a country is liberated and delivered only by the shedding of blood." The civilian interpreted the statement as a claim of responsibility for the assassinations and a strong signal to other potential defectors of the likely costs of their actions.[34]

The deaths of Senyenya, Akuya, and Josua were characteristic of the NRA's tactics in its areas of control. Violence, when used, was perpetrated in a limited fashion. "Assassination wasn't something that happened very often," a former senior commander reported, "but there were Youth Wingers who were armed, and they became legitimate military targets."[35] First, however, efforts were made to convert the defectors.[36] They were identified by the local committees and then arrested by the NRA. The rebels sought to politicize and educate defectors before inviting them to join the guerrilla army or return to their villages.[37] Even when some resisted, they were simply transported to the NRA's rearguard camp for safekeeping during the war.[38] If they did not have information about where the rebels were hiding, some were set free to leave NRA areas of control and live on the government side.[39] Most UNLA supporters fled areas of NRA control rather than face the risk of reprisal by the rebels.[40]

---

[34] Ibid.

[35] Interviews, Kampala, October 25(A), 2000; July 15(A), 2001.

[36] One of the NRA's doctors described how injured prisoners of war would receive medical treatment and political education at the same time. They would be given the option to join; if they refused, they would be released back to the government side. The NRA believed that by treating the prisoners of war well, the rebels could weaken the morale of the government forces. Ibid., October 27(A), 2000.

[37] Ibid., October 24(B), 2000; interviews, Semuto, November 18(B), 19(A), 2000.

[38] Interviews, Kampala, November 2(A), 2000; January 24(A), 2001.

[39] Moses Kamya, a former communal chief, provides a good example. Kamya often informed on the guerrillas before he was arrested by Museveni and taken to the forest. The guerrillas originally planned to kill him, but after talking to him they decided to release him back into the village. He never informed again. A civilian recalled that "it was very uncommon for killings to take place." Interview, Semuto, November 15(B), 2000.

[40] Interview, Kampala, October 25(A), 2000.

But when defectors would not leave, they had to be dealt with seriously. It was critical, an NRA commander recalled, that the NRA use force differently than the UNLA. "We distinguished between friends and enemies," he claimed.[41] Another former NRA officer explained: "If we wanted someone exterminated, we reached the decision with the secret committee and the commanders... we would use [assassination] under desperate circumstances, after all other avenues had failed."[42] Only covert actions were taken against civilians, and often the NRA relied on the UNLA to kill its own supporters by using other civilians to provide false information to the government. The system was not perfect, of course. Mistakes were made, and some were killed unnecessarily by people who used the NRA to resolve old family feuds.[43] But by working through the local committees to identify traitors and gather evidence, the NRA sought to limit the number of mistakes it committed.

The NRA also prohibited behavior such as looting and the destruction of civilians' personal property. Looting was limited to the capture of resources from government facilities and health posts to replenish supplies for the insurgency. Theft from civilians was outlawed in the Code of Conduct, but the decision not to steal had deeper roots for most combatants. "This was not a group taking up arms for self-enrichment or robbery," one former commander said. "There was no interest in taking advantage of the situation for ourselves. It was circumstance, and our actions were in the best interest of the people."[44] Another soldier recalled: "Loot and do what with it? You could only take what you could carry. Our survival depended on discipline. We needed to be different than those we were fighting against."[45] Civilians from Semuto were aware of the discipline of the NRA rebels. One civilian refused to provide his vehicle to Museveni in the earliest days of the war for the transport of goods and people. Museveni's response, he recalled, was, "Fine, I'll walk."[46] Another told me: "If you met a guerrilla on the road with your bike, he would ask you to use it to take goods to the bush and arrange with you to return it the following day. The government would simply take it by force."[47]

[41] Ibid., January 15(A), 2001.
[42] Ibid., October 22(A), 2000.
[43] Interview, Semuto, November 19(A), 2000.
[44] Interview, Kampala, September 27(A), 2000.
[45] Ibid., January 24(A), 2000.
[46] Interview, Semuto, November 14(B), 2000.
[47] Ibid., November 17(C), 2000.

Civilians also recalled that the NRA punished acts of indiscipline. For crimes against civilians, punishments were determined publicly, through the use of disciplinary committees in full view of the civilians who were harmed. Civilians were encouraged to raise charges against NRA soldiers through the resistance councils or directly with NRA commanders. Museveni explained: "Because we were prepared to do this, the peasants were able to see that we were not like the old regimes which covered up crimes committed by their own supporters."[48] Capital crimes were punishable by death; other crimes, such as the looting of civilian property, received lesser sentences, including *kiboko* (a beating) or a short prison term in the rebel camp.[49] The High Command ordered executions for the four or five capital offenses committed by NRA soldiers against noncombatants. One famous case is of a soldier, Zabron, who, with another soldier, killed some villagers near Semuto in 1985. Both were under the influence of alcohol, and during their trial some tried to blame the crime on their drunkenness in an effort to spare Zabron's life. But in order to send clear messages to the population, both soldiers were executed.[50] Civilians knew that the NRA would discipline its own soldiers; as a result, when the NRA arrived in a village or called a meeting, the civilians would gather rather than flee.

Kiwanguzi As it was building a base near Semuto in 1981, the NRA decided not to extend operations into Kiwanguzi on the east side of the Kampala-Gulu road, which cuts the country in two. Although technically not in the Luwero Triangle, Kiwanguzi was also populated largely with Baganda who stood in staunch opposition to the Obote regime and the UNLA. As a consequence, the people of Kiwanguzi suffered the same attacks from UPC cadres and UNLA soldiers in their villages. The case of Kiwanguzi demonstrates the import placed by the NRA on maintaining its reputation for restraint and discipline. Because the NRA left residents of the region to fend for themselves, a group of locals established their own movement – the Vvumbula Armed Forces – to resist the Obote regime.[51]

---

[48] Museveni, *Selected Articles*, p. 134.

[49] Prisons were constructed by digging deep pits. Undisciplined soldiers would be kept in a pit for a particular amount of time as punishment. This was called *andaki*. Interview, Semuto, November 15(A), 2000.

[50] Interviews, Kampala, September 27(A), October 22(A), November 2(B), 2000; January 24(A), 2001. See also Museveni, *Selected Articles*, p. 134.

[51] Interviews, Luwero, December 7(A,B), 8(A), 2000.

Composed entirely of ethnic Baganda, the group set out to recruit members from the surrounding villages. It solicited food and members and sought to organize small committees to assist it. A former soldier in Idi Amin's army was the most experienced military man; he provided recruits with basic training and set in place a strategy of tactical ambushes of government forces in order to raise the arms necessary to survive.[52] But Vvumbula was a disorganized force. The line between combatants and civilians was blurred. Recruits were free to move in and out of the rebel camp, to drink as much as they wanted to, and to roam through the villages.[53] Problems of indiscipline were generally ignored. Civilians accused Vvumbula's soldiers of stealing property and looting shops.[54]

Because the NRA was not operating in the region, there was also a much larger presence of United People's Congress supporters in Kiwanguzi. The UNLA made more frequent incursions and benefited from the information provided by defectors, including UPC cadres and communal chiefs. The region was characterized by an insecurity and distrust that was not evident in areas of NRA control.

Most of Vvumbula's attacks targeted police posts and military patrols. Over the course of one year of independent operations, it amassed forty-six guns. But it also used force against UPC supporters who tried to undermine it in the villages. Like the NRA, Vvumbula saw UPC cadres as legitimate military targets because of their behavior. When I asked whether Vvumbula killed Obote supporters, a former Vvumbula soldier responded: "When they still lived in the villages, or when they came armed with pangas leading UNLA soldiers on their killing sprees?"[55] Defectors necessarily became targets.

In 1982, the leaders of Vvumbula visited an NRA camp in the Triangle to discuss a possible merger of the two fighting forces. There was significant dissension within Vvumbula about whether to link up with Museveni and the NRA or with Andrew Kayiira's group, the Uganda Freedom Movement, led by fellow Baganda. When the Vvumbula leaders could not locate Kayiira, they decided to seek Museveni's assistance for new arms, soldiers, and resources to carry on the war. At this point, my respondents' stories

---

[52] Ibid., December 8(A), 2000.
[53] Ibid., December 1(A), 2(A), 5(A), 2000.
[54] Ibid., November 30(A), December 4(B), 2000.
[55] Ibid., December 1(A), 2000.

diverge. Former NRA commanders remember that Museveni sent an investigative team to the Kiwanguzi area to learn more about Vvumbula and its operations.[56] The team included Paul Kagame, an intelligence operative and Rwandan refugee who is the current president of Rwanda. The team was tasked with taking stock of the insurgent unit, assessing its operations, and conducting reconnaissance of the Kiwanguzi area. One civilian who witnessed the team's arrival put its purpose in the form of an African proverb: "You wouldn't immediately trust a person you have never been digging with to supply your food until you had seen him do it yourself."[57]

The team discovered that Vvumbula was involved in banditry – stealing from, abusing, and killing the civilian population. More troubling for Museveni was the fact that many civilians in Kiwanguzi believed Vvumbula was already a unit of the NRA. In an effort to protect the NRA's reputation with civilians, Museveni authorized a team to arrest the senior leadership of Vvumbula, to take away its weaponry, and to retrain willing Vvumbula combatants as NRA soldiers under new NRA leadership.[58] Three Vvumbula commanders were detained and taken to the NRA's rearguard camp, where they were forced to endure political education and retraining for the rest of the war.

Former Vvumbula commanders tell another version of the story, namely, that the NRA agreed in principle to accept the force as a new unit on one condition: The commander of Vvumbula was ordered to round up all UPC supporters and communal chiefs in Kiwanguzi before NRA commanders and soldiers would arrive.[59] Knowing that the area was more densely populated with defectors than the Luwero Triangle proper, Museveni may have felt the need to lessen the risks of taking on a new operational zone. Vvumbula complied and detained a number of UPC supporters. They were first encouraged to convert. Five refused and were killed. When the area was pacified, the NRA sent a team of new commanders to take over the unit. The transition was muddled, with former Vvumbula leaders unsure of their new role in the merged force.[60] Moreover, the new NRA leadership of the unit was viewed by the old cadres as weak and corrupt. At a meeting of former Vvumbula supporters, three leaders proposed breaking away from

---

[56] Interviews, Kampala, November 2(A), 7(A), 2000.
[57] Interview, Luwero, December 1(A), 2000.
[58] Interviews, Kampala, November 2(A), 7(A), 2000.
[59] Interview, Luwero, December 8(A), 2000.
[60] Ibid., December, 4(A,B), 7(A,B), 8(A), 2002.

the NRA to link up with the Uganda Freedom Movement.[61] Although the members rejected this approach, the leaders insisted and challenged the authority of the NRA commander. For this reason, they claim, Museveni had them arrested and taken to his camp for the duration of the war.

The events in Kiwanguzi point to the importance of maintaining consistency in rebel behavior: the NRA prized its reputation and sought to instill the same discipline in Kiwanguzi as it maintained in the Triangle. Civilians of Kiwanguzi recalled that after the merger guerrillas no longer moved freely in and out of the rebel camps, that looting by insurgents came to an end, and that people enjoyed greater protections from the incursions of the UNLA.[62] Even far from the center of rebel control, the NRA set in place mechanisms to rein in supportive forces and establish an equivalent level of discipline. Regardless of where it operated, the NRA sought to behave with consistency; to punish defectors, even if they were civilians; and to prevent abuses against the civilian population perpetrated from within or from outside the movement. Consistent with its origins as an activist movement, it drew on its shared ideology and its tight linkages to local communities to employ violence strategically and selectively.

A Campaign of Brutality: Renamo

While the NRA operated in a compact region full of potential rebel supporters, Renamo faced a more difficult challenge. The rebels were at a relative disadvantage from the perspective of mobility. To advance on provincial capitals, Renamo had to place soldiers at points throughout the country without access to mechanized transport. The government utilized airplanes, helicopters, tanks, and vehicles to assemble its fighting forces rapidly and to counter rebel advances, but it was at a relative disadvantage from the perspective of territorial control. With limited resources and personnel, it was unable to distribute its forces widely in rural areas and maintain sovereignty throughout its vast territory. There were many places where Renamo could hide and build bases of popular support.

One practical implication of Mozambique's size was that Renamo operated nationwide, both in areas of potential support and in regions of almost total opposition. The central provinces and areas in northern Mozambique were fertile ground for Renamo recruitment: local populations shared the

---

[61] Ibid., November 30(A), December 1(A,D), 2002.
[62] Ibid., December 2(A), 4(D), 2002.

same ethnic identities as Renamo combatants and had resisted Frelimo's socialist innovations in the countryside. The South, by contrast, was a Frelimo stronghold. Renamo could not avoid launching operations in southern provinces if it wished to capture state power, but it faced much greater resistance from local populations there. Thus, in the case of Mozambique, perspectives from both areas of strong rebel control and areas of weak rebel influence are critical in developing a picture of how force was used in Renamo's campaigns.

In spite of the ready-made national divisions, patterns of Renamo violence exhibit surprising consistency both geographically and temporally. While violence was sometimes used selectively to target Frelimo supporters, Renamo rarely showed restraint. Victims of Renamo attacks included Frelimo supporters and Renamo supporters, as well as civilians living in government-controlled zones and those in areas of rebel influence and administration. One civilian recalled: "In the beginning, they only abducted boys and took them. But they came back and said that the objective was to kill everyone who belonged to the Grupo Dinamizador. They began by killing those people, but then began to kill people who had nothing to do with the Grupo Dinamizador or anything else. And they also abducted women."[63]

The distinguishing characteristic of Renamo's actions was the abuse of noncombatants: forced abduction of recruits and civilian supporters, destruction of buildings in government-influenced areas, looting of civilian property, and killing. Such behavior led the government to label Renamo's members *bandidos armados* (armed bandits), and for much of the war analysts characterized Renamo as a disorganized movement of thieves. Yet Renamo was a highly centralized operation, with each of its many units connected by radio to the central command.[64] The rebels transferred arms caches and recruits from unit to unit and coordinated strategy from their headquarters in Gorongosa and later Marínguè. Civilians who lived in fear of violence, abduction, and robbery were not threatened by marauding bands of thieves; the threat emanated instead from an organized insurgency.

As Figure 6.8 makes clear, aggregate data capture this consistency in the character of Renamo's conduct. Rebels were responsible for the vast

---

[63] Civilian quoted in Anders Nilsson, *Peace in Our Time* (Gothenburg, Sweden: Padrigu, 1999), p. 115.
[64] This fact was revealed in an important study conducted by William Minter in 1989. See *The Mozambican National Resistance (Renamo) as Described by Ex-Participants* (Washington, DC: Report Submitted to the Ford Foundation, 1989).

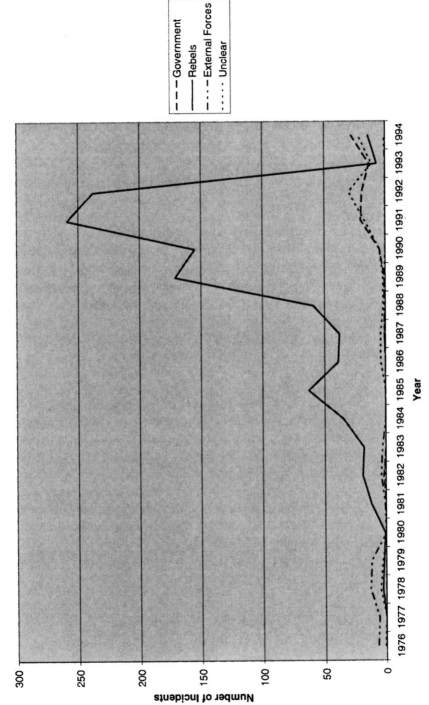

Figure 6.8. Incidents of Violence against Civilians, Mozambique

231

majority of incidents of violence.[65] After the fall of Rhodesia, when external forces no longer played an active combat role in the conflict, Renamo consistently perpetrated the largest number of abuses against the civilian population. These data fit with Africa Watch's assertion that the "vast majority of gross abuses" can be attributed to Renamo.[66] As Renamo grew in size and spread throughout the 1980s, moreover, the number of violent incidents increased. The violence subsided only after 1992, when the majority of Renamo soldiers demobilized as part of the peace agreement.

Whereas NRA violence overwhelmingly targeted individuals and small groups, Renamo's actions often resulted in the deaths of many civilians in each incident: between 1980 and 1992, Renamo committed 112 massacres of more than 15 noncombatants. Massacres were a consistent feature of Renamo's behavior over time, occurring at the earliest stages of the conflict as well as at its conclusion (see Figure 6.9). Renamo violence also appears fairly indiscriminate when broken down geographically: while a greater number of massacres took place in the southern provinces – regions of Frelimo support – the Center and the North were not immune from Renamo's brutality (see Figure 6.10).

The quantitative data provide evidence of Renamo's abuses against noncombatant populations. Its behavior stands in stark contrast to that of the NRA. Renamo actions were violent and often involved killing, looting, and destruction. When civilians were killed, moreover, they died in large groups, and few were identifiable as political leaders, party officials, or communal chiefs. Importantly, the patterns evident in Renamo behavior appear consistent over time and across geographic regions, even as the level of violence varies.[67]

---

[65] Data on civilian casualties in war can be found in the Stockholm International Peace Research Institute, *SIPRI Yearbook 1999* (Stockholm: SIPRI, 1999).

[66] Africa Watch, *Conspicuous Destruction: War, Famine, and the Reform Process in Mozambique* (New York: Human Rights Watch, 1992), p. 1.

[67] This consistency is in marked contrast to a well-known report on the Mozambican conflict by a U.S. State Department consultant, Robert Gersony. Based on interviews with Mozambican refugees during the war, he argued that Renamo operated in three types of zones: tax areas, which it visited only to collect resources; control areas, where it administered the population; and destruction zones, where indiscriminate violence was the norm. Others suggested that these characterizations applied to the North, Center, and South, respectively. See Robert Gersony, *Summary of Mozambican Refugee Accounts of Principally Conflict-Related Experience in Mozambique* (Washington, DC: Report submitted to the U.S. Department of State, 1988).

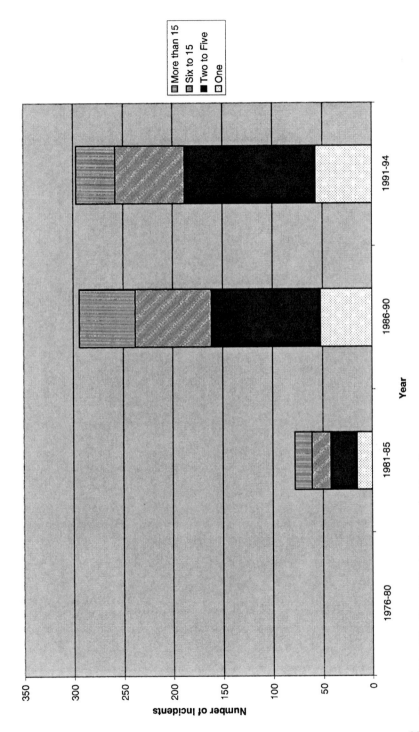

Figure 6.9. The Size of Victim Groups by Year, Renamo

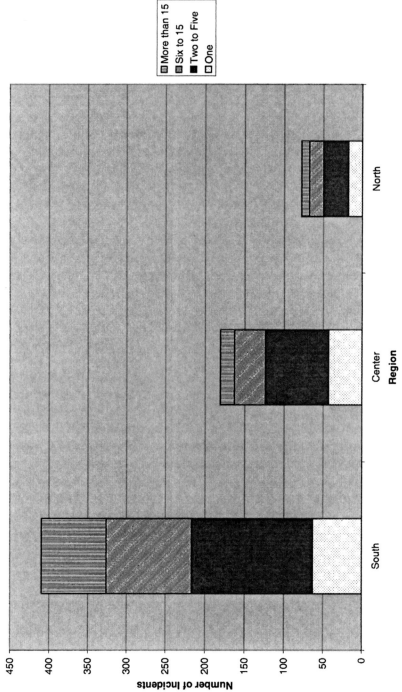

Figure 6.10. The Size of Victim Groups by Region, Renamo

234

Maríngue, Sofala Province, Central Mozambique   A peasant said about the Renamo guerrillas: "They are our sons, but what they want we do not know. As they are making these massacres, when the war ends, with whom will they live? Will they live only with the trees? Their hearts are inside out. They don't think of themselves as with us."[68] Many peasants who live in what was formerly Renamo's stronghold share vivid memories of the group's first attacks on their villages. In Canxixe, Renamo attacked for the first time in 1979, looting shops, destroying equipment, and abducting one man. The rebels gave no advance warning to the population; peasants remembered fleeing as soon as the shots rang out. Three years later, Renamo mounted its second assault on Canxixe. By 1982, Canxixe had a small detachment of government soldiers who stayed in the center of town. But Renamo did not target the government outpost. Instead, it attacked the Nhamaika communal village, setting houses on fire, looting property, and killing ten civilians. The régulo at the time remembered that there was chaos as the attack ensued.[69] Renamo soldiers made no effort to identify victims, he recalled. People tried to flee, and the soldiers shot them.

Renamo's first attacks on Canxixe are characteristic of its behavior in contested zones. The government had posted small numbers of soldiers and militia members in the center of the town and organized communal villages outside of the center of town to centralize the population for security purposes. Yet outside of the town itself, in the fields where civilians went to grow their food, Renamo had unlimited access. Renamo's incursions in these contested zones were brutal and indiscriminate. Efforts were sometimes made to identify Frelimo party secretaries and other government supporters, but violence often careened out of control.[70] The killing extended broadly to anyone whom Renamo encountered.[71] And Renamo burned down the communal villages, looted people's property, and abducted men, women, and children for service in its military and to live as captives in Renamo areas of control. Expecting this behavior, civilians learned to flee immediately when Renamo arrived. "Fleeing was not a social thing," one civilian explained. "You went by whatever path you found."[72]

Such behavior might be expected in zones of governmental control where civilians are already dead-set against assisting a rebel movement,

---

[68] Nilsson, *Peace in Our Time*, p. 124.
[69] Interview, Maríngue District, Sofala Province, May 22(A), 2001.
[70] Ibid., May 18(A), 22(A,B,C), 23(B), 24(A), 2001.
[71] Ibid., May 22(A), 2001.
[72] Ibid., May 21(D), 2001.

but Canxixe was located only kilometers from Marínguè, the heart of the rebel movement. It was near Renamo's command post in Gorongosa, and it housed a civilian population already fed up with the coercive policies of Frelimo's socialist regime. Yet Renamo made few efforts to politicize the local population. Even though it had unfettered access to people in the fields, Renamo opted to destroy communal villages without warning and to forcibly herd people into its zones of control.[73]

Behind Renamo lines, the situation was similar. Nfudzu was a rebel-controlled zone just outside of Marínguè town.[74] Renamo controlled the population through its system of régulos and mudjibas, and attacks by armed combatants were unnecessary. I could find no evidence of large massacres of civilians in Renamo's areas of control. Nonetheless, people experienced high levels of coercion on a daily basis. Most had been forcibly moved into the Renamo zone as part of a rebel attack. When they arrived, the behavior of the combatants rarely improved. Renamo soldiers were known to steal, rape, and kill civilians "without motive."[75] The rebels would demand that residents carry goods and weapons long distances.[76] "Whatever they asked for, a person was required to give," one civilian reported.[77] Another former resident described a similar situation: "When there was a chicken, they asked for it; a goat, they asked for it; if you didn't have the goat, they would take your wife."[78] When this civilian could not provide a chicken, he was beaten severely. Only the intervention of another Renamo combatant prevented his execution.

Of course, government soldiers employed coercion as well. Before leaving Marínguè for good in 1985, Frelimo organized a local militia led by a man named Japão. He terrorized the local population, often using force to bring people back into the communal villages. Civilians who resisted villagization could be killed.[79] In response to rebel attacks, the government instituted further controls on civilian populations, restricting their movement

---

[73] Ibid., May 19(D), 21(A), 22(A), 23(B), 2001.

[74] These findings come from interviews with former residents of Nfudzu who still live in the area – a strong signal of their support for Renamo. Marínguè and its surroundings remain at the center of Renamo's electoral power base in the country. This fact makes the interviewees' willingness to speak frankly about Renamo indiscipline more credible.

[75] Interview, Marínguè, Sofala Province, May 21(A), 2001.

[76] Ibid., May 22(A,C), 2001.

[77] Ibid., May 23(B), 2001.

[78] Ibid.

[79] Ibid., May 19(B), 21(A), 22(B), 2001.

outside of communal villages and forcing them to serve in militias. But in stark contrast to peasants' recollections of Renamo attacks, few could remember the names of any civilians killed by Frelimo in Marínguè.

Ribáuè District, Nampula Province, Northern Mozambique Hundreds of miles away in northern Mozambique, Renamo initiated its operations in 1983 near the town of Ribáuè. The general in charge of Renamo's forces approached the régulo, Metaveia, for permission to operate in an area just outside of the municipality. Metaveia consented and agreed to help the rebels organize resistance to Frelimo.[80] His anger at the government was palpable at the time. Like other régulos, he had lost his position when Frelimo took power and disbanded traditional systems of governance. As in Marínguè, there was a potential base of discontent in the region that was growing in response to Frelimo's socialist policies in the countryside.

Yet attacks on government-influenced areas demonstrated an absence of restraint on Renamo's part.[81] No efforts were made to identify party officials and government supporters or to attack posts of government soldiers or local militias. The first attack near Ribáuè was an ambush on a Land Cruiser in 1983. The driver, who was the director of a state-owned company, Minas Gerais, was killed when the vehicle was set ablaze. Although he was a state employee, he was not a local party functionary. In this same period, Renamo began to abduct students and other civilians to swell its ranks in the area.[82] In 1985, Ribáuè itself came under fire. The rebels entered the town and destroyed the Frelimo party building, the post office, the social club, and a store. They looted supplies and food; three people were killed and seven abducted as Renamo fled. The next year brought an attack on the hospital, school, and some houses in which a teacher was killed and vehicles were destroyed. Incidents of looting followed in 1988 as Renamo raided the cattle holdings of some villagers. Renamo made no effort to organize the population or politicize them during any of these attacks.[83] People fled to the bush to avoid being killed or abducted by the rebels.[84]

---

[80] Interview, Ribáuè, Nampula Province, April 1(B), 2001.
[81] Ibid., March 30(C), 2001.
[82] Ibid., March 31(B,C), 2001.
[83] Ibid., March 30(C,D), 2000.
[84] Ibid., March 31(B), 2001.

A similar situation unfolded in Iapala, a nearby village that also housed a small detachment of government soldiers. Renamo first visited Iapala in mid-1984.[85] Combatants destroyed a number of buildings and looted the village market. No one was killed, as the entire population fled when the first shots were fired. The rebels attacked again in 1986, killing eight people and abducting thirty. The head of the police was one of those killed; another victim was a teacher. No respondents could recall the names or identities of others who died that day. In the course of these attacks, Renamo also destroyed the communal villages surrounding Iapala, forcing civilians to flee from their homes and setting the houses ablaze.

Around Ribáuè, the violence seemed to serve no strategic purpose. The rebels did not target government forces, local police, or even government supporters. Attacks failed to mobilize potential supporters living in government-influenced zones. A former combatant in the area explained that Renamo targeted communal villages to destroy them and loot the property.[86] Commanders would divide up the take when they returned to base, and soldiers could use their shares to trade with local populations living in rebel zones.[87] Renamo proved unable to protect even its own supporters from its attacks. One communal leader in the village of Caiaia only joined Renamo after the rebels kidnapped his wife. The rebels had not realized she was the spouse of a traditional leader – an important ally – and when they did, they returned her to her home and encouraged she and her husband to move into the Renamo zone voluntarily.[88] Another respondent, who assisted Renamo from his home in government-influenced territory, found his shop and cattle ranch attacked and looted during a Renamo incursion. He gave up on the rebels and fled to the provincial capital for the duration of the conflict.[89] Mistakes of this sort abounded: Renamo even ambushed the car of a Portuguese priest working in a local mission and killed him before destroying his vehicle. A Renamo insider admitted that they had not known the victim was a priest.[90]

Renamo maintained its coercive approach behind rebel lines in Nampula Province as well. One régulo who threw his support behind Renamo when it

---

[85] Ibid., April 3(B), 2001.
[86] Ibid., March 30(D), April 2(B), 2001.
[87] Ibid., April 2(B), 2001.
[88] Ibid., March 31(C), 2001.
[89] Ibid., April 2(C), 2001.
[90] Ibid., April 2(A), 2001.

arrived recalled that combatants misbehaved regularly, moving in and out of the base, taking women, and threatening the local population.[91] When there were significant charges of indiscipline, the commanders would promise to punish the soldiers inside the base, outside of the view of noncombatants. Often, civilians never found out if the problem had been resolved. As one civilian recalled, "This was a secret of the guerrillas."[92]

In northern Mozambique, far from the center of rebel control, levels of violence were much lower and attacks more infrequent, yet the character of Renamo's behavior was similar. Combatants showed little regard for the welfare of civilian populations when using violence in areas of government control and even against populations under their administration. Southern Mozambique, which experienced the highest levels of violence over the course of the conflict, has often been described as the epicenter of Renamo's campaign. Because of this region's overwhelming support for Frelimo, analysts have taken high-profile massacres in the South as evidence of Renamo's strategic targeting of Frelimo supporters and non-coethnics in the course of the war.[93] Even though levels of violence were higher in the southern region, the quantitative data indicate that the character of rebel violence was consistent across regions in the Mozambican conflict. The guerrillas avoided engagement with the government and police forces. Instead, Renamo attacked civilian targets in efforts to abduct new members, loot property, and destroy infrastructure. Civilians died in these attacks – some targeted, but most in the chaos of rebel incursions. And Renamo did little to punish abuses committed against civilian populations. The short-term, material motivations of its membership rendered Renamo's commanders unable to police defection within their units; abusiveness was an unintended byproduct of a recruitment strategy that attracted opportunistic joiners first, and then swelled the ranks with abductees.

Patterns of Restraint and Excess: Sendero Luminoso Nacional

Like rebel groups in Uganda and Mozambique, the Shining Path was a rural insurgency with important links to the peasantry. Peasants were recruited

---

[91] Ibid., April 1(B), 2001.
[92] Ibid.
[93] For a review of the standard interpretation of regional variation in the civil war, see William Minter, *Apartheid's Contras: An Inquiry into the Roots of War in Angola and Mozambique* (London: Zed Books, 1994), p. 211.

as members of the Shining Path's armed forces. They also made up the crucial *bases de apoyo* (bases of support) for the guerrilla army. But there was a hierarchy of participation even in the guerrilla zones.[94] The "principal force" was Sendero's professional army. The "local force" remained tied to one region and had as its principal goal the defense of guerrilla zones. The "base force" was a reservoir of manpower.[95] A parallel structure existed within the party. The masses were largely members of the base force. In each zone, they were organized into an open people's committee under the leadership of *responsables* (authorities): a secretary general and secretaries of security, production, communal affairs, and organization.[96] Sometimes, these positions overlapped with the roles of authority in the base force: a *mando politico* and a *mando militar*. Armed militants in the principal force and in higher reaches of the party appointed members of the local population to these positions of authority and invested them with the power to administer civilians and maintain order in guerrilla zones.

These multiple loci of power are critical to understanding the character of rebel violence in Peru. Multiple actors were in a position to use force, and their behaviors were shaped by distinct factors. Patterns of Sendero violence thus reflect a mix of behaviors, from highly selective assassinations to large civilian massacres, which occurred particularly in the later stages of the war. The Shining Path's acts of strategic violence included attacks on members of the armed forces, police, civilian guards, government and party officials, and wealthy landowning elites. Perpetrated by members of the principal and regional forces, sometimes with the assistance of the base force, these actions were Sendero's so-called terrorism, targeted selectively at representatives of state power and wealth.

Sendero Luminoso also utilized violence in an effort to maintain territorial control in guerrilla zones. Its actions included the killing of communal authorities and government supporters through popular trials. More often, the Shining Path killed civilians who refused to live in accordance with the movement's rules. Importantly, these actions were carried out by responsables and mandos invested with authority by Sendero militants. Increasingly over the course of the war, these local authorities were left to their own

---

[94] Ponciano del Pino, "Family, Culture, and 'Revolution': Everyday Life with Sendero Luminoso," in *Shining and Other Paths: War and Society in Peru, 1980–1995,* ed. Steve J. Stern (Durham: Duke University Press, 1998), p. 176.

[95] Interview, Huanta, Ayacucho, December 1(D), 2001.

[96] Ibid., December 4(B), 2001.

devices.[97] The distribution of responsibility for violence led one civilian to comment that Sendero militants ("those who visited us from outside") "did not commit abuses."[98] Rather, it was those who lived with the civilians all the time who were responsible for the majority of the violence.

Aggregate data on violence in Peru reflect the restraint and excess of rebel behavior. Restraint was evident in the activities of Sendero's principal combat forces, while excesses were committed both by Sendero in the later stages of the conflict and by the armed forces as part of counterinsurgency campaigns in the rural areas after 1983. Figure 6.11 charts incidents of violence by Sendero and the government broken down by year.[99] It is now generally accepted that the government and rebels share responsibility for the violence; however, many government abuses committed during the war went unrecorded by the local newspapers from which my events database was constructed.[100] The data presented here thus link Sendero Luminoso to a significant proportion of the attacks against civilians, but connect the government to less than 4 percent of total attacks. Rebel combatants committed, at a minimum, 37 percent of the incidents catalogued between 1980 and 1988, and the number of total incidents steadily increased with each passing year as Sendero and the government forces grew in strength. New data gathered from peasant testimonies by Peru's Truth and Reconciliation Commission paint a more accurate picture of the government's involvement

[97] Ibid., December 1(B,D), 2001.
[98] Ibid., December 4(B), 2001.
[99] The significant drop in the total number of Shining Path incidents after 1983 is mostly a reflection of the coding process rather than of an absolute reduction in violence. Sendero Luminoso was the sole actor in the conflict until the end of 1983, when the government launched its counterinsurgency campaigns and the Movimiento Revolucionario Túpac Amaru became operative. Thus, after 1983, the majority of incidents of violence cannot be specifically tied to Sendero, and responsibility is coded as "unclear." As a consequence, they do not appear in Figures 6.12 and 6.13. Data from the Truth and Reconciliation Commission, however, do suggest that 1983–84 was the period of greatest intensity in the war. Levels of violence did decline in the ensuing years, although murders and disappearances reached a second (lower) peak in 1989 – a period that the incident database described here does not cover. See Comisión de la Verdad y Reconciliación, *Final Report*, Chapter 3, p. 176.
[100] The primary source of incident data for this project is a monthly survey of political violence compiled by DESCO, a local Peruvian nongovernmental organization. See DESCO, *Violencia política en el Peru* (Lima: DESCO, 1989). Where this reporting assigns responsibility to the government, Sendero Luminoso, or the Movimiento Revolucionario Túpac Amaru (a rival rebel group), the database codes the appropriate party as the perpetrator. The majority of incidents, however, have no specific information about perpetration. They have been coded as "unclear."

242

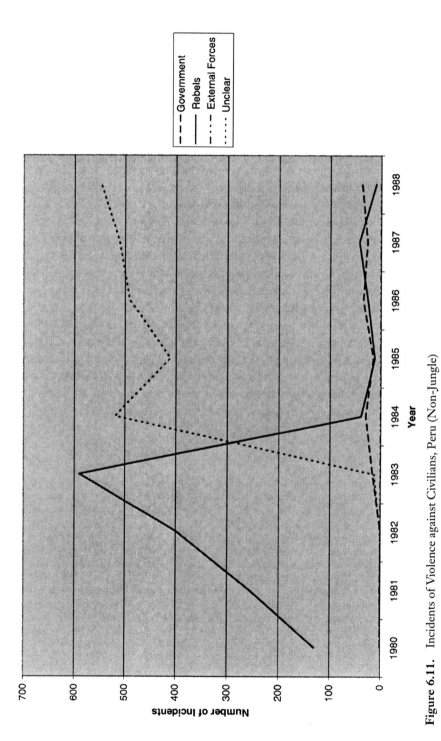

Figure 6.11. Incidents of Violence against Civilians, Peru (Non-Jungle)

in violence and assign responsibility to the military for 37 percent of total deaths.

Data on the character of Sendero violence suggest that the rebels showed significant restraint between 1980 and 1988, even as their reach extended into new geographic zones (see Figures 6.12 and 6.13).[101] Like the National Resistance Army in Uganda, the Shining Path killed civilians individually or in small groups as part of targeted assassinations and executions of defectors. More than 80 percent of rebel killing incidents caused the deaths of fewer than six people. By contrast, government attacks targeted medium and large groups more than 40 percent of the time. The Shining Path tended to kill individuals in slightly larger groups in its principal region of operation (Ayacucho), but its predominant strategy was one of selective and targeted killing across its geographic zones of operation.

But the stories peasants tell, to which we now turn, point to an additional pattern not captured in the quantitative data. In particular, they suggest an increase in the number of Shining Path massacres as the war progressed, particularly after 1988, a period for which data are not available. Civilians were targeted not because of their political or communal leadership positions but because of their active resistance to Sendero's advances. To some extent, these massacres were excesses on the part of Shining Path local authorities. But many were a form of collective punishment. The rebels conducted massacres in villages that were organizing civilian self-defense committees with the support of the government to send a signal of the costs of abandoning the insurgent movement. Understanding when, where, and why the Shining Path resorted to mass selective violence (that is, the targeting of entire villages) requires a closer examination of the experience of two communities in the Peruvian highlands.

Zonas Bajas, Huanta Province, Ayacucho, Peru   "We knew that it was Sendero Luminoso," she said, "because they left the bodies behind." When it was the military or civilian militias who were responsible, this civilian

---

[101] One should be careful in drawing overall conclusions about Sendero's behavior, as the incident database covers the war only through 1988. The Shining Path continued its attacks through 1992 before it was largely defeated. Case study evidence, however, is strongly suggestive of the continued selective character of Sendero attacks, although it also makes clear that collective punishment (of villages rather than individuals) emerged as a common strategy in later years.

244

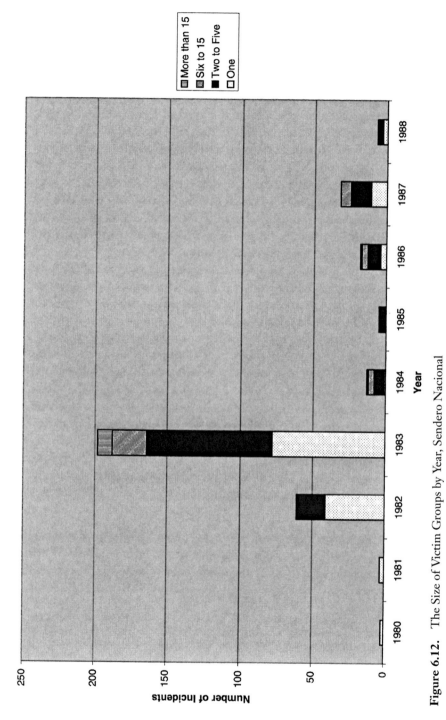

Figure 6.12. The Size of Victim Groups by Year, Sendero Nacional

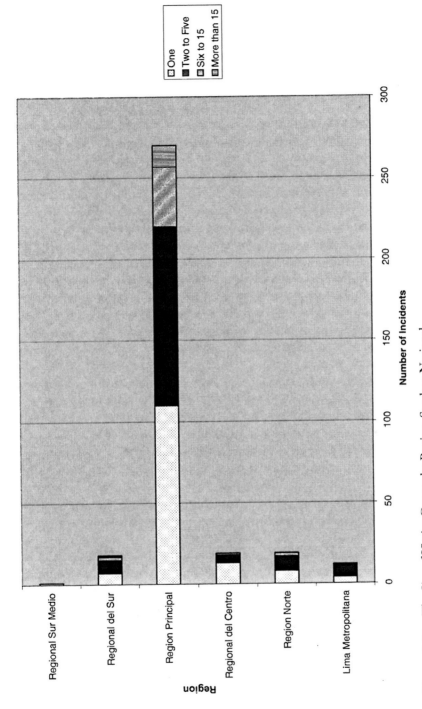

Figure 6.13. The Size of Victim Groups by Region, Sendero Nacional

remembered, people simply disappeared.[102] Sendero used its acts of violence to send strong signals to the civilian population.

The Shining Path established a base of operations in the valley below the town of Huanta. The capital of Ayacucho, the department in which Sendero launched its armed struggle, was nearby. This location provided the militants with access to the senior party leadership for guidance and direction. Operating in the valley was also a strategic choice.[103] The Shining Path had local contacts in the area, the lowland areas were fertile, and peasants had strong memories of the hacienda owners against whom the rebels railed in their propaganda.

Sendero launched attacks on the town of Huanta from its base in the valley. The first incursions were harmless – graffiti on government buildings, the destruction of monuments, and threats to local leaders.[104] But then the Shining Path became more ambitious. The rebels began to assault posts of the police and civilian guard. In April 1981, they attacked the civilian guard in Luricocha, just down the road from Huanta, and stole arms and ammunition.[105] Months later, the militants attacked another guard post in San José de Secce up in the hills above Huanta and stole additional armaments. In 1982, they assassinated a member of the armed forces during an action in the town of Huanta.

Assassinations also extended to noncombatant populations. A former member of the civilian guard was killed in Huanta in late 1982 by a group of eight insurgents. In May of 1983, the rebels launched an attack that killed the lieutenant governor and a teacher in the town of San Francisco. Another government official was executed in August. And a candidate for mayor in Huanta was the victim of an assassination attempt in October of 1983.

Members of the principal or regional force operating in the zone planned many of these actions in advance. Sendero militants or informers carefully monitored the targets beforehand to establish their patterns of behavior. The nascent rebel army had to limit its exposure to government forces while maintaining its capacity to strike in the heart of areas of government control. The basis for these actions was the operational tactical plan put

---

[102] Interview, Huanta, Ayacucho, December 1(A), 2001.
[103] Ibid., December 2(A), 2001.
[104] Ibid.
[105] For a chronology of major incidents of political violence in Peru, see DESCO, *Violencia política en el Peru*.

246

together by the mandos in charge of the military unit.[106] The action committee required the submission of such a plan before the action could be launched. The plan would include information about the target, the responsibilities assigned to each participant, and a rationale for the attack. When the attack was completed, the militants were required to put together a report for higher party and military officials evaluating the action. In it, the mandos evaluated the behavior of each participant in the action. Due to these procedures, attacks were disciplined and targeted, and there was little room for misbehavior.

The Shining Path also used violence in its efforts to establish authority and maintain control behind rebel lines. Even in this context, Sendero was selective, chose its victims carefully, and used its executions to demonstrate publicly its authority and power in the zone. Violence was a tool for "social cleansing," and the Shining Path used public executions to rid local communities of thieves, adulterers, and, most importantly, deserters.[107] This objective was reflected in 1982 propaganda of the Central Committee that called on the militants to "hammer the countryside": "In Hammering, the key is to demolish, and demolish means not to leave anything . . . to dislocate the power of the bosses, disarrange the power of authorities, and hit the live forces of the enemy . . . clean out the zone, leave an empty plain."[108]

Popular trials served as an important forum for the rebels as they sought to indoctrinate their supporters and build an impenetrable base of support. Huanta's victims are remembered by many peasants. In November 1982, Sendero killed a businessman after he was accused of providing information to the government.[109] Later that same month, two peasants were executed for being traitors against the Sendero state. Two female peasants became victims in July 1984 after being accused of "collaborating with the police." And the list goes on.

Civilians tell similar stories about killings outside of the context of popular trials. One woman lost her uncle, a wealthy businessman, after he refused to make contributions to the guerrilla army.[110] A cousin of the same woman was executed after he was caught deserting the Sendero army. Another man

106 Benedicto Jiménez Bacca, *Inicio, desarrollo, y ocaso del terrorismo en el Perú* (Lima: SANKI, 2000), p. 146.
107 Carlos Iván Degregori, "Harvesting Storms: Peasant *Rondas* and the Defeat of Sendero Luminoso in Ayacucho," in Stern, *Shining and Other Paths*, p. 136.
108 Ibid.
109 DESCO, *Violencia política en el Peru*.
110 Interview, Huanta, Ayacucho, December 3(A), 2001.

and his two sons were killed in a popular trial for refusing to participate as mandos in the guerrilla army. In the *zonas bajas* (low zones), because members of the principal and regional forces stayed nearby, violence remained selective throughout much of the war. Civilians could guarantee their own survival only by participating in Sendero activities and refusing to collaborate with the police or government forces.

This behavior presents a marked contrast to that of the government in its counterinsurgency campaigns. One civilian recalled that "when Sendero entered a community, the military would follow and massacre the entire village."[111] "Innocents were killed along with the guilty. They killed because they liked it," another said.[112] The Peruvian military's strategy put peasants in a difficult position: all who had previous contact with Sendero risked execution if they did not remain protected in rebel-held zones. It did not matter whether they had assisted the rebels personally; the government did not care. But peasants who remained in the countryside, unprotected by the guerrillas, were liable to be targeted by the government as potential terrorist supporters. The zonas bajas thus remained under tight rebel control until 1989 and 1990, near the end of the war. Where the military had far greater access to the population in the highlands, Sendero encountered greater difficulties with the local population. If they wanted to stay in their homes, they had to resist the rebels – a strategy that elicited a brutal response from Sendero.

Zonas Altas, Huanta Province, Ayacucho, Peru The roads and paths rise into the mountains as they lead out of Huanta. Huanta has a rich, fertile valley on one side. On the other side are the *zonas alto-andinas* (high Andean zones), where the weather is unpredictable, the land is infertile, and the linkages to the relative prosperity of the lowlands are few. Even today, more than ten years after the war's conclusion, there are no paved roads to most of the high Andean communities.

Sendero Luminoso battled for peasant support in the zonas altas as well. Its connections to the indigenous population were weak. Whereas in the valley the guerrillas could draw on their shared background, language, and familial connections, the rebels lacked any entry into the highlands save for their ideology. Because they openly called for better lives for the

[111] Ibid., December 1(A), 2001.
[112] Ibid., December 1(C), 2001.

peasantry, civilians often welcomed the rebels when they first arrived.[113] But in many ways, Sendero's approach was alien to the indigenous populations.[114] Sendero promoted collective production for subsistence and for the party, but its efforts to close markets for agricultural produce were met with resistance. Sendero replaced older communal authorities with young people; this transition was difficult and often angered long-time community residents. And Sendero used force to punish community members. Many peasants thought that the killing of thieves, adulterers, and deserters was too extreme and that communal laws dictated a more appropriate punishment.

Civilian testimonies suggest that difficulties arose most directly from the behavior of Sendero's appointed local authorities. The mandos moved quickly to establish their authority. They prevented unknown people from entering the community and confiscated people's personal identity documents to stop residents from leaving.[115] They kept track of who attended community meetings and punished those who were absent.[116] And the mandos began to take advantage of their authority for personal gain. Some would raise the warning of an attack, and when people fled, they would rob their belongings from their homes.[117] Others would use popular trials to take revenge on members of the community. One young man described how his father was accused and denounced to the Shining Path by a family member who was jealous of his cattle and his wealth.[118] He was later killed by Sendero. Moreover, the mandos simply ignored rules such as "do not take liberties with women," though adultery was supposed to be punished with death.[119]

The indiscipline of highland mandos and members of the base force was the result of two connected factors. Because the Shining Path maintained its bases in the lowlands, where food and resources were more plentiful, its visits to highland communities were often brief. Authorities were appointed to administer so-called liberated zones and then left to their own devices. Little was invested in the ideological formation of these mandos.[120] In the lowlands, by contrast, many of the mandos were integrally

---

[113] Ibid., December 1(B,D), 2001.
[114] Degregori, "Harvesting Storms," p. 133.
[115] Interview, Huanta, Ayacucho, December 1(B), 2001.
[116] Ibid., December 4(A), 2001.
[117] Ibid., December 4(B), 2001.
[118] Ibid., December 5(A), 2001.
[119] Del Pino, "Family, Culture, and 'Revolution,'" p. 181.
[120] Interview, Huanta, Ayacucho, December 2(A), 2001.

connected to the rebel movement. They had been recruited through university, school, or familial contacts. Over time, they became ideological converts as well as local authorities. Because the formed Sendero militants passed through highland communities infrequently, the monitoring mechanism that restrained abuses in the lowlands was largely absent in the zonas altas. Undisciplined behavior occurred when the principal force had gone, and civilians had nowhere to turn for recourse.

After 1983, when the government initiated a counterinsurgency campaign in Ayacucho, the zonas altas also became more susceptible to government incursions. Because residents of the high Andean communities had welcomed Sendero in the beginning, they became targets of the government forces, regardless of whether they continued to support the guerrillas. Unable to protect themselves from corrupt Sendero authorities and unwilling to die at the hands of barbaric government forces, many civilians decided to organize their own home-grown resistance to the guerrillas. Less than a month after the Peruvian government began its crackdown, peasants in Huaychao assassinated seven Senderistas in retaliation for the killing of three communal authorities.[121] Local self-defense committees, later called *rondas campesinas*, blossomed in the highland zones as civilians realized they would receive infusions of government aid and support for actively resisting rebel incursions. Regardless of their loyalties, active resistance was the only way for them to avoid death at the hands of the government forces.

In response to this resistance, the Shining Path unleashed a campaign of violence against many highland communities. It perpetrated increasingly large massacres of civilian populations in communities known to be organizing resistance to the guerrillas. Caught between brutal actions by the government and the rebels, the civilians of the zonas altas had nowhere to turn. They armed themselves and attempted to protect their homes or, if they could get out alive, fled to the regional cities and to the capital, Lima.

Sendero utilized a strategy of collective punishment in the zonas altas. One woman from a village near San José de Secce recalled that when the rebels received word that peasants were organizing a ronda, the rebels attacked. Most of the people fled, but Sendero stayed to set fire to the homes in the village, killing four in the process.[122] A more famous case is the massacre of Lucanamarca. After civilians killed three Senderistas and captured another seven, the rebels responded with a massacre of over eighty

---

[121] Ibid., December 2(A), 3(E), 2001.
[122] Ibid., December 3(A), 2001.

peasants in February 1983.[123] At least in the highlands, the peace between Senderistas and civilians was irrevocably broken. Nonetheless, even amidst the brutality, the Shining Path exercised selectivity in choosing its targets. Civilians may have had no choice but to resist the rebels, but it was active resistance that brought on massacres and collective punishment.

Free from Central Control: Sendero–Huallaga

The structure of the Comité Regional del Alto Huallaga was similar to that of other regional committees.[124] It established three military forces – principal, regional, and base forces – to operate in its zones of influence along the Huallaga Valley. The CRH also set in place open people's committees led by appointed local authorities to govern the guerrilla zones. And its senior leadership remained in constant contact with the Central Committee. In some ways, combatants in Huallaga also behaved like their counterparts in Ayacucho. Their first actions involved the assassination of political leaders, governmental authorities, and members of the civilian guard, police, and armed forces. Behind rebel lines, Sendero–Huallaga also embarked on a campaign of social cleansing to eliminate the problem of common delinquency. Sendero militants executed drug traffickers, common criminals, thieves, adulterers, and others who threatened the stability of peasant communities.

On the other hand, Sendero–Huallaga exhibited coercive behavior that was unmatched in the highlands, where the national organization maintained its base of support. Some of this was evident in the form of killings, which increased in number and severity at the end of the 1980s and in the 1990s. It was even more apparent in patterns of rebel behavior in the communities Sendero controlled. Violence became the tool of choice for the CRH as it sought to maintain control of the drug trade. Control required unconstrained access to land and peasant labor to grow the crop. Threats to CRH dominance were met with fierce reprisals. And as government efforts to end coca production increased, civilians found themselves in a difficult situation: live with Sendero, make a profit, and risk death from brutal government attacks and Sendero indiscipline or give up coca production, flee to the cities, and risk deadly reprisals from Sendero combatants. One civilian commented: "The campesinos were used by everyone.... It was the

---

[123] Del Pino, "Family, Culture, and 'Revolution,'" p. 163.
[124] Interview with former Sendero commander, Lima, November 5(A), 2001.

military, Sendero Luminoso, and the drug traffickers who survived off of one another."[125]

Data on violence in the Huallaga region demonstrate how combatant behavior in the CRH differed from that in Ayacucho (see Figure 6.14). Sendero–Huallaga began mounting attacks in the early 1980s. By 1988, the rebels averaged between 150 and 200 actions a year, and the level of violence remained consistent until 1998, when they became less active. After Guzmán was captured in 1992, however, the actions taken by the combatants in Huallaga made up an increasingly large part of total Sendero activities. By 1998, Sendero–Huallaga was responsible for more than 40 percent of the total actions launched nationwide.

Information about the identity of victims provides some evidence of Sendero–Huallaga's indiscriminate violence (see Figure 6.15). While combatants in Ayacucho consistently targeted local officials and representatives of the state, the rebels in Huallaga participated in the killing of noncombatants, many of whom had no link to government forces. CRH violence against politicians, government officials, and community leaders reached its high point in 1987, when it made up more than 70 percent of Sendero–Huallaga attacks. But the CRH became increasingly indiscriminate in its use of violence over time. By 1998, attacks on unaffiliated victims made up in excess of 75 percent of Sendero actions in the jungle. This assertion is supported by anecdotal evidence that suggests Sendero–Huallaga's attempts to distinguish between "friends" and "enemies" focused less on the political leanings of victims than on their willingness to contribute to the party coffers.

As Sendero–Huallaga took responsibility for a larger share of national actions, the total number of victims and the percentage that were not affiliated increased. Even in the early 1990s, when Sendero's national movement was more active than the guerrillas of Huallaga, violence in the Upper Huallaga Valley produced a disproportionate number of the total victims nationwide. Violence was central to Sendero–Huallaga's strategy. The political mobilization and targeted assassinations that drove the rebellion in other parts of the country, while present at the committee's inception, largely faded into the background.

Tingo María, Alto Huallaga, Peru By 1986, the CRH had established a guerrilla zone just across the river from the provincial capital of Tingo

[125] Interview, Tingo María, November 17(B), 2001.

252

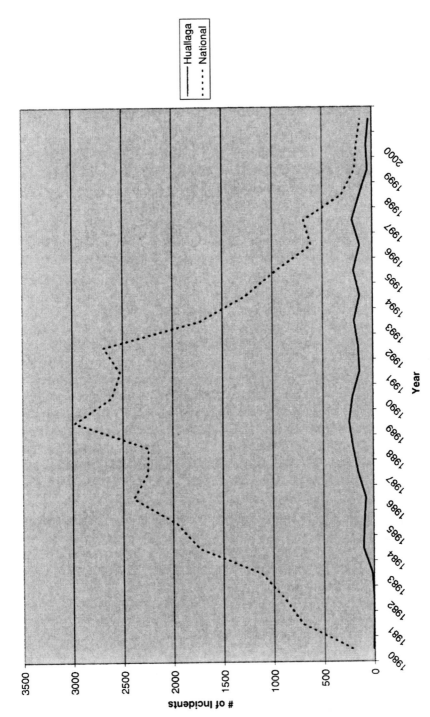

Figure 6.14. Incidents of Violence against Civilians, Sendero–Huallaga

253

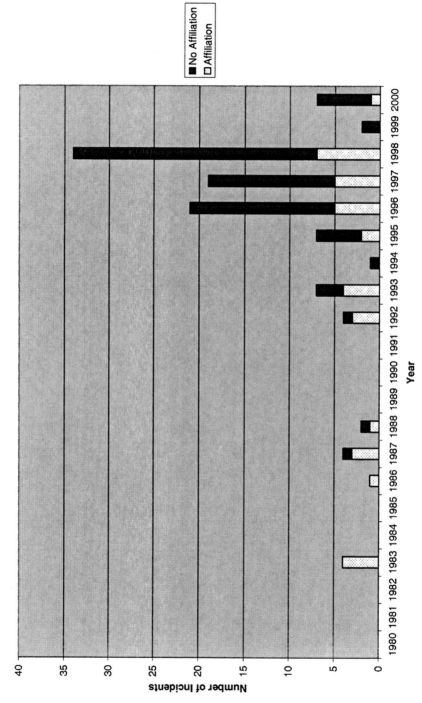

Figure 6.15. The Affiliation of Victims, Sendero–Huallaga

254

María.[126] The left bank of the river was the Comité Zonal Principal, stretching to Uchiza, which included areas where coca was cultivated and labs for the processing of pasta básica. The Comité Zonal Ucayali was on the right bank of the Huallaga River, and deeper in the jungle, the Comité Zonal Fundamental stretched to Tocache. Each subcommittee was subordinate to the leadership of the CRH. In the early years, the CRH directed a campaign of political assassinations of provincial and loyal mayors, government officials, and communal leaders in these regions similar to what was witnessed in Ayacucho.[127] Between 1985 and 1990, Sendero Luminoso assassinated four mayors and two city registrars.[128] The attacks were brazen, often carried out in broad daylight, but they were not unexpected. Each victim was warned in advance, sometimes in writing, to renounce his position in the Peruvian government.

Sendero–Huallaga also exercised revolutionary justice in its areas of control. Often, civilians welcomed these demonstrations of violence.[129] Common criminality had prospered along with the coca boom in the late 1970s, and civilians felt threatened by the behavior of drug traffickers and the newly wealthy, many of whom wielded guns and abused the peasant populations. Sendero–Huallaga set in place a system of rules to govern behavior. Militants and members of the popular committees supervised the civilian population, watching for violations of these rules and for transgressions against unwritten mores, including the prohibition of homosexuality, prostitution, and excessive drinking. When violations occurred, the punishment was severe. Offenses resulted in exile or summary execution; there were few second chances.

But in the process of building a movement around coca production, the reliance on force began to be abused both by Sendero militants and by local authorities. A movement built initially around social endowments was transformed in its new environment as its membership changed. Popular trials began to be used at the whim of commanders for crimes not covered by the rules or understood by the local population. Commanders and their comrades, moreover, began systematically to violate their own rules. The

---

[126] MENADES and CONDECOREP, *La guerra ha terminado...Dónde está la paz?* (Lima: MENADES and CONDECOREP, 2001).

[127] Interview, Tingo María, November 15(A), 2001.

[128] Ibid., November 13(A), 2001. See also Comisión de la Verdad y Reconciliación, *Informe Final: Peru, 1980–2000, Tomo IV* (Lima: Pontificia Universidad Católica del Peru y Universidad Nacional Mayor de San Marcos, 2003), pp. 364–65.

[129] Ibid., November 14(A,B), 2001.

cupos charged by party officials for coca soon extended to all other goods and property.[130] When there was not enough money coming in from the coca trade, Sendero would call the villagers together and demand additional money for food, clothing, and other goods.[131] "This was abuse," one woman explained. "Civilians were punished for the same crimes committed by the guerrillas," but the guerrillas were never held accountable.[132]

When the government launched a new counterinsurgency campaign in the Upper Huallaga Valley in 1989, civilians began to resist Sendero's control.[133] Government forces paraded through the countryside, killing civilians on sight.[134] Anyone living outside of the provincial capitals was assumed to be assisting the rebels. The government, with the support of the United States, constructed antidrug bases inside the areas of rebel control and used them as a foundation for operations against the civilian supporters of the CRH. With helicopters, the Peruvian Armed Forces began to bombard civilian populations with gunfire from the air, forcing them to flee. Efforts to eradicate coca crops and catch traffickers were redoubled, leading to a drop in coca prices to below the cost of production by mid-1990.

The abuses of Sendero–Huallaga's mandos were matched and even exceeded by those of the government forces. Following a Sendero attack on a government patrol in 1990 in which fourteen soldiers were killed, the military bombed the village of Río Azul, killing large numbers of civilians, one woman reported. She lost her husband in that attack.[135] Another woman described how the military invaded her house one morning, taking her husband and two cousins to the base. The soldiers stole their property and accused them of being terrorists. Days later, the military agreed to release her husband for a cash payment of $5,000, but she was unable to raise the money. She never found her husband; the bodies of her cousins

---

[130] Ibid., November 13(A), 14(A,B), 2001.
[131] Ibid., November 19(C), 2001.
[132] Ibid.
[133] An early stage of this counterinsurgency campaign was led by Brigadier Alberto Arciniega. Arciniega resisted a singular focus on the drug war, instead arguing that to be effective the government would need to gain the backing of the cocaleros. At the same time, however, his military units employed a heavy-handed approach that paid little regard to the protection of human rights. The United States was unhappy with Arciniega's level of commitment to the drug war, and he was replaced after seven months. See José Gonzales, "Guerrillas and Coca in the Upper Huallaga Valley," in Palmer, Shining Path of Peru, p. 135.
[134] The National Commissioner of Human Rights launched a special study of government abuses in the Alto Huallaga. See Coordinador Nacional de Derechos Humanos, Los sucesos del Alto Huallaga (Lima: Coordinador Nacional de Derechos Humanos, 1994).
[135] Interview, Tingo María, November 19(B), 2001.

were discovered in the river.[136] In Aucayacu, less than fifty kilometers from Tingo María, the government commander offered to spare people's lives if they would name one hundred rebel supporters in the village. One woman remembered that "people took advantage of the offer to save themselves."[137]

The combination of a precipitous drop in coca prices and the threat of governmental abuses led many to flee Sendero-controlled zones or to organize resistance in the countryside by setting up rondas. But attempts to flee or to fight back were met with still more violence by the Sendero cadres. The National Human Rights Commission reported the torture and massacre of seventeen civilians in one incident in 1994.[138] Later in the same year, six campesinos were assassinated when Sendero–Huallaga rebels attacked two villages and looted the local shops. One of the victims was the president of the defense committee; the others were civilians.[139]

Even as the government launched increasingly successful efforts to move civilians outside of Sendero areas, the rebels fought back. One method was to use force against civilians. Sendero–Huallaga also sought to keep civilians from fleeing by forcing coca prices higher through negotiations with the drug traffickers. But for most, the choice to live with Sendero no longer revolved around profit. They stayed because they had to.

After governmental abuses in Huallaga were publicized in 1994, the military began to withdraw and closed down its internal bases. In the late 1990s, coca prices gradually began to rise again. Sendero–Huallaga reestablished influence in areas that it had lost and continued to attack government forces, the police, and civilians who resisted the rebels' efforts to control the coca trade. The government was relatively passive in its response, afraid of the consequences of another military buildup in the region. Violence continues in the Upper Huallaga Valley even today, even though Sendero has been largely defeated in the rest of the country.[140]

To maintain its presence and prevent defeat, Sendero–Huallaga used increasingly higher levels of violence against the population. After a campaign of assassinations in its early years, rebel violence in the Upper

---

[136] Ibid., November 20(A), 2001.
[137] Ibid., November 20(C), 2001.
[138] See Coordinador, *Los Sucesos*, p. 46.
[139] Ibid., p. 82.
[140] For this reason, a comparison of two communities in the Upper Huallaga Valley was deemed impossible. Instead, this section presents an overview of the violence in the region. More precise theories about how levels of violence varied according to the extent of rebel control simply cannot be tested.

Huallaga Valley became more indiscriminate. The corruption of rebel mandos and authorities meant that no one was safe from attack by Sendero–Huallaga; knowing this, civilians chose to resist or to flee. Many thousands died "in between three fires," said one civilian, referring to the rebels, the government, and the drug traffickers.[141]

Conclusion

This chapter takes what Charles King calls a "micropolitical turn" in the study of social violence. Violence within civil war is its object of inquiry; it disaggregates the concept of conflict that is at the center of much scholarship in comparative politics and international relations. In so doing, it reveals vast differences in the scope and scale of violence perpetrated by rebel groups. Data drawn from multiple sources – the coding of newspaper reports, the testimonies of victims, and the stories told by perpetrators – point to patterns of insurgent violence that vary across groups, across geographic areas, and over time.

Theories that purport to make sense of the victimization of civilians in conflict are then put to the test. The focus on rebel organization adopted in this book has significant explanatory power in addressing why the character of insurgent behavior is so different across civil wars and why patterns of behavior appear persistent over time within each conflict. Recognition of the diversity of membership and the differing structures of rebel groups offers significant insight into the mechanisms through which indiscriminate violence and indiscipline, on the one hand, and selective killing and restraint, on the other, are observed in the context of conflict. Arguments that locate the causes of anticivilian violence in patterns of interaction either with governments or civilian populations perform less well. Neither of the alternative approaches makes predictions about how the character of violence is likely to differ across conflicts, and both suggest much less consistency in rebel behavior than we actually observe within each of the four cases. Even patterns of temporal and geographic variation in abusiveness are not well captured by these approaches: Theories of contestation that predict increasing levels of violence when the rebels are weak find disconfirming evidence in the rising tide of victimization experienced in Mozambique and in the Huallaga Valley as the rebel groups expanded and grew more powerful. Theories of control that suggest levels of violence will be lowest where

[141] Interview, Tingo María, November 13(A), 2001.

258

one party exercises nearly uncontested sovereignty, in turn, are challenged by the enormous number of incidents in southern Mozambique, where government forces faced little effective opposition from Renamo. These same theories, which predict almost no violence in hotly contested zones, cannot account for selective violence by the NRA and indiscriminate massacres by the government in the disputed Luwero Triangle or for massive abuse by both sides in the highland regions of Peru.

Adopting a focus on violence is essential if we wish to lessen the impact of political conflict on noncombatant populations. This book argues that understanding differences in the strategies pursued by groups requires an examination of the organizations themselves – their membership, their structure, and the ties that hold them together. But the stories presented here also point to patterns of change in rebel behavior that may be in tension with the path-dependent predictions of my theory of organizational development. The next chapter turns to the evolution of rebel groups in an effort to identify the conditions under which activist and opportunistic rebellions change course over time.

7

Resilience

Even though they face similar challenges with respect to recruitment, organization, the management of civilians, and the use of force, rebel groups respond to the challenges of organization in different ways. In an effort to make sense of rebel strategies, I began with the nature of a group's endowments: economic resources put groups on a path toward authoritarianism and coercion, while social endowments give rise to groups that embrace participatory structures and eschew the use of force. This story of organizational formation implies substantial path dependence: groups that employ coercive strategies in the early stages of the conflict appear doomed to repeat those strategies throughout; rebel leaders capable of disciplining the use of force and sharing power with civilians find themselves better equipped to replicate the same patterns at later stages of the conflict. Data on how force was used by the NRA, Renamo, Sendero Nacional, and Sendero–Huallaga illuminate a surprising consistency in the character of violence over time and across regions within each conflict.

But how sticky is the organizational structure of a rebel group? Before exploring how my argument fares in a broader set of cases, it is necessary to consider what types of shocks threaten the coherence and stability of the various organizational forms and what effect these shocks have on groups' behavioral patterns. This chapter begins with a discussion of four potential developments in civil conflict that can weaken the internal structures that hold groups together. The chapter then turns to a set of critical events in the wars of Uganda, Mozambique, and Peru in an effort to understand the sources of organizational consistency within each of the organizations. It concludes with a discussion of two additional cases – the civil conflicts in Angola and Colombia – in which rebel groups evolved and changed in substantive ways over time.

Shocks and Expectations

Four broad developments threaten the structure and coherence of rebel groups. First, rebel groups must recover from battlefield losses. Military failures have manifold consequences for rebel groups: they create a need to recruit new infantry soldiers, convince civilian supporters to continue providing support, and prevent defection within the organization. But rebel groups must also respond to success. When an insurgency nears victory, individuals fighting on behalf of the government rush to join the rebel force. Civilians who have remained neutral or disengaged in the conflict reevaluate their choices and often see participation in the rebel group as the best strategy for survival and success in the new climate. Third, rebel groups confront changes in their endowments. Sources of economic wealth are exhausted or disappear as geopolitical considerations alter the calculations of external patrons. Economic endowments can also emerge as groups take control of new territories in the course of the violence or as external actors gain interest in the conflict. Even social endowments may be affected by shocks as civilians reconsider the meaning of particular identities or ideologies. Finally, rebel groups face government opponents with the capacity to alter their counterinsurgency strategies over time. Government forces may rely on overwhelming military force in the early days of the conflict and implement strategies of organized civilian resistance at later points. They can offer amnesty to rebel participants or threaten individuals with punishment if they are caught.

I focus on these four developments because each one has the potential to change the *expectations* of rebels and their supporters, and to keep a force in the field, rebel groups must manage changing expectations over time. The resolution of each organizational challenge hinges on the formation of a set of expectations about the behavior of the rebel group, its members, and civilians in its zones of control. Some groups resolve the recruitment challenge by making payoffs; others employ appeals to the long-term orientation of potential members by making promises or activating a set of reciprocity norms. The utility of these approaches depends on individuals' expectations about whether the group is able to and likely to live up to its end of the bargain.

Internal structures of control also depend on a bargain struck between rebel leaders and soldiers. Norms of cooperation take hold, and discipline emerges where rebel soldiers believe that institutional structures prevent rebel leaders from threatening the viability of the organization and its long-term orientation through defection. Groups dominated by defection also depend on a set of expectations, namely, that the organization will permit individuals to continue realizing short-term rewards.

Likewise, strategies of governance and the use of force rely on shared expectations. Civilians provide or withhold their support and assistance depending on the degree of power that they are given to shape the trajectory of the rebellion and to prevent indiscipline on the part of the rebel leadership. In the same sense, civilians cooperate or resist depending on their judgments about the capacity of the rebel group to use force selectively to punish defectors. Each step on the path of organizational formation thus depends on an underlying system of incentives that shape the relationships that give rise to a rebel group – relationships between rebel leaders and soldiers, between groups and civilians, and between groups and their adversaries. Battlefield losses, impending success, changing endowments, and government strategies each represent shocks to the expectations of participants that must be managed by rebel groups.

Shocks change the calculus of rebel groups and civilians in distinct ways. Mounting losses reduce the probability of a rebel victory and the likelihood that individuals will receive benefits that they have been promised in the future. Successes, on the other hand, increase the relative attractiveness of participation, making it more likely that individuals of all types will rush to join the rebellion. In this context, current members and supporters have cause to reevaluate whether the group will live up to commitments made to its earliest backers.

Changing endowments affect the capacity of a rebel group to provide benefits to recruited members. Groups that lose access to economic endowments may find themselves unable to continue providing short-term rewards. Organizations that gain access to economic resources, on the other hand, may face pressure to provide payoffs to participants in the short run. How a group responds to the introduction of new endowments or the disappearance of old ones may contribute to a change in its membership pool and organizational structure.

Government strategies matter, finally, because they alter the set of alternatives to participation in the rebel group that exist for potential recruits and supporters. Major military campaigns raise the cost of participation in the rebel group, forcing individuals to reevaluate their participation. Amnesty efforts or investments in local populations may increase the benefits of defecting to the other side. In either case, rebel groups must respond to these changes in order to preserve their organizations.

How Organizations Respond

One might imagine that, facing mounting losses, a rebel group would employ coercive means to maintain participation and generate new recruits. With the probability of a rebel victory falling in the eyes of civilians, appeals to the long-term orientation of potential recruits might become a more difficult sell. Alternatively, facing civilian resistance to coercive rebel behavior, one could envision a rebel group enforcing discipline and implementing a new code of conduct as part of a public campaign to win popular support and dampen resistance.

These may appear to be natural responses, but they are not the only strategies available. In the context of losses, rebel leaders might also reinforce the commitment of their supporters by reaffirming the group's long-term orientation and their dedication to it. In facing resistance, rebel leaders might estimate that their members' time horizons are shrinking even further and maintain a permissive environment for indiscipline until the organization eventually collapses.

I argue that three factors play important roles in enforcing organizational consistency, allowing some groups to replicate previous patterns of behavior in response to shocks. Where shocks alter the nature of a group's membership, previous patterns of behavior are difficult to maintain. If the introduction of economic endowments leads an activist group to begin providing short-term benefits to recruit new participants, for example, the time horizons of its membership will change, creating difficulties for the group's leadership as it tries to manage the organization in its interactions with civilians. But if a group manages to maintain selective recruitment by using strategies of information gathering, vouching, or costly induction, the leadership can protect the long-term orientation of the membership. Where groups replicate previous strategies of recruitment and employ new economic endowments for purposes other than recruitment, then we can expect consistent patterns of behavior.

Rebel groups also demonstrate resistance to the impact of shocks when their organizational structure – internal expectations, processes, and codes of behavior – acts as a bulwark against change. In the context of mounting losses, for example, activist organizations draw on the shared beliefs and behaviors of the identities or networks that brought them together to reinforce their long-term orientation and prevent defection to the opposing side. Leaders rely on methods of political education, ethnic mobilization, and community organization to bolster the organization. Established processes for delivering orders and codes guiding individual behavior also make it possible for leaders to maintain organizational coherence in changing contexts. In opportunistic groups, internal norms that enable indiscipline have provided the basis for participation throughout the conflict and are difficult to break down or reverse.

Third, leadership emerges as a critical variable in organizations responding to shocks. Where the leadership restates and reinforces commonly held beliefs, expectations, and behaviors, groups are able to maintain the bargains they have struck with their members and with civilian populations. Leaders communicate important signals about how the organization is responding to change, using messages to reaffirm a group's orientation, its goals, and the commitments of the leadership to its survival. The key here is to minimize doubt and uncertainty. Consistency in message and coherence serve to hold an organization together. Leadership can reinforce a pattern of either cooperation or defection, depending on the nature of the group in question.

Strong reinforcing tendencies are thus created by patterns of recruitment and organization that keep rebel organizations on a consistent path. Activist groups draw on their social endowments, coherent organizational structures, and negotiated bargains with civilian populations to maintain patterns of participatory governance and the selective use of force. Opportunistic groups, dominated by the short-term motivations of their membership, respond to shocks in accordance with their time horizons by maintaining patterns of defection, structures of authoritarian control, and indiscipline throughout the conflict.

Groups do not always remain on their original paths, however, in spite of the powerful constraints imposed by previous strategies and experiences. Beyond looking at cases of organizational resilience, this chapter also explores situations of organizational change. The evidence suggests that it is more likely that activist groups will turn into opportunistic organizations than vice versa. The bargains struck between leaders, members, and civilians in activist contexts depend heavily on the credibility of the commitments made by the rebels. Because individuals make investments in the short term in the hope of receiving long-term benefits, an individual's expectations about the likelihood of achieving victory and receiving rewards must remain unchanged in order for an organization to survive in its activist form. This precarious relationship of trust can be upset by shocks to the system that force rebel leaders to make difficult choices, such as whether to continue to provide security to civilians in zones of rebel control even when such efforts threaten the viability and survival of the rebel group.

But can opportunistic groups shift to an activist strategy? One might imagine that when a group relying on coercion comes to encounter tremendous civilian resistance, it might reevaluate its strategy in favor of more cooperative relationships with civilian populations. The problem is that once trust is broken, it is difficult to reestablish. Because civilians have information about how the conflict is unfolding in other areas, rebel groups face a challenging task when they attempt to change how noncombatants perceive them. The stakes are high for civilians when evaluating rebel groups: a decision regarding whether to flee or to stay in a village when a rebel group arrives may be a decision between life and death. Given the nature of their membership, moreover, opportunistic groups lack the long-term orientation required to establish cooperative relationships and the organizational structure needed to prevent and punish indiscipline. Without internal mechanisms of control, opportunistic groups have a difficult time establishing the credibility of their promises to behave.

The Dynamics of Conflict

Uncovering the determinants of organizational change is a question of specifying the conditions under which groups are transformed by shocks. This section returns to the narrative history of civil war in Uganda, Mozambique, and Peru to identify the critical moments that threatened to undermine or reshape the strategies pursued by each of the rebel organizations. It points to a powerful tendency toward path dependence in the cases that are the focus of this book.

Expulsion and Reemergence: The NRA

Less than two years after the initiation of its guerrilla struggle, the NRA controlled a vast region of territory – the Luwero Triangle – governing close to 10,000 square miles. Only 100 kilometers away in the capital, Kampala, the NRA's successes were an embarrassment to the Obote regime. Given the size of the territory under rebel control, the UNLA was forced into a position of dispersing its forces widely in order to challenge guerrilla advances. But this strategy left it vulnerable to rebel attacks. With government forces broken down into smaller detachments, the highly mobile guerrillas, who possessed knowledge of the territory and information from the local population, were far better equipped to fight hit-and-run battles against the government. With defeat looming, Obote launched his Grand Offensive in January 1983, an operation that employed close to 75 percent of the UNLA's total strength. The government forces attacked the Triangle, using medium- and long-range artillery in an attempt to flush out the rebels and the civilian population. Civilians recalled that the "loud guns" boomed throughout the day and night, upsetting the serenity and freedom that had prevailed under rebel control.[1]

As the UNLA advanced into the Triangle, the leadership of the NRA became convinced that a pitched battle for territory might leave the rebels vulnerable to defeat. Still small, with only 4,000 troops, the NRA was in no position to govern and protect the Triangle against the massed government forces. The NRA ordered its combatants to retreat to the arid plains of Singo and Ngoma. The NRA's evacuation of Luwero was not a simple task. The leadership felt strongly that the area's civilians needed to be protected during the expulsion. One NRA soldier recalled: "If we had left them behind, Obote would have killed them all. There was really no alternative to evacuating them ourselves, because the UNLA had shoot-on-sight orders."[2] Following a series of dramatic battlefield losses, Yoweri Museveni ordered all the resistance committees together to explain the reasons for the evacuation. He made it clear that giving up the Triangle was necessary if the NRA hoped to achieve victory in the struggle, and he pledged that the NRA would assist civilians in leaving the rebel zone safely.[3]

One respondent described the evacuation: "The greatest challenge was how to filter all of these civilians through enemy lines. It took incredible organization and logistical coordination. We gave people the time to move, directions about where to go, for how long to stay at each point, and where to get food and water along the way." Rebel soldiers positioned themselves along the escape route, advising civilians to move from place to place and leading them to areas outside of the range of the government artillery. At the Mayanja River, an area dangerously exposed to government forces, the NRA provided cover for civilians as they made a daring race for the other bank.[4]

A key component of the NRA's strategy was to reinforce its commitment to the civilian population. Patterns of NRA behavior did not change,

---

[1] Interview, Semuto, November 16(A,B), 2000.
[2] Interview, Kampala, November 7(A), 2000.
[3] Interviews, Semuto, November 14(A,B), 15(B,C), 16(A,B), 17(B), 18(B), 22(A), 2000.
[4] Interview, Kampala, November 7(A), 2000; interviews, Semuto, November 15(B), 16(A,B), 18(B), 20(A), 2000.

moreover, even when the rebels and civilians set up a new base in the plains. Singo lacked the food surplus and jungle-like cover of the Luwero Triangle, creating adverse conditions for the survival of the rebel organization. Yet the NRA continued to set in place cooperative arrangements with noncombatants. When villagers arrived in Singo, the rebels directed them to particular areas based on the villages they came from. The NRA attempted to reestablish the RC structure that had governed the population in Luwero.[5] Because there was little to eat in the plains, the rebels led civilians back into Luwero at night in search of food.[6] The rebel leadership negotiated for the few resources that were available, mainly cattle, by making "contracts" with the herders that promised compensation in exchange for their recorded contributions.[7] Meat from the cattle was shared broadly with the civilian population. Soldiers suffered just as civilians did in the harsh climate of Singo.

The expulsion was a major shock to civilian and rebel expectations. Victory had seemed within the movement's grasp. Living on the edge of survival in Singo was a dramatic change, standing in stark contrast to the freedom and security of the Luwero Triangle. But even when the food supply ran out and Obote promised amnesty to soldiers and civilians who fled areas of rebel control, NRA leaders allowed supporters to make their own choices. The chief political commissar called civilians together and explained that they were welcome to return to their home areas to try and live in government zones until the war was won.[8] Recognizing the burdens evacuation placed on the rebel army, the NRA leadership used a political education campaign to explain its decision to encourage civilians to leave, and it reaffirmed the group's long-term commitment to its supporters.[9] In spite of its losses, then, the NRA rejected strategies of coercion, forced recruitment, and violence to maintain its support base. For many civilians, the fact that the NRA stuck to its commitments was further evidence of its long-term orientation and credibility.

The year 1984 was one of reorganization and reevaluation for the rebels. Stuck in inhospitable terrain, the NRA sought a strategy that would demonstrate its continued strength to the government and civilians and provide it with a new base from which to bring down the Obote regime. A series

---

[5] Interviews, Semuto, November 15(C), 16(A), 2000.
[6] Ibid., November 16(A,B), 2000.
[7] Interview, Kampala, November 7(B), 2000.
[8] Interview, Semuto, November 15(C), 2000.
[9] Interviews, Kampala, September 20(A), 27(A), October 25(A), 2000.

of attacks launched by the NRA's Mobile Brigade across the country announced the rebels' reemergence as a credible force. The move to open a western front in 1985 demonstrated the NRA's military capability and readiness to challenge for the capital.

The years 1984 and 1985 also brought with them substantial changes in the NRA's resource base and endowments. Apart from a small cache of arms contributed by the Libyans, the NRA had had little access to economic resources and war material in the first years of the conflict. The rebels were wholly dependent on the civilian population for their survival. Owing to a series of bank robberies in 1984, however, the NRA experienced an infusion of economic resources. The first robbery occurred in June 1984. The Mobile Brigade, led by Museveni himself, attacked the town of Hoima, first overrunning the military detachment and then breaking into the government-owned commercial bank. The NRA desperately needed funds from this bank robbery and the others to purchase food from external sources to resupply the rebel soldiers who were starving in Singo. The leadership also sought funds to purchase weapons and ammunition to support logistical military operations throughout the country. The infusion of Ugandan currency, however, threatened the pattern of organization that had existed in the NRA. The group had not previously had access to significant resources that could be distributed to rebel commanders or combatants.

One might imagine that in a struggling rebel force without access to food, commanders or soldiers, realizing that defeat might be near, would have taken the cash and fled the rebel army. Instead, the NRA leadership invested the resources in the food supply and used it to provide funds to local units for the purchase of supplies.[10] The NRA used its existing structure to distribute these resources, vesting control in unit policy and administrative committees that involved combatants in the oversight of the critical resources.[11] The rebels committed their newfound economic endowments to the goals of the organization rather than use them for personal reward.

This pattern continued in 1985 when the NRA opened a western front. Having gained control over the borders with Rwanda and Zaire, the rebels were in a position to tax the export of the coffee crop from resource-rich western Uganda. Again, however, the NRA established formal mechanisms for governing trade, creating an administrator of finance to arrange taxing

[10] Ibid., September 27(A), 2000.
[11] Ibid., October 24(B), 2000.

268

relationships with coffee farmers and channeling the funds into a central account under the quasi-governmental administration run out of Fort Portal.[12]

Rebel success in establishing the western front presented a third challenge to the National Resistance Army. As it moved toward the capital from both the western provinces and the center, it increasingly appeared that the NRA would sweep into power. In fact, on July 27, 1985, Tito and Basilio Okello, two senior army officers, overthrew Obote in a coup. They called immediately for the NRA to lay down its arms and begin negotiations for a peaceful transition to shared power. The coup was a response in part to mounting battlefield losses on the part of the government. With a firm footing in western Uganda, Museveni's home area, the rebels were picking up steam, recruiting thousands of new soldiers on the march to Kampala. It became clear to most civilians that the rebels offered a winning ticket and the promise of jobs, resources, and security in a post-Obote world.

These developments threatened the survival of the NRA. Many of its combatants had joined early on, when the odds of victory were low and the promises of what might be gained with victory were all that held the group together. As thousands of new members joined, members of longer standing questioned whether the NRA leadership would remember their commitment. Whether the NRA could maintain discipline among massive numbers of new recruits was also open to question.

The leadership of the NRA recognized the centrality of maintaining discipline as the number of troops grew from 4,000 to over 10,000 in 1985. Rigorous courses of political education within the army were maintained to counter indiscipline within its ranks. Museveni set in place a National School of Political Education during the late stages of the war to develop curricula and training programs for new NRA cadres. Its former director explained: "There was a realization that, as the army grew, we wanted not only numbers, but discipline. Our new soldiers needed to know how we wanted the country to run. If we had taken Kampala without properly politicizing the soldiers, they would have behaved like our old soldiers. We wanted them to value property and the lives of the people."[13] Thus, even as success loomed in the distance, the NRA maintained a process of selective recruitment to ensure that its membership pool shared its long-term orientation.

[12] Ibid., September 20(A), 27(A), November 9(A), 2000.
[13] Ibid., November 9(A), 2000.

To preserve the commitment of its first joiners, the NRA also continued on a path of rewarding commitment and merit with internal promotions. Since the beginning, promotion had been based not on ethnic identity or favoritism but on the performance and service of members. This continued even as the army grew. When the NRA captured Kampala, moreover, the new government initiated an effort to compensate soldiers and civilians who had served in the struggle. Throughout the war, the leadership communicated its commitment to rewarding participants; when the NRA achieved victory, it acted on those commitments.

Resistance and Continued Repression: Renamo

In 1984, eight years after the war in Mozambique began, Renamo was operating at full strength. With more than 20,000 men under arms, the rebel army was in a position to extend itself militarily into every province in Mozambique, threatening government forces in their home regions in the South and in geographically distant central and northern provinces. The Nkomati Non-Aggression Pact of 1984 came as a substantial shock to the movement. Two years earlier, Frelimo had initiated contacts with the South African government in Pretoria in an attempt to end external support for the insurgency. South Africa's message to Frelimo was clear: continued Mozambican support for the African National Congress would be met with harsh and repeated retaliation. A South African Defence Forces attack in Matola, a neighborhood in Mozambique's capital city, provided evidence of the South Africans' determination. But both governments had something to gain in striking an agreement. The Mozambicans believed that the end of external support would spell the defeat of Renamo. South Africa sought to weaken the African National Congress by eliminating its external bases. The Nkomati Pact cemented the two governments' commitments to end support for activities that destabilized their neighbors. Immediately following the agreement, Frelimo expelled the leadership of the African National Congress from Maputo, shutting down its training camps and forcing them to move to Zambia. The South African government, in turn, promised to stop sending military supplies and providing logistical assistance to Renamo.

The unexpected loss of South African assistance seemed at first to be a crushing blow to the insurgent forces. Because Renamo had over 20,000 men under arms, however, Frelimo's expectations were at best naïve. But the disappearance of the external patron did represent a challenge for the structure of Renamo's rebel organization: without a consistent flow of guns and ammunition, participation in Renamo became a riskier proposition. The loss of South African assistance also weakened the capacity of the movement to provide immediate payoffs to its supporters.

One might imagine given these new conditions that Renamo was in a position to reverse course – to discipline the behavior of its troops, build cooperative relationships with noncombatants, and reorient the movement toward longer-term gains. In fact, had 1984 been the starting point of the conflict, Renamo might have been unable to organize without building its movement around social identities or preexisting social networks. But Renamo did not change its strategy. It made no attempt to renegotiate relationships with civilian populations, to crack down on rebel behavior, or to communicate a new vision or orientation for the rebel participants. Instead, Renamo sought to open up new sources of finance to continue providing the short-term incentives that held the movement together.

The looting of civilian property was central to the revenue flow. South African support provided salaries to senior members of the Renamo leadership, but even prior to 1984 the organization had diversified its sources of revenue to provide incentives for lower-level combatants to remain in the force. The strategy continued in the wake of the Nkomati Pact. The theft of household goods, products from government stores and cooperatives, and supplies from health posts became a consistent part of Renamo attacks after 1982.[14] Trade in looted goods became a central part of an informal economy that developed around Renamo bases. Infantry soldiers bartered goods to civilians in exchange for farm produce and animals.[15] As the rebel army established firm control over the Mozambican border with Malawi, cross-border trade also emerged as a central source of finance. Renamo forces generated large amounts of foreign currency by selling ivory and game meat. The organization channeled much of this newfound wealth to commanders and senior combatants in an effort to maintain their loyalty and commitment.

Renamo also began to obtain funds through extortion. The rebels negotiated with multinationals operating in Mozambique, exchanging security guarantees for large sums of foreign currency.[16] Lonrho, which operated profitable farms all over Mozambique, provides a good example. As part

---

[14] Interview, Marínguè District, Sofala Province, May 18(B), 23(B), 2001.

[15] Interviews, Ribáuè District, Nampula Province, April 2(B), 4(A), 2001; interviews, Marínguè District, Sofala Province, May 24(C), 2001.

[16] Alex Vines, "The Business of Peace: 'Tiny' Rowland, Financial Incentives, and the Mozambican Settlement," in *The Mozambican Peace Process in Perspective* (Maputo: Accord, 1998).

of agreements struck between the rebels and Lonrho, Renamo received permission to mount infrequent attacks on the company's facilities with minimal damage to keep up appearances. It also extorted funds from the Malawian government, negotiating payments in Malawian currency (to ease the purchase of goods across the border) in exchange for commitments not to attack trains carrying Malawian exports and imports along the Nacala rail corridor in northern Mozambique. Extortion took on a new form when peace negotiations began in 1990, with external actors offering hard currency to Renamo's leadership in an effort to buy the peace. These payments for the "organizational growth" of Renamo as a political party served to fatten the pockets of its leadership.

As it turned out, there was no need to invest newly identified financial resources in the purchase of military supplies because the South African government continued to airdrop basic supplies even after the signing of Nkomati Pact. After expelling Renamo from its mountain base in Gorongosa in 1985, Frelimo uncovered evidence of continued South African military assistance to Renamo.[17] It is believed that South African assistance to Renamo continued until the very late stages of the war, when apartheid was on its last legs.

Renamo faced a second significant shock in 1989–90, when civilian resistance to the rebel movement became formalized under the leadership of Manuel António. Called the Naprama Movement, organized civilian resistance took root in the border areas of Zambézia and Nampula provinces, right in the heart of Renamo control. Inspired by an almost religious fervor, this movement of uneducated civilians was an expression of the realization, as Ken Wilson put it, that "only they, themselves could end their suffering from Renamo's terror and war, and that they could find the means to achieve this from their own cultural resources."[18]

The Naprama Movement was formed within António's Macua-Lowme linguistic group, and it drew on religious representations and visions to

[17] The Renamo leadership kept detailed notes of its meetings with the South African military leadership, recording the explicit promises of armaments and supplies and the timetable for airdrops. A combatant who fought in Nampula described how supplies were delivered at least two times a year to Renamo units in the North even after the Nkomati Pact (interview, Ribáuè District, Nampula Province, March 30(D), 2001). His claims were supported in an interview in Marínguè, as well (May 18(C), 2001).

[18] Ken Wilson, "Cults of Violence and Counter-Violence in Mozambique," *Journal of Southern African Studies* 18, no. 3 (September 1992): 527–82. Wilson's is the definitive description of the Naprama Movement, and the narrative in this section draws heavily on evidence presented by Wilson.

promote the higher calling of resisting Renamo's incursions. To join the movement, recruits went through an elaborate ceremony accompanied by singing and ritual that ended with the "vaccination" of the recruits against the bullets of the enemy forces. This vaccination was said to protect adherents throughout the fighting as long as they stuck to the rules of the movement: not to use firearms, not to duck bullets or run away from the enemy, and not to harm or steal from the peasantry.[19] The movement represented a stark contrast to Renamo. Adherents went into battle without firearms, appreciably raising the risk of death. Looting and rape were explicitly forbidden and punished severely if caught. The group eschewed the use of force, killing only when necessary in the course of battle. Yet the Naprama Movement encountered immediate success in its campaign against Renamo. In 1990, working with government forces, the Naprama soldiers pushed Renamo into a retreat from a key strategic region. Naprama fighters forced the rebels out of bases in the eastern areas of Zambézia, in parts of Nampula, and later in Cabo Delgado and Niassa. The alliance between the Naprama forces and the government was loosely organized; the government gave the Napramas wide latitude in the central and northern regions, where Frelimo forces were viewed as outsiders.

The Napramas mobilized hundreds of participants for each assault on a Renamo base. Rebels found themselves confronted by troops who were willing to face them down; the days of attacks on weak and vulnerable villages were largely over. Due to their religious conviction of invulnerability, Naprama adherents advanced with little fear. A journalist wrote of his discussion with a Naprama commander about the movement's success in battle: "Perceiving our skepticism about the efficiency on the battlefield of such insignificant weaponry when compared to the modern AK-47s, mortars and bazookas, Commander Vinte said that these weapons worked, for they had already killed some enemy with them. 'When they fired at us, we didn't duck in order to crawl away, we didn't hide; on the contrary, we went forward on foot…avoiding the bullets, and advancing on the place from where the enemy bullets were coming. The bullets don't hit us, and if the enemy flees we go after him. Those who don't give themselves up, we kill. But many matsangas have been giving themselves up."[20]

The Naprama Movement posed a substantial threat to the dominance of Renamo in the rural areas of central and northern Mozambique. Rather

---

[19] Ibid., p. 564.
[20] Quoted in ibid., p. 568.

than compete for the affections of the civilian population, Renamo continued its coercive tactics in response to the rise of Naprama. Aphonso Dhlakama himself led an initial military campaign against the new movement, stalling the peace process to fight with his forces in Zambézia and Nampula. Renamo also challenged the Naprama advance by reasserting its hierarchical and unilateral power in village communities. Field reports from areas in which Renamo responded to the Naprama Movement reflected a strategy of violence and coercion no different than what had come before. One journalist reported: "Renamo [is] putting fear into the villagers to wipe out... [the strong belief in] Naprama... and demonstrate Renamo power to overcome what a population thought was untouchable."[21] Another explained that Renamo chose to exploit its "whole history and tradition of using brutalized murders to make political statements."[22] Renamo overran Lalaua, a town near Ribáuè in Nampula Province that had played host to Naprama forces, in June 1991. The official death toll stood at forty-nine, and the attack served to demonstrate the rebels' capacity to a broader audience: severed heads sat on the shelves of shops; the social, political, and economic infrastructure of the town was destroyed; and villagers were forced from their homes. The rebels' militaristic response to a credible challenge to their authority ended successfully with the killing of António in December 1991. Without his charismatic leadership and influence, the strength of the Naprama Movement gradually dissipated.

The emergence and success of the Naprama Movement represented an enormous threat to Renamo's organization and survival. Renamo met this challenge with force and coercion – drawing on previous patterns of violence, abduction, and destruction – rather than with a concerted campaign to capture (or recapture) popular support from the Naprama. Even though we can imagine an alternative strategic response, conditions on the ground made a reversal difficult for the Renamo leadership. Its soldiers were fearful of the Naprama fighters' strength and courage. Only a sustained military campaign led by the leadership and its strongest soldiers could inflict direct damage on the civilian resisters. Infantry soldiers were sent into villages to demonstrate their strength, as they had done before, through killings, destruction, abduction, and looting. Patterns of behavior were reinforced rather than altered, even as losses mounted in Mozambique's civil conflict.

[21] Quoted in ibid., p. 577.
[22] Vines quoted in ibid.

Facing Down the Government: Sendero Luminoso Nacional

The Shining Path also faced an organized civilian resistance – led by rondas campesinas – that operated in almost every region of the country by the end of the conflict. These self-defense patrols were used by every Peruvian president from Belaúnde to García to Fujimori as part of their counterinsurgency strategy. Concerns about arming civilians were widespread: some argued that because civilians supported Sendero, the government would in effect be arming the rebels; others feared that rondas would use their weapons against rival communities rather than the rebel forces. The biggest concern was that civilians would become cannon fodder for the rebels, targeted in response to their organizing.[23] In spite of these concerns, consecutive presidents made the case that peasants had the right to defend themselves. As a consequence, the government supported peasant organization against Sendero as early as 1983. While civilians organized some civil defense committees on their own, the military also forced villagers to mount rondas in many communities.[24]

Rondas were an important challenge to the authority of the Shining Path in peasant communities. The first indication of peasant strength was the massacre of Huaychao, in the highlands above Huanta, in January 1983. Peasants massacred seven young Senderistas in retaliation for the killing of three communal authorities by the Shining Path.[25] This incident took place just as the Belaúnde government was beginning its first military campaign against the rebels. It provided an important warning to Sendero that the movement would face resistance both from military forces and from some civilian communities.

The Shining Path's response to the massacre of Huaychao demonstrated its power and authority over civilian populations. The killing of more than eighty peasants in Lucanamarca in April 1983 served as a demonstration that those who cooperated with the government would suffer Sendero's wrath. Following the organization of community-wide resistance, the range of Sendero targets broadened from communal authorities to entire communities, but the selective character of Sendero's violence remained. As Carlos Iván Degregori, a Sendero expert, explained: "To put it brutally, in

---

[23] Cynthia McClintock, *Revolutionary Movements in Latin America: El Salvador's FMLN and Peru's Shining Path* (Washington, DC: U.S. Institute of Peace Press, 1998), p. 145.
[24] Interviews, Huanta, December 1(C), 2(A), 3(A,E), 5(A), 2001.
[25] Ibid., December 2(A), 3(E), 2001.

these times Shining Path knew those they killed, even in Lucanamarca; the peasants who submitted to Sendero's dictates would survive."[26]

Abimael Guzmán justified the massacre: "Confronted with the use of armed bands and reactionary military action, we responded decisively with one action: Lucanamarca. Neither they nor we will forget it, of course, because there they saw a response that had not been imagined.... [But] our problem was to give a bruising blow to restrain them, to make them understand that the thing was not so easy. In some occasions, such as this, it was the Central Leadership itself that planned the actions and ordered everything, that is how it was."[27] Battles between some civilian communities, particularly in the highlands, and rebel forces continued throughout the war, leading to an increase in the scope and scale of Sendero violence.

But Sendero's response was largely consistent with its initial patterns of behavior. While the range of targets broadened, the use of force remained selective. The Shining Path unleashed violence on individuals and communities that resisted its advance. Such attacks were organized in advance, with responsibilities assigned to members of military units, and they were evaluated for their success or failure after the fact. Decisions to use force were vetted at multiple levels within the regional committees, and the Central Committee played a role in organizing some of the larger attacks. While large massacres can indicate an organization's lack of control, the evidence suggests the opposite interpretation in Sendero's case: the shift to killing greater numbers of civilians was a strategic decision. It was implemented by an organization with a consistent membership, strong mechanisms of internal control and discipline, and an ideology that demanded the killings of defectors. And, importantly, higher levels of violence did not bring incidents of wanton destruction, looting, or individual indiscipline, the behaviors characteristic of opportunistic insurgencies.

The Shining Path also confronted challenges due to the changing strategies of the Peruvian government. From as early as 1985, the governmental leadership recognized that poverty and destitution in Ayacucho and other rural provinces were one key cause of Sendero's expansion. In response, presidents Alan García and Alberto Fujimori significantly increased economic aid to rural areas where Sendero was based. Between 1985 and 1986

---

[26] Carlos Iván Degregori, "Harvesting Storms: Peasant *Rondas* and the Defeat of Sendero Luminoso in Ayacucho," in *Shining and Other Paths: War and Society in Peru, 1980–1995*, ed. Steve J. Stern (Durham, NC: Duke University Press, 1998), p. 143.

[27] Guzmán quoted in ibid., p. 143.

alone, economic aid quadrupled to about $30 million.[28] Interest rates for agricultural loans were reduced to zero, leading to an enormous increase in lending to Andean peasants. Real investment in areas of strong Sendero support continued in the early 1990s as the government constructed roads, schools, and health centers in an effort to appease the civilian population. Pointing to new buildings in his village, one civilian explained that these were the fruits of the civil war.[29] They were not the result of a Shining Path victory, as some had hoped. Rather, they came from a government pushed into making investments by growing civilian support for the insurgency.

At the same time, following García's crackdown on the military between 1985 and 1990, President Fujimori reestablished a permissive environment for military attacks on the rebel force and its civilian supporters. He promoted generals who had been accused of human rights violations and supported an increase in the number of extrajudicial assassinations. Several highly publicized incidents, including the massacre of sixteen people in the Barrios Altos neighborhood of Lima in 1991, provided evidence of Fujimori's willingness to escalate state violence against the rebels and their civilian supporters. At the same time, Fujimori provided additional incentives for rebels and civilians to defect to the government's side. Building on laws passed before his term began, Fujimori set in place the *ley de arrepentimiento* in May 1992, an amnesty program that promised clemency or reduced prison terms to rebel soldiers and civilian supporters who turned themselves in to the authorities.

These combined actions changed the environment in which Sendero Luminoso and its civilian supporters operated. The Fujimori regime heightened the brutality of military actions, raising the probability that civilians living with the rebels would not survive, at the same time that it recognized the need to invest in rural areas and showed its willingness to forgive the crimes of rebel supporters and soldiers. These changes in government strategy caused many in the Shining Path's camp to reevaluate their commitment to the organization. Increasingly, the Shining Path was in retreat, without the security or the resources to reinforce control through popular education and mobilization. This was particularly the case in the Andean highlands, where links between the rebels and the civilian population had never been strong.

---

[28] McClintock, *Revolutionary Movements*, p. 142.
[29] Interview, Huanta, December 1(D), 2001.

The changing government approach weakened Sendero's civilian support base. With each successful incursion by government forces, the risks of continuing to support a rebel movement in retreat grew. Civilians found, moreover, that in their position as residents of popular support bases, the Shining Path militants had no strategy to provide security for civilians against brutal government attacks. The rebel military units preserved themselves, often leaving villagers to weather the storm of government incursions on their own. With the prospect of development and amnesty awaiting them on the other side, civilians began to lose faith in the Shining Path project.

This created a new challenge for the rebel movement as it sought to maintain and enlarge its membership for the next round of military confrontations. Some argue that the Shining Path began to recruit coercively, obligating young men to join the rebel forces.[30] As compared to the militants of earlier generations, who volunteered for and endured extensive periods of indoctrination before admission to Sendero, many of the new recruits participated out of fear. New militants who were not steeped in the ideology and hierarchy of the movement resisted orders and created fractures within the organization. Sendero also began to employ more coercive tactics to maintain popular participation in its zones of control. Resistance was met with force, and militants played a far greater role in maintaining the territorial integrity of support bases. It appeared to many that Sendero Luminoso was losing control.

But by and large, Sendero maintained its organizational structure and membership in spite of these challenges. The rupture with highland peasants had begun long before the shocks described here and was likely irreparable. Yet in regions where the Shining Path had constructed popular organizations and mobilized the masses, its capacity remained. Cadres within the organization did not take advantage of the amnesty offer; only civilians caught between Sendero and the government fled rebel zones. Internal processes of selection and promotion, mechanisms of choosing targets and assigning responsibility, structures of political education and indoctrination – most of these were largely unchanged by the developments of the late 1980s and early 1990s. Remarkably, the Shining Path also preserved its capacity to act in a disciplined manner. Although the potential population of targets broadened with the organization of civilian resistance, experts argue that the rebels' violence remained selective

---

[30] Ponciano del Pino, "Family, Culture, and 'Revolution': Everyday Life with Sendero Luminoso," in Stern, *Shining and Other Paths*, p. 164.

until the end.[31] This was a consequence of the consistency of Sendero's membership, structure, and hierarchy. Even with a growing gulf between Sendero and noncombatant populations, the organization managed to survive through the early 1990s. Because of its committed combatants, clear ideology, and established organizational structure, defeating Sendero was not an easy task. As it turned out, it took the capture of its senior leaders in a sudden raid in 1992 to weaken the links that held the militants together.

A Changing Local Economy: Sendero–Huallaga

As U.S. involvement in counternarcotics operations in the Upper Huallaga Valley increased in the 1980s, Sendero–Huallaga confronted a series of major shocks to its organization. The first significant U.S. contribution to Peru's antiterror campaign in Huallaga came in the form of an antidrug base in Santa Lucía in the UHV. Opened in 1988, the base housed twenty-five Drug Enforcement Administration agents, eight U.S.-supplied helicopters, and nearly five hundred Peruvian military personnel. Located centrally in the valley abutting areas of Sendero control, the antidrug base was a major indication of the government's priority of weakening the resource base that held the CRH together.

U.S. military assistance enabled the Peruvian government to threaten Sendero–Huallaga's territorial hegemony in the coca-producing zones. While the government had previously been limited to its bases in major regional cities such as Tingo María, the new funds and equipment helped the military move into zones of rebel control. Moreover, helicopters allowed the government to track Sendero's progress, monitor the production of coca, and direct eradication campaigns. It became increasingly clear that the government was in a position to challenge the security of coca production in rebel-held zones. One consequence was that Colombian traffickers began to encourage coca production in Colombia in an effort to protect their assets.

Falling coca prices accompanied increases in U.S. assistance to the Peruvian government. Drug flights from Colombia declined, and a surplus of coca resulted. Between 1989 and 1990, prices dropped precipitously from two dollars to thirty cents per kilo of coca leaf, which was below the cost of production.[32] For the first time, crop substitution became a real possibility.

---

[31] Interview with former DINCOTE commander, Lima, October 2001.
[32] José Gonzales, "Guerrillas and Coca in the Upper Huallaga Valley," in *Shining Path of Peru*, ed. David Scott Palmer (New York: St. Martins Press, 1992), p. 137.

With resources now available to fund alternative development programs, a government victory seemed to be on the horizon.

The introduction of an amnesty law made the government's success seem all the more likely. It promised reduced sentences to Senderistas and supportive civilians who switched sides. As the security of coca producers and the prices they earned for their crops both declined, amnesty offered an opportunity that was impossible for many to turn down. Soldiers and civilians began to defect from the rebel side in droves. One civilian explained: "It was the ley de arrepentimiento that liberated civilians and members of Sendero Luminoso who wanted out. It was incredibly generous, enabling people to turn themselves in and turn in others in order to lessen their punishment. Outside of the police station, there would be lines of people waiting to turn themselves in."[33] The head of the counterterrorism police in Tingo María estimated that more than five thousand Senderistas and civilian supporters gave themselves up to the police in the Upper Huallaga Valley.[34] Given that Sendero Luminoso had at most ten thousand soldiers and tens of thousands of supporters nationwide in 1990, the capitulation of five thousand in Huallaga alone was a significant blow.

Sendero–Huallaga's response was consistent with its previous patterns of behavior. Its central goal was to preserve its dominance over the coca trade. This required it to prevent defection, maintain territorial hegemony, and combat government incursions. To prevent civilians from escaping, the CRH sought to create financial incentives for its lower-level soldiers and civilians to remain committed. It artificially raised prices in the UHV, demanding that Colombian traffickers pay more than the market price for kilos of coca leaf. Such actions increased the incentives for Colombians to look elsewhere, of course; coca cultivation continued to shift to Colombia and to areas farther south in Peru in the Apurímac and Ene River Valleys.

The CRH also employed violence to prevent civilians from leaving its areas of control. Defectors were targeted even after reaching safety in government-held zones, demonstrating Sendero–Huallaga's capacity to unleash force. Still, local mandos and commanders realized that their support base was shrinking and sought to maximize their take before the whole

---

[33] Interview, Tingo María, November 14(A), 2001.

[34] Ibid., November 14(B), 16(A), 2001. The Truth and Reconciliation Commission estimates that in the area around Tingo María alone, more than ten thousand people turned themselves in for amnesty. See Comisión de la Verdad y Reconciliación, *Informe Final: Peru, 1980–2000, Tomo IV* (Lima: Pontificia Universidad Católica del Peru y Universidad Nacional Mayor de San Marcos, 2003), pp. 362–63.

venture collapsed. Defection from the leadership was common, with commanders disappearing with tens of thousands of dollars at a time.[35] Theft of people's household goods, the stripping of products from passing trucks, killings for land and revenge – all of these continued as Sendero's hold on power in the UHV weakened.

In this period, Sendero Nacional lost its leadership when DINCOTE (Dirección Nacional Contra el Terrorismo, or the National Counterterrorism Directorate) captured Guzmán and other members of the Central Committee. While most of the other regional committees collapsed in the wake of the capture, Sendero–Huallaga struggled along, maintaining a small core of supporters and producers. Prices remained low, government assistance for alternative development continued to arrive, and crop production shifted to Colombia, but Sendero–Huallaga survived. By the mid-1990s, Colombia had surpassed Peru as the world's leading supplier of coca. Aerial interdiction and crop eradication continued, reducing Peru's area of cultivation from over 100,000 hectares in 1995 to 45,000 in 2001.[36] In this same period, the price of coca remained low, creating few incentives for defectors to switch back to the rebel side. Continued international investments in alternative development – amounting to at least $6 million annually from the United Nations alone – provided the opportunity for civilians to develop new sources of revenue from legal agricultural production.

The consequence of the collapse of the Peruvian drug trade has been a gradual depletion of the forces of the CRH. Continued military operations in the UHV led to the capture of members of the regional committee in the late 1990s, leaving it without the key figures who had promoted its rise and evolution in the 1980s. According to Peruvian government estimates, the CRH retains a force of just under one thousand men today. They live deep in the jungle, remain involved in the coca trade, and demand civilian compliance, though most coca producers have defected to the government side.[37]

The most unlikely path of organizational change is from opportunism to activism, but it may be the case that Sendero–Huallaga is on this path. In 2001, the CRH was reportedly engaging in mass mobilization activities, drawing the attention of civilians to the excesses of the now-defunct Fujimori government and the failures of the new Alejandro Toledo regime.[38]

[35] Ibid., November 17(A), 2001.
[36] United Nations Drug Control Program, *Peru: Annual Coca Cultivation Survey 2001* (United Nations Drug Control Program, Peru Country Office, 2001).
[37] Interview with former DINCOTE Commander, Lima, October 2001.
[38] Interview, Tingo María, November 14(B), 2001.

Forced to hide deep in the jungle, members of the CRH emerge carefully, organizing meetings with villagers to explain the reasons for carrying on the struggle. Unlike in the past, rebel soldiers hide their guns, looking to build popular support rather than to inspire participation through fear.

It is far too early to say whether a reborn CRH will be able to leave its opportunistic path behind it. The challenge is significant: coca prices are again on the rise, and production is shifting from Colombia back to Peru in the face of U.S.-backed Plan Colombia.[39] Continued attempts by the Peruvian government to suppress drug production will most likely create strong incentives for coca producers to band together under a rebel force capable of establishing security for the trade, and such a force is most likely to resemble the CRH of the past. But for the moment, a transformation of the CRH appears underway. This change in behavior became possible following the near-total defeat of the organization, the collapse of its leadership, and the depletion of its resource base. Only under these conditions could the organization hope to reshape civilian expectations about its motivations and strategies.

Sources of Organizational Change

The narrative accounts of war in Uganda, Mozambique, and Peru underscore the path-dependent nature of rebel behavior. For the National Resistance Army, Renamo, Sendero Nacional, and Sendero–Huallaga, patterns formed early as a consequence of who was recruited to participate, the sorts of rules and codes that guided behavior, the channels for engaging civilian populations, and the mechanisms for maintaining control. These organizational patterns were largely reinforced over time as the UNLA expelled the NRA from its internal base, Renamo faced down a credible civilian resistance, and Sendero responded to increasingly successful government counterinsurgency campaigns. Barring substantial changes in membership and new ways of doing business within each organization, and responding to the signals sent from the leadership, each rebel group replicated its structure and its strategies, relying on past approaches to meet new challenges.

The empirical record of rebellion in other contexts, however, hints at a more complex story of change and adaptation. Some rebel groups *do* seem

---

[39] Kevin Hall, "Plan Colombia: Antidrug Effort Is Fearful of High Coca Prices in Peru," *Philadelphia Inquirer*, March 27, 2003.

to reverse course and change the nature of their interaction with civilian populations over time. The case of Sendero–Huallaga may suggest the existence of a path from opportunism to activism following defeat, but the more likely transition seems to be one from mobilization to coercion. This raises a key question for future research, one that can only be touched on in brief here: Under what conditions do shocks lead to reversals in groups' organizational structures in the midst of war? To uncover some possible explanations, I turn to two additional cases, those of the National Union for the Total Independence of Angola (União Nacional para a Independência Total de Angola, or UNITA) and the Revolutionary Armed Forces of Colombia (Fuerzas Armadas Revolucionarias de Colombia, or the FARC). I begin with a brief review of the evolution of these groups and then discuss the lessons we might draw from their experiences.

A Switch from Self-Reliance: UNITA

The Maheba refugee camp in western Zambia houses tens of thousands of refugees from the southeastern regions of Angola. The camp began as an informal resting place for displaced persons, but as the Angolan civil war continued over a twenty-year span, Maheba became a city, with row after row of mud houses. On any given block, one can encounter refugees from the very same villages in Moxico or Kuando Kubango provinces in Angola. What differs from house to house is when its residents fled Angola. Some escaped in the mid-1970s, and others departed in the late 1990s or at some point in between.

Interviews with refugees in Maheba document a transformation in the civilian experience of Angola's rebellion: as the endowments of UNITA changed, so too did its behavior.[40] UNITA began as an anticolonial independence movement in the early 1960s, and it fought the Portuguese mainly from its base in the South, capturing weapons from the colonial army. Refugees from the southern provinces of Angola describe a pattern of rebel-civilian relations in the 1960s and 1970s that mirrors the experiences of civilians in Uganda and parts of Peru: Soldiers from UNITA would arrive in a village and call a meeting of its inhabitants. The rebels would invest

---

[40] I conducted interviews in the Maheba refugee camp in July 1999. Over the course of a week in the camp, I had formal and informal conversations with approximately thirty refugees. I intentionally solicited information from a mix of recent arrivals and long-time Zambian residents.

energy in explaining the political purposes of the struggle and ask for the support of the population. Recruitment was voluntary, and rebel leaders approached elders in the community in an attempt to convince them of the need to "donate" their sons to the cause of the rebellion.

The 1980s brought about a fundamental change in the dynamic of Angola's internal conflict. As in Mozambique, the South African government offered its military and technical support to UNITA as part of its anticommunist foreign policy in southern Africa. UNITA also penetrated further into the northern diamond-producing regions of Angola, which provided a heretofore untapped source of wealth to the rebel organization. Refugee accounts plot the transformation of the rebel group. Processes of political indoctrination and mobilization disappeared entirely. The rebels began to arrive in villages without warning, abducting civilians to participate in the army and looting food and household goods.

Making sense of UNITA as an organization requires a careful analysis of three distinct periods of the guerrilla struggle. UNITA emerged first as an anticolonial movement – one of three distinct streams of Angolan nationalism – centered mainly among the Ovimbundu peoples of the South, who comprise more than 40 percent of the national population. In contrast to the other two anticolonial movements in Angola, UNITA was distinguished by its internal orientation.[41] Few of its leaders had access to overseas education, so the expatriate influence on the emerging group was minimal. Its base of operations was in Angola, and it lacked substantial support from external patrons vying for influence in Africa. Indeed, the two other anticolonial groups, the Popular Movement for the Liberation of Angola (MPLA) and the National Liberation Front of Angola, were polar opposites of UNITA: both had their primary bases outside of the country, their leadership consisted entirely of expatriate Angolans, and both received significant financial support from other countries.

Jonas Savimbi officially launched UNITA in 1966 when he crossed into southern Angola with a small group of trained guerrillas and a handful of weapons – knives, pangas, and a single Tokarev pistol. The guerrillas' first operations were disastrous, with large numbers of recruits killed. Savimbi initiated a self-reliance program of attacks planned and executed against achievable targets to yield returns of hardware and ammunition for the

---

[41] Richard Cornwell, "The War for Independence," in *Angola's War Economy: The Role of Oil and Diamonds*, eds. Jakkie Cilliers and Christian Dietrich (Pretoria: Institute for Security Studies, 2000), pp. 44–67.

new rebel movement.[42] At the same time, UNITA focused its energies on political mobilization by educating the Ovimbundu population, engaging it in the political campaign, and establishing tight linkages to local systems of custom and authority. Even though Savimbi attempted to cultivate some forms of external support at this early stage, the movement largely followed the teachings of Chairman Mao in its commitment to depend on the resources it could generate internally.

The armed forces coup that brought down the Portuguese regime in April 1974 paved the way for a rapid transition to Angolan independence in 1975. UNITA attempted to consolidate its political position in the Center and South of the country, stepped up recruitment to increase its physical strength, and began to reach out to other Angolans, especially whites, in an effort to build support. A short-lived agreement to establish a government of national reconciliation was threatened in mid-1975 as infighting between the three revolutionary movements turned violent. Following the transition to independence in November 1975, the MPLA established itself as the official government in Luanda, effectively ending the tripartite arrangement and plunging the country back into civil war. UNITA vowed to return to the bush and wage a guerrilla struggle.

In the second phase of the guerrilla war that began at this time, UNITA was at a major military disadvantage. Savimbi returned to the South, where his support base was strong, and began to set up a sustainable state within a state, formalizing structures of administration and control over the local population. At the same time, his primary focus was on building UNITA's military capacity. The new government was already receiving significant support from its external patrons. Soviet military advisors were attached to each army brigade, Cuban and Eastern European pilots staffed the Angolan air force, Cuba had placed more than nineteen thousand soldiers in Angola by 1979, and the Angolan government began to mortgage its future oil revenues for substantial flows of conventional arms and ammunition.[43] An arms race had begun, and UNITA's survival depended almost entirely on its capacity to keep up.

In an effort to secure consistent and stable flows of arms, ammunition, and logistical supplies, UNITA began to exploit the competition between

---

[42] Jakkie Potgieter, "'Taking Aid from the Devil Himself': UNITA's Support Structures," in Cilliers and Dietrich, *Angola's War Economy*, pp. 255–73.

[43] Hannelie de Beer and Virginia Gamba, "The Arms Dilemma: Resources for Arms or Arms for Resources?" in Cilliers and Dietrich, *Angola's War Economy*, pp. 70–93.

the United States and the Soviet Union. With the collapse of the National Liberation Front of Angola, UNITA became the only alternative to MPLA rule in the country. A flood of external support followed from the United States and, more importantly, from South Africa. U.S. assistance was modest, though it increased during the Reagan administration. South African assistance, on the other hand, was substantial. By the mid-1980s, UNITA was receiving roughly US$200 million annually from the South Africans. Moreover, South Africa sent some of its best troops to fight alongside the UNITA cadres. For much of the 1980s, South African troops were participating in and often leading UNITA attacks on MPLA garrisons.

Superpower interest and competition in Angola declined in the late 1980s as the Soviet Union and its allies suffered economic exhaustion and the region was awash in political transition, including Namibian independence and the weakening of the apartheid state in South Africa. The warring parties, conscious of the changing interests of their backers, focused on one pressing objective: reducing their dependence on external support and procurement. While the MPLA further developed offshore oil fields, UNITA sought to establish effective sovereignty over resource-rich areas, including the diamond mines. By one estimate, UNITA's revenues from diamond mining increased from US$4 million in 1984 to over US$14 million by 1989.[44] The Bicesse Accords legitimized UNITA's territorial gains and committed both parties to a national election in 1992 to determine a postwar political arrangement.

Following an election in which the MPLA bested UNITA in both the presidential and legislative votes, the collapse of the Bicesse Accords gave rise to the third period of the guerrilla struggle. UNITA pushed quickly into the rest of the diamond areas in the Northeast, using its new source of revenue to procure weapons from Eastern Europe. The MPLA was recognized by the United States, and the arms embargo was lifted, paving the way for U.S. weapons to make their way into the hands of the Angolan government. With UNITA controlling close to four-fifths of the country, the MPLA dramatically increased its arms procurement and ramped up the size of the army, nearly quadrupling military spending. In this final period of the guerrilla struggle, the costs of waging war continued to increase. The MPLA plunged its oil revenues into the military, and United Nations sanctions on UNITA dramatically increased the cost of exporting diamonds

[44] Christian Dietrich, "'UNITA's Diamond Mining and Exporting Capacity," in Cilliers and Dietrich, *Angola's War Economy*, pp. 275–94.

and importing arms and logistical supplies. To maintain its force, UNITA created an infrastructure of diamond mines and export networks to produce the resources needed to fight the war. The rebel organization managed close to 10 percent of global diamond production in the 1990s, and its annual revenues approached US$600 million.

UNITA constructed industrial capacity in its zones of control, moving away from inefficient taxes on local diggers toward in-house trained managers and supervisors who oversaw operations in diamond zones. Savimbi centralized the flow of funds by relying on foreign operators under UNITA protection to oversee much of the industry. UNITA cadres were deeply involved in the extraction and management of diamonds in a period that was otherwise marked by a relative calm in the military struggle. This changed in the late 1990s as MPLA offensives challenged UNITA control over the diamond regions. With fighting ongoing, it became more difficult for Savimbi to maintain his industrial infrastructure. He turned instead to a form of "diamond democracy" in which UNITA cadres were encouraged to extract and use diamond revenues to supply their units and even for personal gain – a development one analyst suggests began early in the 1990s.[45] Industrial mining maximized UNITA's control, but small bands of UNITA cadres operating in a more fluid military environment were able to return to earlier patterns of taxing the diamond diggers in the final stages of the war. Although international pressure on UNITA continued to mount, this pattern of conflict funded by extraction might have continued if not for the death of Jonas Savimbi in a major government offensive in 2002.

Under the Influence: The FARC

While peasant recollections reinforce broader currents of thought about how UNITA changed over time, the evolution of the FARC in Colombia remains contested analytical terrain. With the war ongoing and significant external interest in its outcome (especially from the United States), scholars and policy makers have a great deal at stake in debates about the extent to which participation in the drug trade has undermined the FARC's peasant origins. Yet it is a case that bears mention if for no other reason than the high levels of violence experienced by civilians in Colombia and the FARC's role in those abuses. It is now estimated that the FARC is responsible for

---

[45] Ibid., p. 279.

16 percent of the massacres committed during the civil war.[46] Although this pales in comparison to the atrocities reportedly committed by the paramilitaries, levels of violence by the FARC against civilians have been on the rise in the past decade. The annual number of civilians killed in FARC attacks, which numbered approximately two hundred in the early 1990s, more than doubled after 1995, reaching a peak of nearly one thousand in 2002.[47] Newspapers report regularly on FARC violence against the civilian population – the brother of Colombia's education minister killed after being held for ransom for over three years,[48] thirty-four peasants massacred in San Martín in June 2004,[49] a bomb planted by the rebels in a discotheque in a northern city that killed five and wounded fifty-two,[50] and attacks with hand grenades on popular nightspots in downtown Bogotá.[51] The FARC is now known as much for its kidnappings, assassinations, drug production, and massacres as for the political causes that motivated its founders.

The FARC traces its earliest members to a number of self-defense organizations founded by peasant squatters organized against the incursion of the state and large landowners into parts of Sumapaz and Tanquendama. Many were participants in the Communist Party, and after the assassination of Liberal Party leader Jorge Eliécer Gaitán in 1948, these self-defense groups became increasingly militarized. They had little choice, as the Colombian government launched a full-scale military campaign and later a spate of assassinations to weaken the support base of what was an undeclared insurgency. The FARC became a formal guerrilla movement in the mid-1960s when the Colombian government, with active U.S. support, stepped up its campaign to defeat the peasant rebellion. The FARC's military efforts were officially launched at a conference of the self-defense groups in 1966 at which the peasants agreed on a mobile guerrilla war strategy and an

---

[46] See Comisión Colombiana de Juristas, *Panorama de los derechos humanos y el derecho internacional humanitario en Colombia 1999* (Bogotá: Comisión Colombiana de Juristas, 1999), p. 3.

[47] Jorge Restrepo and Michael Spagat, "Civilian Casualties in the Colombian Conflict: A New Approach to Human Security" (unpublished manuscript, Royal Holloway College, University of London, 2004).

[48] Sibylla Brodzinsky, "Colombia Rebels Kill Minister's Brother," *Manchester Guardian*, July 9, 2004, p. 16.

[49] Juan Forero, "Attack by Colombia Rebels Threatens Fragile Peace Talks," *New York Times*, June 17, 2004, p. A3.

[50] World Digest, *St. Louis Post Dispatch*, May 24, 2004, p. A4.

[51] Nicole Karsin, "Bogota Defiant in Face of Rebel Attacks," *Montreal Gazette*, November 17, 2003, p. A17.

agrarian reform plan, which later formed the basis for the FARC's political program.

The FARC's early composition reflected its roots in the peasant self-defense leagues.[52] Seventy percent of its members were peasants; only 30 percent came from the lower middle class or from urban areas. In line with its base in the Communist Party, the FARC had an educated, intellectual core, but its main foundation was in rural areas. Most of the commanders of fronts and columns were of peasant origins. The militants hailed largely from regions that were formerly "independent republics," where locals had rejected colonization by the state and large landowners. The peasant origins of the FARC became even more pronounced in the late 1980s when the rebels severed their relationship with the Communist Party.

Using data gathered from the judicial prosecutions of captured combatants, one analyst explained the FARC's recruitment practices (and the profile of its membership) in terms similar to those employed to describe activist movements in Chapter 3.[53] Participation in the FARC has always been risky. It is a life engagement, and it requires burning bridges to the establishment. The organization is built around mechanisms of tight control: everything in a guerrilla's daily life is managed. And the general rule is that soldiers get their equipment and no more; according to deserters, the absence of a salary is one of the major reasons they leave the organization.[54] Generating conviction, as distinct from employing individualist incentives, is thus central to the FARC's mobilizing strategy.

Between 1966 and 1980, the FARC focused its military activities in rural areas, particularly in regions affected by colonization, where smallholders and sharecroppers were prominent. The war was generally of low intensity, and there were few major confrontations with the government forces. The FARC's priority was building a collective identity and a political platform that its peasant base could support.[55] Its recruitment efforts capitalized on the crisis of the agrarian sector in Colombia, which left many young peasants without educational opportunities, subject to untenable labor conditions,

[52] Nazih Richani, *Systems of Violence: The Political Economy of War and Peace in Colombia* (Albany: State University of New York Press, 2002), pp. 62–64.
[53] Francisco Gutiérrez Sanín, "Telling the Difference: Guerrillas and Paramilitaries in the Colombian War" (unpublished manuscript, 2003).
[54] Human Rights Watch, *You'll Learn not to Cry: Child Combatants in Colombia* (New York: Human Rights Watch, 2003).
[55] Juan Guillermo Ferro Medina and Garciela Uribe Ramón, *El orden de la guerra: Las FARC-EP entre la organización y la política* (Bogotá: Centro Editorial Javeriano, 2002).

and without means to emerge from poverty. Political formation, a process that gave new recruits a sense of agency and possibilities for advancement that did not exist outside of the movement, was central to participation in the FARC. The FARC filled a gap of state authority in the communities in which it organized, providing a voice for the peasants and a more legitimate structure of authority.

The situation in rural areas changed dramatically with the increasing penetration of coca and poppy cultivation into Colombia in the early 1980s. Francisco Thoumi calls this period the "coca boom," as prices skyrocketed in response to substantial interdiction policies in Bolivia and Peru.[56] Prior to the boom, the FARC had only limited exposure to the production of illicit drugs and opposed any involvement of its cadres in their cultivation.[57] But the agricultural sector in Colombia was under tremendous stress, and illegal crops began to sprout in areas of FARC control. Economic liberalization was wreaking havoc on the peasant economy: foodstuffs faced competition from cheaper imports; cash crops, such as cotton, were being displaced by synthetic imports; and sugar exports were limited by quotas set by the United States. Under increasing strain, many peasants were attracted to a booming industry in illicit crops fed by increasing demand in the United States, decreasing supply in neighboring countries, and a relative absence of government control in the regions amenable to planting.

The FARC was compelled by its supporters to accept the shift to illicit crop plantations as a source of supplementary income. Coca and other crops rapidly became fundamental to the peasant subsistence economy, helping the FARC's base of support meet its basic needs. The spread of illegal crops throughout rural areas of Colombia brought with it an influx of migrants. The rural areas experienced reverse migration as the unemployed migrated back from the city to the countryside in the "coca rush."[58] As in the Huallaga region of Peru, cultural codes, values, and the political culture were transformed by the influx of easy money. At the same time, narcotics traffickers infiltrated the rural areas, offering to purchase peasants' coca crops and get them to market. They brought with them increasing crime, competition between merchants, and violent disagreements between the producers and the traffickers.

---

[56] Francisco Thoumi, *Economia politica y narcotrafico* (Bogotá: Tercer Mundo, 1994).
[57] Ferro Medina and Uribe Ramón, *Orden de la guerra*, p. 96.
[58] Richani, *Systems of Violence*, p. 72.

The FARC, as the main source of political authority in these regions, watched as the influence of illicit crops dramatically transformed the local subsistence economy. The organization attempted to preserve its revolutionary ideals of self-sacrifice at the same time it sought to manage the growing tensions between peasants and traffickers, which threatened stability in its regions of influence. Peasants were encouraged to continue growing foodstuffs and to limit the amount of land they dedicated to coca production. FARC cadres also interceded on behalf of the peasantry by demanding that traffickers pay a decent wage to their workers and the market price to producers. The FARC took up the charge of policing criminal and delinquent activity in an attempt to minimize the negative ramifications of the growing drug trade. To pay for these services on behalf of the peasantry, the FARC implemented a system of taxation that became increasingly formalized and wide-ranging over time. Estimates of FARC tax income range from $60 million to $100 million per year, and these funds are supplemented with revenues generated from protection rents and ransom money.

This infusion of resources contributed to a substantial change in the military strategy of the FARC. At a 1982 military conference, the FARC committed to double the size of its fronts; to expand its operations to middle-sized cities; to invest in more powerful armaments; to improve its command, control, and communications systems; and to develop a stable economic infrastructure that could fund much of the organization's growth.[59] Between 1982 and 1989, it is estimated that membership of the FARC's guerrilla army increased from fewer than nine thousand to over eighteen thousand combatants. Because of the new resources, capacity, and strength involved in it, the war in Colombia came to be characterized by much larger military operations and confrontations.

Debate about the FARC centers on the extent to which the coca economy has affected its internal organization.[60] The FARC centralized revenues drawn from the taxation of coca production in an effort to channel those resources to their most productive uses. Much of that money was invested in licit enterprises in Colombia's major cities. The FARC's centralized, efficient administration of the revenue from coca differs dramatically from the strategy of the Shining Path. While Sendero maintained a

[59] Ibid., p. 76.
[60] See Ferro Medina and Uribe Ramón, *Orden de la guerra*, pp. 93–105, for a detailed description of how the FARC was transformed by its involvement in drug production.

decentralized operational approach, the FARC insisted on strict control of the revenues, expressing serious concern that the money might be misused by its unformed masses. As a national organization, the FARC became a real competitor to the narcotics traffickers and the paramilitaries, fundamentally changing the nature of the military struggle. At the micro level, analysts insist that "all the goods coming from military or illegal economic activities go to the organization." Salaries are still not paid, even though the FARC is flush with cash, and "looting for individual benefit is nearly inconceivable."[61]

At the same time, other analysts argue that the FARC has experienced a significant decline in its political activities as a result of its engagement in the drug economy.[62] The organization faced a difficult intellectual quandary: engagement in the coca trade was in clear tension with the ideals of the revolution. But the difficulties were also more concrete. Political education – the formation of the masses – became a less important priority in the organization, and tensions between the uneducated base and the "formed" commanders, which were prominent early in the war, became more pronounced. The logistical necessity of responding to government counterinsurgency efforts drove the FARC to continue expanding its membership and gaining military strength, but the new recruits were of a different mold and rarely received the indoctrination that was characteristic of the movement early on. Juan Guillermo Ferro Medina and Garciela Uribe Ramón suggest this transformation is part of what accounts for the guerrillas' increasing violence and violations of international humanitarian law.[63]

Drawing Lessons

UNITA and the FARC experienced significant endowment shocks. For UNITA, the influx of resources came first from external patrons that sought influence in Africa's Cold War–era conflicts. In the Andes, interdiction policies drove narcotics traffickers from Peru and Bolivia to search for new regions that could serve as the basis for illicit plantations. The traffickers stumbled on an agrarian economy in crisis in Colombia. The easy money to be made in the coca trade transformed the rural economy, changing the resources available to the FARC. But resource shocks on their own do not

---

[61] Gutiérrez Sanín, "Telling the Difference."
[62] Ferro Medina and Uribe Ramón, *Orden de la guerra*.
[63] Ibid.

necessarily lead to changes in behavior: the NRA robbed banks in the later stages of the war, but much of the money was channeled directly into the organization's growth without negative ramifications. We must ask what the cases of UNITA and the FARC suggest about the *conditions* under which shocks lead to reversals of strategy.

Rebel groups in Angola and Colombia experienced endowment shocks for different reasons. In Angola, the endowment shock was not exogenous: Jonas Savimbi actively went in search of external patrons to fund his guerrilla campaign against the MPLA government. Superpower competition made this possible, but it was not determinative, as the first phase of UNITA's campaign suggests. After Angolan independence, UNITA faced an enormous supply constraint. The rebels were in an arms race with the government. The MPLA received logistical, technical, and financial support from a whole host of international partners, including many who were willing to put their own troops on the ground. The Angolan government could mortgage enormous oil wealth in order to procure the best weapons and train its troops. Soviet technical advisors professionalized the Angolan army, transforming what had been a weak anticolonial movement. As the government army grew stronger, battlefield losses for UNITA mounted, and the likelihood of a rebel victory grew dimmer. In this climate, Savimbi knew it would be difficult to maintain his membership, fill his ranks, and compete with government forces. The choice to seek out new endowments and to abandon an initial strategy of self-reliance was driven by a pressing need to overcome standard supply constraints on insurgency. UNITA needed to grow rapidly in order to remain a credible opponent in Angola's civil war.

The experience of the FARC reveals a different path: demand-side considerations played a far more prominent role in Colombia. The FARC explicitly avoided involvement in the coca trade when illicit plantations began to sprout in the late 1970s because cadres saw illegal drugs and easy money as anathema to the FARC's ideology, which emphasized self-reliance. Instead, its commanders focused on building a collective identity and establishing legitimate structures of authority in peasant communities largely beyond the reach of the state. With the subsistence economy in crisis, however, demand for the revenues from coca came from the FARC's support base. Coca and other illicit crops yielded significant income for peasant farmers, and the FARC could do little to stop their spread. The organization also faced increasing demands from its constituents for the FARC to act as an intermediary with the narcotics traffickers and criminal gangs

293

who began operating in rural zones. Grappling with these new responsibilities and managing the infusion of resources sapped valuable attention, resources, and capacity from the political work that was at the core of the FARC's revolutionary model.

Endowment shocks, then, transformed the internal structures of UNITA and weakened the political basis of the FARC as both rebel organizations became enmeshed in the trade of illegal goods. Extracting diamonds in Angola required the creation of downstream partnerships with a series of criminal organizations – groups that were willing to flout United Nations sanctions in order to transit and sell Angolan diamonds on the international market. Involvement in the coca trade put the FARC in direct competition with the traffickers and paramilitaries who sought to exploit producers to meet the growing demand for drugs in the northern hemisphere. Downstream partnerships risked criminalizing both movements and spreading corruption through the senior ranks. At the same time, for both diamonds and drugs, the local nature of extraction or production attracted waves of individuals interested in easy money to regions that came under rebel control.

Yet the evidence suggests that UNITA experienced a more rapid and complete transformation from an activist insurgency to an opportunistic one, while the FARC has resisted (at least in part) a shift in the character of its rank-and-file membership. The nature of the process of resource extraction may be of some consequence here because UNITA confronted an increasingly decentralized diamond extraction operation (under constant assault from the MPLA), and the FARC operated a centralized revenue management system in a territorial zone left largely under its control. Preventing the corruption and defection of cadres was thus much easier for rebel leaders in Colombia than it was in Angola. But differences in the process of resource extraction cannot be the entire story. In Colombia, the internal institutions forged in the early years of the insurgency appear to have been more resilient than those in Angola. Leaders of the FARC have so far resisted pressures to distribute resource wealth, instead investing new assets in the growth of the military movement (just as the NRA did in Uganda). UNITA, on the other hand, abandoned self-reliance when the South Africans and the United States came calling in the 1980s, even before it gained access to diamond regions. The increasing military power of the government in Angola is likely an important variable, as it placed a premium on UNITA's capacity to grow in size and strength. Strategic considerations then drove Savimbi's decision to seek external support. But why the influx of material resources could not be managed in such a way that the organization's decay was prevented remains a puzzle. Perhaps, Savimbi faced a growing chorus of demands for remuneration from his members, exhausted after more than a decade of fighting. It is possible also that rapid expansion required a more efficient recruitment strategy; abduction may have replaced political mobilization as UNITA moved into areas outside of its Ovimbundu base and sought quickly to counter the government's growing strength. Maybe UNITA's leadership was itself corrupted by the influx of resources, leading to a breakdown in the norms and practices that had been constructed in the movement's first decade. These are questions for future research, but they suggest that the dynamics of organizational change are not explicable simply in terms of changing endowments; substantial shifts in strategy, once groups begin down a particular path, may be shaped in important ways by the demands of constituents within and outside the movement, strategic considerations, and the choices of a group's leadership.

Conclusion

Rebel groups face a series of challenges in civil war that threaten the organizational structures they have built and may necessitate changing strategies in response. These challenges include the need to recover from battlefield losses, manage success, respond to changing endowments, and react to new government counterinsurgency strategies. New developments that arise during conflicts act as a shock to the expectations of the participants – rebel soldiers and civilians alike – causing many to reevaluate the choices they have made, the commitments voiced by commanders, and their expectations about what they are likely to gain from continued participation.

My exploration of how the four rebel groups central to this study responded to shocks during war reinforces a central point emphasized throughout this study: because patterns of behavior form early on in conflict, they are difficult to change over time. Rebel behavior is not simply a function of the strategic situation that groups encounter. It is shaped by the nature of the group's membership, the mechanisms established to manage and control combatants, and the types of relationships a rebel group builds with noncombatants. Change is difficult because soldiers and civilians form expectations about how others are likely to behave, and, to the extent that those expectations are continually reinforced, rebel groups maintain their earliest patterns of behavior.

But the experiences of some groups suggest that patterns of behavior can change. The most likely path of change is from a structure of governance emphasizing social mobilization to one that employs coercion. New endowments, particularly those that involve linkages to illicit industries, can undermine the internal structure of rebel groups. If not managed, they have the potential to change a group's membership and its patterns of interaction with noncombatants. When routines that engender trust are broken, civilians and combatants quickly lose faith and look for alternatives. A cycle of resistance and repression begins that is difficult to bring to an end. An alternative path from opportunism to activism may also be possible, but the road is littered with obstacles. Near-total defeat may be required before groups can refashion civilians' expectations and build trust, thereby reversing previous patterns of behavior.

PART III

Beyond Uganda, Mozambique, and Peru

8

Extensions

In the preceding pages, I have sought to shed light on the question of why some insurgents abuse noncombatants and others exhibit restraint and discipline in the use of force by exploring the behavior of rebel groups in Uganda, Mozambique, and Peru. The four organizations, which vary in the initial conditions they confronted, the strategies and tactics they pursued, and the ultimate behaviors they exhibited in relation to civilian populations, invite a controlled comparison that helps to identify key determinants of rebel behavior.

The specific outcome I sought to explain is why the National Resistance Army and the Shining Path's national organization used force systematically and strategically to punish defectors, while Renamo and the Shining Path's regional committee in the Upper Huallaga Valley perpetrated indiscriminate violence, looted villages, and employed much higher levels of coercion in the governance of civilian populations. I began by showing how the access of rebel groups to economic endowments in Mozambique and the jungles of Peru enabled their leaders to make appeals for participation rooted in short-term material interests, while the absence of such endowments in Uganda and the Peruvian highlands forced leaders to develop credible appeals about the private and public benefits that would come with an uncertain victory, to activate community networks and norms of reciprocity, and to build ideological foundations that reflected (and sometimes changed) the interests of potential members. Appeals to identity and ideology by the NRA and the Shining Path yielded an activist core of members, making it possible for the rebel leadership of both groups to decentralize operations, share power with civilians, and build a reputation for restraint. Mobilization strategies that employed short-term rewards, characteristic of Renamo and the CRH, instead produced movements full of opportunists and organizations where defection was the norm, civilian populations were governed with an iron fist, and repeated patterns of indiscipline generated substantial civilian resistance.

In its more general form, the central argument of this book is that the initial endowments to which rebel leaders have access shape the strategies these groups pursue and the ways in which they employ violence. Economic endowments lend themselves to recruitment on the basis of short-term material interests, generating a flood of opportunistic joiners. Social endowments enable mobilization strategies that appeal to long-term interests or draw on norms, networks, and values, producing a selective pool of activist recruits. The profile of recruits then conditions the choices rebel leaders make about how to manage and control behavior within the organization and to govern noncombatant populations. The strategic dilemmas that groups face are thus endogenous to the resource environment in which they emerge. With a pool of committed recruits who share beliefs, norms, or identities, leaders of activist rebellions are in a better position to develop organizational cultures that reinforce cooperation. Strong norms guide behavior in activist organizations and are complemented by systems of training and promotion and structures of delegation that reinforce the shared commitments of a movement's members. But misbehavior and indiscipline plague opportunistic organizations, as individual members take advantage of their positions of authority over civilians for personal gain. Training and promotion depend more on personal allegiance than performance, and structures of delegation sometimes involve a high degree of centralization – because local units cannot be trusted to follow the orders of the central command – or significant decentralization, with only a loose alliance joining largely independent fighting units. Unable to police the behavior of their combatants effectively, opportunistic insurgencies encounter civilian resistance and resort to authoritarian forms of governance in their territory as they seek local resources to maintain the struggle. Activist organizations strike bargains with noncombatant populations that exchange civilian manpower, information, and other resources for shared authority in zones of rebel control.

When it comes to explaining patterns of violence against civilians, variation in the origins and organization of insurgency matters because it affects the *capacity* of rebel groups to discipline their membership and the *expectations* of civilians about how soldiers are likely to behave. Selective violence can be an effective tool for preventing and punishing civilian defection, but to employ it, an organization must be able to collect quality information, direct violence at some targets and not others, and deal effectively with mistakes or indiscipline. When used in an indiscriminate fashion, violence generates resistance from noncombatant populations. Groups that are incapable of preventing indiscriminate violence or punishing it appropriately when it occurs find themselves in a cycle of violence and resistance. To the extent that this picture of organizational formation is correct, combatants perpetuate high levels of indiscriminate violence not because little support exists for their insurgency in the region in which they live or because their rebellion is losing to government forces. The brutal and widespread abuse of noncombatants by insurgent groups is instead often an unintended consequence of an organizational strategy that appeals to the short-term material interests of potential recruits.

The argument I advance in this book may account for the variation we observe in the behavior of rebels in Uganda, Mozambique, and Peru, but that does not necessarily mean it is portable. To determine whether differences in a group's initial endowments correlate with distinct recruitment profiles in other contexts, the next section turns to rebellions in Sierra Leone and Nepal for evidence that supports the causal importance of the recruitment process. I then examine quantitative evidence that exploits macro-level variation in the resources available to rebel groups across conflicts to make sense of patterns of violence in civil war since 1945. I conclude by examining four anomalous cases in which high levels of violence are observed in wars in which insurgent groups have access to limited material resources.

Endowments and Recruitment in Other Contexts

When Nepal's Maoists – the Communist Party of Nepal (Maoist), or CPN(M) – launched their guerrilla war in 1996, few believed that a small communist splinter group could offer a serious challenge to the Nepali regime. However, less than a decade later, with ten thousand men and women under arms, the Maoists control much of Nepal's territory. Based initially in some of the poorest regions of rural Nepal, the Maoists quickly captured the attention and allegiance of a wide range of excluded ethnic and caste groups suffering under the weight of extreme poverty and discrimination. But their primary base was among disaffected communist party sympathizers, many of whom were unhappy with the pace of political change. The monarchy's grudging acceptance of a transition to multiparty democracy in 1990 had only temporarily placated aspirations for wholesale political reform. While many Nepali elites saw the elections of 1991/1992 as an opportunity to rein in the power of the monarchy, leaders of the Maoist wing of the Communist Party grew disillusioned with the reforms and advocated armed struggle as the only means to establish a republic and end the monarchical system.

The Revolutionary United Front of Sierra Leone launched its insurgency in 1991 in an effort to unseat the ruling single-party state of the All People's Congress, which had overseen Sierra Leone for twenty-three years. The RUF challenged an increasingly bankrupt state that was seeking to maintain networks of patronage through its manipulation of the diamond trade. The weakening of the All People's Congress's shadow state in the 1980s gave rise to a political movement of young students on the campus of Freetown's Fourah Bay College that began to mobilize in opposition to the Congress's rule. The students linked up with Libya, which was actively engaged in supporting African revolutionary causes, before state security services flushed the intellectual movement off the college's campus. As the student movement melted away in response to repression, the revolutionary fervor shifted to a much different population of potential insurgents: the unemployed urban youth of Freetown, known for their antisocial behavior, including marijuana smoking, petty theft, and violence.

Like the four rebel organizations discussed in this book, the Maoists and RUF launched insurgent movements in poor, rural areas. They challenged governments that increasingly lacked popular legitimacy, and each faced an asymmetry of power with the government forces. Yet the two movements differed most substantially at their founding with respect to what participation in insurgency meant for potential recruits. When the Maoists initiated the armed struggle, they had no organized military force and little weaponry; two rifles, one of which was broken, represented the totality of their armaments.[1] As they extended their operations, the insurgents constructed muskets, took shotguns and other weapons from local residents, and captured guns from the police, at first, and later the military. Because of the Maoists' precarious military position in the first years of the struggle, participation was a risky venture. It also offered few immediate benefits. Guerrillas were not paid a salary but given instead a monthly allowance of less than two dollars for items such as toothpaste and soap. Without material

---

[1] For a more comprehensive discussion of the Maoist insurgency, see International Crisis Group, "Nepal's Maoists: Their Aims, Structure, and Strategy" (International Crisis Group, Washington, DC, October 2005). See also Robert Gersony, "Sowing the Wind: History and Dynamics of the Maoist Revolt in Nepal's Rapti Hills" (Mercy Corps International, Washington, DC, October 2003).

support from overseas, the Maoists sought financial self-sufficiency inside Nepal by raising their own taxes, soliciting voluntary contributions and donations, and, as they grew in size, conducting bank robberies and practicing extortion to meet their growing military costs. Their strategies in a resource-poor environment mirror those of the NRA and the Shining Path.

While the Maoists committed themselves to self-reliance, Sierra Leone's Revolutionary United Front embraced wholeheartedly the support and resources provided by Charles Taylor in neighboring Liberia. The leaders of the RUF purportedly struck a deal with Taylor in 1989, pledging to help him liberate Liberia in exchange for an external base and assistance in launching an internal struggle in Sierra Leone.[2] While a small number of the initial RUF cadres received training in Libya in 1987 and 1988, the bulk of the organization and preparation took place in Liberia before the group's 1991 launch. Participation in the RUF offered recruits an opportunity to partake of new patronage networks, which was an advantage because many in Sierra Leone were increasingly excluded from the benefits of government largesse in the capital of Freetown. Both Foday Sankoh, the RUF leader, and Charles Taylor, the rebel head in neighboring Liberia, were typical "warlord rulers" of West Africa who used the "extortion of aid organizations, manipulation of drug and diamond trades, profit from forced labor, official looting operations, and control of markets through alliances with foreign commercial partners" to reward their supporters and build a base of political power.[3] The RUF became a vehicle for personal enrichment, and the diamond mining area of eastern Sierra Leone was its first target.

The different incentives offered by the Maoists and the RUF yielded substantively different pools of recruits. The Maoist leadership is highly educated, some with university degrees from outside Nepal; only one member of the standing committee is self-taught. This reflects an initial recruitment process that actively sought the defection of members of mainstream communist parties to the insurgency.[4] This ideologically sophisticated core of educated members was critical to the movement's expansion. In rural areas,

---

[2] A detailed discussion of the RUF movement can be found in Ibrahim Abdullah, "Bush Path to Destruction: The Origin and Character of the Revolutionary United Front/Sierra Leone," *Journal of Modern African Studies* 36 (1998): 203–35. See also Paul Richards, *Fighting for the Rain Forest: War, Youth, and Resources in Sierra Leone* (Oxford: James Currey, 1996).

[3] William Reno, "War, Markets, and the Reconfiguration of West Africa's Weak States," *Comparative Politics* 29 (1997): 493–510.

[4] On the Maoist's recruitment process, see International Crisis Group, "Nepal's Maoists," pp. 14–16.

its early campaigns, using political education and indoctrination, expanded the support base of the rebels to include ethnic and caste groups long ignored or exploited by the central government. New cadres were carefully selected, screened, and educated in Maoist doctrine before they were given responsibilities in the movement. Urban strategies included the creation of above-ground front organizations to engage student populations and trade union members. A Maoist campaign to reduce private school fees won support from Nepal's large lower middle class, after the student organization was able to shut down 30,000 schools in a strike in late 2000.

The RUF, on the other hand, drew what one of the original student leaders called the "wrong kind of individuals."[5] As the original Fourah Bay College student movement disintegrated under pressure from the government, a small number of nonstudent revolutionaries began to mobilize the population of lumpen youth, the so-called rarray boys in Freetown. These youths were mostly unlettered second-generation residents of the city. They had roots all over the country, and they lacked access to employment. They were known first and foremost as thugs, drug users, and, when dirty work was required, as tools of the political elite. Sankoh and his colleagues did not have networks among the educated classes, nor had their marginal existence in urban and peripherally urban areas given them community ties in rural areas. So they turned to the population of unemployed young men in Freetown and, later, to that of the hinterland near the Liberian border.[6]

The distinct recruitment profiles of the Maoists and the RUF correlate with differences in the nature of rebel behavior in the two conflicts. The RUF is widely thought of as the Renamo of the 1990s, responsible for a decade of killing and mutilation in Sierra Leone. Its commanders now sit in the docks at trial, charged by the Sierra Leone Special Court with crimes against humanity. The Maoists, on the other hand, have implemented a military campaign marked by selective violence, with attacks on police posts, military barracks, and political leaders as their dominant strategy. Cadres responsible for mistaken killings of civilians and abusive extortion have been punished by the Maoist leadership, and the insurgents have taken to warning civilians of impending attacks in populated areas in order to allow them to escape. Of course, this out-of-sample test is merely illustrative. The comparison is meant only to demonstrate that the logic linking endowments

---

[5] Abdullah, "Bush Path."
[6] Ibid.

to the recruitment profile of rebel groups finds some immediate support outside of the sample. More systematic analysis, in particular analysis that utilizes cross-national statistics, is an important next step in assessing the strength of my argument.

Explaining Patterns of Violence across Civil Wars

Extending the geographic scope of the analysis to all civil wars since 1945 provides an opportunity to assess the general applicability of the argument advanced in this book. While it is not possible to carry out investigations of the micropolitics of rebellion as detailed as those presented in previous chapters, I can estimate statistical relationships between the key independent variables and measures of the *level* of violence committed against noncombatants in civil war. Assessments of the *character* of rebel violence are more accurately measured at the micro level, as shown in Chapter 6, because judgments depend on accurate information about violent incidents that occur within conflict. But I take a preliminary look as well at patterns of violence in ten randomly selected cases from the post–Cold War period using proxies for the character of rebel behavior. Large-N analysis of the type utilized here complements the theory-generation aspects of this study with a test of its cross-national (or cross-conflict) validity. Yet such approaches, in spite of their strengths, involve abstracting away from the individual and group-level processes and mechanisms given priority throughout the book.

To explain variation in levels of violence, I employ a dependent variable – combat-related deaths – that includes all soldiers and civilians killed in civil war.[7] Recently collected by scholars associated with the International Peace Research Institute in Oslo (PRIO), the data capture best-guess estimates of direct casualties drawn from a multitude of sources, including compendia of casualty statistics and the reports of conflict monitoring organizations. This measure excludes indirect deaths, which are often substantial and encompass both those that follow from war-induced famine and disease and casualties of one-sided military campaigns in which either the government or an opposition force faces no military challenger. (Think of state violence outside of the context of war and attacks by terrorist groups, for example.) Linked to James Fearon and David Laitin's dataset of civil

---

[7] Bethany Lacina and Nils Petter Gleditsch, "Monitoring Trends in Global Combat: A New Dataset of Battle Deaths," *European Journal of Population* 21 (2005): 145–66.

wars between 1945 and 1999, the measure of combat-related deaths varies from deaths in the low hundreds in Haiti, Mali, and Nepal to more than one million in China and Vietnam.[8] The median civil war killed about ten thousand in combat, although the mean is almost seven times that.[9] I log transform the dependent variable in order to address its tremendous skew.

Combat-related deaths are the best measure of the scale, scope, and intensity of violence committed in civil war. They can be misleading as a measure of rebel violence, however, for two reasons. The first is that combat-related deaths include the killings of both soldiers and civilians. Even though no high-quality measures of combat-related deaths that can accurately distinguish military and civilian victims exist, rough assessments have been produced for the post-1945 period and published by the World Bank.[10] Log-transformed measures of civilian and total deaths in the World Bank paper correlate at above 0.95, suggesting that civil wars with large numbers of overall casualties tend to have significant civilian casualties as well. A second concern is that an aggregate measure of combat-related deaths conflates killings perpetrated by rebel groups and governments. In order to more accurately capture variation in levels of rebel violence, I exclude from the sample twenty-four civil wars where government-sponsored mass killing accounts for at least fifty thousand deaths.[11] Data on the remaining ninety-five cases more credibly capture the level of violence perpetrated by insurgent organizations in civil war.

To assess the impact of a rebel group's resource wealth on levels of violence, I employ two proxies. I look first at how levels of violence in wars in which rebel groups have access to material resources differ from those in conflicts where insurgents are resource-poor. As a proxy for the material wealth of the insurgents, I employ James Fearon's measure of contraband

---

[8] James Fearon and David Laitin, "Ethnicity, Insurgency, and Civil War," *American Political Science Review* 97 (2003): 75–90.

[9] This measure correlates at 0.75 with the International Institute for Strategic Studies' measure of war deaths, so although all the results presented here are robust to the use of either dependent variable, I include only results using the International Peace Research Institute measure.

[10] The data were collected by Milton Leitenberg and published in Robert S. McNamara, "The Post–Cold War World: Implications for Military Expenditures in Developing Countries," *Proceedings of the World Bank Annual Conference on Development Economics* 1991.

[11] Benjamin Valentino, Paul Huth, and Dylan Balch-Lindsay code all civil wars in the post-1945 period in terms of whether the government perpetrated mass killing, defined as more than fifty thousand civilians killed. See "Draining the Sea: Mass Killing and Guerilla Warfare," *International Organization* 58 (2004): 375–407.

Table 8.1. *Resource Wealth and Violence*

	Dependent Variable: Log of Combat-Related Deaths (Excluding Mass Killing)			
Duration	0.123	0.045	0.120	0.056
	[3.60]***	[2.17]**	[3.20]***	[3.33]***
Contraband	0.961	1.249		
	[2.29]**	[3.19]***		
Pro-Rebel intervention			0.820	1.226
			[1.75]*	[3.60]***
Constant	8.057	8.260	7.913	8.028
	[25.77]***	[31.30]***	[22.07]***	[28.21]***
Observations	42	78	42	78
R-squared	0.33	0.16	0.35	0.20
Sample	Wars fought over state control	All civil wars	Wars fought over state control	All civil wars

Notes: OLS estimates. The dependent variable is combat-related deaths, excluding mass killing. T-statistics (calculated with robust standard errors) in parentheses. *** Significant at 0.01 level; ** Significant at 0.05 level; * Significant at 0.10 level.

resources. Fearon coded civil wars for whether it was reported that rebels relied on income from trade in contraband, including drugs and diamonds.[12] His decision to code the presence of contraband, however, was not in any way related to an apparent relationship between contraband financing and levels of violence. I also utilize a second proxy for a group's resource wealth: whether an external patron intervened on behalf of the rebel side. Patrick Regan's measure of external intervention captures whether outside actors supported the rebel group militarily or economically in the course of the fighting.[13]

To estimate the relationship formally, I use ordinary least squares regression analysis, as reported in Table 8.1. Regression analysis is a statistical tool that enables us to identify the causal effect of one variable upon another and to assess the statistical significance of the estimate – that is, the degree of confidence that the relationship we observe in the data is close to the true relationship. The statistical analysis is conducted from a cross-sectional

[12] James Fearon, "Why Do Some Civil Wars Last So Much Longer Than Others?" *Journal of Peace Research* 41 (2004): 275–302.
[13] Patrick Regan, "Third-Party Interventions and the Duration of Intrastate Conflicts," *Journal of Conflict Resolution* 46 (2002): 55–73.

perspective using data on all civil wars that occurred between 1945 and 2000, excluding those where governments perpetrated mass killings of noncombatants. In columns 1 and 3, I report results on a sample of civil wars in which insurgent groups sought control of the state; columns 2 and 4 replicate the analysis on the full sample of civil wars, including secessionist struggles. Conscious that revenue sources might increase the level of violence simply by prolonging the war, I include an additional control in each regression: the duration of the conflict.[14]

The results of the analysis are robust and compelling. In wars in which combatants seek to capture the state, the use of contraband resources to finance an insurgency is statistically associated with higher levels of violence, controlling for the duration of the war. Moving from a civil war in which rebels are not involved in illicit trade to one in which they are is associated with an increase in the level of combat-related deaths of nearly one-half a standard deviation. In terms of civilian deaths, the presence of contraband resources is equivalent to nearly ten years of additional fighting. External support for rebellion also significantly increases the level of civil war violence. The size of the effect is similar to that of material resources. Moreover, external support appears to have mattered just as much during the Cold War, when it was typically motivated by grand ideological debates, as it does in the post–Cold War period, when a variety of actors intervene for other reasons. The statistical results are consistent with my theory but also with rival explanations of violence, including one that links material resources to a greater capacity to inflict harm on noncombatants through the purchase of more effective armaments. Further cross-national research is needed to distinguish among competing explanations. Yet the addition of robust cross-national findings on both material resources and external support to the evidence for micro mechanisms outlined in previous chapters should give added confidence that my hypothesis is at work.

---

[14] The results are robust to the inclusion of a control for population size as well. I also explored the impact of a potential omitted variable, rebel troop strength. It is possible that more resources allow leaders to expand their militaries and thereby produce more combat-related deaths. The evidence for this is not strong, however. No statistically significant relationship exists between the proxies of resource wealth and the size of opposition forces (from the Valentino, Huth, and Balch-Lindsay dataset). And although including a control for opposition force size in the multivariate regressions renders insignificant the coefficients for the proxies described earlier, this is likely due to a reduction in sample size by twenty-six conflicts. Those conflicts for which data on opposition troop strength are not available tend to be resource-poor by Fearon's measure (25 of 26) and have an average level of combat-related deaths that is lower by thirty thousand than those cases that remain.

It is interesting to note that the relationship between material resources and levels of violence is replicated in the full sample of civil wars (columns 2 and 4). Throughout the book, my focus has been on insurgent movements that intend to capture control of the state. I argued in the introduction that a combatant group's desire to govern the population of an entire country might affect the organizational strategies it can pursue. Focusing on groups that seek state power provided us with significant leverage in identifying a set of shared organizational choices. It may be the case, however, that aspects of a group's internal structure shape patterns of violence in a wider range of contexts. Indeed, the statistical results suggest that the relationship I describe holds in secessionist conflicts as well. The results linking a group's material wealth to levels of violence are stronger when secessionist conflicts are included in the analysis. Whether this is evidence in support of my theory or not requires an in-depth analysis of the organization of secessionist movements. But it is possible to imagine that low barriers to insurgency, even in contexts where groups have articulated a claim to ethnic or regional autonomy, may produce a similar sorting of types to those chronicled in this book.

Resource wealth is associated with higher levels of violence, I argue, because opportunistic groups tend to use violence in such a way (indiscriminate, brutal) that it generates resistance from civilian populations, leading to a cycle of repression and resistance. Measuring the character of violence cross-nationally is a more difficult enterprise; without micro-level event data, temporal trends, or geographic patterns, judgments about overall insurgent behavior must be approached with caution. Nonetheless, as a preliminary cross-national test of my intuitions, I randomly selected a set of ten civil wars in the post–Cold War period. Consistent with the relevant proportion of cases in the overall sample, four civil wars were contested by resource-rich rebel groups, while in the remaining six, insurgents had no access to external support or contraband resources. I then identified a set of proxies for indiscriminate violence: large numbers of refugees, the occurrence of massacres (defined as killings of more than six people in a single incident), and reports of rape, looting, and forced recruitment. The refugee data are from the United Nations High Commissioner for Refugees and have been employed by others as a measure of violence.[15] Using annual U.S. State Department reports of each country's human rights practices

---

[15] Jean-Paul Azam and Anke Hoeffler, "Violence against Civilians in Civil War: Looting or Terror?" *Journal of Peace Research* 39 (2002): 461–85.

Table 8.2. *Resources and the Character of Insurgent Violence*

Country	War Years	IISS Battle Deaths	UNHCR Refugees	Massacres	Rape	Looting	Forced Recruitment
Resource-Rich							
Angola	1997–99	5000	333,700	✓	✓	✓	✓✓
Burundi	1993–99	206,000	809,200	✓	✓	✓	✓
Indonesia	1997–99	4000		✓	✓	✓	
Sierra Leone	1991–99	40,000	478,900	✓	✓	✓	✓
Resource-Poor							
Bosnia	1992–95	90,000		✓	✓		✓
Central African Republic	1996–97	1000			✓	✓	✓
China (Uighur Rebellion)	1991–99	1000					
Nepal	1997–99	1000					
Russia	1991	167				✓	✓
Somalia	1991–99	355,000	716,600	✓	✓	✓	

as a dataset, I also coded for the presence or absence of massacres, rape, looting, and forced recruitment for the duration of the conflict. Although State Department reports do not have the detail that might come from country experts, their consistent reporting requirements and structure of presentation allow for (at least) some preliminary analysis of cross-conflict patterns.

The results of my inquiry are reported in Table 8.2. Across the four conflicts in which insurgent groups had access to material resources, a clear picture of indiscriminate, brutal violence emerges. Three of the four produced large outflows of refugees (each above the median number of refugees for wars in the post–Cold War period); reports of insurgent-perpetrated massacres, rape, and looting were identified in State Department documents for all four. Resource-rich rebel groups appear also to have participated in the forced recruitment of combatants, at least in Angola, Burundi, and Sierra Leone. The results on resource-poor insurgent groups are more mixed. Aside from Somalia, none of the conflicts produced large numbers of refugees. Yet massacres were reported in two of the six cases, and descriptions of rape, looting, and forced recruitment appeared in State Department documents for half of the conflicts. The Somali case, while classified as resource-poor, is likely consistent with the logic I advance: extraordinarily low barriers to insurgency are present in a country that has been without a ruling central government for nearly fifteen years. But without a more fine-grained analysis of patterns of violence within each conflict, I am hesitant to draw conclusions. The fact that proxies for indiscriminate violence are observed universally in resource-rich cases, but not in resource-poor cases, provides some additional support for my argument, although further cross-national work is needed.

Learning from Outliers

Although the cross-national evidence suggests a good fit between my theory and the data, there are anomalous cases in which insurgents perpetrated high levels of violence even when they lacked access to material resources or external support. Figure 8.1 shows a partial scatter plot of combat-related deaths against a measure of rebel resources, conditional on the duration of the war. The measure of rebel resources, as I define it here, captures whether groups employed contraband resources or received assistance from external actors. The strong relationship described in the previous section is visible in the graph; access to material resources is associated with high levels of

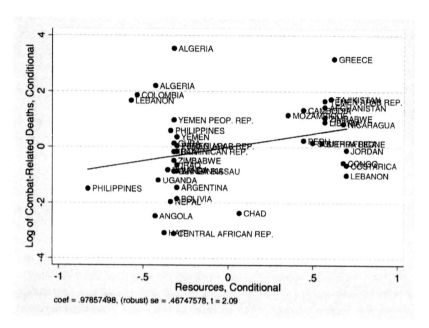

Figure 8.1. Outliers in the Relationship between Resources and Violence

violence. At the same time, the figure reveals four outliers: Algeria (1962–64), Algeria (1992–2000), Colombia (1949–63), and Lebanon (1975–91).

A closer examination of these cases is important for theory testing and theory building on the causes of rebel violence. It may simply be that the cases are miscoded; estimates of combat-related deaths may be too high, or insurgent groups might have had access to material support that was difficult to observe. It is also possible that the mechanisms I have described as generating high levels of violence are present in these conflicts but are spurred by a different independent variable. Perhaps groups had no access to material resources but emerged in an environment in which the state had collapsed, reducing significantly the barriers to insurgent organization. Most importantly, these cases might reveal an entirely different factor associated with high levels of violence. In this way, anomalies can open up new questions for exploration and explanation.

Algeria, 1962–1964

Algeria's descent into civil conflict in 1962 immediately followed its independence from France. Contending elites from the Front de Libération

National (FLN) – the anticolonial army – engaged in a bloody struggle for power. Although the anticolonial movement had never been a monolithic organization, its leaders had maintained the appearance of unity for the duration of the war against France. With the departure of the colonists, however, numerous factions within the movement jockeyed for a position in the future leadership of Algeria. These internal fractures were already visible during the previous decade. In contrast to many independence movements, the FLN was not dominated by one party or a single personality; instead, it was a fragile coalition of factions held together by a pact that called for "collegial" leadership.[16] The vicissitudes of the war against France hardened the divisions between these factions. An external "state" in waiting in Tunis waged a diplomatic campaign and housed the army leadership, while guerrillas in charge of military regions (or *wilayat*) within Algeria enjoyed significant autonomy and bore the brunt of the campaign against the French. At independence, the grand coalition collapsed as political leaders split the anticolonial army and sought alliances with the quasi-autonomous wilaya leaders in the country as they battled for the capital.

Yet there is some disagreement about how to characterize the violence that followed. The PRIO dataset estimates that the fighting caused 150,000 combat-related deaths. Its source is Anthony Clayton who suggests that "revenge killings of indigenous after the March (1962) cease-fire [totaled] at least 151,000, almost certainly more."[17] But other estimates are far lower. Milton Leitenberg estimates 1000 military deaths and 1000 civilian deaths over a two-year period; Barbara Harff and Ted Gurr offer an uncertain estimate of between 12,000 and 60,000 deaths.[18] The scholarship on Algeria is consistent with these more modest estimates of the scale of the violence. David and Marina Ottaway, in their comprehensive account, refer to the violence as a "summer crisis" or "summer struggle" rather than a war.[19] Quandt describes "open fighting" between factions in August and

---

[16] David Ottaway and Marina Ottaway, *Algeria: The Politics of a Socialist Revolution* (Berkeley: University of California Press, 1970).

[17] Anthony Clayton, *France, Soldiers, and Africa* (London: Brassey's Defence Publishers, 1988), pp. 188–89.

[18] A detailed description of the conflicting estimates (and their corresponding sources) is provided in Bethany Lacina, "Monitoring Trends in Global Combat: Documentation of Coding Decisions I (Uppsala/PRIO Data)" (Centre for the Study of Civil War, Oslo, Norway, September, 2004), pp. 26–30.

[19] Ottaway and Ottaway, *Algeria*, pp. 69, 92, 177.

September of 1962 but estimates no more than "several thousand" casualties.[20] Neither offer descriptions of mass violence; instead, the historiography chronicles competition between factions, the settling of old scores, and revenge killings made possible by instability during the transition. Rather than being an anomalous case, it appears that Algeria in the aftermath of independence is simply miscoded. The estimate of 150,000 deaths probably includes casualties from the anticolonial conflict. It seems that interfactional fighting in 1962–64 caused fewer than ten thousand deaths.

If, as I have argued, Algeria's brief civil war resulted in many fewer casualties than some have estimated, it would be natural to ask whether the patterns of violence are consistent with the logic of insurgent organization advanced earlier. While specifics on the Algerian transition are somewhat hazy, there is some evidence that high barriers to organization prompted leaders to invest in building disciplined organizations. Postindependence battles pitted highly organized military factions forged during the anticolonial struggle against one another. In particular, political elites previously based outside of the country formed alliances with wilaya leaders who had fought the French from inside. These factions of the internal guerrilla army had the most to lose as representatives of the new government returned from Tunisia. A centralized state and military threatened the significant political and military autonomy wilaya leaders gained during the war. Fighters in the wilayat were Algeria's battle-hardened insurgents: members joined to struggle for independence against great odds, exposing themselves to significant risks. William Quandt suggests that these factions of the anticolonial movement were consistently different than the revolutionaries that operated from abroad; the guerrillas had a strong sense of common identification with the peasants and placed a high value on equality, collective decision making, and self-criticism.[21] Seeking to maintain the autonomy they had garnered during the war, wilayat commanders allied with competing political elites in the summer struggle. Lasting only three months and ending when the capital fell to Ahmed Ben Bella, the initial crisis resembled more of a coup d'etat as "palace politics spilled onto the streets of Algiers."[22] But some wilayat leaders kept out of the new Ben Bella regime continued

---

[20] William Quandt, *Revolution and Political Leadership: Algeria, 1954–1968* (Cambridge: The M.I.T. Press, 1969), p. 171.

[21] Ibid., p. 115.

[22] For a narrative summary of the dynamics of Algeria's first civil war, see David Laitin, "Algeria" (unpublished manuscript, Stanford University, June 2005). Laitin describes the civil war as akin to an urban overthrow of the government (see Laitin, p. 14).

their fight, orchestrating a small-scale insurgency that persisted for nearly two years. They returned to their base among the Berbers in the region of Kabyle, where their tight linkages with the close-knit and relatively independent communities allowed them to maintain a struggle for autonomy.[23] Rooted in their own rural communities, insurgent leaders continued to show the discipline and restraint that had marked their behavior during the war of independence. And as in the summer clashes, the fighting was of low intensity. Eventually, a well-equipped Algerian army quelled the uprising, and Algeria's growing authoritarianism put at least a temporary stop to the country's internal violence.

Algeria, 1992–2000

Following its unstable transition to independence, Algeria experienced uninterrupted authoritarian rule for more than two decades.[24] Oil revenues proved useful to the country's authoritarian leaders who placated the population through generous social service provision; at the same time, with few incentives to tax and make productive investments, successive regimes oversaw economic policies that destroyed the agricultural sector and contributed to massive urbanization. A drop in world oil prices in 1986 undermined Algeria's fragile economy, and increasingly active Islamist organizations took advantage of rising urban unemployment to bring substantial pressure on the government for political change. When waves of urban protest in 1988 degenerated into rioting, a strong-armed government response earned the moniker "Black October" as more than five hundred people were killed. Facing now unrelenting pressure from a chorus of independent organizations, the government offered a new constitution paving the way for competitive, multiparty elections. The Islamic Salvation Front (FIS) swept to victory in the 1990 local and provincial elections and in the first round of elections in 1991. To prevent an FIS victory in the run-off, the military staged a coup, martial law was reimposed, and the FIS was banned. Military repression spawned an insurgency as the FIS fractured into a mix of moderate and radical groups. The most radical group, the Armed Islamic Group (GIA), rejected any compromise with the government and the stage was set for Algeria's second civil war.

[23] Laitin, "Algeria," pp. 14–15.
[24] This historical summary draws on a range of sources including Laitin, "Algeria"; Stathis Kalyvas, "Wanton and Senseless: The Logic of Massacres in Algeria," *Politics and Society* 11 (1999): 243–85; and Hugh Roberts, *The Battlefield Algeria: 1988–2002* (London: Verso, 2003).

The scale and scope of violence in Algeria's second civil war is uncontested. The PRIO dataset estimates more than 85,000 combat-related deaths since 1988, a number about which there is little disagreement in the source literature. Evidence has also accumulated about the character of violence in the conflict. Stathis Kalyvas contends that insurgent groups (the GIA in particular) have employed massive "yet targeted and selective violence" as part of a rational strategy to punish and deter civilian defection.[25] He lists seventy-eight GIA massacres perpetrated in 1996–98 and offers evidence that attacks targeted particular villages, neighborhoods, families, and individuals; victims included local opponents, defectors, and former sympathizers; and violence was carried out by teams of insurgents with the help of local collaborators that provided information about those who plan to assist the government or already have defected. Based on this evidence, Algeria's second civil war appears to be an anomalous case in one respect. Consistent with the theory, the GIA, a resource-poor rebel group, has committed acts of selective violence. However, high levels of violence, I have argued, tend to follow from an escalation dynamic in which indiscriminate violence drives civilian resistance, which in turn opens the door to more coercion. Here, large numbers of civilian casualties result not from indiscriminate violence and escalation but from another factor. A closer examination of the case may offer some additional insights about the origins of rebel violence.

The insurgency had its origins in the process of political mobilization that gave rise to the FIS in the late 1980s. Islam was not a deep cleavage in the country, but discontent among fundamentalists in the 1970s led to state support for the growth of religious institutions – a policy choice with unintended consequences. The inflow of resources enabled clerics to expand their connections to urban populations through religious instruction and social service provision, just as the state began to face a crisis of legitimacy and capacity following the drop in oil prices. The FIS drew upon a growing network of urban mosques to build its membership and lay the groundwork for widespread strikes and protests in the late 1980s. When the party was banned in 1992, it split into two guerrilla groups: the GIA, which initiated acts of urban terrorism, and the Islamic Salvation Army (AIS), which waged a more traditional guerrilla struggle and concentrated its attacks on military bases. Both groups were met, at least initially, with sympathy from noncombatant populations that had supported the FIS in local and national elections. But the tactics of the FIS-sponsored AIS reflected the more cautious

[25] Kalyvas, "Wanton and Senseless," p. 243.

316

perspective of the political movement's leadership; consistent with a willingness to engage the government toward some form of accommodation, it targeted security forces and political actors in an effort to make the continued political isolation of FIS too costly for the government.[26] The GIA always opposed the constitutionalist strategy of the AIS; in addition to its publicized attacks on urban targets, it moved quickly to kill civilians associated with the government in urban and suburban areas where it sought to establish control.[27]

The massacres often viewed as characteristic of Algeria's civil war became a prominent feature of the conflict only in the mid-1990s. The increasing intensity of violence followed an adjustment of military strategy in which Algerian forces sought to reclaim guerrilla-held areas in the suburbs of Algiers. Instead of employing a centralized counterinsurgent strategy, the Algerian government initiated a massive campaign of militia formation using coercive tactics and economic incentives to attract urban youths to the government side. Efforts to encircle and suffocate GIA-held zones increased the costs of collaboration with the rebels; supplies of arms and cash raised the benefits of changing one's allegiance in support of the regime. Kalyvas argues that this shift in incumbent strategy fragmented the insurgents' control without eliminating them; at the same time, mass defections substantially increased the number of government sympathizers living in areas vulnerable to insurgent attacks. Insurgent massacres thus became a strategic tactic for the rebels as they confronted these mass defections and sought to maintain bases of support in the areas around Algiers.

An initial look at the second civil war in Algeria raises questions about the broader applicability of the escalation dynamic discussed in this book. A resource-poor rebel group in Algeria committed acts of selective violence, but the massive scale of that violence comes as a surprise. Civilian resistance did not emerge (per our expectations) as a result of the insurgents' indiscriminate tactics; massive countermobilization was a consequence of a new Algerian military strategy that changed the costs and benefits of providing support to the insurgency for a large number of urban, civilian sympathizers. With their support base rapidly undermined, the GIA launched a string of massive and selective massacres in an attempt to impede militia formation, driving up the level of violence. This dynamic has some parallels with the experience of the Shining Path in Peru; government efforts to form civilian

---

[26] Roberts, *The Battlefield Algeria*, p. 154.
[27] Kalyvas, "Wanton and Senseless," p. 261.

militias led to an increasing number of massacres over time, particularly in highland areas on the fringe of rebel control. I previously linked escalation in Peru to the growing discontent of Quechua-speaking indigenous populations with the local Shining Path cadres who lacked ideological formation and were not restrained by the internal structures present in other parts of the movement. But such discontent also contributed to the Peruvian government's success in forming self-defense militias; as in Algeria, the opportunity for massive defection, substantially increased the scale of violence in the country. The Algerian case thus points to the importance of shifts in government strategy for understanding patterns of rebel violence. Governments able to move quickly and efficiently to change the costs and benefits of support for the insurgents alter the strategic calculus of rebel groups. Facing mass defection, insurgent groups may shift from patterns of restraint and the targeted killings of individuals to massive, selective violence directed at villages that choose to defect.

Colombia, 1948–1963

"La Violencia" – a period of Colombian history in which more than 135,000 people perished – provides a third anomalous case that merits further investigation. Violence erupted after decades of political conflict between two traditional political groups: the Liberal and Conservative Parties.[28] Fifty years of Conservative Party hegemony came to an end in 1930, as the Liberals seized on growing discontent among working classes to take the Presidency. Economic change in the 1920s had been accompanied by growing social disparities that contributed to the rise of strong class movements outside the two-party system. A communist party was formed in 1930, and its ability to mobilize discontented peasants strengthened with the Great Depression. But the Liberals' electoral victory only laid bare internal contradictions within its coalition, fractures that had prevented it from achieving success at the polls in the past. On the one hand, Liberal elites sought a capitalist transformation of the agrarian system which would not antagonize the traditional landholders; the worker and peasant masses, however, demanded and expected a much deeper set of changes in which the excluded

---

[28] This brief presentation of the history draws on the narrative structure of Gonzalo Sánchez and Donny Meertens, *Bandits, Peasants, and Politics: The Case of "La Violencia" in Colombia* (Austin: University of Texas Press, 2001), pp. 10–17.

voices of the lower classes would achieve prominence in the political debate. Failing to co-opt peasants and workers, the Liberal Party found itself under attack from the left; Jorge Gaitán, a radical politician with socialist ideals, challenged the Liberals' official candidate, throwing the 1946 election to the Conservative Party. The Conservatives' victory emboldened the *gaitanista* movement further as it took control of the fractured Liberal Party, and Gaitán appeared to be a lock for the presidency in 1950. But he was assassinated in 1948, plunging the country into more than a decade of widespread violence.

The masses responded to the assassination with an insurrection; when it was crushed by the army, gaitanistas, workers, and peasants took to the countryside where they formed popular governments, peasant militias, and the first nuclei of what would become full-fledged guerrilla armies. The national government initiated a campaign that can only be characterized as state terrorism. This included the silencing of the working class in the cities, and an effort to crush Liberals and Communists that had fled to the countryside. Terror perpetrated by both parties reshaped social relations in rural areas as regions became more politically homogenous. Areas of Liberal Party strength became home to organized guerrilla movements, but the rise of Communist self-defense units reopened an old fracture in the party between the dominant classes and the peasants. To stem the revolutionary tide, Liberal and Conservative elites joined in a National Front, agreed to first in 1956, which officially brought La Violencia to an end. In fact, the parties' pledge to cooperate did little to stem the insurrection, and Colombia's experience of large-scale violence continued until 1963 when an energetic army offensive rendered leaderless many of the guerrilla units that remained in the fight.

Empirical work on violence in Colombia is useful in identifying the aspects of La Violencia that account for its place as an outlier with respect to my theory. While few disagree that upwards of 135,000 people were killed during the conflict, there is a growing consensus among scholars that La Violencia should be divided into two distinct periods. The first, lasting from 1948 until the mid 1950s, was an epoch of political violence between the Conservative-dominated state and Liberal and Communist Party sympathizers in the countryside; the second, stretching from the launch of the National Front until 1963, is now consistently thought of as a period of *bandolerismo*, or banditry. Juan Fernando Giraldo presents evidence on the evolution of homicides in Colombia which suggests that nearly two-thirds of the killing associated with La Violencia occurred after 1955.[29] Consistent with the idea that different dynamics of violence were at work in the two periods, systematic analysis of homicide data identifies the following relationship: for the years between 1948 and 1953, the degree of party polarization in a given geographic area is a strong predictor of the level of violence, but the relationship disappears in the subsequent period.[30] Mary Roldán's qualitative account of the beginnings of La Violencia in Antioquia points to the "selective, concentrated" nature of violence, spurred by national-level partisan battles, but refracted through the interests of local elites in environments where the state's presence was weak.[31] Something fundamentally different, however, was at work in the subsequent period when La Violencia was at its most brutal. It is to this period I now turn.

Even as Colombia's dominant parties forged a joint effort to end the fighting, the countryside remained awash in violence. More than one hundred armed groups persisted until 1964, indicative of a scale of military organization far greater than that experienced in most civil wars. These groups were not remnants of the militarized partisans of the previous period; they were political bandits funded and protected by ruthless rural power brokers engaged in local struggles for power.[32] Unlike the peasant self-defense militias of the previous period that were linked together through national political leaders, armed groups now forged "direct and compromising" relationships with local landowners and elites, fragmenting the opposition to Colombia's dominant two-party system. These alliances created significant internal tensions: peasants viewed the bandit groups as an extension of the discontent activated initially by Gaitán, while regional and local bosses employed the armed peasants as paid assassins in their efforts to secure control of land and resources. The mass of armed peasants grew steadily in the late 1950s, as the armed groups incorporated large numbers of adolescents who, by virtue of their experiences of partisan violence, sought avenues

---

[29] Juan Fernando Giraldo, "Colombia in Armed Conflict, 1946–1989" (unpublished manuscript, Uppsala University, Stockholm, Sweden, 2003).

[30] Fabio Sanchez, Andres Solimano, and Michel Formisano, "Conflict, Violent Crime, and Criminal Activity in Colombia" (unpublished manuscript, Research Program of The Economic and Politics of Civil Wars, Yale University, October 2003); Mario Chacón, "Dinámica y Determinentes de la Violencia durante 'La Violencia' en Colombia" (CEDE Working Paper 2004–16, Universidad de los Andes, Colombia, March 2004).

[31] Mary Roldán, *Blood and Fire: La Violencia in Antioquia, Colombia, 1946–53* (Durham: Duke University Press, 2002), pp. 5–13.

[32] Descriptions of banditry and the structure of armed groups come from Sánchez and Meertens, *Bandits, Peasants, and Politics*, p. 22.

to achieve retaliation, vengeance, and personal enrichment. This process of incorporation further blurred the original motivations of the struggle against the government.

Reflecting Colombia's regional diversity, there were many different paths to political banditry, and I cannot do justice to the complexity and specificity of local patterns of violence here. Yet Gonzalo Sánchez and Donny Meerten's stories of bandolerismo share some commonalities that bear on the question of what causes insurgent violence. Participation in the armed bands was driven in many places as much by the prospect of economic advancement as by political vendettas from the previous period.[33] Economic incentives grew in importance over time, such that by the early 1960s, few that joined could claim a connection to the violence that followed Gaitán's assassination. The cozy relationship between bandit leaders and their powerful backers enabled this transformation in the motivation of participants. More important than securing the backing of peasant communities, bandit leaders sought financing and protection from regional political leaders who were, in the words of Sánchez and Meertens, the "intellectual authors" of the bandits' activities, paying for certain tasks to be completed.[34] These economic motivations undermined the cohesion of the bandit organizations: they generated individualism and led to internal rifts, disloyalty, and a weakened capacity of group leaders to shape the behavior of their members.[35] One consequence of this lack of cohesion was a significant rise in property crime, as bandits robbed agricultural produce and demanded money. A second was an inability to police the use of force by combatants; mid-level commanders often carried out operations on their own and for their own benefit.[36] Violence committed by bandit groups was thus disconnected in many ways from their implicit political challenge to the sovereignty of the state. Many groups were simply composed of criminal wage-earners, paid by backers to assassinate individuals or sow terror in rural communities. Importantly, their operations were not impeded significantly by peasant resistance largely because past and present tactics of state repression drove civilians into the bandits' camp. When police and military forces arrived in rural communities, they used brutal tactics indiscriminately against peasants; more commonly, when the state was absent, rural

---

[33] Ibid., pp. 66, 105, 115.
[34] Ibid., p. 105.
[35] Ibid., p. 67.
[36] Ibid., p. 58.

communities were entirely at the mercy of the local power brokers and their armed bandits.

Upon closer examination, the dynamics of violence in La Violencia are explicable, in part, with reference to the internal characteristics of the fighting organizations. Much of the killing during Colombia's civil war took place following the bipartisan commitment to a National Front; instead of being orchestrated by national political elites, violence followed the formation of many, distinct bandit groups across rural Colombia. Like combatants in Mozambique and the Huallaga Valley, participants in La Violencia (at least in the second stage) were distinguished by their economic motivations. They joined groups marked less by formal military hierarchies and political platforms and more by a lack of cohesion and too much indiscipline. Economic endowments, as I define them in the book, were mobilized by the bandit group leaders: most received financial backing from internal (rather than external) patrons that enabled them to build and maintain their military organizations. The local nature of these patronage arrangements, however, is not captured in the cross-national data. But the fragmentation of the peasant opposition to the dominant two-party system appears also to have been the result of an utter lack of state presence in many of the rural areas where La Violencia took its toll. The fact that few barriers existed to the formation of bandit groups – indeed, local patrons consistently sought to finance groups of their own – undermined the incentives for the peasant opposition to build a cohesive, national organization with an effective internal structure. Colombia's experience of violence suggests that the absence of state power, like the presence of material resources, reduces the dependence of military organizations on their constituents for the support needed to wage a struggle.

Lebanon, 1975–1991

As a final exploration of the theory's applicability, I turn to Lebanon's civil war, which killed 144,000 people. My cross-national measure of material resources codes Lebanese insurgents as resource-poor, making the Lebanese case an outlier that requires explanation. Although important socioeconomic and regional disparities existed, Lebanon's civil war erupted in a climate of sustained economic growth and rising per-capita income. The source of confrontation was largely political: a sectarian system for power sharing among three religious communities (the Maronites, Sunnis, and Shi'a), which had been negotiated at independence in 1943, exacerbated tensions between the groups.[37] An informal arrangement guaranteed each community equitable representation in the government, and an overall balance of Christian and Muslims was maintained in the cabinet for the first thirty years of independence. But the agreement also stipulated that the Maronites would hold the post of the presidency, with all of its executive powers, while the Muslims would occupy the seats of speaker of the assembly and prime minister. With the benefit of presidential powers and a guaranteed majority of parliamentary seats, the Maronites emerged as the dominant religious community in the pre-1975 period. The delicate power-sharing arrangement prevented outright conflict by acting as a check on the powers of the presidency, although regular cabinet crises and disagreements in parliament contributed to the emergence of a weak state characterized more by nepotism and corruption than efficiency. Increasing domestic calls by Muslim leaders for more equal power sharing began to strain the Lebanese political system. Islamic leaders capitalized on patterns of unequal development in the country as they mobilized their religious communities. The Maronite elite ignored these roiling tensions, fearing the consequences of any change in the political arrangement. The likelihood of a confrontation continued to grow with the rising military power of resident Palestinian organizations which sought to keep the cause of Palestinian liberation alive, at the same time that they began to align with Muslim communities in Lebanon against the Maronite-dominated state. The civil war itself broke out following an initial armed clash between Maronite political parties and Palestinian organizations in April 1975, which quickly spiraled out of control as members of both groups took to the street.

Lebanon's civil war was particularly costly in terms of human life. But of the 144,000 combat-related deaths, experts estimate that nearly 40,000 were military deaths suffered by combatant groups on both sides.[38] The extent of military casualties is perhaps not surprising as Lebanon experienced a more conventional civil war with clear front lines and entrenched positions. Experts also suggest that between 50,000 and 70,000 civilian casualties occurred in the midst of Syria's invasion of Lebanon in 1975–76, with a

[37] This description of the background to the conflict draws from Samir Makdisi and Richard Sadaka, "The Lebanese Civil War, 1975–90," in *Understanding Civil War: Evidence and Analysis Volume 2*, eds. Paul Collier and Nicholas Sambanis (Washington, DC: World Bank, 2005), pp. 59–86.

[38] William Eckhardt, "Wars and War-Related Deaths, 1900–1995," in *World Military and Social Expenditures 1996*, ed. Ruth Ledger Sivard (Washington, DC: World Priorities, 1996), pp. 29–31.

large percentage of the remaining noncombatant deaths taking place around and in the aftermath of Israel's intervention in 1982.[39] These data suggest that the overall estimate of 144,000 dead obscures more information than it reveals: slightly more than one-quarter of the deaths were suffered by military actors, and much of the noncombatant suffering occurred in the context of external military interventions rather than as a consequence of actions or behaviors of the internal combatant groups. Once we account for these factors, Lebanon's civil war no longer appears to be an outlier.

Yet the case deserves a closer look as our key independent variable is also miscoded. The cross-national statistics treat the insurgents as resource-poor; nevertheless, resident Palestinian organizations and their Lebanese Muslim partners received significant financial support from outside of the country, external backing in the form of military support, and consistent revenues from the control of trade routes, looting, and smuggling. The question can thus be reframed to ask whether the behavior of Lebanese insurgents, with access to material resources, fits with the predictions of the model. The evidence is largely supportive.

Various militias that fought on behalf of both warring sides were firmly enmeshed in an illicit war economy that offered combatants perhaps the only remaining opportunity for economic advancement.[40] Soldiers were paid more than the prevailing wage, and many earned additional income on the side through illegal activities made possible by their positions of author-ity.[41] Beyond financial support from external patrons, militias accumulated the resources needed to maintain their organizations through thievery, the confiscation of property, taxation, the trading of drugs and other contraband, bank robberies, and extortion. These economic gains were a major factor in sustaining the conflict, and many faction members and leaders accumulated substantial personal wealth. Competition in this economic environment led to significant in-fighting within the militias, and violence was often seen to be the responsibility of "uncontrollable elements" operating with the permission or oversight of the militia leaders themselves.[42]

---

[39] As before, a detailed description of the conflicting estimates (and their corresponding sources) is provided in Lacina, "Monitoring Trends in Global Combat: Documentation of Coding Decisions I (Uppsala/PRIO Data)," pp. 280–83.

[40] Nazih Richani, "Systems of Violence: The Political Economy of War and Peace in Lebanon and Colombia" (unpublished manuscript, Kean University, 2001).

[41] Makdisi and Sadaka, "The Lebanese Civil War," pp. 66–72.

[42] Stathis Kalyvas, "Warfare in Civil Wars," in Rethinking the Nature of War, eds. Isabelle Duyvesteyn and Jan Angstrom (Abingdton: Frank Cass, 2005), p. 97.

But the elaborate economic position of militias in Lebanon was accompanied by a substantial social role as well. Militia leaders invested some of their material wealth in the provision of social services – including scholarships for children's schooling, medical assistance, and food subsidies – and public relations, both inside Lebanon and abroad. These state-building activities are inconsistent with the behaviors we have come to expect from opportunistic organizations.

An explanation for this seeming inconsistency lies in the fact that leaders of the Lebanese militias confronted a strategic situation quite different from that faced by the insurgent leaders in Uganda, Mozambique, and Peru. The asymmetry of power that renders insurgent groups vulnerable to defection and weak in the face of government forces was simply not present in Lebanon. Soon after the conflict began, the government collapsed into a set of competing militias. The dividing line between the warring actors, the so-called Green Line, was stabilized soon after the fighting began and combat occurred at this boundary, while relative calm prevailed on either side.[43] Lebanon's conflict was characterized much more by a balance of power between the Muslim and Christian sides rather than by an asymmetry. Within their sectarian enclaves, militias flush with financial resources acted as if they were oppressive, corrupt governments. Beyond managing internal factional struggles, they faced few challenges to their hegemony from the other side. Sniper-style fighting and shelling were the dominant form of fighting across the Green Line; this explains why large numbers of civilian casualties accompanied the external interventions, rather than being generated from battles between militias. That being said, with the collapse of the Lebanese state and the wealth of resources flowing to military actors exercising unchallenged control of their enclaves, few incentives existed for militias to discipline their behavior. Some social services were provided to maintain the quiescence of the population, but cooperation was even more frequent across militia groups that sought to secure trading routes than it was between militias and their purported constituencies. As in Colombia, the Lebanese case suggests that when barriers to insurgency are low, such as when the state collapses entirely, the military actors that emerge in this vacuum exhibit behaviors consistent with opportunistic insurgency.

The findings presented here complement the micro-level analysis presented in earlier chapters. Measures of rebel resource wealth – in particular, whether groups used contraband to finance their organization or whether

---

[43] Richani, "Systems of Violence," p. 6.

they received outside assistance – are strongly associated with higher levels of combat-related deaths in civil war, controlling for the duration of conflict. They also appear to correlate with a series of proxies for indiscriminate violence. A closer examination of four outliers also offers tentative support for the importance of material resources. Groups in Colombia and Lebanon with access to material wealth not captured by the measures collected crossnationally exhibit behaviors not unlike those seen in opportunistic insurgencies in Mozambique and Peru. In contrast, Algeria's experience of civil war is one of selective, targeted violence in spite of its significant scale. Shifts in government strategy similar to what we observed in Peru help to account for this escalation. Resource differences across conflicts likely influenced the organizational strategies and behaviors of insurgent organizations in countries beyond Uganda, Mozambique, and Peru. And although large-N approaches do not lend themselves to an assessment of causal mechanisms, the macro-level relationships they illuminate lend support to the overall argument advanced in this book.

9

―――――――――――――――――――――――――――――――――――――

Conclusion

In its search for factors contributing to the brutal, indiscriminate violence that characterizes some civil wars, this book has concentrated on the significance of rebel organizations. It is because of variation in the characteristics of insurgent movements that, despite the presence of conditions that facilitate armed opposition to the state, some civil wars produce insurgents that seek to transform governance while others give rise to predatory organizations that sow terror among noncombatant populations. I have argued that variation in the barriers that exist to the organization of insurgency – in particular, whether insurgent groups have access to material resources – helps us to account for the different characteristics of rebel groups.

The theory is simple and concise. It is also consistent with the logic of state building in the modern world. Leaders that face strong incentives to secure the consent of the governed, and the tax revenues that accompany consent, have tended to build states that protect the security and rights of their constituents. But it may be too simple. In emphasizing structure over agency, it underlines the importance of constraints and ignores the ability of political actors to shape the environments in which they operate. Perhaps differences in leadership are what explain the divergent behavior of insurgent groups.

This requires a return to an issue first raised in the introduction: the fact that a group's initial endowments may be shaped by the actions of its leaders. In this chapter, I begin by considering why some rebel leaders invest in the mobilization of social endowments while others do not and, if patterns of indiscriminate violence *may* be counterproductive for an insurgency in the long run, why insurgent groups in resource-rich environments fail to bank their material resources and mimic the behavior of activist organizations. In answering these questions, I present evidence that opportunistic insurgencies tend to quickly dominate civil wars in resource-rich environments, cutting short a process of social mobilization that might have produced an activist movement.

This emphasis on structure provides a general set of guidelines for thinking about when and why rebel groups are likely to commit mass atrocities against noncombatants. It also provides a conceptual framework useful for differentiating civil wars from one another and offers a new perspective on the internal mechanisms that drive insurgent behavior, some of which might be amenable to outside influence. The applications of the argument are potentially far reaching. I conclude by addressing the implications of my argument for social scientists interested in processes of civil war resolution and state building and for policy makers concerned with shaping the behavior of nonstate armed groups.

The Curse of Resource Wealth

Early in the book, I asked why rebel groups in resource-rich environments make appeals to the short-term, material interests of potential recruits rather than employing economic endowments to build the capacity of their organizations and invest their energies.[1] This question makes it clear that while resource wealth at the country level is perhaps a necessary condition for the emergence of groups that employ economic endowments to motivate participation in insurgency, it is not a sufficient condition. An organization's initial stock of economic and social endowments and its decisions about how to utilize them may be themselves a function of leadership, ideology, and strategy. A convincing explanation for variation in rebel behavior thus must account for how differences in resource environments (at the country rather than the group level) shape the nature of the competitors that emerge in civil conflict.

The primary advantage of using economic resources to appeal to the material interests of recruits is that it enables groups to get off the ground more quickly. First movers are in a better position to dominate territory,

---

[1] Although I make no claims in this book about the relative effectiveness of different organizational strategies, one might assume that opportunistic approaches, because they generate significant civilian resistance, are counterproductive for insurgent groups in the long run. If this is the case, the puzzle is more stark: knowing that such approaches might undermine their chances of victory, why would rebel leaders employ economic endowments for recruitment? In principle, a rebel leadership with more material resources should be able to do at least as well as one with less if it simply mimics the strategies of the poorer group.

control access to resources, capture the attention and interest of those pre-disposed to oppose the state, gain the lion's share of risk-seeking potential recruits, make a claim for external assistance, and actively prevent the emer-gence of competing groups. Importantly, the marginal benefits of moving quickly are much higher in resource-rich environments. Potential rebel leaders know that if they adopt a more time-consuming strategy of social mobilization, others might accept offers of external assistance, capture lootable resources, or beat them to the capital. So leaders in resource-rich environments will tend to choose the first strategy, and processes of social mobilization will be short-circuited, with such groups stopped in their tracks or never able to get off the ground in the first place.[2]

I explore evidence for two observable implications of this theory. The first is that where barriers to the organization of insurgency are low, more rebel groups will emerge to fight, putting a premium on speed in the process of organizational formation. Second, in such contexts, opportunistic rebel groups will be the first movers and crowd out the development of activist organizations that mobilize along lines of identity or ideology. Testing the first assumption requires cross-national evidence on the number of rebel groups engaged in civil war; exploring the second involves looking inside a set of resource-rich cases to consider the character of the groups that emerged (and did not emerge) to challenge the state.

Using data from PRIO, I began by constructing a list of all opposition organizations for each civil war between 1945 and 2000. From this data, I produced a measure of the maximum number of rebel groups that fought in a given civil war. Three independent variables are used to proxy for the ease of rebel organization. The first is a measure of "resource-related" conflicts. Michael Ross created a sample of active civil wars between 1990 and 2000 in which "scholars, non-governmental organizations, or United Nations agencies suggested that natural resource wealth, or natural resource

---

[2] One could imagine an alternative explanation for the puzzle of why rebel leaders use eco-nomic endowments to appeal to short-term material interests. Suppose leaders of insurgent organizations make decisions about how much discipline to instill in their movements. More discipline is costly, but it increases the odds that the organization will succeed in capturing the state. If the marginal cost of increasing discipline is higher in a resource-rich environ-ment because the temptations for rebels are greater, then insurgent leaders in such contexts will invest less in discipline. This explanation is similar in structure to the one I advance. Whether a leader faces competitive countermobilization from the outside or criminalization from the inside, he recognizes that a technology of short-term, resource-based mobilization exists and that if he does not take advantage of it, someone else may. I thank James Fearon for pointing out this alternative argument.

Table 9.1. *Resources and Insurgent Competition*

	Dependent Variable: Total Number of Opposition Groups Engaged in Civil War		
Duration	−0.01	0.05**	0.04*
	(−0.14)	(2.20)	(1.70)
Resource wealth	1.43**		
	(2.37)		
Pro-rebel intervention		0.47	
		(1.11)	
Log GDP per capita			−0.68**
			(−2.32)
Constant	1.91***	1.52***	6.60***
	(5.28)	(4.61)	(3.18)
Number of observations	36	98	64
R-squared	0.20	0.06	0.11

Notes: OLS estimates. The dependent variable is the total number of opposition groups engaged in civil war. T-statistics (calculated with robust standard errors) are in parentheses. *** Significant at 0.01 level; ** Significant at 0.05 level; * Significant at 0.10 level.

dependence, influenced the war's onset, duration, or casualty rate."[3] His subjective measure allows for a good first cut at assessing the impact of resource wealth on the number of insurgent groups. The second, Patrick Regan's measure of external intervention, was employed in the previous chapter. I also include a measure of GDP per capita at the start of the war as a proxy for the strength of the state.[4] The evidence is supportive of the first observable implication of the theory. As reported in Table 9.1, conflicts believed to be linked to resources exhibit significantly larger numbers of rebel groups than those in which resource wealth was not central to the violence. Higher GDP per capita is also associated with fewer rebel groups, consistent with the argument that high barriers to organization impede the formation of multiple challengers to the state. The data reveal, finally, that external interventions on behalf of one side are not correlated with the number of rebel groups. This is not surprising, as external support is not as divisible as lootable resources spread over a geographic terrain, and outside

[3] Michael Ross, "How Does Natural Resource Wealth Influence Civil War? Evidence from 13 Case Studies," *International Organization* 58 (2004): 34–67.
[4] James Fearon and David Laitin, "Ethnicity, Insurgency, and Civil War," *American Political Science Review* 97 (2003): 75–90.

actors interested in toppling an existing government might tend to support only one group to maximize its chances of victory.[5]

If competition in resource-rich environments leads to the organization of more rebel groups, perhaps there is evidence at the micro level that opportunistic insurgencies form first, crowding out the development of activist movements. The story of the Mozambican conflict seems to provide such evidence. Renamo was not the only claimant for the mantle of opposition to Frelimo. Opposition to the new ruling party had its roots in the independence struggle, which was fragmented along ethnic and regional lines. Frelimo was seen as the party of southerners, while the Comité Revolucionário de Moçambique sought to represent the ethnic groups of central and northern Mozambique. As Frelimo took power in Maputo in 1974, it faced immediate challenges from a host of opposition groups.[6] But Frelimo fought back, suppressing political activity and forcing opposition leaders into reeducation camps in the countryside. Despite this harassment, antigovernment organizing continued among the Macua and Makonde ethnic groups in the North and among local leaders in central Mozambique. Peasants collectively resisted Frelimo's policies by sabotaging state farms and refusing to work.[7] Even in southern Mozambique, communities rejected government pressures to move into communal villages.[8] With the support of the Rhodesians, Renamo began its military campaign just as this domestic political opposition was beginning to grow and solidify. Renamo's leadership took up the rhetoric of the excluded nationalists, yet it was surprising how few of the ideological elite joined its military campaign. Renamo was the first rebel group out of the gate, and it quickly became the central opposition player in the country. A second movement, called Africa Livre, emerged soon after in Zambézia Province with the active support

---

[5] If rebel groups face less competition where external actors intervene, one might ask why leaders of groups that receive outside support do not reserve that money for military capacity rather than recruitment. There are two possible answers. On the one hand, attracting external assistance requires showing some initial strength, so rebel leaders may organize the first group of recruits by offering material rewards to beat others to the punch. On the other hand, pressure from outside actors to move quickly, complemented with contributions of military hardware, may leave rebel leaders with surplus cash that can be disbursed among the leadership and the cadres to maintain morale.

[6] Margaret Hall and Tom Young, *Confronting Leviathan: Mozambique since Independence* (Athens: Ohio University Press, 1997).

[7] Jean-Claude LeGrand, "Logique de guerre et dynamique de la violence en Zambézia, 1976–1991," *Politique Africaine* 50 (1993): 88–104.

[8] Joanne McGregor, "Violence and Social Change in a Border Economy: War in the Maputo Hinterland, 1984–1992," *Journal of Southern African Studies* 24 (1998): 37–60.

of the Malawian government. Because its resources paled in comparison to those of Renamo, it never emerged as a serious challenger.[9] Africa Livre merged with Renamo in 1982. Despite widespread opposition to the policies of Frelimo, no other rebel movement was able to generate the manpower and resources to challenge Renamo's place on the stage.

Evidence drawn from the civil wars in three other resource-rich countries also supports the idea that opportunistic insurgencies emerge first and crowd out the development of other rebel groups. In the previous chapter, I argued that a combination of external support from Liberia and the looting of diamond mines in Sierra Leone enabled the leadership of the RUF to recruit rebels based on tangible, short-term payoffs. The RUF was not alone in its opposition to the All People's Congress regime, however. Following nearly two decades of authoritarian misrule exacerbated by a collapse in state capacity and the provision of basic services, student radicals on the campus of the national university had been the most outspoken opponents of the regime throughout the 1980s.[10] Their first major confrontation with government occurred in 1977, when the annual university convocation was disrupted by a demonstration that drew attention to the corruption and brutality of Siaka Stevens's regime.[11] A counterprotest orchestrated by the government brought more than five hundred thugs to campus in a campaign of destruction and violence, which was accompanied by the arrests of a number of student leaders and lecturers. This precipitated a massive protest in downtown Freetown, where secondary school pupils mobilized from around the city to join Fourah Bay students in demonstrating against the closing of the national university. The police fired on this crowd, killing more than forty people, and as protests erupted around the country, the Stevens regime was forced to declare a state of emergency. By the mid-1980s, student activism had coalesced into a set of radical groups – the Green Book Study Club, the Pan-African Union, and the Socialist Club – that eschewed the drug culture in favor of serious ideological engagement.[12] Talk of resistance quickly turned to discussion of revolution as these new student groups organized seminars, meetings, and rallies on campus. Attention focused on Stevens' attempt to become a

---

[9] João Cabrita, *Mozambique: The Torturous Road to Democracy* (New York: Palgrave, 2000).

[10] William Reno, *Warlord Politics and African States* (Boulder, CO: Lynne Rienner, 1999), Chapter 4.

[11] Ishmail Rashid, "Subaltern Reactions: Lumpens, Students and the Left," *Africa Development* 22 (1997): 19–43.

[12] Ibid., p. 33.

life president, and protests organized by the new student groups led to a second closure of the college campus in 1984. When it reopened in 1985, a coalition of student radicals was elected to campus leadership under the banner of Mass Awareness and Participation, and they launched a campaign of propaganda and mobilization against the government. The government responded by declaring the student leaders ineligible to attend the college and forcibly removing them from campus. Most ended up in exile in Ghana. Remnants remained behind in Freetown and turned their attention to the mobilization of urban and rural youth. These experiences of confrontation followed by repression fractured the emerging opposition in Sierra Leone.

The RUF had its origins in connections between some of the exiled students who fled to Ghana and the Libyan government.[13] The Libyans provided financial assistance to the exiles and encouraged them to identify recruits for military training. In 1987, when it was time to deliver recruits, the network of student radicals in Freetown had been substantially weakened, and ties between them and their counterparts in Ghana were somewhat frayed. Requests for volunteers to the Pan-African Union were met with skepticism by the membership and precipitated a split in the organization between those opposed to a "premature adventure" in revolution with the Libyans and those in favor of training in Libya, who were in the minority.[14] Subsequently expelled from the student movement, a number headed to Libya. Since the Pan-African Union had rejected participation as an organization, the decision to acquire training in insurgency was largely an individual one, and the unemployed youths and thugs of Freetown became the main source of early recruits. While the incipient RUF acquired training and forged a partnership with Charles Taylor, social mobilization among students in Freetown continued, albeit at a lower level of intensity, until 1991, when students launched an effort to promote multiparty politics in the country. Demanding that president Joseph Momoh resign, the students at Fourah Bay College called for a massive demonstration. Beleaguered, the regime conceded to multiparty politics and elections in 1991. As the elections drew nearer, the RUF made its entry into Sierra Leone. The movement quickly captured territory and plunged the country into civil war. With an insurgency already dominant in the eastern part of the

---

[13] Ibrahim Abdullah, "Bush Path to Destruction: The Origin and Character of the Revolutionary United Front," *Journal of Modern African Studies* 36 (1998): 203–35.

[14] Ibid.

country, the student radicals and opposition continued to focus their energies on developments in Freetown, pressing for political reform and regime change throughout the duration of the war. Most had not been ready for revolution in the late 1980s when the call to Libya came, but by 1991, the war was upon them, upending the political transition they sought and cutting short their mobilization of a broader constituency to transform the country.

The trajectory of the civil war in neighboring Liberia offers additional support for the theory. Charles Taylor's National Patriotic Forces of Liberia (NPFL) began its challenge to the government of Samuel Doe in 1991. It was quickly joined by a host of other rebel groups: the United Liberation Movement for Democracy, the Johnson faction of this group, the Liberian Peace Council, and an offshoot of the NPFL, its Central Revolutionary Committee. Many factors contributed to the onset of civil war, including Doe's patronage politics and discriminatory use of power, which reinforced a preexisting elite in the capital; the favoritism he showed to his Krahn ethnic group in key appointments; massive corruption, which enriched him and his henchmen; a collapse in the national economy that lasted for a decade; and the near-total loss of external aid in the late 1980s.[15]

What is so striking about the Liberian case, however, is the nature of the rebel groups that emerged in this environment. Charles Taylor, a former Liberian government official who escaped from prison in the United States after embezzling U.S. government money, launched the NPFL in December 1989. By June of 1990, less than six months later, the NPFL was in the suburbs of Monrovia, Liberia's capital. In marching toward the capital, Taylor employed a large group of fighters from more than a dozen ethnic groups, at least three foreign countries, and a team of professional commandos from Burkina Faso.[16] His mobilization strategy was "quick, easy, and efficient," and it depended on the accumulation of significant amounts of revenue through external and commercial alliances.[17] The NPFL sold abandoned assets in areas of captured territory, sought deals with foreign companies to initiate logging operations in its regions of control, forced outside companies to pay taxes and fees in foreign exchange, and inserted itself in informal, cross-border trading networks in diamonds and other valuable resources. William Reno estimates that the value of "warlord trade" in Liberia surpassed US$200 million during the five-year war. Taylor plunged

---

[15] Reno, *Warlord Politics*, Chapter 3.
[16] Ibid., p. 92.
[17] Ibid., p. 98.

these resources into building a military organization, but he channeled them as well into the recruitment of massive numbers of unemployed rural youth.[18] Their most consistent source of income was looting: combatants armed to the teeth but often unpaid turned their arms on the civilian population. Many in fact joined "to acquire property and riches," but they found that the vast majority of captured wealth resided with the commanders. Other insurgent groups formed quickly and effectively, attracting dissatisfied recruits with promises of a bigger share of the booty. The United Liberation Movement for Democracy wrested control over the trade networks on the Guinea–Liberia border, the Johnson faction controlled mining operations in Bomi County and distributed mining opportunities to combatants to keep them under control, the Liberian Peace Council captured Liberia's rubber plantations, and the Central Revolutionary Committee of the NPFL split off to monopolize trade on the Ivorian border.[19] In the resource-rich environment of Liberia, spurred on by internal sources of wealth and external patrons, rebel groups engaged in fierce competition to dominate territory and capture the state. Throughout this war, political opposition to the Doe regime was almost nowhere to be found. Leaders of Liberia's opposition parties were largely discredited former members of the government or representatives of narrow ethnic constituencies.[20] Many fled into exile as soon as the fighting began and only returned in the mid-1990s in anticipation of the 1997 election. Although Doe's corruption was evident from early in his rule, Taylor moved first to capitalize on the growing weakness of the state following the end of U.S. assistance in 1988. By 1990, opposition politicians who might have been in a position to consider challenging the government for control had been usurped in authority, power, and public attention by Liberia's warlords. The consequences of Taylor's emergence were significant, as perhaps 8 percent of the population (as many as 200,000 people) died in the fighting, and more than half of the country's people became refugees.[21]

The repeated insurgencies in eastern Congo since 1996 provide a final laboratory in which to explore the implications of this theory. The first war lasted only eight months, as the Alliance of Democratic Forces for

---

[18] Stephen Ellis, "Liberia's Warlord Insurgency," in *African Guerillas*, ed. Christopher Clapham (Oxford: James Currey, 1998), p. 162.

[19] Reno, *Warlord Politics*, pp. 103–06.

[20] David Harris, "From 'Warlord' to 'Democratic' President: How Charles Taylor Won the 1997 Liberian Elections," *Journal of Modern African Studies* 37 (1999): 431–55.

[21] Reno, *Warlord Politics*, p. 79.

the Liberation of Congo–Kinshasa (AFDL) swept to the capital, backed by Rwandan forces, and ejected President Mobutu Sese Seko from office. A second, which began in 1997, has persisted, involving combatants from the Congolese Democracy Rally, the Congolese Liberation Movement, and external forces from Angola, Zimbabwe, Rwanda, Uganda, and a number of other countries. These insurgencies emerged in an environment of tremendous state decline.[22] GDP per capita dropped by more than 50 percent between 1975 and 1996, when the first war began.[23] Mobutu privatized the state budget, underwriting his patron–client network and generating enormous personal wealth. Economic activity moved underground, spurred by Mobutu's use of state power to facilitate clandestine trade in Congo's rich natural resources. And when the international community cut the country off from outside assistance, Mobutu reasserted political authority by giving loyal military units permission to plunder the country's resources for their own personal benefit.[24] When more than 1.2 million Rwandan Hutu refugees, including former Rwandan soldiers and Interhamwe militiamen, flooded eastern Congo in June 1994, the situation deteriorated quickly. The ethnic balance tilted against Banyamulenge of Tutsi origin in the region, and the presence of large numbers of Rwandan Hutus just across the border posed a major security threat to the new Rwandan government.[25]

With external support from Rwanda, Uganda, and Angola, the AFDL, led by Laurent Kabila, launched an insurgency in October 1996 from its bases in eastern Congo. Kabila had a "chequered political background" that included participation in uprisings against the Mobutu regime in the 1960s, a period of warlordism and despotic rule at the local level in eastern Zaire in the 1970s, and most of the 1980s spent in Tanzania exporting gold and running nightclubs.[26] He managed to build a coalition of Congolese Banyamulenge, who feared the growing dominance of Rwandan Hutus, and other local groups opposed to the misrule of Mobutu. Kabila's "easy" victory over Mobutu followed a rapid march through the countryside spurred by resources and logistical support from the Rwandans. The resulting

---

[22] Ibid.

[23] Léonce Ndikumana and Kisangani Emizet, "The Economics of Civil War: The Case of the Democratic Republic of the Congo," in *Understanding Civil War: Evidence and Analysis*, vol. 1, eds. Paul Collier and Nicholas Sambanis (Washington, DC: World Bank, 2005), pp.63–87.

[24] Reno, *Warlord Politics*, p. 159.

[25] Ndikumana and Emizet, "Economics of Civil War," p. 76.

[26] See Wm Cyrus Reed, "Guerrillas in the Midst," in Clapham, *African Guerrillas*, p. 146.

movement was nothing more than a shell.[27] Kabila promoted himself from spokesperson to uncontested leader of the AFDL in the early stages of the rebellion; after taking Kinshasa, he named himself transitional president of the Congo without consulting political leaders and organizations involved in the rebellion. The so-called alliance was essentially a military one, and the army of liberators quickly became one of occupiers as Congolese citizens gained awareness of the presence of Rwandan army officials in the leadership of new Congolese national army. It was staffed mainly by professional soldiers from across the border, but Kabila's contribution of manpower to Congolese liberation was *kadogos*: uneducated young men and boys from eastern Congo. At the political level, the AFDL was composed of Kabila's inner circle of supporters from exile, none of whom had an internal base. Marching quickly toward the capital and capturing most of the resource-rich regions of the country along the way, the AFDL was given a "hero's welcome," but the ease of its victory made unnecessary a process of social mobilization that could have laid the groundwork for political transition in the country.

Kabila's term as president was short-lived. Soon after his victory, accusations began to fly. International actors accused the AFDL of committing mass atrocities during its insurgent campaign. Human Rights Watch reports detailed the massacres of unarmed elderly men, women, and children in areas heavily populated by Rwandan Hutus and their Congolese supporters.[28] Even as polls of the public showed widespread support for a partnership between Kabila and Congo's vibrant democratic opposition, he refused to engage in such a partnership, and the opposition warned that the former guerrilla would return the country to the decadent days of Mobutu's corruption.[29] Popular opinion turned against the rebel leader after his government appointments sent the signal that he was concerned primarily with promoting the interests of Rwanda and Uganda.[30] In a bid to rescue his regime just over a year after taking power, Kabila announced the end of military cooperation with Rwanda and Uganda and ordered all foreign troops to leave the country. Days later, with the help of Congo's neighbors, an anti-Kabila revolt broke out.

[27] Osita Afoaku, "Congo's Rebels: Their Origins, Motivations, and Strategies," in *The African Stakes of the Congo War*, ed. John Clark (New York: Palgrave Macmillan, 2002), p. 112.

[28] Human Rights Watch, *Democratic Republic of Congo: What Kabila Is Hiding* (New York: Human Rights Watch, 1997).

[29] Afoaku, "Congo's Rebels," p. 112.

[30] Ndikumana and Emizet, "Economics of Civil War," p. 76.

Congo's most recent civil war has persisted at varied levels of intensity for nearly a decade. At its start, the August 1998 rebellion was composed mostly of Rwandan and Ugandan soldiers. The senior leadership of its local partner, the Congolese Democracy Rally, admitted later that "the military side was better prepared because military intelligence had actually plotted the way in which Kabila had been moving steadily away from the objectives we all had."[31] The political side of the rebellion was virtually nonexistent until nearly one month after it began, when a group of Congolese politicians convened in Goma to form officially the Congolese Democracy Rally. Agreeing on what they disliked about the regimes of Kabila and Mobutu was easy, but committing to work together to overthrow the government was far more difficult. Osita Afoaku argues that "the rebel movement was a collection of strange bedfellows; the members were loosely held together by a common objective of overthrowing a government they detested for different reasons."[32]

Although the war continued, the anti-Kabila alliance failed rather quickly. The Congolese Liberation Movement emerged in northern Congo, headed by the son of a former Mobutuist. The Congolese Democracy Rally split into two rival factions, one supported by Uganda and the other by Rwanda. Each movement sought to establish control of a distinct territory and to set in place mechanisms for financing its war effort. Outside assistance played a crucial role, and internal fractures were often precipitated by battles among the war's external patrons. Competing interests in the extraction of natural resources contributed as well to the alliance's demise. Congo was carved into fiefdoms by the various rebel groups and their outside backers, enabling rebel leaders to finance their insurgencies and external actors to "make the war pay for itself."[33] The established Congolese democratic opposition, which had challenged Kabila just as it had Mobutu, rejected participation in the anti-Kabila activities. It perceived that these rebel groups were a front for Rwanda and Uganda and preferred to continue its own mobilizing activities. By April 2001, the estimated death toll of the wars in eastern Congo surpassed three million.[34] Human Rights

---

[31] Afoaku, "Congo's Rebels," p. 115.

[32] Ibid., p. 118.

[33] Ibid., p. 120.

[34] The International Rescue Committee released the results of a mortality survey in 2000 cataloguing the total deaths caused by the war. See Les Roberts, *Mortality in the Democratic Republic of the Congo: Results from Five Mortality Surveys* (New York: International Rescue Committee, 2000).

Conclusion

Watch detailed the systematic massacres, rape, and pillaging that insurgent groups and their collaborators perpetrated throughout the countryside.[35] These atrocities reached a scale such that the prosecutor of the International Criminal Court elected to begin an investigation of war crimes committed by Congo's rebels and government forces during its long-running civil war. As in Mozambique, Sierra Leone, and Liberia, the ease with which rebel organizations could finance insurgency in Congo short-circuited a process of social mobilization that might have offered citizens hope for a better political future, an escape from poverty, and a transition from the violent and corrupt misrule that characterized its postindependence period.

Implications for the Study of Civil War and Insurgency

The argument presented in this book challenges scholars and analysts of revolution and insurgency to reevaluate the categories and approaches they have employed to study civil war. It demonstrates, first, that rebel groups emerge from diverse starting points. The conventional view that insurgency implies a dependence on civilian populations for the resources needed to build an organization does not hold up to closer scrutiny. Prospective rebel leaders actually face two different states of the world. In one, external or internally generated material resources can be mobilized to meet organizational challenges. In the second, leaders must generate the resources they need to fight by striking bargains with noncombatants in the countryside they wish to rule. These different environments throw out distinct problems that leaders need to solve. Examining the strategic challenges rebel leaders confront thus requires recognition of the resource environment in which groups organize. There is no single model of rebel organization or one optimal path to victory.

Second, my approach challenges scholars to move beyond cross-country studies of civil war onset toward investigations of the micropolitics of violence. Macro-level factors may correlate with the onset, duration, and intensity of violence, but only careful examination of the choices, and constraints faced by individuals and groups can reveal the mechanisms linking poverty, resources, and identities to the practice of violence. Anecdotes drawn from a range of conflicts motivated now-tired debates about "old"

---

[35] See, for example, Human Rights Watch, *Eastern Congo Ravaged: Killing Civilians and Silencing Protest* (New York: Human Rights Watch, 2000), and *Uganda in Eastern DRC: Fueling Political and Ethnic Strife* (New York: Human Rights Watch, 2001).

versus "new" civil wars in the 1990s. Attention focused on variation in the recruitment strategies groups employed and the ways in which violence was used against noncombatant populations, but these studies linked violence only to a change in the international environment as grand ideological debates between capitalism and communism melted away. Without a theoretically grounded explanation for why some rebel groups employ abusive practices while others do not, such debates foundered when other anecdotal evidence revealed that economic motivations, brutal practices, and coercion existed in rebellion during the Cold War and before. This book suggests that wars may in fact differ from one another in important and measurable ways, but it moves the discussion beyond a simple classificatory scheme to suggest the causal pathways through which variation in the resource environment potential rebels confront shapes the strategies they ultimately pursue.

This study also raises new questions that might occupy the next generation of researchers. It uncovers variation in the membership, internal structure, and practices of insurgent organizations but remains silent on the consequences of these differences for a range of important outcomes. Perhaps most significantly, I make no claims about the relative efficacy of activist or opportunistic strategies for achieving victory. Intuition might suggest that cohesive organizations constructed around long-term relationships among members are better equipped to challenge national governments. Yet Laurent Kabila's AFDL captured Kinshasa in less than a year; the RUF fought its way to Freetown, joining forces with the Armed Forces Revolutionary Council in the later stages of the war; and the Shining Path still persists in the jungles of Peru more than ten years after its national organization collapsed. Activists do not always win, and opportunistic rebellions are not guaranteed to lose. Whether differences in the membership, structure, and practice of insurgencies matter for military effectiveness is a question that remains unanswered.

As rebellion is sometimes an integral part of the state-building process, future research might also inquire into the postwar trajectory of activist organizations that achieve military victory. The NRA invested in representative structures of local governance during the war in order to obtain the resources it needed to finance the movement. These structures reshaped power dynamics at the local level, setting in place participatory, democratic institutions of power long before the organization achieved victory. But what becomes of such a movement in the postwar period? Do activist organizations produce more democratic governments after they win? Do these movements deliver public goods more effectively than the governments that came before them? Uganda's success as a reforming African nation in the 1990s was a positive development: the foundations for its democratic decentralization of power, constitutional revision, and programs of poverty reduction were undoubtedly laid during its guerrilla struggle. But its adventurism in eastern Congo and the long-running war in northern Uganda suggest that the equation for state building may not be so simple after all. Insurgent state building may represent a viable alternative to external intervention in civil war, but its efficacy must be further examined.

Implications for Policy Makers

Understanding why some rebel groups commit high levels of abuse against noncombatants while others do not is also important for policy makers focused on the prevention of violent conflict and the resolution of ongoing civil wars. In particular, stories of violence in Uganda, Mozambique, and Peru suggest a transparent and actionable conclusion for policy makers: civil war will be less costly for civilian populations if war can be made more expensive and more difficult for insurgent groups to initiate.

This conclusion puts primary attention on the capacity of governments. Many states in the developing world lack the resources and legitimacy to govern and control their territories. These weak states provide fertile ground for the evolution of opportunistic rebellions. Where governments lack capacity, the barriers to organization are so low that it is possible for small bands of organized individuals to credibly and successfully challenge the state. One unfortunate consequence is that rebellion in these environments is unlikely to deliver the political and economic reforms necessary for development. Instead, such rebel organizations will tend toward criminal enterprise, taking advantage of the absence of state control to extract resources from the territory or population and, if successful, will implement authoritarian structures no different than those set in place by their predecessors. This suggests the importance of a renewed global commitment to supporting the development of state capacity in the world's poorest countries.[36] Strong and effective states are important for development, but they are also essential for weeding out opportunistic rebellions.

[36] Francis Fukuyama, *Statebuilding: Governance and World Order in the 21st Century* (Ithaca, NY: Cornell University Press, 2004).

This book also adds to the growing chorus calling for attention to the problems of resource-rich states. One might imagine that resource wealth is a blessing for development. Drawing on empirical evidence from across the developing world, however, scholars have demonstrated the myriad ways in which resource booms distort the macroeconomy and undermine the incentives that exist for states to deliver public goods and protect the rights of their citizens.[37] I have identified an additional resource curse that plagues developing countries: where combatant organizations can access economic resources with which to finance rebellion, they face few (if any) incentives to strike important and constraining bargains with civilian populations. This study thus complements recent research by the World Bank that pinpoints resource wealth as a proximate cause of civil war.[38] But resource-rich states are not only more likely to face civil conflict, they are also more likely to be challenged by opportunistic insurgencies – groups organized around short-term benefits that are prone to use high levels of coercion and force. Finding better ways to manage resource wealth for the benefit of the population is important for preventing conflict and may reduce the costs of conflict to civilian populations as well.

This understanding of how rebel groups form also offers a cautionary note to foreign governments as they consider providing military and financial assistance to rebel groups. External support for insurgent groups was a fundamental part of foreign policy during the Cold War as the United States and the Soviet Union sought to construct spheres of influence in the developing world. In the new global campaign against terrorism and state sponsors of terrorism, the United States has already engaged in an effort to identify friendly opposition forces as it has mounted challenges to regimes in Afghanistan and Iraq. External aid to rebel groups may help states meet their foreign policy objectives, but it fundamentally changes the incentives facing rebel leaders and foot soldiers within a conflict. Flows of foreign resources in Mozambique, Sierra Leone, Liberia, and the Democratic Republic of the Congo enabled the growth of movements with little or no interest in

---

[37] See, for example, Alan Gelb, *Oil Windfalls: Blessing or Curse?* (New York: Oxford University Press for the World Bank, 1988); Terry Karl, *The Paradox of Plenty: Oil Booms and Petro-States* (Berkeley: University of California Press, 1997); and Michael Ross, *Timber Booms and Institutional Breakdown in Southeast Asia* (New York: Cambridge University Press, 2001).

[38] Paul Collier, V. L. Elliott, Hvard Hegre, Anke Hoeffler, Marta Reynal-Querol, and Nicholas Sambanis, *Breaking the Conflict Trap: Civil War and Development Policy* (Washington, DC: World Bank, 2003).

political and economic change. A similar danger presents itself whenever and wherever foreign governments finance rebellion and back that support up with military assistance.

The experience of the U.S. military in Afghanistan suggests that this warning is well founded. U.S. intelligence agents purchased the support of tribal warlords as the United States prepared for a full-scale invasion of Afghanistan in late 2001. Briefcases of cash were provided to Northern Alliance commanders and warlords in the southern provinces, along with promises of aerial bombing campaigns to support the advance of their ground forces. Although successful in the short run in defeating the Taliban regime, this strategy of building alliances has had unfortunate long-term consequences. Warlords used external patronage to reinforce their political and military positions, making it more difficult for the new government to consolidate control in the regions outside of Kabul. Realizing that the American interest in a centralized authority threatened their capacity to maintain economic and political control of lucrative trade routes and drug-producing areas, warlords have undermined the transition process at almost every stage. Foreign patronage purchased opportunistic allies in the war against the Taliban. Unfortunately, America's allies during the war have shown little commitment to nation building in the aftermath. To this day, the government of Hamid Karzai remains holed up in Kabul as America's partners in the war to overthrow the Taliban enjoy the fruits of their victory in the countryside.

In addition to its evident implications for the prevention of violence, this approach offers useful insights for policy makers who seek to minimize the human rights abuses committed by insurgent groups in ongoing conflicts. Under significant pressure from the humanitarian and human rights communities, rebel groups are increasingly held to the same standard of behavior as states. In 1977, the Geneva Conventions, the foundational document of international humanitarian law, were extended to victims of noninternational armed conflicts. Key human rights organizations, including Amnesty International and Human Rights Watch, have broadened their definition of what constitutes a human rights violation to cover acts of violence committed by rebel groups. But even though expectations about how armed groups should behave have changed, the capacity of the international community to influence the actions of rebel groups has seen innovation only at the margins. The policy tools available are too blunt, too ineffective, or wholly irrelevant to the task of changing the way armed groups conduct war.

If insurgent organizations are to be held accountable for violations of international humanitarian law, instruments must be developed and refined to reflect the diverse structures of these groups. The ability of the international community to influence the behavior of a group is undoubtedly shaped by a host of factors, including the motivations of its combatants, internal incentives within the organization, the structure of command and control, the financing of the group, the degree of outside influence, and the likelihood of victory. By focusing on the origins of rebel movements, this book offers policy makers a starting point for thinking about how instruments of influence might vary in their effectiveness across rebel organizations. In conclusion, I examine three critical instruments outsiders employ to influence or constrain the actions of insurgent groups in light of the theory advanced in this book.

Naming and Shaming

Naming and shaming, probably the most commonly used instrument, treats armed groups as targets of national and international action. Fact finding and denunciation are the critical tools used in monitoring human rights. National and international organizations gather information on human rights violations, assess its validity, and write reports that are quickly made public and placed in the hands of key policy makers and the media. The goal is simple: to use publicity to change the behavior of the group. Methods of naming and shaming armed groups have been developed by "norms entrepreneurs" at the international level who are committed to the expansion of international legal instruments.[39] Human Rights Watch and Amnesty International are the obvious examples, but international donors have also rushed to provide financing for local human rights monitoring organizations.

Jeffrey Herbst aptly summarizes the fundamental problem with naming and shaming: "Regulating rebel entities without recognizing them is an extraordinary conundrum."[40] Herbst offers as an example a paragraph taken from a Human Rights Watch report on northern Uganda. It recommends

---

[39] Margaret Keck and Kathryn Sikkink, *Activists beyond Borders: Advocacy Networks in International Politics* (Ithaca, NY: Cornell University Press, 1998).

[40] Jeffrey Herbst, "International Laws of War and the African Child: Norms, Compliance, and Sovereignty," in *International Law and Organization: Closing the Compliance Gap*, eds. Michael Doyle and Edward Luck (Lanham, MD: Rowan & Littlefield, 2004), Chapter 7.

that the Lord's Resistance Army "immediately stop abducting children; immediately stop killing children; immediately stop torturing children; immediately stop sexually abusing children; immediately release all children remaining in captivity; [and] ensure that Lord's Resistance Army combatants respect the human rights of civilians in areas of conflict."[41] Undoubtedly, public denunciation and shaming works in many contexts by shaping either how a group behaves or how it is viewed by the international community, but the challenges involved in making it effective are immediately apparent. In this particular case, it is not clear what the Lord's Resistance Army will gain from complying with the demands of Human Rights Watch.

The use of dialogue, cooperation, and negotiation with armed groups might provide a significant opportunity for persuasion, enabling external actors and armed groups to come to consensus on a set of principles that should guide behavior. But on its own, naming and shaming does not offer an opportunity for persuasion. Instead, denunciation is a strategy whereby unacceptable patterns of behavior are made public, and, due to negative publicity, armed groups are shamed into changing their behavior. Often, the target is an armed group committing atrocities. But naming and shaming has been used effectively to challenge the governments of developed countries to alter policies that allow human rights violations to continue.

To work, naming and shaming requires that groups put a high value on their reputation. Rebel leaders must care what others think. They must be concerned that negative publicity has serious consequences for their operations either within or outside of the country. Where reputation does not really matter, groups can be easily pushed into a corner, isolated in such a way that behavioral change produces almost no benefits in terms of increased legitimacy. A second key condition for effectiveness is that groups have the capacity to reverse course, that is, to implement changes in the rules of conduct of their constituent units. That capacity cannot be taken for granted and is likely to vary in important ways across different types of rebel groups. Given their commitment to weeding out opportunistic joiners, maintaining the character of their movements, and punishing indiscipline, activist leaders are more likely to exhibit the concerns for reputation that naming and shaming requires and to have the capacity to change formal and informal patterns of behavior within the organization.

[41] Ibid., p. 197.

Sanctions as a Source of Leverage

Sanctions are a second instrument often used to influence the behavior of armed groups. Sanctions have traditionally been applied to governments or against specific individuals within governments, but pressure mounted in the 1990s to develop punitive instruments that can apply to nonstate armed groups as well. These take multiple forms, including foreign travel bans, bans on investment in areas under rebel control, restrictions on arms transfers, the freezing of foreign assets, and prohibitions on a group's political activities abroad, but the most significant innovations have come in the arena of economic sanctions against legally traded commodities emerging from conflict areas.

Sanctions in this context are designed to criminalize specific suppliers within an otherwise licit industry.[42] The impact on prices in a competitive world market should be nil. This operates entirely differently than the illegal trade in narcotics, in which interdiction policies have only served to increase prices, providing strong incentives for nonstate armed groups to remain engaged in trade activities. Two specific forms of sanctions are relevant to the armed groups considered in this book.

A *sanctions regime* seeks to gain economic leverage over combatant factions by limiting their capacity to trade in particular commodities. These regimes are flexible enough to target states, groups, or individuals. With the cooperation of member states, particularly in global bodies such as the United Nations, sanctions regimes can be extremely effective in cutting off the flow of financing to combatant organizations. The challenge in making sanctions work is that it requires effective on-the-ground monitoring and cooperation from major states. The record of commodity sanctions as they were applied in the 1990s is mixed at best. In most cases, in nations to which sanctions were applied, the conflicts were resolved with outside military intervention rather than as a result of the collapse of the group targeted by the sanctions regime. At the same time, there have been examples of success. Indeed, after the death of rebel leader Jonas Savimbi, UNITA officials admitted that United Nations sanctions played a decisive role in weakening the rebel infrastructure over time.

An alternative approach, a *certification regime*, has recently evolved to address the challenges posed by conflict diamonds. Here, the goal is to

---

[42] Philippe Le Billon, "Getting It Done: Instruments of Enforcement," in *Natural Resources and Violent Conflict*, eds. Ian Bannon and Paul Collier (Washington, DC: World Bank, 2003), pp. 215–86.

prevent the trade in a specific commodity from particular producers at the national or subnational level. Certification regimes work by controlling access to the market for commodities that have not been certified. Total cooperation on the part of firms that purchase and states that consume these commodities is required to make such regimes effective. With respect to their impact on armed groups, these regimes provide less leverage over a particular group in a particular conflict, but they effectively put "the writing on the wall" that one source of finance will likely come to an end. The Kimberly Certification Process is a prominent example of this alternative approach. It seeks to establish a voluntary system of industry self-regulation in which participants commit not to trade with nonparticipants, to provide certificates for all shipments, to establish controls that eliminate trade in conflict diamonds, to track exports and imports closely, and to be transparent to external review. Although the initiative is a remarkable step forward in restricting trade in conflict commodities, the plodding pace of its implementation and its voluntary nature have significantly hampered its effectiveness.

The goal of sanctions and certification regimes is to choke the lifeline that sustains nonstate armed groups. Sanctions can help to starve belligerents of revenue, make the benefits of peace more attractive, or raise the costs of trade sufficiently to dampen profit margins. Such regimes also undermine comfortable stalemates in which both sides benefit from continued conflict. An added benefit is the stigmatization that comes from UN or regional condemnation. Choking the lifeline has its costs, however, as a strategy for influencing the behavior of armed groups. Lacking access to the regular flow of resources, some groups may turn to predation, leading to a spike in human rights violations rather than their diminution. Combatants with only a limited commitment to the organization may peel away, leaving core believers who will be more difficult to engage in negotiations. The stigma itself may be sufficient to back groups into a corner, making it more difficult for them to exit the conflict. And the impact of sanctions on trade diversion – in particular, the shifting of trade to other nonstate groups – is an issue that has received far too little attention.

Sanctions can be effective if a number of conditions are met. First, the rebel organization must be sufficiently dependent on a particular resource flow to make the organization and implementation of sanctions worth the costs of mobilizing compliance and enforcement mechanisms. Second, the leadership must be able to bring the members of the faction along if the lever is powerful enough to provide incentives for settlement or behavioral change. Barring substantial dependence on a single resource and an internal capacity to deliver peace, sanctions may be wholly ineffective or even counterproductive. Sanctions are an appealing strategy for dealing with opportunistic insurgencies, as they generate an internal crisis in which the glue holding an organization together melts away. The result, however, may be a short-term increase in predation and violence as the organization turns to looting to maintain its membership, with a long-run improvement in the prospects for peace as its capacity is weakened.

Formal Instruments of Accountability

International criminal trials and tribunals are now perhaps the most important tool employed by international actors to constrain insurgent groups. Trials and tribunals seek to hold individuals responsible for violations of international humanitarian law, or domestic law when applicable, that limit the exercise of violence. Many international legal conventions (most of which apply to states alone) already require the establishment of procedures for punishing individuals who have committed abuses.[43] Contemporary practice, driven by a growing embrace of individual accountability, has seen the rise of domestic prosecutions, ad hoc criminal tribunals, the formation of the International Criminal Court, and the exercise of universal jurisdiction as strategies for deterring and punishing the human rights violations committed by nonstate armed groups.

The most prominent recent examples of international jurisprudence around war crimes are the International Criminal Tribunals for Yugoslavia and Rwanda. But recent innovations have extended legal instruments to include hybrid judicial structures, such as the Special Court of Sierra Leone; the use of domestic legal processes abroad, as in the Alien Torts Claim Act in the United States; and home-grown domestic prosecutions, such as investigations into rights violations in post-Fujimori Peru. The Special Court of Sierra Leone, a hybrid structure combining elements of national and international judicial structures, is representative of a growing tendency to push for prosecution in the immediate postwar period. Even though amnesty offers had been provided during peace negotiations in the late 1990s, the final resolution of the conflict came through a decisive victory on the part of

---

[43] Chandra Lehka Sriram, "Achieving Accountability for Non-State Armed Groups: Use of Domestic Mechanisms for International Crimes" (paper prepared for the Armed Groups Project, University of British Columbia, 2004).

the government with the active support of a contingent of the British military. Reluctant to continue establishing unwieldy international structures of justice, the United Nations supported the design of a hybrid structure, which had the added benefit of making investments in rebuilding local judicial capacities. The Special Court is largely resourced from abroad, and it has a narrow mandate: to punish those who "bear the greatest responsibility" for crimes against humanity committed during the war. Targeting the senior leadership of each faction, the Special Court has issued indictments against state and nonstate officials alike.

Trials and tribunals are designed to send a strong signal to perpetrators and would-be perpetrators that they will be held individually accountable for the human rights violations they commit. Deterrence is central to arguments about the efficacy and importance of prosecution. Trials also help to build the foundation for systems of impartial justice in postconflict settings. It is argued that when particular individuals are made to pay for their actions, the potential for future violence along group lines is somehow defused.[44] To make trials and deterrence an effective strategy for influencing groups, it is critical that a reasonable expectation exists that such trials and tribunals will be formed. Particularly in Africa, however, that expectation is not commonly held.

With respect to the character of groups, trials and tribunals depend on the ability of outsiders to determine responsibility for the violations committed against noncombatants. In particular, the mandate to prosecute those who bear the greatest responsibility assumes a traditional structure of command and control in which the senior leadership of a movement authorizes harmful actions. Two other group-specific considerations also affect the efficacy of trials. The fear of punishment on the part of individuals within a group must outweigh other motivations for fighting. Indeed, this sort of logic is central to the spread of stiff mandatory sentencing for criminal activities. The targeted group must also be weak enough not to be able to strike back when the threat or practice of prosecution is advanced. The same concern that rears its head in discussions of naming and shaming and sanctions – that is, the extent to which these instruments isolate particular groups – is also relevant in the context of criminal prosecutions.

A focus on the internal structures of rebel groups raises important questions about the efficacy of trials and tribunals as a strategy for constraining

---

[44] Jack Snyder and Leslie Vinjamuri, "Trials and Errors: Principle and Pragmatism in Strategies of International Justice," *International Security* 28 (2003/2004): 5–44.

anticivilian violence. Mechanisms of deterrence depend on the fact that individuals care about the future. Opportunistic groups filled to the brim with consumers tend not to exhibit that characteristic. It is often difficult to make sense of the command and control structure in these groups, moreover, in order to assign individual responsibility. Although many opportunistic groups exhibit a high degree of centralization in military command, much of the violence for which they are responsible is committed in a decentralized fashion as a result of a culture of indiscipline – one that goes unpunished by local, rather than national, commanders. Moreover, the absence of a reasonable expectation of punishment makes this instrument unlikely to have a deterrent effect. With activist groups, the situation is equally dire. Even though investors tend to care about the future more than consumers, a fear of being held accountable down the road may not outweigh the powerful incentives maintaining an organization in the short run, especially given the climate of uncertainty that characterizes rebellion. Common expectations, beliefs, and interests reinforced through education, indoctrination, and practice are difficult to overcome. Even if prosecutions can begin to unravel an organization by picking off some of its leaders, moreover, activist groups may be strong enough to strike back.

Looking Forward

As long as individuals live together under the authority of sovereign governments, rebellion will be employed as a strategy of resistance. Sometimes, rebellion will be a force for positive change. Groups will overturn corrupt regimes and set in place institutions of participatory, democratic, and just governance. In other contexts, insurgents will perpetrate atrocities that are broadcast around the globe, capturing resources for their own personal benefit as they rampage through the countryside. This book represents an attempt to make sense of these patterns, to identify the conditions under which citizens can expect state-building – as opposed to state-destroying – insurgent organizations. The argument is simple, and its implications are clear. Protecting the lives of noncombatants in civil war requires a commitment to starving rebel organizations of the resources they use to finance insurgency and forcing insurgents to confront the difficult task of building states with the consent of the governed.

Appendix A

THE ETHNOGRAPHY OF REBEL ORGANIZATIONS

My research strategy relied principally on the collection of grassroots accounts of rebellion from diverse perspectives. The overriding goal was simple: to bring the tools of ethnographic research to bear on the internal dynamics of rebel organizations. To understand why rebel groups abuse civilian populations in some contexts and not in others, I spoke to rebel commanders, foot soldiers, civilians who lived in war zones, and government forces. I asked them to share their experiences of the war. The stories of commanders and combatants typically began with an account of how they came to join. Civilians shared first the rumors they heard about rebels living in the bush. As our conversations unfolded, my respondents talked about the internal characteristics of the organizations they built or their experiences of mobilization and repression. Together, these individual perspectives tell a story about the formation of rebel groups and their attempts to negotiate access to and acquiescence from those around them.

The challenges of conducting interviews in the midst or aftermath of conflict – often with the perpetrators of violence themselves – were complex. But for the comparative analysis of strategies, participant accounts offer unique and powerful insights into the choices individuals make and the operation of groups – insights that cannot be easily gleaned from traditional sources.

Because I interviewed participants to understand rebellion from the inside, I am able to shift focus away from the memoirs of elite revolutionary leaders that have been so important to the study of previous peasant insurgencies. The concerns inherent to relying on memoirs of rebellion are many: the narrator is often not representative of the participants in the movement, post hoc representations of a rebel group are frequently little more than constructed (and possibly imagined) narratives, and elite memoirs provide few avenues for fact checking or the testing of alternative explanations. I drew inspiration instead from a methodological approach first pioneered during the Vietnam War that relies primarily on open-ended interviews with participants. Between 1965 and 1971, the Rand Corporation conducted more than four hundred interviews with prisoners and defectors from the communist side, producing almost twelve thousand pages of transcripts. Scholars flocked to these individual accounts of the war in an effort to make sense of why people participated, what ideologies guided their actions, how the insurgency was organized, and what fractures and fissures were experienced and overcome. A recently published study by one scholar involved in the collection of these participant accounts combines records of these interviews with detailed social histories of the populous rural province of My Tho.[1] Data from cadet interviews and provincial records enable David Elliott to describe the origins and character of a revolution in a way that reflects both individual calculations and the broader social conditions that shaped those choices. In my own study of insurgency, I seek to capture that back and forth between the experiences of combatants and civilians and the broader context in which they lived. And for Elliott, as for me, "interviewing these simple peasants was a transforming experience." Elliott writes: "I was astounded by the political sophistication and analytic skills...as well as the truly remarkable ability to relate their experiences with concision and introspection."[2]

Peasant perspectives have been important to studies of more recent civil wars as well. They have been used most frequently in efforts to understand the calculations individuals make about whether to join insurgent movements. Elisabeth Wood interviewed hundreds of participants and nonparticipants in the civil war in El Salvador, drawing on these oral histories to advance a theory of participation rooted in the desires of peasants to affirm their dignity and autonomy through purposive action.[3] A comparison of the accounts of participants and nonparticipants enabled Wood to challenge existing theories about the role of material gain and selective incentives in motivating action. Roger Petersen, too, emphasizes the voices of ordinary

---

[1] David W. P. Elliott, *The Vietnamese War: Revolution and Social Change in the Mekong Delta, 1930–1975* (Armonk, NY: M. E. Sharpe, 2003). See also Paul Berman, *Revolutionary Organization: Institution-Building within the People's Liberation Armed Forces* (Lexington, MA: Lexington Books, 1974).

[2] Elliott, *The Vietnamese War*, p. xiii.

[3] Elisabeth Wood, *Insurgent Collective Action and Civil War in El Salvador* (New York: Cambridge University Press, 2004).

people in exploring the dynamics of civilian resistance to oppressive states in Eastern Europe. Petersen probed the factors that account for the movement of individuals from one level of participation (such as vocalizing opposition to the existing regime by attending a rally) to another (such as becoming an armed member of a rebellion). His empirical treatment of participation focused on the experiences of approximately forty elderly Lithuanians who opposed the Soviet occupations in the 1940s and 1950s. Drawing on their experiences, Petersen was able to link individuals' movements along the threshold of participation to broader factors, including community ties and networks.

Participant accounts have also contributed to the development of theory about the interaction of insurgent groups and noncombatant populations. Norma Kriger's research on peasant support for the insurgency in Zimbabwe complicates the view that revolutionary movements depend on civilian support to emerge victorious.[4] By doing fieldwork in one district that was heavily affected by the conflict, Kriger was able to uncover the strategies peasants used to manage the guerrillas and the governments, minimizing the risks they faced from both sides while protecting their livelihoods and gradually shaping the revolution itself. Stathis Kalyvas employs an innovative microcomparative research design that exploits variation in the intensity of violence during the Greek civil war across geographic zones to test a new theory about the conditions under which governments and rebel groups use violence.[5] Intensive fieldwork in Greece among those who experienced the conflict provides him with heretofore unavailable quantitative and qualitative data about the strategies employed by the warring parties.

It is possible that survey research, which draws on large, representative samples of respondents, might provide more leverage for understanding the dynamics of civil war than participant accounts, which suffer from a small sample bias. But such approaches to large-scale data collection in the midst of violence are still in their infancy. The data that are available from war-torn countries focus on the basic socioeconomic characteristics of households, bypassing difficult questions about individuals' interactions and experience with rebel and government forces, and the data's coverage,

---

[4] Norma Kriger, *Zimbabwe's Guerrilla War: Peasant Voices* (New York: Cambridge University Press, 1992).

[5] Stathis Kalyvas, *The Logic of Violence in Civil War* (New York: Cambridge University Press, 2006).

particularly in areas outside of government control, is patchy. Although such approaches were not employed for this project, survey research is potentially a fruitful avenue for gathering data on individual motivations for participation, the dynamics of conflict, and the transition from war to peace, as I have shown in more recent research on Sierra Leone.[6]

For this project, I conducted ethnographies of four different rebel organizations. My principal source of information was open-ended interviews with former commanders and combatants who participated in the rebellion, residents of communities who lived through the experience of rebel control, and members of the government forces that fought against these rebellions. Through in-depth exploration of the experiences of many individuals, I sought to uncover the structural conditions these groups faced, the information they had available to them as the war progressed, the constraints that limited their options, the choices they made, and the consequences that followed from those choices. My basic strategy was the same across all four cases, although points of access differed. In this appendix, I discuss the obstacles to conducting social science research on the micropolitics of rebellion and the strategies I used to overcome them.

Distinct Challenges of Ethnography

This book advances an argument that reflects my interpretation of the stories told by individuals who participated in and experienced rebellion in Uganda, Mozambique, and Peru. I sought diverse respondents and asked them to describe their personal histories of the war – the conditions that preceded it, how they came to know of the rebel group, in what ways they participated (or did not participate) in the movement, and how the organization itself operated and changed over time as the war took its course. My choice to draw heavily on personal perspectives on rebellion raised a number of distinct challenges of interpretation, which I took seriously in designing the fieldwork for this study.

First, I was concerned that I would not be able to trust what I heard from the respondents. Those who have experienced high levels of violence or perpetrated it themselves are a difficult pool from which to elicit information. The accuracy with which individuals recall events they experienced in the past is open to question, and, regardless of how well events are

[6] Macartan Humphreys and Jeremy Weinstein, "What the Fighters Say" (Working Paper no. 20, Center for Globalization and Sustainable Development, Columbia University, 2004).

354

remembered, social and cultural processes may shape how they are retold. The nature of the postwar outcome (whether a group won or lost), for example, can influence how individuals describe their motivations for participation and evaluate the choices their leaders faced. What people say, finally, is shaped in part by their own personal agendas – by what they would like to get out of participating in the interview, what messages they would like the world to hear, and what their present political loyalties dictate they should say.

Second, I was conscious that the perspectives offered by my respondents might not provide me with the complete story. Unable to conduct interviews with a random sample of respondents, I was concerned about forms of bias that might weaken my ability to draw inferences from the set of interviews I conducted. I had to pay attention to a number of different forms of bias, but two were of particular concern. It was critical that my respondents represent a broad range of political views, from government supporters to rebel collaborators, from disaffected ex-combatants to true patriots of the movement. A bias in any direction could substantially undermine the representativeness of the views that were presented to me. There was also a significant concern with capturing both local and national dynamics. Elite-level interviewing has the advantage of providing a bird's-eye view of a movement's organization, but to tell a coherent story I needed to cross-check stories of organization with what was experienced by rank-and-file combatants and civilians who experienced the war far from the commanders' camps and far from the national political debate. Of course, even if I had been able to draw a random sample, I still would have been unable to capture one population in particular: those who perished during the war.

Third, while personal narratives of participation may offer significant insight into the dynamics of rebellion, it is possible that they miss broader structural and demographic factors that drive individual choices and group strategies in the context of conflict. Individual narratives are necessarily individual: they provide the interviewer with one person's perception and interpretation of the structures and processes that may be at work. Aggregating these personal narratives provides a basis for comparison – a means of validating particular stories and drawing out patterns. Yet to make sense of structural and demographic factors, the analyst must maximize variation at a more aggregate level, something that can be easily done by examining how groups change over time, how they behave in different regions, and how their evolution varies across countries.

The Research Method

My field research occurred in the aftermath of conflict in regions where political violence was severe and rebel groups had exerted some form of sovereignty during the war. The National Resistance Army was victorious in Uganda more than ten years before I arrived there, and its commanders and combatants now serve in the senior leadership of the government and the military. In Mozambique, Renamo committed to a peace agreement eight years before my work began, it fully demobilized six years ago, and its former commanders and combatants returned to their home regions or areas in which they built ties during the course of the conflict. Peru, in spite of the collapse of the Shining Path in the early 1990s, still struggles with the remnants of Sendero Luminoso, and in the Upper Huallaga Valley, where I conducted some of my fieldwork, groups of combatants remain active deep in the jungle.

The choice to work in a postconflict setting was not an obvious one. My first explorations of this topic involved interviews with refugees from the eastern parts of the Democratic Republic of Congo and Angola. It quickly became clear to me while conducting these interviews, however, that achieving a representative sample would be extraordinarily difficult in the context of war. Moreover, respondents wore their political agendas on their sleeves, and many of the questions to which I sought answers – about strategies of violence, mechanisms for disciplining combatants, and structures of command and control – were off limits. When combatants did choose to speak, I found it difficult to obtain responses that deviated from a very obvious party line.

Even in a postconflict setting, the challenges of conducting interviews were substantial. My interviews sought to uncover the political differences that gave rise to the violence, the strategies that groups employed to build their organizations, the tough decisions commanders and combatants made about how and when to use violence, and the painful experiences of hunger, frustration, violence, and loss that combatants and civilians alike experienced during war. Asking these questions often put me in an uncomfortable position and sometimes placed me at personal risk; answering them and making public (at least to me) their reflections on how the war was fought entailed its own set of risks for those I interviewed. When I had successfully gained entry into someone's home to conduct an interview, I undertook a process of gaining informed consent: emphasizing the interview's voluntary nature, ensuring privacy in the interview setting, guaranteeing confidentiality to respondents in my writing, and offering my assurances that the written records of our discussions would be protected. But finding means to gain the trust of my respondents in the first place so that they would be willing to expose themselves and their organizations to outside scrutiny was a challenge that became fundamental to my fieldwork.

Despite these difficulties, I managed to interview nearly two hundred combatants and civilians in three countries. My access to combatants and civilians came via national political elites and local leaders, depending on the context. In Uganda and Mozambique, I met with senior officials in the various rebel movements and asked them to broker introductions to the various commanders and combatants who would serve as my sources for this book. These initial interviews focused on the purposes of my research project, my plans for using the information I expected to gather, and my background: in essence, my contacts evaluated whether I could be trusted. A similar process of establishing means of access took place in the various communities in which I worked. First, contact was established with local party leaders and officials, and after I received permission to work in the region, many offered their assistance in identifying potential sources. I was also free to develop my own contact lists, and I regularly sought to do so in an effort to balance the sample of respondents.

My experience in Peru was slightly different, particularly at the national level. With the insurgency still ongoing in some parts of the country, access to rebel combatants was more restricted and, given the anti-American views of Sendero rebels in the Upper Huallaga Valley, potentially more dangerous. Before working in local communities, I sought to develop contacts in the capital, relying heavily on interviews with incarcerated members of Sendero Luminoso and with informers who were cooperating with news organizations. Interpreting the responses of prisoners and informers raises difficult questions, of course, but I was able to validate their stories through an examination of detailed records of the Shining Path that had been captured by the counterterrorism police – a veritable treasure trove of documents from the movement's history to which I was granted unrestricted access.

To address the challenges enumerated earlier, I developed an ethnographic approach with three main components. I gathered data on four different rebel groups in order to gain leverage on the structural and demographic factors shaping rebel group behavior. My choice of cases enabled me to generate variation on both dependent and independent variables of interest, and the comparison of two groups within Peru provided me with

Table A.1. *Distribution of Formal Interviews*

National Level	Uganda			Mozambique	Peru	
Political and military leaders	22			6	5	

Local Level	Semuto	Kiwanguzi	Ribáuè	Marínguè	Huanta	Tingo María
Combatants	3	10	10	10		
Civilians	29	11	19	14	21	16

some additional controls as I sought to tease out potential causal mechanisms. The key to employing multiple cases effectively was the use of a parallel research strategy in each context, one in which the profile of interviewees, the selection of sites, and the questions I asked were similar.

Second, although I did not attempt to build a random sample of respondents, I did interview combatants and civilians from a broad range of backgrounds and perspectives. While in the capital cities, my interviews were largely with soldiers who had served in the leadership of the various rebel organizations. In rural areas, however, I actively complemented elite-level perspectives with information I obtained from one-on-one interviews with rank-and-file soldiers. In total, I interviewed over fifty commanders and combatants. My strategies for identifying rebel leaders and combatants differed across countries, as Table A.1 demonstrates. In Uganda, my contact with the rebel leadership occurred largely through interviews with senior military officials and government officers, as most NRA commanders now live in the capital, Kampala. Conversations with combatants in Mozambique, by contrast, were more likely to take place up-country in my two fieldwork sites, as only a small number of former Renamo soldiers live in the country's capital, Maputo, in southern Mozambique. Peru represented the most difficult challenge in terms of accessing combatants. Many are locked in prison, and those who are not are either reluctant to admit to their participation in Sendero, particularly if they live in the hotly contested region of Ayacucho, or are still active as insurgents in the Upper Huallaga Valley and are actively anti-American. With the assistance of the counterterrorism police, I conducted five extended interviews with prisoners who are former leaders of Sendero's regional committees. The interviews I carried out in Huanta and Tingo María (labeled "civilians" in the table) also included some conversations with combatants, most of whom would not admit directly to their participation but spoke freely about the internal structure of the group in a way that reflected an in-depth knowledge of it. The fact that Peru's Truth and Reconciliation Commission was undertaking work in both areas just as I arrived further increased the sensitivity of asking people whether they had personally participated as members of the Shining Path; some feared any public knowledge of their role in the war and others worried about the prospect of punishment even though the Commission had no prosecutorial role.

My fieldwork in the rural areas focused as well on generating local histories of the conflicts. In each country, I worked in two different regions – one close to the center of rebel control and one on the fringes. As Maps A.1, A.2, and A.3 indicate, the two fieldwork sites in Uganda were near to one another: Semuto represents the heart of the Luwero Triangle, where the NRA had its internal base, while Kiwanguzi borders the Luwero Triangle but is a region in which the NRA had only limited influence until it sought greater control two years into the war. In Mozambique, I explored the organization and behavior of Renamo in its strongest area of support, Sofala Province, basing myself in Maríngue, the location of the group's headquarters in the later stages of the war. I also conducted fieldwork in northern Mozambique in a town called Ribáuè, where Renamo faced greater difficulties in contesting for territory with government forces based in Nampula. My field research in Peru focused on two different regional committees, one based in Huanta, where the Shining Path originated, and the other in Tingo María, where the group did not operate until years after the war commenced. At each of these sites, I made an effort to conduct interviews in the areas where the rebels were strong and in more contested territories.

In building these social histories, I aimed to identify and interview a broad range of former combatants and civilians. On the civilian side, a conscious effort was made to gather information from government supporters and members of opposition parties. My goal was to establish a timeline for the conflict, to identify the key players in each community, to bring to light critical events that shaped the course of the conflict, and to provide a basis for the comparison of competing accounts of the struggle. In each community, I interviewed between twenty and thirty civilians in an effort to develop a coherent version of the local history. I supplemented regional variation with temporal variation, explicitly identifying sites and individuals that experienced different periods of the war. It is difficult to paint a single accurate picture of a complex rebel organization when local contexts exert powerful influences on behavior, but the diverse perspectives I sought at

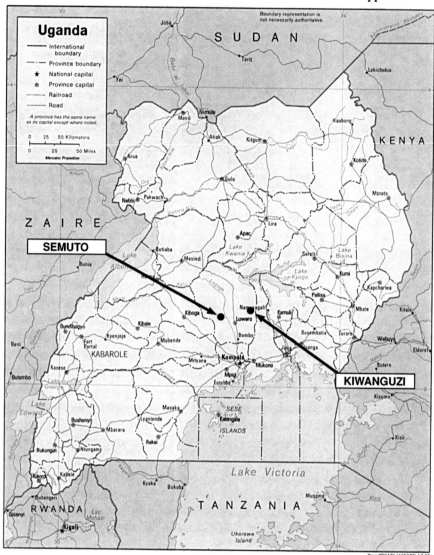

Map A.1. Location of Fieldwork in Uganda
Source: Central Intelligence Agency

both national and local levels enabled me to generate a profile of the four
rebel organizations with confidence.

It is important to offer some thoughts on the interviews themselves.
All interviews were conducted in private. I explicitly avoided group

360

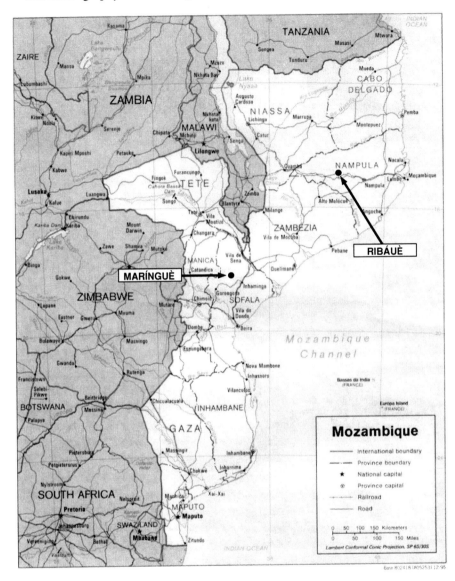

Map A.2. Location of Fieldwork in Mozambique
Source: Central Intelligence Agency

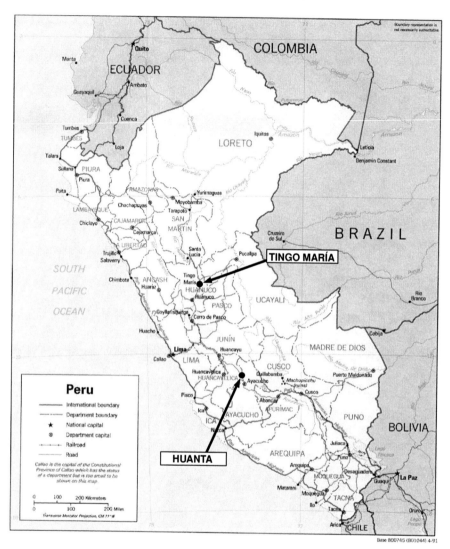

Map A.3. Location of Fieldwork in Peru
Source: Central Intelligence Agency

discussions whenever possible, preferring to visit people in their homes. Although I developed a semistructured interview format, with a specific series of questions I hoped to have answered, the evolution of the conversations in practice was more open-ended. I found through experience that providing respondents with the opportunity to tell their own story of the war yielded significantly more information than did attempting to guide the interviews, and it eventually yielded the information I sought. The interviews lasted for two to three hours on average, with some stretching on far longer. I visited the homes of some respondents on multiple occasions, although most conversations were single visits. Where possible, I conducted the interviews in English (Uganda), Portuguese (Mozambique), and Spanish (Peru) – three languages in which I am proficient. I also employed three research assistants, one in each country, who acted as translators when local languages were required. Each was in training or had completed training as a social scientist at the national university, so they became partners in the process of gathering, recording, and interpreting the information we collected. Significant time was invested in developing a structure for asking questions and translating responses, and each of us took detailed notes during interviews and wrote up interpretations of those notes every evening. Importantly, I promised all the respondents that we would not reveal their identities. Although notes were taken, I did not record any of the conversations. For this reason, throughout the book, I refer to interviewees only in terms of the location and the date of my interviews with them.

As the third component of my research strategy, I employed multiple data-gathering methods to complement what I could learn from participatory accounts. In each country, I actively sought to obtain records of the rebel organization. Political propaganda was by far the easiest material to access, but I also succeeded in identifying records that described the internal dynamics of some of the groups. The National Resistance Army, for example, produced a list of its collaborators broken down by region that enabled me to identify and validate stories that I heard in my local fieldwork. One NRA commander also kept a detailed diary of his first year or so in the bush that he graciously shared with me. His hour-by-hour, day-by-day account provided an unusual window into the first months of an insurgency. The Shining Path, notorious for its record keeping, produced reams of information that now rest with the counterterrorism police in Peru. Memoranda sent from one regional committee to another updating progress on recruitment, organization, plans for attack, and disciplinary problems revealed enormous amounts of information about how the internal structure of Sendero evolved over time. These documents also provided powerful evidence of the fissure between the Shining Path and its regional committee in the Upper Huallaga Valley.

I also employed a team of research assistants to develop a quantitative events database charting patterns of political violence over time during the war. My research assistants worked from a common template, combing through archived local newspapers, publications, and nongovernmental reports to capture the dynamics of violence over time. This quantitative work is described more fully in Appendix B.

Finally, I turned to the primary and secondary literature to place my own research in context. I looked for local analyses of the conflict in master's and doctoral theses at key universities in each country, I identified and interviewed journalists and academics who had followed the violence to obtain their perspectives, I uncovered bits and pieces of the doctrine developed by each government to counter the growing insurgencies, and I pored through the analytical and empirical work of outsiders who have examined various aspects of these movements previously.

Conclusion

It is clear that one must be careful in interpreting the participatory accounts of former combatants and civilians that serve as the basis for this book. But the potential biases that this methodological approach introduces can be identified, and explicit steps were taken to minimize their impact. Indeed, the key challenge in assembling accurate accounts of violence from the perpetrators themselves is one of gaining their trust. The access I achieved and the honesty that characterized the testimonies I received proved possible for a number of reasons. Undoubtedly, the fact that the war was over, at least in Uganda and Mozambique, made it possible for my interviewees to speak openly and honestly about events that have gradually lost their political salience. Moreover, I was an outsider – an American who arrived in small villages on local transport with not much more than a backpack and remained for weeks at a time, getting to know members of the various communities in which I worked. That approach capitalized on my status as an outsider but made me an insider, too, by demonstrating that I was willing to make myself a part of their world, to live as they live, in order to understand what many experienced during war. National and local contacts also eased my entry. Often, a letter from someone in the capital who was known to people in the community helped to open doors; just as often, the translators I worked with from the national universities were able to broker initial introductions and gradual acceptance.

I can also be confident that the testimonies I heard represent credible accounts of the violence because my efforts were met with the enthusiastic cooperation of combatants and civilians alike, regardless of the side they took during the war, the depth of their participation, or how their position is now viewed in the aftermath of conflict. For most, speaking with me was their first opportunity to tell their story, to describe how their families and communities experienced a traumatic period of political change. Because I allowed interviews to proceed in an open-ended fashion, my respondents felt ownership over their narratives, resisting when I tried to skip steps or guide the conversation in a different direction. And many of my contacts repeatedly expressed their pressing desire that I "get the story right." Interviews stretched for hours not because I had an unending list of questions but because those who spoke with me made a conscious commitment to tell their story. In doing so, it was essential that they tell it in its entirety.

Recognizing the challenges inherent in interpreting participatory accounts, I also made every effort to check my facts, validate claims, and utilize other sources of information. By focusing on two communities within each country, I was able to compare and contrast the oral testimonies of different individuals, making it possible to develop a credible timeline of the conflict, outline the roles of particular combatants and civilians, and understand critical events. At the same time, I made a conscious effort to develop independent sources of information from a diverse group of respondents with different agendas, analysts with local and international ties, written documentation of how groups emerged and evolved, and a quantitative record of the political violence that characterized the countries where I did research. No single method is sufficient to avoid the biases described previously, but together I believe they allowed me to produce a substantial and credible picture of how the NRA, Renamo, Sendero Nacional, and Sendero–Huallaga were organized to fight for political and economic change.

Appendix B

DATABASE ON CIVIL WAR VIOLENCE

Over the last two decades, the quantitative study of civil war has gained prominence in the literature of political science. Analyses of large-scale databases have provided for fruitful cross-country comparisons. In particular, statistical analysis has yielded new insights into the causes of civil war, the forces impacting its duration, and the factors shaping its termination. The quantitative data that exist, however, have limited the questions scholars have been able to ask about civil war. Specifically, researchers have focused on "civil war" as the unit of analysis. At this level, databases are composed of country-level indicators including whether there was a civil war, how long it lasted, when it came to an end, and a set of political and economic indicators of country-level characteristics.

Without more fine-grained information, it is impossible to examine systematically an additional set of issues, including the geographic spread of civil war, the variation in the incidence of civil war over time, and the characteristics of civil war violence. These characteristics include the types of violence committed by soldiers during a conflict, their prevalence, the location of violence, and the details about the victims.

Scholars interested in quantitative research should not be limited to studies of the structural determinants of civil war initiation, duration, and termination. While studies of the incidence and character of civil war violence have traditionally been conducted largely by anthropologists and sociologists, it is feasible to develop a method for the systematic collection of cross-national quantitative data on the incidence and character of civil war. In this appendix, I present the outline of one such method.

Structure

The violence database that I constructed for this study was collected with the following assumption in mind: civilians are often the primary and deliberate target of combatants in civil wars. This is the result of a set of interrelated factors, including the weakness of military structures in irregular war, the absence of clear front lines on which the parties fight, and the blurred line between combatants and civilians. Accordingly, an appropriate indicator of the "incidence" of civil war is the use of violence against noncombatant populations. A database constructed on this foundation yields significant information about the geographic location of civil war, how the level of violence varies over time, and the characteristics of those who are affected by the conflict.

In the database, the basic unit of analysis is the event. An "event" refers to any interaction between soldiers (rebel or government) and civilians in which a violation is committed. "Violations" are instances of violence, including killings, mutilation, abduction, detention, injury, destruction, rape, looting, forced displacement, and overkill.[1] As a result, any one event may include a set of violations committed against the civilian population. Each event is characterized within the database in terms of the violations it includes. Importantly, in the statistics presented in Chapter 6, the unit being counted is always the event.

In addition to coding the violations that occurred as part of an event, the database also includes important identifying characteristics for each event. These include its geographic location, when it happened, who perpetrated the violence, the form of weapons they used, and whether rebel or government soldiers were also killed during the event. An effort is also made to capture detailed characteristics of the victims of civil war violence, including the number killed and injured, the number identified by name, and their age, sex, and affiliation. For purposes of understanding who suffered from civil war violence, victims are categorized into the following affiliation groups: religious leaders, professors and teachers, students, political leaders, traditional authorities, civilians (with a specified occupation), and those without any identifying characteristics.

---

[1] Each of these violations was defined in a codebook. The one violation whose meaning may not be immediately clear to readers is overkill. Overkill is coded for an incident in which bodies are mutilated or burned in the course of killing or after the person is dead.

Method

The violence database consists of events drawn from press sources. Local coders were trained to collect detailed event descriptions from daily newspapers in collections at national archives and local libraries and from press reviews produced by local nongovernmental organizations. Coders gathered information from each published newspaper for each day during the entire period of armed conflict. More than fourteen hundred events were collected in a review of both government and opposition newspapers for the period 1976–94 in Mozambique. Over eight hundred events were coded in Uganda, and more than four thousand were recorded in Peru.

Of course, the same events often appear in different sources. One newspaper might report that six individuals were killed, while another has information about only three. One story might indicate that a range of violations were committed, while another might limit its description to the killing alone. Coders were required to complete a full event description each time the event was reported. In the process of building the quantitative database – transforming the event descriptions into numerical data – every effort was made to eliminate overlapping incidents, and a simple set of coding rules was established to resolve conflicting information about the same event.

In many cases, the data for an event are incomplete. A newspaper may report that individuals were killed but lack information about the identities of the victims and the perpetrators. More often, specific identifying information, including the affiliation, sex, and age of the victims, is unavailable. The final structure of this database incorporates the incomplete information. Where no clear evidence is provided with which to code the individual variables, those entries are left blank. The events are still included in the dataset, however, even when some variables cannot be coded. Therefore, the summary statistics represent the *certain* information recorded with respect to each variable.

Biases and Limitations

Importantly, the violence database does not present a complete picture of civil war violence. Newspapers are unable to report every incident of violence that takes place in a conflict due to material and security limitations. As a result, each database understates the level of violence experienced by noncombatants. Nonetheless, it is possible to theorize with some certainty about the characteristics of the bias likely to be apparent in the data.

Particularly in the African context, where resources are limited, reporting on rural incidents is likely to be the weakest. Therefore, I expect that were complete information available about the course of the conflicts, an even greater weight of incidents (in all cases) would be committed in rural areas.

Those incidents most likely to be reported, moreover, are those that involve attacks in highly populated areas or on state institutions or that are targeted at "important" individuals. Of course, the vast majority of these reported incidents will be true events; as a proportion of the total population of events, however, they will be overrepresented. Accordingly, each database will systematically understate the level of violence that is directed at civilian institutions and "unimportant" populations, namely peasants. Thus, if the gathered data suggest a trend toward the killing of peasants in rural areas, we can expect that such crimes were committed more regularly in reality than is represented in the data.

Incidents in which individuals are killed tend to receive more media coverage than actions in which individuals are robbed, their property is destroyed, or people are beaten and threatened. This suggests that data gathered on incidents of killing will most closely approximate the level and character of actual civil war violence. Each database therefore understates the extent to which insurgent groups engaged in other abuses of the civilian population. Nonetheless, this bias is likely to be consistent across countries; differences in rebel behavior apparent in the data are not likely to be the result of this bias alone.

A large number of the news stories (in most cases, the majority) come from government sources, though an effort was made in each country to supplement government sources with reporting from independent newspapers and opposition sources in order to cross-check the facts. It is widely recognized that governments systematically underreport rebel successes and overassign responsibility for civilian deaths to insurgent groups to divert attention away from government misbehavior. Even though it is possible that this bias could lead one to believe that rebels committed a high level of violence when the government was in fact responsible, careful analysis using qualitative sources gives us a sense of the magnitude of the bias. In Mozambique, for example, where the data suggest that rebels perpetrated nearly 90 percent of incidents of violence, fieldwork indicates that the level of rebel violence was in fact this high and was not just a result of the bias. The reader should discount the total number of incidents assigned to the rebels to take account of this bias. Again, however, where patterns are evident across countries – that is, where rebels are massacring civilians in

Mozambique and not in Uganda – those results are unlikely to be driven by the bias.

A final source of bias is the capacity of the press. Because a newspaper in country A has better access to the rural areas than one in country B, a comparison of the number of incidents across countries might reveal that the war in A was more violent than that in B when in reality the reverse was true. For this reason, I do not compare the levels of violence across countries using the incident database. Using reported events, comparisons of levels are more realistically made over time and across regions. Actual numbers of dead reported by the international press are slightly more reliable for comparing the level of violence across conflicts. For analyzing the character of violence, however, differences in the absolute level of violence do not introduce a significant bias unless almost no incidents are reported for one country. Because I have a significantly large number of incidents in each case, I am confident that the characteristics of violence are representative of behavior within each country and, as a result, are comparable across countries.

Conclusion

Importantly, the geographic, temporal, and characteristic patterns identified in each dataset closely match the trajectory of civil war violence established in the historical record and narrative reports about each conflict. This method enables the systematic collection of data on civil war violence across conflicts. It is likely that the limitations in any one case are similar across countries. As a result, the data gathered, despite their weaknesses, are comparable across conflicts, allowing for fine-grained comparisons of the incidence and characteristics of violence within civil war.

Appendix C

THE NATIONAL RESISTANCE ARMY
CODE OF CONDUCT (ABRIDGED)

A. Dealing with the Public

(1) Never abuse, insult, shout at, or beat any member of the public.

(2) Never take anything in the form of money or property from any members of the public, not even somebody's sweet bananas or sugar-cane on the grounds that it is mere sugar-cane, without paying for the same.

(3) Pay promptly for anything you take and in cash.

(4) Never kill any member of the public or any captured prisoners, as the guns should only be reserved for armed enemies or opponents.

(5) Return anything you borrow from the public.

(6) Offer help to the members of the public who may be in the territory of your unit.

(7) Offer medical treatment to the members of the public who may be in the territory of your unit.

(8) Never develop illegitimate relationships with any woman because there are no women as such waiting for passing soldiers yet many women are wives, or daughters of somebody somewhere. Any illegitimate relationship is bound to harm our good relations with the public.

(9) There should be no consumption of alcohol until the end of the war. Drunken soldiers are bound to misuse the guns which are given to them for the defence of the people.

The complete NRA code of conduct is reprinted in Ondoga Ori Amaza, *Museveni's Long March from Guerrilla to Statesman* (Kampala: Fountain, 1998), pp. 246–51.

B. Relationships among the Soldiers

(1) The lower echelons of the army must obey the higher ones and the higher echelons must respect the lower ones.

(2) In decision making, we should use a method of democratic centralism where there is democratic participation as well as central control.

(3) Every officer, cadre, or militant must strive to master military science in order to gain more capability so that we are in a position to defend the people more efficiently.

(4) The following tendencies can be injurious to the cohesion of the army and are prohibited:

    (i) Quest for cheap popularity: on the part of officers or cadres by tolerating wrongs in order to be popular with soldiers.

    (ii) Liberalism: which entails weak leadership and tolerating of wrongs or mistakes. In case of liberalism, the person in authority knows what is right and what is wrong, but due to weak leadership, he does not stand firmly on the side of right.

    (iii) Intrigue and Double Talk: this can cause artificial confusion even when there is no objective basis for confusion.

(5) The following methods should be used in correcting mistakes within the army:

    (i) Open criticism of mistakes instead of subterranean grumbling which is favored by reactionaries.

    (ii) The holding of regular meetings at which all complaints are heard and settled.

    (iii) A distinction should always be made between errors due to indiscipline, corruption or subversion and treatment of each should be different.

(6) All commanders should ensure that all soldiers, depending on particular circumstances, should at any one particular time either be fighting, studying military science or undertaking self-improvement in academic work, taking part in recreational activities, or resting. There should not be idleness whatsoever which breeds mischief.

(7) Political education should be mandatory every day so that the cadres and militants can understand the reasons for the war as well as the dynamics of the world we live in. "Conscious discipline is better than mechanical discipline."

(8) Formation of cliques in the army is not allowed, at the same time the principle of compartmentation should be strictly adhered to and understood. We should adhere to the principle of "the need to know" and avoid the mistake of soliciting information for its own sake. The strategy of the NRA and the regular tactics should be known to all officers, cadres, and combatants. But operational matters should be known to those who need to know.

(9) (i) There shall be a High Command consisting of the Commander-in-Chief, who shall be Chairman, and eight other members to be appointed by the Commander-in-Chief.

(ii) All members of the High Command shall be members of the Army Council.

(iii) The High Command shall perform such functions as may be conferred upon it by any law in force in Uganda; or as the President may direct.

(10) (i) There shall be a General Court-Martial which shall be the supreme trial organ under this Code.

(ii) This General Court-Martial shall consist of
(a) a Chairman;
(b) two senior officers;
(c) two junior officers;
(d) one Political Commissar; and
(e) one non-commissioned officer.

(11) (i) There shall be a Unit Disciplinary Committee for each Army Unit which shall consist of
(a) the Second in Command who shall be the Chairman;
(b) the Administration Officer of the Unit;
(c) the Political Commissar of the Unit;
(d) The Regimental Sergeant-Major or Company Sergeant-Major of the Unit;
(e) Two junior officers;
(f) One private.

(ii) The Unit Disciplinary Committee shall have powers to try all combatants below the rank of Provisional Junior Officer II for all offences except the following:
(a) murder;
(b) manslaughter;
(c) robbery;

     (d) rape;

     (e) treason;

     (f) terrorism;

     (g) disobedience of lawful orders resulting in loss of life.

(iii) A Unit Disciplinary Committee may refer any case which in its opinion is of a particularly complex nature to the General Court-Martial.

Appendix D

NORMS OF BEHAVIOR FOR A SENDERO LUMINOSO COMMANDER

(1) Know your function.
(2) Know yourself and work to improve yourself.
(3) Know your men and look after their well-being.
(4) Keep your men well-informed.
(5) Act as an example to your men.
(6) Ensure that the orders are understood, controlled, and followed.
(7) Train your men as a team.
(8) Take decisions correctly and in a timely manner.
(9) Act with initiative and develop a sense of responsibility among your subordinates.
(10) Employ their unity and agreement to achieve all that is possible.
(11) Assume the responsibility for their actions.

Report of the second national conference April 21–June 6, captured Sendero document, 1982, DINCOTE Sendero collection, Lima, Peru.

Index

abductions, by Renamo, 113–15,
  145–47, 183, 230
accountability, formal instruments of,
  348–50
activists
  changes/shifts from, 259, 265,
    281–83, 294, 296
  opportunists and, 9–11, 53, 126, 199,
    204–08, 259, 265, 281–83, 294,
    296, 299–300, 327–28, 329–32,
    340, 349–50
  resilience, norms and expectations
    of, 11
  responses to shocks by, 263–65
  violence by, 198, 204–08, 229
adverse selection, 41, 43, 102, 130
AFDL. See Alliance of Democratic
  Forces for the Liberation of
  Congo-Kinshasa
affiliation of victims
  NRA and, 215, 216, 252
  Renamo and, 215, 216, 252
  Sendero–Huallaga and, 215, 216,
    252, 254
  Sendero Luminoso Nacional and,
    215, 216, 252
  violence and, 215, 216, 252,
    367
Afghanistan, 6, 342–43
Afoaku, Osita, 338
Africa Livre, 331–32

Africa Watch, 232
African National Congress, 76, 270
agency
  model of managerial behavior, 13
  structure and, 20–22, 327
agrarian reforms, in Peru, 187–89
agriculture. See also coca production;
    food resources; poppies
  in Mozambique, 74
  as resource, 48, 173
  taxation and, 67, 190–91
AIS. See Islamic Salvation Army
Algeria
  1962–1964, 312–15
  1992–2000, 315–18
Alien Torts Claim Act, 348
All People's Congress, 302, 332
Alliance of Democratic Forces for the
    Liberation of Congo-Kinshasa
    (AFDL), 335–37
Alto Huallaga. See Huallaga Valley;
    Sendero Luminoso–Huallaga
Alur group, in Uganda, 219–20,
    222–24
Amin, Idi, 227
  deaths during dictatorship of, 64
  economy under, 56, 64, 67
  insurgency against, 57
  Obote v., 64, 66
  overthrow of, 61, 62, 64, 67–69
  regime collapse of, 56

377

amnesty, 261, 348. *See also ley de
arrepentimiento*
  Obote promising, 267
  in Peru, 277, 278, 280
Amnesty International, 343, 344
anarchy, in states, 36–37
andaki (prisons), 226
Angola, 260, 283–87, 311
  arms purchases by, 285–87, 293
  Congo and, 335–37
  endowment shocks in, 292–95
  interviews in, 356
  oil and, 285, 286, 293
  Portugal and, 283–84, 285
  refugees in Zambia, 283, 284
  South Africa, diamonds and, 284,
    285–87, 293–94
anticolonialism, 283–87, 312–15
António, Manuel, 272–74
apartheid, 79, 80
  in South Africa, 79, 272, 286
apprenticeship, 105
Arciniega, Alberto, 256
Armed Forces Revolutionary Council,
  340
Armed Islamic Group (GIA), 315–17
Armenia, ethnic genocides in, 6
arms purchases, 93, 101
  by Angola, 285–87, 293
assassinations, 201, 222–24
  of Adda, 222–24
  of Akuya, 222–24
  of Jaime, 89, 91
  of Josua, 222–24
  of Lutta, 222–24
  massacres *v.*, 215
  NRA and, 219–29
  of Senyenya, 222–24
asymmetric conflict, 55
  between state and insurgency,
    325
asymmetries, information, 41–42,
  43, 100, 103, 208–09
authoritarianism
  in Algeria, 315

economic endowments, coercion
  and, 260
  in Sendero–Huallaga, 164, 192–95
authorities
  centralized, communism and, 31
  traditional, Renamo and, 164,
    181–86
autocratic rule, democracy *v.*, 165–67
Ayacucho, Peru
  Sendero Nacional in, 57–58, 81–83,
    87, 89, 117, 120, 125, 150, 156,
    187–88, 217, 243–51, 276
  violence in, 243–48

Baganda tribe, in Uganda, 36, 55–56,
  142, 176–80
  Kabaka Yekka and, 66
  opposition to Obote regime, 63–64,
    65–66, 109, 110, 222, 226–28
bandidos armados (armed bandits), 230
bandits, 230
  in Colombia, 319–22
  roving, 169
  stationary, 169
bank robberies, by NRA, 268, 293
Banyankole, in Uganda, 36, 55–56, 57,
  67, 68, 108–11, 142
bargains
  governance and, 164, 168–72,
    174–75, 196
  for resources, 339, 341–42
  violence and, 208–09
barriers to organization
  initial conditions and, 7, 14–15,
    20–22
  resources and, 329–30
  social endowments and, 24, 48–49
  weak states and, 341
bases de apoyo (bases of support), 240
Bates, Robert, 54
batongole (chiefs), 176–77
Belaúnde, Fernando, 81–82, 85–87, 275
Ben Bella, Ahmed, 314
Berbers, 315
Bermúdez, Francisco, 81

Index

Index

Index

Index

Index

responsables (authorities), 240–41, 243
Revolutionary Armed Forces of
  Colombia. *See* FARC
Revolutionary United Front (RUF),
  301–05, 332–34, 340
  manifesto for, 32–33
revolutions, civil wars *v.*, 35
Rhodesia
  Renamo and, 57, 72, 111–12, 232,
    331
  Renamo, Portugal and, 57, 72, 96,
    111
  Renamo, South Africa, 57, 75–79,
    112, 146–47
  Zimbabwe and, 76
Ribáuè District, Nampula Province,
  Mozambique, 237–39
Roldán, Mary, 320
Rommel, 152
rondas campesinas (self-defense
  committees), 250, 257–58, 275
Ross, Michael, 329–30
RUF. *See* Revolutionary United Front
Russia, 5
Rwanda
  Congo and, 335–37
  ethnic genocides in, 6
  International Criminal Tribunals for,
    348
  Kagame and, 228

Sánchez, Gonzalo, 321
sanctions
  defection and, 43
  in Sendero Nacional, 152–53
  as source of leverage, 346–48
  by United Nations, 286–87, 294, 346
Sankoh, Foday, 303, 304
Savimbi, Jonas, 284–87, 293–95, 346
Schmitter, Philippe, 165
Sebirumbi, Hajji Musa, 219–20
secessionist movements/wars, 17, 309
security
  governance and, 163, 168, 175, 180
  states and, 36–38, 168

self-interest, pursuit of, 41–43, 48, 98
Selznick, Philip, 39
Semuto, the Luwero Triangle, Uganda,
  222–26
Sena, in Mozambique, 36
Sendero Luminoso–Huallaga, 14
  affiliation of victims and, 215, 216,
    252, 254
  authoritarianism in, 164, 192–95
  autonomy and, 155–58
  changing local economy and, 279–82
  chronology of, 92
  cocaleros and, 122–25, 256
  codes and rules for, 156–58
  Colombia and, 91, 92, 94, 193,
    279–80, 281
  comparisons with other groups,
    55–58, 61, 88, 95, 125–26, 196–97,
    258–59, 299–301
  control and, 127, 155–58, 251–58
  corruption in, 55, 157, 194–95
  drugs and, 14, 36, 55, 58, 89–95, 96,
    122–25, 155–58, 192–95, 251–58,
    279–82, 291–92
  governance and, 164, 173–74,
    192–95
  history of, 89–95
  ideology of, 156–58, 196–97
  inclusion in, 192–95
  indiscipline in, 14
  mandos for, 256
  opportunism and, 156–58, 281–83
  recruitment and, 96, 122–25
  resilience of, 279–82
  resources and, 58, 91–93, 95
  structure of, 251
  in Tingo María, 89, 90, 122–23, 124,
    252–58
  victims of violence by, 218
  violence against civilians and, 252,
    253
  violence by, 55, 89, 94–95, 212–13,
    215–17, 251–58
Sendero Luminoso Nacional, 13–14,
  340, 356

396

Index

stationary bandits, 169
  roving *v.*, 169
Stevens, Siaka, 332–33
strategies
  constraints on, 45–50
  for control, 135–40
  initial conditions, resources and,
    20–22, 23, 101–02, 125, 327–28
  as problem of institutional choice,
    27–28, 38–39
  for recruitment, 7–11, 22–23, 45, 48,
    96–126, 263, 340
  resources and, 20–22, 23, 54, 339
  violence and, 201–02
structure(s)
  agency and, 20–22, 327
  of database on civil war violence,
    367
  of governance, 5, 6, 23, 44
  membership, violence and, 198,
    204–08, 210–11, 217–19, 259, 340
  of organization, 6–7, 20–23, 217–19
  resources and, 23
Sudan, 32
survey research, 353–54
sympathizers, 97
  militants *v.*, 99
Syria, invasion of Lebanon by, 323

Taliban, 343
tangible and intangible assets, 47
Tanzania
  Kabila and, 336
  NRA and, 62, 67–68, 108–11
  UNLF and, 64, 67–68
taxation, 7, 47
  agriculture and, 67, 190–91
  drugs and, 92–93, 124, 156, 192–95,
    255–56, 291–92
  governance and, 164, 176, 192–95
  in Uganda, 67, 176, 268–69
Taylor, Charles
  Liberia, RUF and, 303, 333–34
  NPFL and, 334–35
Taylor, Michael, 45

team production function, 129–30
Ten-Point Programme, NRA and, 70,
  177
territorial control, 17, 20, 56
  contestation and, 11–13, 37–38
  governance and, 163, 164, 169, 195
terrorism, 17. *See also* counterterrorism
  global campaign against, 342–43
  Guevara on violence and, 30–31
  by Guzmán, 87
  in Peru, 94
  signaling and, 208–41
thick description, 54
Thoumi, Francisco, 290
Tilly, Charles, 28, 31
Tingo María, Alto Huallaga, Peru, 89,
  90, 122–23, 124, 252–58
trials
  for indiscipline, 145
  Sendero–Huallaga and, 255
  Sendero Nacional and, 247–48
  tribunals and, 348–49
trust, 296
  in governance, 134, 167–69
  during interviews, 357, 364
  between rebel leaders and recruits,
    101
Truth and Reconciliation Commission,
  Peru, 44, 88, 212, 213–17, 241–43,
  359
Tunisia, 313, 314

Uganda, 341. *See also* National
  Resistance Army; *specific
  cities/regions*
  Alur group in, 219–20, 222–24
  Baganda tribe in, 36, 55–56, 63–64,
    65–66, 109, 110, 142, 176–80, 222,
    226–28
  Banyankole in, 36, 55–56, 57, 67, 68,
    108–11, 142
  British colonialism in, 55–56, 65, 176
  Buganda region in, 63–64, 65–66,
    110
  bush war in, 108

399

Index

Vietnam, 98, 306, 352
violations, coding of, 367
violence, 198–59. *See also* specific
  countries
by activists, 198, 204–08, 229
affiliation of victims and, 215, 216,
  252, 367
bargains and, 208–09
character and intensity/level of, 6,
  10–11, 18–19, 23, 24, 27, 59,
  198–02, 210–19, 305–10, 311,
  317–18, 370
within civil war, 16, 217–58
civil wars, organization and, 16–20,
  199
civilians and, 16, 24, 199–200
against civilians, Sendero–Huallaga
  and, 252, 253
coercion and, 198, 199, 202
consequences of, 198
data on, 59, 202, 258, 366–67
defection and, 198, 209–10, 224–25,
  227, 228–29, 299–300, 317–18
definitions of, 6, 198, 199–02
duration of war and, 308, 311,
  326
expectations and, 205–08, 217–19
external patronage and, 209
Geneva Conventions on, 200,
  201
industrial organization of, 27–60
lingering effects of, 5
measuring, 53, 202, 213–15, 305–11
micropolitics of, 339
mistakes/errors with, 198, 205–06,
  225, 238
nature of perpetrators of, 204,
  205
non-state actors' role in, 16
opportunists and, 199, 204–08,
  217–19, 239, 276, 309,
  326
organization and, 16–20, 199,
  203–08
organizing, 39–50

patterns of, 6–7, 18–19, 20, 198–202,
  217–19, 300–01, 305–11
practice of, across countries, 210–17
as rational, 208
resistance and, 44, 206–08, 217–19
resources and, 7, 11–13, 15–16,
  20–22, 23, 306–07, 310, 311–26
responsibility for, against
  noncombatants, 211–12
selective *v.* indiscriminate, 6–7,
  10–11, 13–14, 18, 44, 45, 198,
  203–04, 206–08, 209–10, 213–15,
  217–19, 258–59, 299–301
as social cleansing, 247, 251
by states, 5–6, 18
strategies and, 201–02
structures, membership and, 198,
  204–08, 210–11, 217–19, 259,
  340
targets/identification for, 210–11,
  215, 217, 232, 252
across time and regions/geographic
  space, 199, 202, 207–08, 209–10,
  217–19, 232, 258–59, 260
types of, against noncombatants,
  212–13
variations in, 14, 15
victim group size and, 213–15
vipingamizi (enemy agents), 220
vouching, 105, 106–07, 263
  Sendero Nacional and, 118, 124
Voz da Africa Livre (Voice of a Free
  Africa), 72, 111–12
Vvumbula Armed Forces, 226–29

Weingast, Barry, 167–69
wilayat (military regions), Algeria,
  313–15
Wilkinson, Steven, 202
Wilson, James Q., 127, 135–36
Wilson, Ken, 272
wives, taking, 3, 79, 184, 236
Wood, Elisabeth, 19
  on collective action, 45
  on El Salvador, 99–100, 352

Richard Snyder, *Politics after Neoliberalism: Reregulation in Mexico*

David Stark and László Bruszt, *Postsocialist Pathways: Transforming Politics and Property in East Central Europe*

Sven Steinmo, Kathleen Thelen, and Frank Longstreth, eds., *Structuring Politics: Historical Institutionalism in Comparative Analysis*

Susan C. Strokes, *Mandates and Democracy: Neoliberalism by Surprise in Latin America*

Susan C. Strokes, ed., *Public Support for Market Reforms in New Democracies*

Duane Swank, *Global Capital, Political Institutions, and Policy Change in Developed Welfare States*

Sidney Tarrow, *Power in Movement: Social Movement and Contentious Politics*

Kathleen Thelen, *How Institutions Evolve: The Political Economy of Skills in Germany, Britain, the United States, and Japan*

Charles Tilly, *Trust and Rule*

Joshua Tucker, *Regional Economic Voting: Russia, Poland, Hungary, Slovakia, and the Czech Republic, 1990–1999*

Ashutosh Varshney, *Democracy, Development, and the Countryside*

Stephen I. Wilkinson, *Votes and Violence: Electoral Competition and Ethnic Riots in India*

Jason Wittenberg, *Crucibles of Political Loyalty: Church Institutions and Electoral Continuity in Hungary*

Elisabeth J. Wood, *Forging Democracy from Below: Insurgent Transitions in South Africa and El Salvador*

Elisabeth J. Wood, *Insurgent Collective Action and Civil War in El Salvador*